OXFORD BIBLE SER

THE LIBRARY
UNIVERSITY OF
WINCHESTER

General Editors
P. R. Ackroyd and G. Stanton

There are many commentaries on individual books of the Bible but the reader who wishes to take a broader view has less choice. This series is intended to meet this need. Each volume embraces a number of biblical books. To provide general orientation, there are two volumes of a more introductory character: one considers the Old Testament in its cultural and historical context, the other the New Testament, discussing the origins of Christianity. Four volumes deal thematically with different kinds of material in the Old Testament: narrative, prophecy, poetry/psalmody, wisdom and law. Three handle different aspects of the New Testament: from the Gospels, Paul and Pauline Christianity, to varieties of New Testament thought. An additional volume looks at the nature of biblical interpretation, covering both Testaments.

Discussion in detail of selected biblical passages provides examples of the ways in which the interpretation of the text makes possible deeper understanding of the wider issues, both theological and historical, with which the Bible is concerned.

KA 0293936 3

OXFORD BIBLE SERIES

General Editors: P. R. Ackroyd and G. Stanton

Introducing the Old Testament
Richard Coggins
Second Edition

Narrative in the Hebrew Bible
David M. Gunn and Danna Nolan Fewell

The Poems and Psalms of the Hebrew Bible
S. E. Gillingham

Prophecy and the Biblical Prophets
John F. A. Sawyer
Revised Edition

Wisdom and Law in the Old Testament
The Ordering of Life in Israel and Early Judaism
J. Blenkinsopp

The Origins of Christianity
A Historical Introduction to the New Testament
Schuyler Brown
Revised Edition

The Gospels and Jesus
Graham Stanton
Second Edition

Variety and Unity in New Testament Thought
J. Reumann

Pauline Christianity
John Ziesler
Revised Edition

Biblical Interpretation
Robert Morgan with John Barton

THE GOSPELS
AND JESUS

Second Edition

Graham Stanton

OXFORD

UNIVERSITY PRESS

OXFORD
UNIVERSITY PRESS

Great Clarendon Street, Oxford OX2 6DP

Oxford University Press is a department of the University of Oxford.
It furthers the University's objective of excellence in research, scholarship,
and education by publishing worldwide in

Oxford New York

Auckland Cape Town Dar es Salaam Hong Kong Karachi
Kuala Lumpur Madrid Melbourne Mexico City Nairobi
New Delhi Shanghai Taipei Toronto

With offices in

Argentina Austria Brazil Chile Czech Republic France Greece
Guatemala Hungary Italy Japan South Korea Poland Portugal
Singapore Switzerland Thailand Turkey Ukraine Vietnam

Published in the United States
by Oxford University Press Inc., New York

© Graham Stanton 2002

The moral rights of the author have been asserted
Database right Oxford University Press (maker)

First published 1989
Second Edition 2002
Reprinted 2003, 2004

All rights reserved. No part of this publication may be reproduced,
stored in a retrieval system, or transmitted, in any form or by any means,
without the prior permission in writing of Oxford University Press,
or as expressly permitted by law, or under terms agreed with the appropriate
reprographics rights organizations. Enquiries concerning reproduction
outside the scope of the above should be sent to the Rights Department,
Oxford University Press, at the address above

You must not circulate this book in any other binding or cover
and you must impose this same condition on any acquirer

British Library Cataloguing in Publication Data

Data available

Library of Congress Cataloging in Publication Data

Data available

ISBN 0–19–924616–5

5 7 9 10 8 6

Typeset in Adobe Minion
by RefineCatch Limited, Bungay, Suffolk
Printed in Great Britain by
Biddles Ltd., King's Lynn, Norfolk

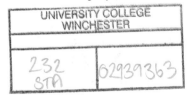

UNIVERSITY COLLEGE
WINCHESTER

232
STA

62939363

GENERAL EDITORS' PREFACE

There are many commentaries on individual books of the Bible, but the reader who wishes to take a broader view has less choice. This series is intended to meet this need. Its structure is thematic, with each volume embracing a number of biblical books. It is designed for use with any of the familiar translations of the Bible; quotations are normally from RSV or NRSV, but the authors of the individual volumes also use other translations or make their own where this helps to bring out the particular meaning of a passage.

To provide general orientation, there are two volumes of a more introductory character: one considers the Old Testament in its cultural and historical context, the other the New Testament, discussing the origins of Christianity. Four volumes deal with different kinds of material in the Old Testament: narrative, prophecy, poetry/psalmody, wisdom and law. Three volumes handle different aspects of the New Testament: the Gospels, Paul and Pauline Christianity, the varieties of New Testament thought. One volume looks at the nature of biblical interpretation, covering both Testaments. This is designed both to draw together some of the many themes touched on in the other volumes, and also to invite the reader to look further at the problems of understanding an ancient literature in the very different cultural context of the present time.

The authors of the individual volumes write for a general readership. Technical terms and Hebrew or Greek words are explained; the latter are used only when essential to the understanding of the text. The general introductory volumes are designed to stand on their own, providing a framework, but also to serve to raise some of the questions which the remaining volumes examine in closer detail. All the volumes other than the two general ones include discussion of selected biblical passages in greater depth, thus providing examples of the ways in which the interpretation of the text makes possible deeper understanding of the wider issues, both historical and theological, with which the Bible is concerned. Select bibliographies in each volume point the way to further discussion of the many issues which remain open to fuller exploration.

P. R. A.

G. S.

PREFACE TO THE SECOND EDITION

For some time now I have been in two minds about a revised and extended edition of this book. This book has been reprinted many times and read much more widely than I ever envisaged. As I am a firm believer in the dictum, 'if it works, don't fix it', a new edition has been low on my agenda.

However, scholarly study of the gospels and of the historical Jesus has moved on apace over the last decade. So much so that a revised edition of this book became imperative. The new edition takes account of recent developments and includes a largely new Bibliography. In Part I there is fuller discussion both of literary approaches to the gospels and of the Gospel of Thomas. In nearly all the chapters in Part II there is additional material. In a number of ways I have tried to make this edition more 'user-friendly'.

On some points I have changed my mind, but I have not been tempted to change the main thrust of the book. When the first edition was published it was rather unusual to insist that the present form of the gospels should be studied *before* tackling issues concerning the historical Jesus. The unconventional has now become conventional! Although this edition gives more attention to current scholarly debates, I have not tried to catalogue opinions on all disputed points. In accordance with the aims of the Oxford Bible Series, I have focused on the text of the gospels. Scholars come and go, but the text remains for us to 'read, mark, learn, and inwardly digest'.

A number of readers made helpful comments on the first edition. I am particularly grateful to Professor Joel Marcus, now of Duke University, for sharing his suggestions and wisdom with me at some length.

During the preparation of this second edition my Alma Mater conferred on me an honorary D.D. degree. As a token of my deep gratitude, I dedicate this book to the University of Otago, New Zealand. During my visit to Dunedin for the conferral, I was delighted to learn from Professor Paul Trebilco that this book is used in the University's Department of Theology and Religious Studies, and also in distance learning courses all over New Zealand. I hope that the new edition will continue to interest readers in many countries in the gospels and in the One they portray.

CONTENTS

KEY PASSAGES DISCUSSED

NOTE

The Scripture quotations in this book are normally from the New Revised Standard Version of the Bible, copyright 1989, Division of Christian Education of the National Council of the Churches of Christ in the United States of America. Used by permission. All rights reserved.

The Bibliography provides suggestions for further study and also gives details of publications referred to in the main text by the name of the author and the date of publication.

PART I

THE FOUR GOSPELS

1

FROM THE GOSPELS TO JESUS

Jesus of Nazareth and the four New Testament gospels continue to fascinate people from many cultural and religious backgrounds. From time to time television and radio programmes attempt to peer behind the gospels to reveal the 'real' Jesus. Lavishly illustrated coffee-table books try to give the modern reader of the gospels some insight into first-century Judaea and Galilee. Many who claim to be agnostic about the existence of God insist, nonetheless, that they try to live by the ethical principles of the Sermon on the Mount.

Christians of all persuasions acknowledge Jesus as the Son of God. But does the historical evidence support such a claim? Christians accept that in the teaching and actions of Jesus, as well as in his death and resurrection, God revealed himself to humanity in new ways. Are we able to reconstruct the life and character of Jesus with a sufficient degree of confidence to make such claims meaningful?

Many modern Jews have a keen interest in Jesus. Some insist that Jesus can be understood as a slightly unconventional Jewish teacher or prophet from Galilee. Does this assessment do justice to the evidence? And if it does, why was Jesus put to death? Most Jews and many Christians would agree that Jesus did not intend to found a new religion. Can the 'parting of the ways' between Christianity and Judaism be traced back in any way to the lifetime of Jesus?

Occasionally critics of Christianity have claimed that Jesus did not exist. On this view the gospels were written after AD 100, at a time when, as a new religion, Christianity felt the need to anchor its mythical Saviour-figure, Christ, in history and to present him as a striking human teacher. Is this a plausible reconstruction?

This wide range of questions—and more could be added—simply confirms that Jesus and the gospels raise a whole series of issues which are of great interest today. Unless one is satisfied with pat answers based on one's own religious convictions, these questions cannot be answered quickly. Almost all our evidence for Jesus is found in the four New Testament gospels, but serious study of the gospels is far from easy.

The gospels were not written until between thirty-five and sixty years after Jesus was crucified. The evangelists all wrote in Greek for urban Christians who were very different from the first Aramaic-speaking followers of Jesus in rural Galilee. According to Matthew, Mark, and Luke, Jesus was very reluctant to make grandiose claims about himself. The evangelists, on the other hand, are all clearly convinced that Jesus was the Messiah–Christ and the Son of God and they either assume or intend that their readers should share their convictions. For these various reasons there is a gap between the Jesus who lived and taught in Galilee and the Jesus portrayed by the evangelists, a gap often referred to as the difference between the Jesus of history and the Christ of faith.

For many modern readers the gospels pose fewer problems than Paul's letters, which seem to be profound, and, at times, terse and tortuous. But the apparent simplicity of the gospels is an illusion. Since at least seven of the letters in the New Testament were written by Paul himself, they provide direct access to the teaching of the apostle. We can date Paul's letters fairly accurately. And we know a little about the localities and communities to whom Paul wrote. Would that we had such direct access to Jesus and would that we knew as much about the origin of the gospels!

But we need not despair. With a keen appreciation of the difficulties and with careful use of the appropriate methods of study, progress is possible. As we shall see in Part II of this book, we can say a good deal about the teaching and actions of Jesus with some confidence. And in Part I we shall see, perhaps to our surprise, that the four gospels have their own distinctive and fascinating features which can be explored with profit. We do well to resist the temptation to bypass the teaching of the evangelists in an over-anxious rush to reach the teaching and actions of Jesus.

Story and significance

Where should we start? As we shall see in Chapters 7 and 8, the four gospels contain virtually all the evidence we have. We must start by asking what kind of evidence the evangelists intended to provide. Did they intend to write biographies, histories, novels, or theological treatises? What are the distinctive features and emphases of the four gospels? Have the evangelists allowed their Christian convictions about Jesus to hide the 'real' Jesus from us? And why do we have four gospels, no more, no less? Only on the basis of provisional answers to these questions can we dare to probe behind the gospels and seek to examine the teaching and actions of Jesus. For this reason the opening chapters of this book are devoted to the individual gospels.

A number of recent books, some scholarly, some popular, have sought to elucidate *either* the teaching and actions of Jesus *or* the distinctive teaching of one or more of the evangelists. In this book both tasks are attempted because I am convinced that only in this way can justice be done to the dual perspective of the evangelists. In the chapters which follow we shall see that Matthew, Mark, Luke, and John have written very different gospels. But all four evangelists are concerned to set out both the story of Jesus of Nazareth and also what they took to be the significance of his actions and teaching. Story and significance are intertwined.

It should not surprise us to learn that the gospels can be approached from either one or both these angles, for this is also the case in some modern writings. Biographers may (perhaps inadvertently) tell us almost as much about their own interests, convictions, and prejudices as about those of their subjects. Historians or historical novelists may focus on an earlier era, but one of their main concerns may well be to encourage their readers to reach particular conclusions about the partly different political, economic, or even religious issues of their own day. Some music can also be considered from more than one angle. In his symphony 'From the New World', the Czech composer Dvořák uses several American melodies and for many listeners the symphony is distinctively American. But for other listeners (and for the composer himself) the music genuinely reflects his own Czech cultural background.

The relationship between these two levels in a piece of literature or music may shift within the same work and may be discerned differently by different readers or listeners. That is part of their fascination. And so it is with the gospels. The evangelists do intend to tell us the 'story' of Jesus, but they are also addressing the needs and circumstances of their own Christian congregations. They do not do this directly, as Paul does, but they reinterpret the earlier traditions on which they have drawn in order to make them relevant for their readers. It is sometimes said that the gospels (especially Matthew and John) are transparent: behind the followers and opponents with whom Jesus speaks in Judaea or Galilee we may discern Jesus addressing Christians and critics in, say, Antioch or Ephesus in the evangelists' own day some fifty years after the ministry of Jesus.

There are, then, two ways of approaching the gospels. The evangelists inform us both about the 'past' story of Jesus of Nazareth and also about the present significance they attach to Jesus who, they claim, is the Messiah–Christ, the Son of God. There is in fact a third set of questions which may be asked in the study of the gospels, but we shall not be directly concerned with them in this book. How may the teaching both of Jesus and of the evangelists be related to Christian theology today? And is that teaching of any importance to non-Christians? How is the historical and cultural gap between the first and twenty-first centuries to be bridged? How does one decide which parts of the gospels are so firmly rooted in the quite different cultural setting of the first century that they are of little or no relevance to us today? These broader questions can be considered only on the basis of a firm grasp of the nature and purpose of the gospels themselves.

The Lord's Prayer

At this point it may be helpful to examine the best-known passage in the gospels in order to clarify further the main issues at stake in the serious study of them.

Matthew 6: 9–13	Luke 11: 2–4
	And Jesus said to them:
Pray then in this way:	When you pray, say:
Our Father in heaven,	Father,
(1) hallowed be your name	hallowed be your name.
(2) Your kingdom come,	Your kingdom come.
(2a) Your will be done,	
On earth as it is in heaven.	
(3) Give us this day	Keep on giving us each day
our bread for the coming day	our bread for the coming day

(4) And forgive us our debts,	And forgive us our sins,
As we also have forgiven our debtors	For we ourselves forgive everyone indebted to us
(5) And lead us not into temptation	And lead us not into temptation.
(5a) But rescue us from evil (or the evil one).	

(NRSV modified)

Very soon after the gospels were written the longer version of the Lord's prayer in Matthew 6 was used regularly in worship and soon became popular in Christian teaching and preaching. By comparison, the shorter version in Luke suffered neglect. In later centuries some scribes who were making copies of the text of Luke 11 were so convinced that the Matthean version of the prayer was the correct version that they expanded the text of Luke in order to bring it into line with Matthew. But as we shall see in a moment, on the whole it is the shorter Lucan version which is closer to the teaching of Jesus.

We must start by considering the way the two evangelists have understood and used this prayer, which is a succinct summary of many of the main themes of the teaching of Jesus. As we do this, it becomes easier to recover the words of Jesus. Matthew's version forms part of the Sermon on the Mount (Matt. 5–7). Although Luke has a shorter equivalent passage, often called the Sermon on the Plain (Luke 6: 17–49), the Lord's Prayer is not included there, but in a very different context in response to a request from one of the disciples of Jesus: 'Lord, teach us to pray, as John taught his disciples' (Luke 11: 1).

Which setting is more likely to be original? When we look closely at Matthew 6 we find that the first half of the chapter is made up of Jesus' instructions to his followers on the appropriate way to carry out three traditional Jewish forms of piety: almsgiving (6: 2–4), prayer (6: 5–15), and fasting (6: 16–18). In all three cases the reader is told not to follow the example of the hypocrites, but to give alms, pray, and fast in a different way. The three paragraphs (or pericopae as they are usually called in study of the gospels) all have exactly the same structure: 'When you . . . , do not act like the hypocrites who . . . , but when you . . . , (do it this way).'

The second pericope, on prayer, has been extended considerably by an exhortation not to follow the example of the Gentiles but to pray 'in this way'—and the Lord's Prayer then follows. At the end of the prayer, teaching on forgiveness of sins has been added (Matt. 6: 14–15); it is taken partly from Mark 11: 25. No doubt Matthew made the addition at this point since forgiveness of sins forms the fourth petition of the Lord's Prayer.

The Lord's Prayer and the teaching on forgiveness, which are both found elsewhere in the gospels, rather spoil the precisely balanced parallel structure of the pericopae on almsgiving, prayer, and fasting, passages which are not found elsewhere. So there is a strong probability that the Lord's Prayer has been inserted into the short pericopae on almsgiving, prayer, and fasting. In its present setting in Matthew 6 the Lord's Prayer is intended by the evangelist to be an example of an appropriate way to pray: do not show off like the hypocrites and do not babble like the Gentiles (6: 5–8).

So the setting of the Prayer in Matthew 6 is probably secondary. What is its setting in Luke? At Luke 11.1 Jesus is praying 'in a certain place'. Luke lays particular stress on Jesus at prayer. In no fewer than five passages (3: 21, just before the baptism of Jesus; 5: 16; 9: 18, before Peter's confession that Jesus is the Messiah; 9: 28, before the Transfiguration; and 11: 1) Luke the evangelist adds a reference to Jesus at prayer. In four of these five passages Luke depicts Jesus at prayer just before something especially important is disclosed to the reader.

In Luke the Lord's Prayer is given to the disciples in response to a request for a prayer comparable to the prayer taught by John the Baptist to his disciples. At the time of Jesus, individual religious groups had their own distinctive prayers; so Jesus is asked for a prayer which would be characteristic of his followers. Although the reference to Jesus himself at prayer comes from the hand of Luke, the immediate context is much more likely to be original than the setting of the Prayer in Matthew 6.

By the very way they have introduced the Lord's Prayer, both Matthew and Luke have interpreted the words of Jesus which follow. This process of adaptation and interpretation continued after the gospels were written. In many manuscripts of Matthew 6 we find the familiar doxology, 'For the Kingdom and the power and the glory are yours for ever. Amen.' This was certainly a very early traditional ending to the Lord's Prayer, for it is found already in the Didache, a Christian writing which dates from about AD 100. The extra words are almost certainly taken from David's prayer recorded in I Chron. 29: 11–13, where strikingly similar phraseology is used. Familiar biblical phrases already associated with prayer have been used to 'round off' the rather succinct Lord's Prayer in order to make it more appropriate for worship.

The same process of later reinterpretation can be discerned in phrases added to the second petition in just a few Greek manuscripts of Luke: 'May your Holy Spirit come upon us and cleanse us.' The additional words probably reflect use of the prayer in baptismal services. Their origin is uncertain, but this form of the Lord's Prayer may have been used in some Christian circles as early as the middle of the second century.

But back to the text of the Lord's Prayer as it exists in the most reliable manuscripts of Matthew and Luke. In Matthew's version there are two extra petitions which are not found in Luke—(2a) and (5a) as printed above. But they are not fresh petitions, for they are both closely related to and interpret the immediately preceding words. How, one might well ask, does God's kingdom or kingly rule come? In Matthew there is an answer: when God's will is done on earth as it is in heaven. Since almost exactly the same words are added by Matthew at 7: 21 to a saying of Jesus which is found also in Luke 6: 46, we can be fairly sure that the evangelist himself has expanded the second petition of the Lord's Prayer. This is not an arbitrary expansion, but an explanatory addition. Similarly, in (5a) the additional clause 'But rescue us from evil' is partly a 'filling out' or explanation of the preceding words, 'And lead us not into temptation.'

There are two other important variations between the versions of the Prayer in Matthew and Luke. In Matthew God is addressed in traditional Jewish liturgical phraseology: 'Our Father in heaven.' In contrast Luke has simply 'Father', behind which stands the Aramaic *Abba*, a word not often used at the time as an address to God in prayer. Jesus speaks of God as Father simply and directly, without any of the qualifying phrases which were often used to safeguard the transcendence of God. Jesus encourages his disciples to address God as Father and to share the relationship of sonship with the Father which he enjoyed.

The same emphasis on 'sonship' is found in Paul's writings. The Aramaic word *Abba* is used twice by Paul (Gal. 4: 6; Rom. 8: 15). In both passages the gift of God's Spirit confirms to Christian believers that they are adopted as sons or children of God and enables them to pray '*Abba*, Father'. Paul has used this Aramaic word in two letters written in Greek to readers who did not know any Aramaic! This suggests that *Abba* was a particularly important word. In a similar way some Christians today who do not know any Latin or Greek nonetheless use the Latin phrase *Pater Noster* (Our Father) or the Greek words *Kyrie Eleison* (Lord, have mercy). Paul's use of *Abba* suggests that Jesus' encouragement to his disciples to address God in prayer as 'Father' was understood in the early church to be an important theme in his teaching. For our present purposes it is important to note that by examining closely two very different versions of the familiar words of Jesus in the Lord's Prayer, it is possible to uncover the striking way Jesus addressed God in prayer.

This observation is supported by one further difference between Matthew and Luke. In the text of Matthew set out above the Greek has been translated as 'Give us this day our bread for the coming day'. The precise meaning of the adjective *epiousion* ('coming day') is uncertain since the word is not found elsewhere. It may refer to bread to be enjoyed in the future in the Kingdom of God; the sense would then be, 'Give us bread today as an anticipation of the feast we may expect to enjoy in heaven.' Not surprisingly, some later church fathers understood the bread as 'eucharistic bread'. But originally *epiousion* may well have a quite different meaning— not 'spiritual' bread of any kind, but ordinary bread which was sorely needed in a very poor rural setting: 'Give us this day bread to sustain our physical existence.'

Luke has certainly understood the petition in this second sense. Luke's opening verb is best translated 'keep on giving'. Instead of 'this day' Luke has the phrase 'each day' or 'daily'. By means of these two changes Luke elucidates the meaning of the unusual word *epiousion* for his readers. Luke's petition means 'Keep on giving us day by day the bread we need to keep us alive.'

The evangelist makes a similar modification to another equally puzzling saying of Jesus: 'If any want to come after me, let them deny themselves and take up their cross and follow me' (Mark 8: 34). At Luke 9: 23 the phrase 'daily' is added in order to stress the need for a daily act of self-denial on the part of a Christian disciple. In both passages the evangelist does not hesitate to alter the text in order to make it more readily applicable for his readers. He does this not because he wishes to put fresh words into the mouth of Jesus, but because he wants his readers to understand and to appropriate an otherwise puzzling saying of Jesus.

So much, then, for the adaptations and additions made both by Matthew and by Luke. The other words in the Lord's Prayer almost certainly go back to Jesus himself. There are no traces of later post-Easter Christian convictions; as we shall see in Chapter 9, this is one consideration which is used in reconstructions of the teaching of the historical Jesus. While a number of individual phrases, as well as the structure, rhythm, and rhyme can be paralleled in early Jewish prayers, the words of Jesus are no mere mosaic of traditional liturgical phrases. The prayer is unusually succinct: it summarizes several of the distinctive themes of the teaching of Jesus.

As we saw above, Jesus teaches his disciples to address God as *Abba*, Father. When the petitioner asks God that God's name (which stands for his person) may be hallowed, he or she asks that God may act (especially, as the next petition indicates) in the full and final disclosure of his kingly rule: men and women will then reverence and worship him.

The final two petitions refer to the needs of disciples. God is entreated to forgive their sins, but not because they have forgiven others—which would suggest a bargain with God. They know they can seek God's forgiveness only if they are willing to forgive others. 'Lead us not into temptation' does not necessarily conflict with James 1: 13 which insists that God himself tempts no one. Rather, the petition is for divine protection from all kinds of evil which threaten the disciple's relationship with God—especially apostasy which was expected to accompany the expected arrival of the last days. This is brought out in the wording used in the NRSV (and in similar wording in many other modern translations): 'Do not bring us to the time of trial, but rescue us from the evil one.'

This brief examination of the Lord's Prayer has illustrated both the difficulties and the fascination of serious study of the gospels. This passage has given us an excellent example of the ways earlier material is reinterpreted by the evangelists. At least partial reinterpretation occurs whenever, as frequently happens, the evangelists themselves provide either introductory phrases or a particular context for earlier traditions. From time to time they also adapt their source material in order to clarify its meaning for their readers.

Consideration of the distinctive literary and theological features of the individual gospels is an important first step towards recovery (as far as this is possible) of the actions and teaching of Jesus of Nazareth. So in the chapters which follow in Part I we shall concentrate on the individual gospels. We shall start with a discussion in Chapter 2 of the main ways the gospels have been studied since the late eighteenth century. We shall then turn to Mark because it is our earliest gospel and because it was used extensively and reinterpreted both by Matthew and by Luke.

In the four chapters on the individual gospels (Chapters 3–6), we shall concentrate on the evangelists' methods and distinctive themes. Only at the end of each chapter will the authorship and date of each gospel be considered briefly. These latter questions have often been given priority (sometimes at the expense of study of the text itself), but they can be considered only in the light of such evidence as we have for the evangelists' methods and purposes. The comments of second-century Christian writers on the origins of the gospels (which are often referred to as 'the external evidence') are interesting and will be discussed briefly, but they must not be given precedence over the internal evidence of the gospels themselves.

In Part II, we shall first discuss evidence about Jesus from outside the gospels, including archaeological evidence (Chapter 8). The methods and criteria which may be used in reconstructing the actions and teaching of Jesus will be considered in Chapter 9. Only then, in Chapters 10–18, will it be appropriate to tackle some of the questions about the teaching, intentions, and ultimate fate of Jesus of Nazareth which were raised at the beginning of this chapter.

2

WHAT IS A GOSPEL?

In reading or interpreting any writing, whether ancient or modern, the first step must always be to determine what kind or genre of writing it is. We do not read a poem and approach it as if it were a piece of history. When we pick up a novel, even before we have any idea at all of its contents, we have certain expectations about the kind of writing it is. The novelist may, of course, surprise us by breaking some of the accepted conventions. But if our novel turns out to be totally unlike other novels we have read, we shall be very confused indeed; we may not be able to read it with enjoyment or understanding.

What is a gospel? How do we know what kind of writing it is? We form a judgement about the genre of a writing quite instinctively by comparing it with other similar writings with which we are familiar. So what were the expectations of the first readers of the gospels? Did they assume that they were biographies, or histories, or travel tales, or religious propaganda? Paul's readers came to his letters with clear expectations, for the letter genre was well-known in the first century AD. The first readers of Revelation were less bewildered by this writing than many modern readers, for they were acquainted with the form of Jewish apocalypses.

The gospels raise a whole series of interesting questions. Are they intended by the evangelists to be read as accurate records of the life of Jesus? Or are they theological treatises cast very loosely in a narrative framework? Were the evangelists simply editors, compilers, or anthologists? Or were they self-conscious authors? Are the gospels stories whose purpose is to engage the reader whose understanding or knowledge is expected to progress from the beginning to the end of the narrative?

These questions will be discussed in this chapter. Unless at least provisional answers are found, there is a real risk that the gospels will not be properly understood. In the past inappropriate answers to these questions have sometimes led to a good deal of misunderstanding. Many readers of the gospels have assumed that they are intended to be accurate records of the life of Jesus, perhaps from eyewitnesses. They are then very puzzled by the differing accounts of the same incident in two or more gospels.

In this chapter we shall consider several different ways of approaching the gospels. For a long period in the nineteenth century the gospels were seen as historically reliable records or as biographies. In the early decades of the twentieth century the gospels came to be seen as anthologies of traditions which had been shaped by the life and faith of the early Christian communities in which they were transmitted. The gospels were 'proclamation' and not in any sense 'records' of the past. Following the Second World War attention turned to the distinctive emphases of the individual evangelists. Finally, and most recently, many scholars have used insights drawn from modern literary criticism and interpreted the gospels as stories with characters and dramatic plots.

It is worth noting at the outset that scholars have often mistakenly assumed that these are mutually exclusive ways of approaching the gospels. In our opening chapter we have already emphasized that 'story' and 'significance' are intertwined. We shall consider this point further at the end of this chapter.

The gospels as biographies

Is the literary genre of the gospels closely comparable with some Old Testament or Jewish writings, or with Graeco-Roman writings? Until recently, the generally accepted view was that the form of the gospels was unique and that Mark had no literary models at all. Discussion of these questions is not new. In the middle of the second century in his *Dialogue with Trypho* Justin Martyr referred to the gospels as 'memoirs of the apostles', thus aligning them with Xenophon's well-known 'memoirs' or 'biography' of Socrates. However, fifty years later Clement of Alexandria wrote, 'John, perceiving that the external facts had been made plain . . . and inspired by the Spirit, composed a spiritual gospel.' Clement was insisting that the Fourth Gospel should not be read as if it were comparable with Matthew, Mark, and Luke as a life of Jesus, or as a memoir of the apostles;

its form was distinctive and it should be approached with quite different expectations.

In the nineteenth century the gospels were often assumed to be biographies or accurate historical records. Many writers attempted to stitch together pieces from all four gospels in order to write a modern biography of Jesus. Quite often psychological explanations of the motives and intentions of Jesus were provided. Gaps in our knowledge were often filled out with imaginative reconstructions. For example, Luke 2: 40–52, the only passage in the gospels which tells us anything about the childhood of Jesus, was often filled out with intelligent (and at times unintelligent) guesswork about 'the hidden years of Jesus'.

On this general approach, Peter's confession of the Messiahship of Jesus at Mark 8: 27–30 was seen as a crucial turning point in the life of Jesus. In the opening chapters of Mark the miraculous deeds of Jesus are prominent, his teaching (which is limited in extent) is given mainly to the crowds, and there is very little discussion of his Messiahship. But after Peter's confession there is a clear change. Jesus frequently teaches the disciples, but rarely the crowds. In his teaching, his Messiahship and in particular his impending passion become much more prominent. There are very few healings.

If Mark's gospel is read as a biography of Jesus, it is natural to ask why Peter's confession, 'You are the Christ', led to a change in the tactics of Jesus. The usual answer given in the nineteenth century ran as follows: following the persistent failure of the crowds to grasp his intention, Peter's reply encouraged Jesus to concentrate his attention on the disciples in the hope that ultimately they might be more responsive than the crowds. This analysis of the motives of Jesus is based squarely on the assumption that Mark is a chronologically accurate biography of Jesus.

In 1915 the American scholar C. W. Votaw made a serious attempt to put this long-standing approach to the gospels on a proper scholarly footing. He compared the gospels with ancient popular biographies, especially Arrian's *Discourses of Epictetus*, Philostratus' *Life of Apollonius of Tyana*, and Xenophon's *Memorabilia*.

However, within a decade or so this approach to the gospels as biographies was abandoned quite suddenly. Why was there such a dramatic shift in scholarly opinion? Under the influence of form criticism (see below, pp. 27–9), the traditions behind the gospels were linked closely to the needs of the early Christian communities, especially their missionary preaching, catechetical instruction, argument with opponents, and worship. It was frequently claimed that the early church was so taken up with its proclamation of the Risen Christ that it was not interested at all in the past of Jesus. On this view the gospels stemmed from the proclamation of the early church and should not in any sense be seen as 'memoirs' or 'records'.

Rudolf Bultmann, the most influential New Testament scholar at that time, reacted vigorously against nineteenth-century scholars who had made a reconstructed biographical account of the life and personality of Jesus the very heart of the Christian message. For Bultmann the Risen Christ was central to Christian faith, not 'gentle Jesus meek and mild', not indeed the historical Jesus at all. Bultmann insisted that in its missionary preaching the early church was not concerned with more than the mere fact that Jesus of Nazareth had existed. The gospels may tell us a few things about the life and the teaching of Jesus, but this was, as it were, incidental or even contrary to their original intention.

To many of the form critics the very word 'biography' was like a red rag to a bull. For a long time nearly all the standard books on the gospels stated confidently that the gospels are not biographies. It was often said that Mark was a Passion narrative with an extended introduction. In other words Mark was seen as an exposition in narrative form of the preaching of the early church with its sharp focus on the significance of the cross and the resurrection. For the form critics the traditions behind the gospel and the gospels themselves were concerned almost entirely with the 'significance' of Jesus and hardly at all with 'story'.

It eventually became clear that some of the form critics had overreacted against the tendency prevalent at the end of the nineteenth century to make Jesus into a 'nice Victorian gentleman', or into a hero whose example could be imitated. In their over-emphasis on the theological intention of the gospel traditions, many form critics seriously confused ancient and modern conventions in biographical writing. They insisted that the main features of biographical writing are missing in the gospels: the evangelists are not concerned with precise chronology; they do not describe the personal appearance of Jesus; they do not attempt to unravel the development of his personality, nor do they set Jesus in the historical context of his own day.

In 1974 I defended an approach which was then unfashionable. I insisted that the gospels must be read against the backdrop, not of *modern* biographical writing, but of their own times. The features of biographies which were said by the form critics to be missing from the gospels are all part of the expectations with which a modern reader approaches a biography, but they were not hallmarks of ancient biographical writing.

A careful study of the methods of the Greek and Roman biographers leads to a positive conclusion of some importance. Even though ancient biographers did not trace character development and rarely summed up their subject's character in their own words, they were interested in the character of a person and knew how to portray it by using an indirect method of characterization. They allowed the actions and words of a person to speak for themselves. This simple and rather obvious technique was widely used even in sophisticated ancient biographical writing with its long literary tradition. So if we find that the gospels appear to portray the character of Jesus by reporting his actions and words, we are certainly not (as some of the form critics would have us believe) misunderstanding their intention.

Richard Burridge (1992) has undertaken a full-scale comparison of the gospels and Graeco-Roman 'lives'. He underlines the extent to which there is a clear family resemblance. Burridge accepts that while the gospels do diverge from Graeco-Roman biographies in some respects, they do not do so to any greater extent than ancient biographies differ from one another.

Nonetheless, it is worth noting that some features of Mark's gospel would have puzzled readers familiar with the conventions of ancient biographical writing: the evangelist's enigmatic opening which sets out 'the beginning of the gospel' as the fulfilment of prophecy and seems to assume that his readers know something about Jesus; his very full account of the last days of Jesus; and his curiously abrupt ending. With the possible exception of the story of the death of John the Baptist (Mark 6: 14–29 = Matt. 14: 1–12), the gospels do not use the stock in trade of the ancient biographer, anecdotes which are intended merely to satisfy curiosity or to entertain the reader.

There is little doubt, however, that early Christian readers of the gospels did read them as biographies. Matthew and Luke extended the trend set by the earliest evangelist, Mark: with their stories of the birth of Jesus and their more polished style and structure, the genre of the two later gospels is even more clearly that of an ancient biography than Mark.

As we shall see in Chapter 6, John's gospel differs considerably from the other three gospels, and is probably not directly dependent on them. However when the four gospels are set alongside all the other 'gospels' and related writings which flourished for a time in some circles in the early church (see Chapter 7), it is their similarities rather than their differences which are striking. In terms of its literary genre, John's gospel belongs to the same tradition as Mark, Matthew, and Luke.

The gospels, then, should certainly not be compared with *modern* biographies. Comparison with ancient biographies has established the gospels' resemblance to them in terms of their literary genre, and underlined their 'story' element. The gospels are undeniably Graeco-Roman biographies, though their distinctive features should not be overlooked.

Do Old Testament and later Jewish writings provide close parallels? Some parts of the Old Testament, especially the portrayal of David in I and II Samuel, the Elijah–Elisha cycles of traditions, and some of the 'biographical' traditions about the prophets provide partial parallels. But no part of the Old Testament is closely comparable with the genre of the gospels, or with their concentration on the teaching and actions of one person and of his varied relationships with different groups of followers and opponents.

Nor do we fare much better when we consider later Jewish writings. The Qumran community was established close to the eleven caves where most of the Dead Sea Scrolls were found. It was founded by the Teacher of Righteousness whose teaching was respected and retained. But we know very little about the Teacher's life and there are no Qumran writings remotely comparable with the gospels.

The gospels as history: source criticism

The second half of this book is concerned with the question: What can the historian say about the life and teaching of Jesus of Nazareth? Questions of this kind have been asked only since the eighteenth-century Enlightenment. H. S. Reimarus, the father of modern historical inquiry into the gospels, recognized that by pressing rigorously historical questions he would be perceived to be undermining traditional Christianity, so he decided not to allow his writings to be published in his lifetime. Six years after his death in 1768, the philosopher—theologian Lessing began to publish extracts from Reimarus's writings anonymously under the title *Wolfenbüttel Fragments*. In 1788 Lessing published his own book about the origin of Matthew and its relationship to Mark and Luke. Once the possibility of a literary relationship between these three gospels was accepted, the quest for the earliest gospel and for sources behind the gospels began. It was driven by the assumption that the earliest gospel or source would have the greatest *historical* value in reconstruction of the teaching and intention of Jesus. And so began intensive historical study of the gospels and their sources which continues to this day.

Historical issues had been considered in a limited way in the sixteenth century. Martin Luther was well aware of mistakes and inconsistencies in Scripture, as was Origen over a thousand years earlier. Luther recognized that Matt. 27: 9 mistakenly cited Jeremiah for Zechariah. He knew that there was a serious discrepancy between Matthew and John over the date of the cleansing of the temple: Matthew placed it at the end of the ministry of Jesus, John at the beginning. But Luther refused to settle such questions, insisting that they did not affect the proclamation which was the primary concern of the evangelists.

Not all Luther's colleagues took the same relaxed line. Andreas Osiander was convinced that proven contradictions in the gospels would undermine faith, so with great ingenuity he tried to harmonize the apparent discrepancies. This led him to conclude that Jesus must have been crowned with thorns twice, and that Peter must have warmed himself four times in the high priest's courtyard! Such harmonizations became impossible once it was recognized at the end of the eighteenth century that there is a close literary relationship between the gospels.

Scholars searched intensively for a hypothesis which would account for both the similarities and the differences between Matthew, Mark, and Luke. In 1835 Karl Lachmann built on and developed earlier proposals, and offered a solution which eventually won wide acceptance. On this view, which came to be known as Marcan priority, Mark's gospel was not the Cinderella among the gospels, as it had been in the early church, but the first gospel to have been written. It was therefore the gospel with the highest claims to be accepted as a reliable historical source.

Marcan priority

Why did Mark so quickly overtake Matthew and Luke in scholarly esteem? The reasons are worth setting out briefly. (For a more detailed discussion of the relationships between Matthew, Mark, and Luke—the synoptic problem—it will be necessary to consult one of the standard Introductions to the New Testament listed in the Bibliography.) There are five main reasons, not all of which were advanced by Lachmann, why Marcan priority is widely accepted by scholars as the most plausible solution of the synoptic problem.

(i) It is not at all difficult to see why both Matthew and Luke should want to expand Mark's much shorter gospel with further material about the life and teaching of Jesus to which they had access. But it is less easy to explain the reverse procedure. Why should Mark want to abbreviate either Matthew or Luke, or both? If he has done so, he has left out nearly every verse of the Sermon on the Mount, but he has managed to find room to expand Matthew with details which seem quite unimportant.

In the example set out below, Mark contains a number of additional phrases, most of which add little or nothing to the corresponding account in Matthew.

Mark 1: 29–31	Matt. 8: 14–15
And as soon as they left the synagogue, they entered the house of Simon and Andrew, with James and John. Now Simon's mother-in-law was in bed with a fever, and they told him about her at once. He came and took her by the hand and lifted her up. Then the fever left her and she began to serve them.	When Jesus entered Peter's house, he saw his mother-in-law lying in bed with a fever; he touched her hand, and the fever left her, and she got up and began to serve him.

For a further example, Mark 5: 1–20 should be compared with the very much shorter account in Matt. 8: 28–34. A synopsis is very useful for detailed comparisons: it sets out gospels in parallel columns so that they can be viewed at the same time (see the Bibliography).

The evidence is very impressive, but not absolutely decisive. There might just have been special reasons why Mark should want to abbreviate

Matthew and Luke in ways which seem to us to be distinctly odd, and yet at the same time add material which seems to us to be redundant.

(ii) Arguments based on the order of the material in Matthew, Mark, and Luke have been especially prominent in discussion of the synoptic problem. Lachmann noted that Luke very rarely changes Mark's order, and that Matthew does so only about seven times. While it is not difficult to account for the changes in order made by Matthew and Luke to Mark, it is very much more difficult to explain Mark's methods if he has used either Matthew, or Luke, or both.

In the past some scholars have developed a second argument from the order of the gospels. They have noted that Matthew and Luke never agree in order against Mark: they seem to have made occasional changes to Mark's order quite independently. But it is now generally accepted that while this observation does support Marcan priority strongly, it can also be used to support rival hypotheses.

(iii) Matthew and Luke frequently modify or omit redundant phrases or unusual words found in Mark, and improve his rather unsophisticated literary style. Mark begins a high proportion of his sentences with 'and'; he often links clauses within the same sentence with 'and'. Both Matthew and Luke, on the other hand, frequently 'improve' his rather unsophisticated Greek style.

Two specific examples are instructive. At Mark 1: 32 we read, 'When evening had come and when the sun had set . . .'. Of course the sun always sets when evening comes—and vice versa! Both Matthew and Luke have noted that one or the other of these clauses is redundant: Matthew includes only the first, Luke the second. Neither Matthew nor Luke includes Mark's rather curious reference to the cushion on which Jesus was asleep in the boat during the sudden storm on the lake (4: 38).

So many examples of the alleged later improvement of Mark's style have been noted that some scholars have claimed that this line of argument offers 'decisive' support for Marcan priority. Once again there is very strong cumulative evidence, but it falls short of proof. Some modern editors have occasionally been known to spoil the nicely turned prose of an accomplished writer by adding clumsy or redundant phrases!

(iv) A number of Marcan passages which seem to place Jesus in a bad light have been modified by Matthew and Luke. For example, Mark 3: 21 notes that some people were saying that Jesus 'was out of his mind'.

Neither Matthew nor Luke includes this strongly critical comment. Mark 6: 35 suggests that Jesus was unable to heal more than a few sick people 'in his own country'. Matthew carefully explains that this was the result of their unbelief, not the powerlessness of Jesus. In Mark 4: 38 the disciples say, 'Teacher, do you not care if we perish?' Both Matthew and Luke omit 'do you not care?', thus removing any suggestion that Jesus was indifferent to their plight. There is so much similar evidence that the most plausible hypothesis seems to be that the first gospel to be written has been 'tidied' by the two later gospels.

But once again an alternative explanation can be offered, though it has convinced few. Mark may have used Matthew and Luke and introduced changes which seem to us either to be awkward or to place Jesus in a bad light. Such changes may possibly have arisen simply as a result of Mark's personal preference.

(v) While the arguments given above (and more could be added) have persuaded most scholars that Mark is the earliest gospel, they do not amount to clear-cut proof. In recent decades some dissenters have noted (quite correctly) that Marcan priority is not the only possible explanation of some of the phenomena noted above. A rival hypothesis, which was first set out in 1789 by J. J. Griesbach, has been defended vigorously by a small number of scholars. On this view Mark is not the earliest but the *last* of the synoptic gospels to have been written, for Mark has used both Matthew and Luke. The modern version of Griesbach's hypothesis is often called the 'two gospel' hypothesis, in order to contrast it with the generally accepted view that Matthew and Luke have used 'two sources', Mark and a collection of the sayings of Jesus called Q (discussed below).

A full discussion of the 'two gospel' hypothesis cannot be included here, but it is worth noting the most damaging criticism that can be levelled against it. If an early Christian writer knew both Matthew and Luke, it is difficult to see why he would ever want to write what eventually became Mark's gospel. Who would want to produce a much-truncated version of Matthew and Luke? Why was Mark unwilling to include either Matthew's Sermon on the Mount in chapters 5–7 or the shorter version in Luke 6: 17–49?

When particular passages are examined carefully on the basis of this alternative to Marcan priority, it is not at all easy to understand Mark's literary methods. But as we shall see in Chapters 4 and 5, on the basis of

Marcan priority we can readily understand why Matthew and Luke should want to modify and expand Mark, and the methods and distinctive theological emphases of Matthew and Luke can be discerned with some confidence. In short, one of the strongest arguments which can be used to support the hypothesis of Marcan priority is that it has proved to be more plausible and more serviceable than any of its rivals.

By now it should be clear why study of the interrelationships of the synoptic gospels has been pursued so vigorously for so long. Marcan priority and the 'two gospel' (or Griesbach) hypothesis lead to utterly different understandings of the evangelists' methods and emphases and of the setting of their gospels in early Christianity. Is Mark our earliest gospel, the foundation on which both Matthew and Luke have built their gospels? Or is Mark but a pale shadow of the two gospels he has abbreviated?

The Q hypothesis

Luke shares with Matthew about 230 verses which are not found in Mark. For over a century this material has been known as Q. We must consider briefly at this point the five main arguments which have been advanced in support of the view that both Matthew and Luke have used Q as well as Mark.

(i) There is often very close verbal agreement between Matthew and Luke, extending over several verses. As examples, the following passages should be compared carefully: Matt. 3: 7–10 = Luke 3: 7–9; Matt. 11: 4–11, 16–19 = Luke 7: 22–8, 31–5. Even though Matthew and Luke are two very different gospels, they have both used Mark extensively. Thus it is likely (so the argument runs) that where they agree closely in non-Marcan sections, they are both using the same source, Q.

Verbal agreement between Matthew and Luke is often close—but not in every tradition the later gospels seem to share. Compare, for example, Matt. 7: 13–14, 22–3 and Luke 13: 24–7; and also Matt 22: 1–10 and Luke 14: 16–24. These passages (and many others with similar limited verbal agreement) are usually said to stem from Q.

Why is there close verbal agreement in some so-called Q passages, but not in others? This baffling phenomenon is often glossed over by supporters of Q. The explanations which are offered often look like special pleading. So the close verbal agreement between Matthew and Luke in some passages by no means proves that Q existed.

(ii) Although Matthew weaves his sources together (especially in his five large discourses) and Luke places them in 'strips' or blocks, there are some striking agreements in the *order* in which the non-Marcan traditions are found in Matthew and Luke. These agreements in order cannot be coincidental and strongly suggest the use of a common source.

(iii) In several passages in Matthew and Luke we find that essentially the same tradition is repeated; these repetitions are known as doublets. These occur where Matthew and Luke both use the Marcan form of a saying, but elsewhere they also both use a non-Marcan or Q form of essentially the same saying. As an example the following doublet should be examined in a synopsis: 'To those who have, more will be given . . .': Mark 4: 25 = Matt. 13: 12 = Luke 8: 18; a similar saying is found at Matt. 25: 29 = Luke 19: 26. And as a second example of a doublet: 'If any want to become my followers, let them deny themselves . . .': Mark 8: 34 f. = Matt. 16: 24 f. = Luke 9: 23 f.; there is a similar saying at Matt. 10: 38 f. = Luke 14: 27, 17: 33.

(iv) The Q material 'hangs together' as an entity: the traditions betray a similar theological outlook. Q did not survive beyond its incorporation into Matthew and Luke, but the Gospel of Thomas does consist of a collection of sayings of Jesus, and this suggests that other collections of the sayings of Jesus may have been made. (See below pp. 123–30.)

(v) Any alternative explanation of the non-Marcan material shared by Matthew and Luke is much less plausible, especially the suggestion that Luke has used Matthew, the main rival hypothesis to Q which we must now consider briefly.

If Luke has used Matthew, then we may dispense with Q. Since the Griesbach (or 'two gospel') alternative to Marcan priority (see above pp. 20–3) also insists that Luke has used Matthew, this possibility has to be considered seriously in discussions of the synoptic problem. If Luke has used Matthew, then he has used this major source extremely freely indeed: he has 'dismantled' Matthew in order to write his own very different gospel. So we must ask whether it is at all likely that Luke has used Matthew (as well as Mark) as a major source.

For the following reasons this alternative to the Q hypothesis is most unlikely and has attracted few supporters. (a) If Luke has used Matthew, what has happened to Matthew's five impressive discourses? On this view, a small part of Matthew's Sermon on the Mount in chapters 5–7 reappears in Luke 6: 20–49, but the rest of the material is either scattered (apparently haphazardly) right through Luke's gospel and set in very different contexts or it is omitted completely. Matthew's second discourse in chapter 10 reappears in no fewer than seven different chapters in Luke! While attempts have been made to account for Luke's rather odd treatment of the Matthean discourses, they have convinced few.

(b) If Luke has used Matthew, we would expect him to have adopted some of the expansions and modifications Matthew makes to Mark. But hardly a trace of them can be found in Luke. On this alternative to the Q hypothesis, where Matthew and Mark have the same tradition, Luke opts for Mark's version and ignores Matthew's; and at the same time he rearranges Matthew very considerably. Why did Luke find Matthew so unattractive, when in almost all other parts of early Christianity it became the favourite gospel? Peter's confession at Caesarea Philippi provides a good example. At Luke 9: 18–21, Mark's account (8: 27–30) has been used, but there isn't a sign in Luke of the major addition Matthew makes to Mark at 16: 16–19. Here several sayings of Jesus addressed to Peter, including the words 'On this rock I will build my church', have not been used.

(c) This alternative to the Q hypothesis has to assume that in the non-Marcan traditions Matthew and Luke share, it is always Luke who has changed the earlier form of the tradition found in Matthew. This claim cannot be sustained when the traditions are examined in detail. On the view that Luke has used Matthew, Luke has *abbreviated* Matthew's version both of the Lord's Prayer (see above pp. 6–11) and of the Beatitudes (see below pp. 67–70). Why should Luke wish to do this? It is difficult to discover reasons.

(d) After the temptations of Jesus (Matt. 4: 1–11 = Luke 4: 1–13), Luke and Matthew never use the non-Marcan sayings they share (i.e. Q) in the same Marcan context. If Luke has used Matthew, then he has carefully removed every non-Marcan (Q) saying from the Marcan context it has in Matthew and placed it in a different context!

(e) We may mention one final point which in fact sums up several of the above observations. If we accept that Luke has used Mark, then with the help of a synopsis we can readily discover the changes of various kinds which he has made to Mark. On the whole he has retained Mark's order and has considerable respect for the content, especially of the teaching of Jesus. If Luke has also used Matthew, we would expect him have to have modified his second source in broadly similar ways. But this is by no means the case.

Most scholars accept that on the whole Luke has retained the order and content of Q more fully than Matthew, so reconstructions of Q are usually based on Luke. Q was probably originally a little larger than the 230 or so verses shared by Matthew and Luke. Since both Matthew and Luke omit some Marcan material, why should we suppose that they have both incorporated Q in full? Hence some of the 'M' or 'L' material (i.e. traditions found only in Matthew and Luke) may have belonged originally to Q, though the precise extent of such additional Q traditions is far from clear.

Before we proceed, we must note that supporters of Marcan priority and of the Q hypothesis do have to contend with evidence which seems to some to undermine these two pillars of most modern study of the gospels. If we accept Marcan priority, why do we find that in a number of passages where Matthew and Luke are apparently using Mark independently, the two later evangelists *agree* in their phraseology? These unexpected agreements are usually dubbed 'the minor agreements'. But are they minor? Or are there so many of them that they are the Achilles heel of the two-source hypothesis? The 'minor agreements' are almost always the starting point for rival explanations.

The phrase 'who struck you?' which Matt 26: 68 and Luke 22: 64 add to Mark 14: 65 is a good example of a 'minor agreement'. Is it simply a coincidence that both later evangelists expand Mark in precisely the same way? Do they both draw on continuing oral tradition? Or is it possible that Matthew and Luke used a version of Mark which included this phrase? In fact some (mainly later) manuscripts of Mark do include the phrase! Most scholars accept that in nearly every case explanations along the various lines just mentioned can be offered.

There are, then, strong reasons for accepting the two-document hypothesis, i.e. for supposing that Matthew and Luke have used both Mark and Q. Alternative hypotheses are much less plausible, but there are two main reasons why the two-document hypothesis does not amount to mathematical proof of the synoptic problem. The phenomena of the 'minor agreements' and the considerable variations in the extent of verbal agreement in so-called Q passages remind us that certainty eludes us. Marcan priority and Q are working hypotheses and on this basis impressive results have been achieved in modern study of the gospels. The later chapters of this book assume that these two hypotheses are the most plausible available.

The gospels as proclamation: form criticism

In the first three decades of the twentieth century the gospels came to be seen not as biographies, but as profoundly theological writings. They were said to be so strongly stamped with the Easter faith of the early church that their value for the student of the life and teaching of Jesus was strictly limited. The gospels were anything but straightforward historical accounts of the life and teaching of Jesus of Nazareth.

This complete change of direction was closely related to the development of a fresh way of analysing the traditions behind the gospels. Scholars noted that Mark was largely made up of short accounts of the actions and teaching of Jesus. These pericopae (or paragraphs) fell into set patterns or forms, hence the term 'form criticism'. Since Mark's pericopae were only loosely linked to one another, if at all, the early form critics concluded that they represented originally independent oral traditions. The evangelist, who was seen very much as an anthologist, was responsible for gathering them together.

If one reads the opening chapters of Mark it is not difficult to see that it is rather like a block of chocolate: it can be broken apart quite easily into separate small blocks. Mark 1: 40–5, the account of the healing of the leper, is fairly typical. There is no explicit geographical or chronological setting: this story could be positioned without difficulty at many other points in the gospel. So it is quite possible that its present position has been determined by Mark himself, rather than by genuine historical reminiscence.

The form critics claimed that the traditions behind the gospels could be analysed according to their structure. Some pericopae which reach their climax with words of Jesus were called 'pronouncement stories'. For example, in Mark 2: 17 Jesus replies to his critics who were outraged at his conduct in eating with tax collectors and sinners: 'I have come not to call the righteous, but sinners.' This comment concludes the dispute: there is nothing more to be said. There are some fourteen 'pronouncement stories' in Mark; see, for example, Mark 2: 23–8; 10: 2–9; 10: 17–22; 12: 13–17.

Other traditions focus not on a word of Jesus, but on his miraculous action. They end with a comment on the response to a miracle of Jesus; see, for example, Mark 1: 28; 1: 31; 1: 45. The sayings as well as the accounts of the actions of Jesus were closely analysed according to their 'form'. The parables, for example, are clearly a special group of sayings. The sayings of Jesus were analysed into several other more technical categories.

Some form critics claimed that close study of the 'forms' of both the narratives and the sayings of Jesus shed light on their origin and development in the early church. For three decades the traditions on which Mark drew had been used and shaped (and sometimes even created) in the life of the early Christian communities. On this view, the gate and path from Mark's gospel to a reconstruction of the life of Jesus was not as wide and easy as had been supposed in the latter half of the nineteenth century. On the other hand, several scholars insisted that analysis of the gospel traditions according to their forms does not necessarily solve the question of their historicity. We shall return to this much-disputed area in Chapter 9.

The various types (or 'forms') of traditions were often related by scholars to the diverse needs of the early church—to missionary preaching, to catechetical instruction, to debate with opponents, or to worship. There are, however, difficulties with this suggestion. We do not know as much as we would like about the earliest Christian communities which transmitted the gospel traditions. So reconstruction of the kind of traditions they needed must be tentative. And some of the 'forms' sketched above seem appropriate for more than one setting in the life of the church.

A more general point made by the early form critics does seem valid: the first followers of Jesus only retained traditions which were relevant to their life and faith. It is for this reason that the gospels fail to satisfy modern curiosity concerning the physical appearance or psychological make-up of Jesus. Some form critics, however, went a good deal further. They claimed that historical and biographical reminiscence was of no interest at all in the early church. Jesus was worshipped as 'Lord' and his *parousia* (coming) or return was expected soon. He was not a 'hero' whose actions and attitudes were to be imitated.

Many form critics appealed to the words of Martin Kähler written in 1896: 'Just as the light of the sun is reflected in every drop of the bedewed meadow, so the full person of the Lord of the church's proclamation meets the reader of the gospels in each little story.' In other words, every single pericope is itself 'gospel' or proclamation.

This understanding of the traditions behind the gospels was also applied to the gospels themselves. They were not intended to be biographies. They are 'gospels' which proclaim the Christ of the faith of the post-Easter church. They continually disclose to the perceptive reader, often partially and indirectly, not so much who Jesus of Nazareth was in his earthly life, but who the Risen Lord is now. In the words of Martin Dibelius written in 1919, Mark is 'a book of the secret epiphanies of Jesus'.

Not all the claims of the early form critics have stood the test of time. Their fundamental insight that the traditions behind the gospels reflect, at least in part, the theological convictions of the post-Easter period is both undeniable and valuable. But there is no need to insist that the early church was not interested in setting out the 'past' of the life of Jesus. As we saw in our opening chapter (pp. 4–6), the gospels are concerned both with the story of Jesus, and with his significance for his later followers.

The evangelists as authors: redaction criticism

In the preceding paragraphs we noted that the form critics saw Mark as an anthology or as a collage—a collection of various shapes and sizes of originally independent pieces. With few exceptions, little attention was paid to the contribution of Mark or of the other evangelists. But as with a collage, the gospels are undoubtedly more than merely the sum of their individual parts. Have the evangelists themselves reshaped some of the traditions at their disposal—or even contributed some pieces? What are the distinctive features of the individual gospels? With hindsight, these questions were bound to be raised in the wake of form criticism. In fact they have dominated study of the gospels for the last forty years.

This general approach is known as 'redaction criticism'. In the first phase of redaction criticism, close attention was given to the modifications made by the evangelists to their sources; the 'redaction', it is usually alleged, is consistent and reveals the evangelist's own theological stance and his particular purpose in writing. Little or no attention was given to traditions the evangelists retained without modification.

In the second phase of redaction critical study, which is sometimes referred to as 'composition criticism', the evangelists' use of *all* the traditions at their disposal (both 'redacted' and 'unredacted' traditions) was studied. 'Composition criticism' considers the overall structure of each gospel, the structure of individual sections and sub-sections, and the order in which the evangelists have placed the traditions at their disposal. Once again conclusions about the evangelists' intentions are drawn from study of their literary methods.

If we can be reasonably certain that Matthew and Luke have both used Mark, it is not difficult with the use of a synopsis to trace the changes or additions the later evangelists have made to Mark's traditions. Some of the changes are no more than a tidying of some of Mark's awkward phrases and constructions. But again and again modifications reflect a different theological point of view.

In 1948 G. Bornkamm published what has become a classic study of Matthew's reinterpretation of Mark's account of the stilling of the storm. This lucid short essay, which is listed in the Bibliography, still repays careful study. Mark's account in 4: 35–41 begins a series of miracle stories which are geographically grouped around the sea of Galilee. The scene is set at 4: 1 where Jesus teaches the large crowd on the shore from a boat on the sea. The long 'parables discourse' follows (4: 2–34). Jesus and the disciples then leave the crowds and cross to the other side of the sea of Galilee. Mark's account of the stilling of the storm is a miracle story. It ends with a reference to the awe of the disciples: 'Who then is this, that even the wind and the sea obey him?'

The setting in Matt. 8: 23–7 is quite different. Matthew's version forms part of a cycle of miracle stories in chapters 8 and 9; they have been carefully set immediately after chapters 5–7, the Sermon on the Mount. Matthew has introduced and concluded this major section of his gospel with similar sentences (4: 23 and 9: 35), thus confirming that these chapters form one long single section.

The immediate context in Matthew is striking. Matthew's account of the stilling of the storm is preceded by two short incidents about following Jesus in discipleship (8: 19–22). In Mark the disciples take Jesus with them in the boat (4: 36), but in Matthew we read: 'And when he got into the boat, his disciples followed him' (8: 23). The verb 'followed' links this pericope with the preceding verses. According to Bornkamm the preceding sayings about discipleship serve to illustrate the meaning of what takes place in the stilling of the storm.

Bornkamm observes that Matthew has made a number of other changes. In particular he notes that whereas in Mark the disciples refer to Jesus as 'Teacher' (4: 38), in Matthew Jesus is called 'Lord', a change the evangelist has made in numerous other places. 'Lord' is not a human title of respect (as is 'Teacher'), but a 'divine predicate of majesty'. Bornkamm concludes: 'Matthew is not only a hander-on of the narrative, but also its oldest exegete, and in fact the first to interpret the journey of the disciples with Jesus in the storm and the stilling of the storm with reference to discipleship, and that means with reference to the little ship of the Church' (p. 55).

This is a good example of redaction criticism. Attention is drawn to the structure of Matthew's gospel and to the new context in which the evangelist has placed the Marcan miracle story ('composition criticism'). Matthew's 'redaction' of Mark often appears at first to involve incidental details, but close study reveals that it is part of a consistent and thoroughgoing reinterpretation of Mark.

In this essay Bornkamm noted that in future it would be necessary to inquire about the motives in the composition of the individual gospels. Over the past half-century many scholars have taken up that challenge. But they have not always heeded Bornkamm's further warning: 'Care will have to be taken to guard against reading out of the text or into it more than is warranted' (p. 57). All too often theological reinterpretation has been discerned in what are simply stylistic preferences.

If Matthew and Luke have clearly reshaped and reinterpreted their traditions, we must surely expect Mark to have done likewise. But in the case of Mark, it is very much less easy to distinguish between the traditions on which the evangelist drew and the changes (or redaction) for which he was responsible. Careful attention to the evangelist's methods of composition does not always take us much further. Redaction criticism of Mark will always be more hazardous than in the case of Matthew and Luke. The problem will be considered further in the next chapter.

Redaction criticism has directed attention to the distinctive features of the individual gospels. In a sense this book is a product of redaction criticism: we have emphasized that study of the gospels must start with the teaching of the evangelists; only then is it possible to consider the teaching

of Jesus. Forty or fifty years ago a book on the gospels would have concen-
trated solely on the teaching and intention of Jesus. Redaction critical
study of the gospels has led to a new appreciation of their purposes. There
have been many gains—some of which will be considered in the next three
chapters.

The gospels as stories: literary criticism

In the last two decades or so a wide range of insights drawn from the work
of literary critics has been applied to the gospels. An appreciation of the
importance of literary genre for interpretation (discussed at the beginning
of this chapter) is one such literary insight. Two further types of literary
criticism will be considered in this section: narrative criticism and reader
response criticism.

Narrative criticism of the gospels began with the publication in 1982 of
Mark as Story, written jointly by a New Testament scholar, David Rhoads,
and a colleague based in an English department, Donald Michie. The title
signals its main thrust. The gospels are seen as narratives with a carefully
constructed plot and with finely drawn characterization of individuals and
groups. The evangelist (or narrator) invites the reader to enter a 'story
world' which is full of conflict, suspense, and unexpected reversal. The
reader is encouraged to sympathize with some of the characters, but not
others. Terms which dot the pages of books on modern English literature
suddenly appear in a study of Mark's gospel.

A year later Alan Culpepper's *Anatomy of the Fourth Gospel* adopted a
similar approach. Plot and characterization are considered, as well as the
gospel's use of symbolism, irony, and the misunderstanding motif.
Narrative critical studies of Matthew and of Luke soon followed; details
are included in the Bibliography.

Narrative criticism deliberately turns its back on attempts to separate
tradition and redaction. The gospels are not seen as 'windows' through
which the reader (after careful historical reconstruction) might be able to
'see' the teaching of Jesus or the make-up of the community for whom the
evangelist is writing. The text of the gospels is a 'mirror' in which readers
'see' the world in which they themselves live. The narrators are seeking
to persuade the reader that the story they tell and its central character

reveal something profoundly true about the 'real' world in which the reader lives.

A narrator often reveals to the reader the full significance of what is happening in the story. Mark contains a number of asides addressed directly to the reader. These often take the form of explanations. In chapter 7, for example, Jewish hand-washing customs are explained (vv. 3–4), and the Hebrew word *Corban* (v. 11) and the Aramaic word *Ephphatha* (v. 34) are translated for Mark's Greek-speaking readers. In verse 19 the evangelist himself comments directly on the preceding words of Jesus in order to make sure that the reader has grasped what Mark took to be Jesus' radical rejection of Jewish ideas about clean and unclean food: 'Thus he declared all foods clean.'

Matthew frequently introduces quotations which stress that in particular incidents the Old Testament has been fulfilled. In Matt. 8: 16 there is a general reference to the healing activity of Jesus which has been taken from Mark 1: 32–4. The verse which follows is not found in Mark. It may be seen as an 'aside' of the narrator which sets out for the reader the significance of what is taking place in the story: 'This was to fulfil what was spoken by the prophet Isaiah, "He took our infirmities and bore our diseases."' (On Matthew's 'fulfilment citations', see further below, pp. 70–3.)

Even more important than the evangelists' asides and explanations to their readers are the ways they disclose to the reader at the very outset of their stories the true identity of the main character. Mark does this in his opening line: 'The beginning of the gospel of Jesus Christ, the Son of God.' As the story unfolds the true identity of Jesus is either kept secret from the participants in the story or is misunderstood by them, but for the reader there is no secret.

In Matthew 1 and 2 and also in Luke 1 and 2, which are usually known as the infancy narratives, the true identity of Jesus is repeatedly made clear before the story proper unfolds. The important prologue to the Fourth Gospel, John 1: 1–18, functions in the same way. The evangelists use the simple literary technique of 'foreshadowing' at the outset of their stories' themes which will be developed as the 'plot' unfolds.

At first sight this approach seems to mark a sharp break with earlier scholarship, but there are some lines of continuity. In some respects narrative criticism is an extension of 'composition criticism' with its strong insistence that the gospels must be viewed as whole units whose various parts are interrelated.

To some scholars it seems inappropriate to apply to ancient writings methods developed in study of sophisticated modern novels. While redaction criticism has taught us that the gospels are not 'artless', they are a far cry from the novels of James Joyce or Thomas Mann. As we saw above, some of the techniques and conventions of modern biographical writing were unknown to ancient biographers. Some of the methods used by modern novelists were unknown to ancient storytellers, so caution is necessary.

However, some of the devices of the storyteller which are universal undoubtedly do help us to read the gospels more sensitively. A good story will contain a memorable beginning and ending, a strong plot with climactic moments, dramatic scenes, and vividly drawn characters. All are present in the gospels, as we shall see in the chapters which follow.

Narrative criticism has made a major impact on study of the gospels. The traditional concerns of biblical scholars with historical reconstruction are being complemented by literary criticism. Consideration of the ways the narratives of the gospels make their impact on the reader and force a response increase still further our appreciation of the evangelists' skills. However, it is important to note that since the 'story world' of the evangelists is not a timeless world, but one set in a particular first-century religious and cultural setting, historical studies are still essential.

There is a further ground for hesitation. Narrative criticism takes seriously (and helpfully) the 'story' element of the gospels. But the gospels are more than 'stories'! Hence the phrase 'story and significance' is used repeatedly in this book in order to draw attention to their dual perspective. The evangelists inform us about the 'past' story of Jesus of Nazareth, and also about his continuing significance as Messiah–Christ and Son of God.

But how do we as readers of the gospels respond? The 'story' and the 'significance' of the text are, and always have been, construed differently by different readers. The evangelists do not always tell us all we want to know, so as readers we are forced fill the gaps in the texts. We may not be disposed to accept what they do tell us. Inevitably we respond on the basis of our own presuppositions.

The points just made take us to the heart of what is known as 'reader response criticism'. The focus of attention is no longer the author or evangelist, or even the text itself, but the reader and her or his responses to the text. Once again the work of literary critics, especially Wolfgang Iser and Stanley Fish, has been influential in raising fresh questions for the serious student of the gospels.

Reader response critics have given most of their attention to the responses of modern readers. They insist that meaning is constructed by the reader who receives the text. However, as we saw in our discussion of the gospels as biographies, ancient and modern literary conventions often differ, and if they are ignored confusion results. So we need to bear in mind that ancient and modern responses to the text may differ. The responses of the first readers of the gospels need to be taken seriously. How did they 'hear' the texts? What assumptions about miracles, for example, would have been in their minds?

Two further points need to be mentioned. The gospels were intended for *oral performance*, not silent personal study. Silent reading of texts was almost unknown in antiquity. The gospels would have been read aloud repeatedly. Hence many of the stylistic techniques used by the evangelists (repetition of words and phrases, for example) were intended to assist *oral* communication of the text.

The first listeners may have taken for granted some of the features of the gospels which make little impact on us. So consideration of the assumptions the first readers would have brought to the text is always important. The first listeners to Matthew's gospel would have been familiar with the technique of comparison, for it was a feature of education at all levels. Comparisons were regularly made between persons who were similar, but different. As we shall see in Chapter 4, Matthew draws a sustained set of comparisons between Jesus and Moses, between Jesus and John the Baptist, between Jesus and the disciples, and between Jesus and the scribes and Pharisees.

In emphasizing the importance of the responses of the first listeners to the gospels, I do not intend to imply that the responses of modern readers are unimportant. We all bring our presuppositions and prejudices to the text. Reader response critics remind us that these assumptions play a much larger role in interpretation than we imagine.

Study of the gospels has undoubtedly been enlivened by the new perspectives and questions brought to their interpretation in recent decades. Feminist writers and liberation theologians, for example, have brought fresh readings and a range of stimulating issues to the fore.

In the interpretation of the gospels the intention of the evangelists must be taken seriously, as must the design and narrative contours of the text itself, and the responses of readers—whether ancient or modern. Author, text, and reader all have their place; a one-sided concentration on any one of the three leads to mayhem in interpretation. (For a fuller introduction to literary criticism and to the principles of interpretation, see Robert Morgan's book *Biblical Interpretation* in this series.)

In this chapter we have examined the approaches to the gospels which have dominated modern study. We have seen how the pendulum of scholarly opinion has swung from a one-sided view of the gospels as biographies to the equally lopsided view of some form critics who saw the gospels (correctly) as concerned with proclamation, but denied that the traditions were concerned with the 'past' of Jesus. The evangelists, we have insisted, have two concerns: to tell the story of Jesus (as they understand it) and to spell out their convictions concerning the continuing significance of Jesus after Easter. 'Story' and 'significance' are intertwined and sometimes tangled. In Part II we shall consider ways of 'unravelling' the gospels in order to reconstruct the teaching and intention of Jesus.

3

MARK'S GOSPEL:
THE WAY OF JESUS

In modern times Mark's gospel has been studied more intensively than any of the other gospels. Since most scholars accept that it was the first written gospel, it has usually been given pride of place in attempts to recover the teaching of the historical Jesus. In the early church, however, Mark was rather neglected. Scribes copied it less frequently than the other gospels; preachers rarely referred to Mark, and it was read only occasionally in church services; few commentators discussed it in detail.

The reasons for this neglect are not hard to find. With the exception of only about forty verses, the whole of Mark's gospel is found in Matthew, and about half is found also in Luke. Mark does not include stories about the birth of Jesus, and his account of the resurrection is terse to say the least. Whereas nearly two-thirds of Matthew's much longer gospel is taken up with the teaching of Jesus, words of Jesus take up only just over one third of Mark. Familiar parables such as the Good Samaritan and the Prodigal Son are found in Luke, but not in Mark. In Mark's gospel there is hardly a trace of the sayings of Jesus found in the Sermon on the Mount in Matt. 5–7.

In AD 400 Augustine, one of the most influential of the early church fathers, claimed that Mark was the 'follower and abbreviator' of Matthew. In the early church generally it was Matthew, not Mark, which was the most popular gospel. So why was Mark accepted into the New Testament, and why did it survive as one of four canonical gospels? The most important single factor was undoubtedly the tradition—accepted almost universally in the early church—that Mark was written by a disciple of Peter. In Chapter 7 (pp. 135–9) we shall discuss briefly some of the reasons why the early church eventually accepted four gospels as authoritative

Scripture even though Matthew, Mark, and Luke overlap to a considerable extent.

Tradition and redaction

As we saw in the previous chapter, modern study of the gospels has been dominated by redaction criticism. In the case of Matthew and Luke, it is not at all difficult for the beginner to trace the changes Matthew and Luke have made to Mark. With careful use of a synopsis, even in an English translation, it soon becomes clear that Matthew and Luke have reshaped and reinterpreted their traditions. But what about Mark? Surely we may expect him to have done likewise with the traditions he incorporated into his gospel. But it is much less easy to distinguish between the traditions on which Mark drew and the changes (or redaction) for which he was responsible.

Most form critics accepted that Mark gathered together originally independent pericopae or paragraphs. But once redaction critics began to ask about the evangelist's own contribution, attention turned to Mark's possible use of blocks of traditions. Some exegetes suggested that perhaps the evangelist simply took over as one unit the cycle of controversy stories from Mark 2: 1 to 3: 6. Similar suggestions were made about chapter 4: 1–34, chapter 13, and parts of chapters 14–16.

But in spite of very detailed studies it has proved notoriously difficult to separate tradition and redaction in Mark. In some passages, however, we are able to trace the evangelist's own hand reasonably confidently. In two verses in Mark chapter 13 adds a direct comment to the reader. In the words of warning in 13: 14 concerning the impending destruction of the Temple and of Jerusalem, reference is made to 'the desolating sacrilege which will be set up where it ought not to be'. The evangelist adds an aside which is often placed in brackets in modern translations: 'let the reader understand what this means'. At the end of this chapter, following repeated warnings to the disciples, readers of the gospel as well as the disciples are addressed in verse 37: 'And what I say to you, I say to all: Watch.' There are further examples of comments from the evangelist himself in Mark 7: 3–4 and 19b.

If the evangelist has used originally independent traditions, then he himself is probably responsible for the summaries and linking passages in the gospel. In Mark 1: 32–4 there is a rather general statement concerning the healing activity of Jesus which is usually seen as a 'summary' which the evangelist himself has provided: 'That evening, at sundown, they brought to him all who were sick or possessed with demons. And the whole city was gathered around the door. And he cured many who were sick with various diseases, and cast out many demons; and he would not permit the demons to speak, because they knew him.' There are similar summaries at 3: 7–12 and 6: 53–6, and a much shorter one at 6: 6b: 'Then he went about among the villages teaching.'

In some cases it is possible to isolate the evangelist's own favourite vocabulary and style. In forty-three places the Greek word *euthus* is used. In the later and much longer gospels this word falls out of favour: it is used only eight times in Matthew, three in Luke, and three in John. *Euthus* is often translated as 'immediately', though some modern translators (correctly) accept that Mark does not intend this word to be understood literally, and so they translate it as 'soon', or 'then'. Mark uses the word as one way of linking originally independent traditions into a continuous story.

Mark uses 'to teach' and 'teaching' more frequently than the other evangelists and always with reference to Jesus. Yet the content of the teaching is often not referred to, or is summarized only briefly. Why is this so? Is Mark primarily interested in the authority with which Jesus taught (1: 22, 27) and with the world's astonishment at his teaching (6: 2; 11: 18)? If so, then his main concern may be to proclaim that in Jesus' teaching God himself has broken into this world; a full account of the teaching of Jesus would, on this view, be superfluous. This is a good example of the way possible conclusions about Mark's purpose may be based on study of the evangelist's vocabulary.

Isolation of Mark's redaction from the traditions which he has used is rarely as straightforward as the examples just given. More often than not close study of Mark's vocabulary and style leads to an impasse. So scholars often place more weight on that other form of redaction criticism known more accurately as 'composition criticism' (see p. 30). Particular attention is paid to the structure of the gospel, to Mark's choice of traditions, to the sequence in which they are placed, to the way his juxtaposition of traditions seems deliberate, and to the way he begins and ends his gospel.

A dramatic story

Narrative criticism (see above pp. 32–4) usefully complements this way of approaching the gospel by insisting that the gospel should be treated as a whole writing. Once we do this, we rediscover Mark's genius as a story-teller. The evangelist has not compiled an anthology of traditions roughly grouped by theme. He has written a lively story with several major turning points and climaxes. Perhaps Mark should be seen not so much as a block of chocolate (form criticism) or as a string of pearls (redaction criticism) but as a piece of rope with interwoven strands. Nearly all Mark's themes are introduced in chapter 1 and then developed as the story unfolds.

Mark's gospel is a dramatic story with a Prologue (1: 1–13 to which we shall turn in a moment) followed by five sections or acts—as in a modern drama. Some scholars have argued that Mark was familiar with the great tradition of Greek tragedy, and borrowed some of its conventions. This must be left as an open question. However, it is helpful to view Mark as a drama with five acts though the ancient Greeks did not divide their tragedies this way.

Act I (1: 14 to 3: 6) opens with a summary of the proclamation of Jesus, who announces the gospel of God: 'The time is fulfilled, and the kingdom of God has come near; repent and believe in the good news' (1: 14–15). These words link Jesus with John, whose role has been set out in the Prologue. Both are portrayed as prophets who proclaim a message from God. Although John stresses that his role is inferior to that of Jesus ('I have baptized you with water; but he will baptize you with the Holy Spirit', 1: 8), they both call for repentance.

The two pericopae which follow introduce four themes which will be developed not only in this opening section, but in later parts of the gospel: discipleship (1: 16–20); teaching which is at odds with that of other Jewish teachers (1: 21–2 and 27–8); Jesus' power over those possessed by demons (1: 23–6); and his reluctance to allow his identity to be disclosed (1: 24–5). The second half of this first section is taken up with a cycle of controversy stories (2: 1 to 3: 6) which reaches a dramatic climax with the reference to the plot by Jesus' opponents to destroy him (3: 6).

While the second act (like the first) starts with a summary (3: 7–12), its conclusion is less easy to locate. Does it end (like the first) with rejection of

Jesus—this time in his home town (6: 6a)? If so, then the third act also opens with a summary statement (6: 6b) and, like the first, starts by focusing on the call of the disciples (6: 7–13).

It is in fact difficult to be certain about the structure of this part of the gospel. But there is little doubt that a major section runs from 8: 27 to 10: 52; its main themes will be considered below under the heading 'The Way of the Cross'. Where does this section begin? Does the account of the healing of the blind man at Bethsaida (8: 22–6) conclude the third section (as many have claimed), or does the gift of sight serve to introduce the account of Peter's 'spiritual sight' or insight concerning the identity of Jesus?

The penultimate act in Mark's dramatic story is set in or near Jerusalem (11: 1 to 13: 37) and sets out Jesus' final confrontation with the Jewish religious leaders and his teaching concerning the future. The final act reaches a dramatic climax with the crucifixion—and a further climax as the women flee in fear from the empty tomb.

While it is not possible to be certain about all the structural divisions of the gospel, even this short sketch confirms that Mark's gospel can be read as a dramatic story. As the evangelist unfolds the story, it becomes clear that he is more concerned with the deeper theological significance of what is happening than with a carefully worked-out biographical, chronological, or geographical framework.

The Prologue: Jesus Christ, the Son of God: 1: 1–13

Before the dramatic story begins with the arrival of Jesus in Galilee preaching the gospel of God (1: 14), Mark sets out an important Prologue. The Prologue functions like the chorus in a Greek drama: these verses explain to the reader right at the outset the significance of the story which follows. The familiar title 'The Gospel according to Mark' almost certainly did not form part of the original writing, but was an addition early in the second century. Thus the opening line, 'the beginning of the gospel of Jesus Christ, the Son of God', contains the evangelist's very first words to the reader or listener.

Most modern translations separate verse 2 from the opening line, which is then set out as a heading to the Prologue. But in the New Testament the phrase 'as it is written' never introduces a new idea; it always refers primarily to the preceding words. For Mark, then, the beginning of the gospel is the Prologue, the whole of which is seen as the fulfilment of what is written in Isaiah the prophet. (Most of the words in the composite quotation from the Old Testament in vv. 2–3 come from Isa. 40: 3, but the opening line 'Behold, I send my messenger before thy face' seems to be a combination of Mal. 3: 1a and Exod. 23: 20.)

The appearance of John the baptizer is undoubtedly seen as being in keeping with Isaiah's promise: he is the one sent by God, 'the voice crying in the wilderness'. The 'coming One', i.e. Jesus (v. 7), also appears in the light of Isaiah, for, from Mark's perspective, the 'way' referred to in both vv. 2 and 3 is the 'way of Jesus'.

Isaiah's words are also in mind in the account of the baptism of Jesus (vv. 9–11). There the Spirit descends on Jesus and a voice from heaven declares, 'You are my Son, the Beloved; with you I am well pleased.' These words are reminiscent of Isa. 42: 1 which speaks of the gift of God's Spirit to his chosen one, his Servant.

The opening line of the Prologue confirms that Mark's story is distinctive: it is 'good news' and its beginning is set firmly in the context of Scripture. The Old Testament citation which follows stresses that the action of the story is initiated by God: he has sent John as his messenger. God's role is also underlined in the baptism of Jesus. The reference to the heavens split open (v. 10) confirms that God is about to act and speak in answer to the ancient prayer that he 'rend the heavens and come down' (Isa. 63: 19). God bestows his Spirit on Jesus; the voice from heaven is the voice of God who attests solemnly that Jesus is his Son.

The opening line announces that Jesus is the Messiah–Christ, a term which is used only six times in Mark. It is usually qualified by other ways of spelling out the identity of Jesus. In 14: 61 'Son of God' elaborates 'Christ', as does 'King of Israel' at 15: 32 and 'Son of David' at 12: 35. In this verse, as in 9: 41, 'Christ' is used as a personal name for Jesus rather than as a title.

In Mark's gospel 'Son of God' is a much more important title than 'Messiah–Christ'. In most modern translations it occurs in the opening line. But there is a puzzle here. The phrase 'Son of God' is not found in many important manuscripts. Did later scribes add the phrase, or omit it? Deliberate omission is very unlikely, but it is just possible that a very early scribe's eye jumped over the phrase inadvertently. In antiquity Greek manuscripts were written in what we call capital letters, without any gaps between letters. Sometimes (as here) groups of capital letters looked very like an adjacent group of letters. The evidence and the arguments are evenly balanced, though the early addition of the phrase is probably more likely.

At the baptism of Jesus he is addressed by the voice from heaven as 'God's beloved Son' (1: 11). As we have just noted, Isa. 42: 1 is in view here, but so too is Psalm 2: 7 where God announces to the king of Israel, 'You are my son.' The king of Israel was declared to be God's viceregent on earth, precisely the role marked out for Jesus, who is God's royal Messiah.

An alternative explanation of 'Son of God' has been advanced by a number of scholars. On this view 'Son of God' is to be understood against a Hellenistic rather than a Jewish background. When the Spirit enters Jesus he is transformed into a supernatural being, a 'divine man'. The Jesus who is able to calm storms, walk on water, and raise the dead arouses deep awe: he is a mysterious divine hero. It has frequently been claimed that in the first century there was a well-established 'divine man' concept and that Jesus is portrayed in the miracle traditions of Mark in these terms. Some scholars note that since Mark himself scarcely views Jesus as a triumphant divine being, he is 'attacking' this view, which in fact represents the disciples' misunderstanding of the identity of Jesus!

But this view is unlikely. Recent research has shown that the 'divine man' concept was never a technical term or a fixed expression in the first century: it was not known until about one hundred years after Mark was written. And evidence from Qumran suggests that there is no need to look for Hellenistic categories: to be 'God's Son' was recognized in Jewish circles at the time of Jesus as one of the characteristics of the Messiah. In any case we shall note in the next section that Mark is not engaging in polemic with the 'heretical' views of the disciples.

The term 'Son of God' recurs in a number of important passages in the gospel. In the account of the Transfiguration the voice from heaven declares, 'This is my beloved Son; listen to him' (9: 7). The words are almost identical with the words at the baptism (1: 11), but there the words are heard only by Jesus, whereas at the Transfiguration the identity of Jesus is disclosed to Peter, James, and John.

In the parable of the vineyard (12: 1–12) the owner (God) repeatedly sends servants (the prophets) to the tenants of the vineyard (Israel) to collect its fruit. The servants are rejected and some are killed. But God had 'still one other (servant), a beloved son; finally he sent him to them, saying, "They will respect my son"' (12: 6). He too is killed and cast out of the vineyard. The reference to Jesus as 'God's beloved son' strikingly recalls the words of the voice from heaven at the Baptism and Transfiguration.

In the trial of Jesus before the Sanhedrin the high priest asks, 'Are you the Christ, the Son of the Blessed (God)?' (14: 61). At the climax of this crucial scene Jesus affirms, 'I am', a claim declared by the opponents of Jesus to be blasphemous and worthy of death. For Mark, however, Jesus has revealed his true identity.

Jesus' claim to be 'Son of God' leads directly to his death at the instigation of the Jewish leaders. But in a note of supreme irony the Gentile centurion standing facing Jesus on the cross confesses, 'Truly this man was God's Son!' (15: 39).

The conclusion of the Prologue also introduces a theme which is especially prominent in Mark. Immediately after the baptism Jesus is engaged in conflict with Satan in the wilderness (1: 13). Later in this chapter (1: 23–8) and in numerous other passages Jesus confronts the 'unclean spirits' who hold individuals in Satanic bondage. At 3: 22 scribes from Jerusalem even claim that Jesus himself is possessed by Beelzebul–Satan. But from Mark's point of view Jesus has triumphed over Satan: the strong man's house has been entered and Satan himself has been bound by Jesus (3: 27). If, as seems likely, Mark considers that Jesus has overcome Satan in the Temptation, then the Prologue ends on a triumphant note. On this view, which has been carefully defended by E. Best (1983), the exorcisms are the 'mopping-up operations' of isolated units of Satan's hosts; they are certain to be successful because Satan himself has already been bound and immobilized.

The disciples and discipleship

The reader of Mark can hardly fail to notice that the weakness, failures, and even the stupidity of the disciples seem to be underlined, even though Jesus frequently takes pains to clarify and to expound his teaching for them. At the end of the cluster of parables in chapter 4, the evangelist adds his own summary: 'With many such parables he spoke the word to them (i.e. the crowds), as they were able to hear it; he did not speak to them except in parables, but he explained everything in private to his disciples' (4: 33–4). On three occasions Jesus withdraws from the crowds and gives the disciples further instruction 'in the house'. At 7: 17, for example, we read: 'And when he had left the crowd and entered the house, his disciples asked him about the parable. He said to them . . . '. (See also 9: 33 and 10: 10.)

But in spite of this preferential treatment, the disciples frequently misunderstand points which seem obvious to the reader! Even after a second miraculous feeding of large crowds, they lack both insight and understanding. Jesus says to them: 'Why are you talking about having no bread? Do you still not perceive or understand? Are your hearts hardened? . . . And do you not remember?' (8: 17–18).

The modern reader is not the first to be puzzled by the disciples' lack of understanding and the generally poor light in which they are cast. Both Matthew and Luke frequently omit or tone down Marcan passages in which Jesus criticizes the disciples. For example, in the passage just referred to Mark's Jesus uses familiar Old Testament phrases to underline the 'hardness' of the disciples' hearts. 'Do you have eyes, and fail to see? Do you have ears, and fail to hear?' (8: 18). Matthew not only omits these phrases, but in another context he applies them to the crowds, and emphasizes that the disciples *do* understand! 'But *blessed* are your eyes, for they see, and your ears, for they hear' (Matt. 13: 13–16). Since it is more probable that a later Christian writer would defend rather than criticize the disciples of Jesus, the more favourable portrait of the disciples in Matthew and Luke strongly supports Marcan priority.

The disciples even discourage those who are bringing children to Jesus. Not surprisingly, Jesus is indignant: 'Let the little children come to me; do not stop them' (10: 13–14). Although the disciples are given authority to exorcize (3: 15 and 6: 7) they are failures as exorcists themselves (9: 18, 28). And they even have the audacity to stop someone who is casting out demons in the name of Jesus (9: 38)!

Although Simon Peter is the first disciple to be mentioned (1: 16) and heads the list of the twelve (3: 16), Jesus rounds on him and calls him 'Satan' (8: 33). Peter ultimately denies Jesus three times. At the arrest of Jesus Mark adds a poignant note: 'And the disciples all forsook him and fled' (14: 50). In contrast, the only one who 'follows' Jesus is the young man 'with nothing but a linen cloth about his body' who narrowly escapes arrest and runs away naked (14: 51–2).

Some scholars have claimed that Mark's harsh portrait of the disciples is related to his polemical purposes. On this view the disciples are 'ciphers' whom the evangelist is using to repudiate false or even heretical views in his own day. Some have suggested that the disciples are representatives of 'conservative' Jewish Christians (perhaps the leaders of the church in Jerusalem) whom the Gentile evangelist wishes to denigrate. Disputes among Christians do lie behind Galatians and other New Testament writings, but we may well wonder whether they explain Mark's purposes satisfactorily. There is hardly a trace in Mark of the issues which are mentioned in Galatians and Acts as divisive in the lifetimes of James, Peter, and Paul.

Other scholars accept that Mark's gospel is a polemical writing, but account for the evangelist's presentation of the disciples along very different lines. Also on this view the disciples represent Christians in Mark's day. They have a completely mistaken, even heretical, view of Jesus. For them Jesus is a 'divine man', a miracle-working hero whose amazing feats confirm his divine status. Mark counters this false view by stressing the suffering and rejection of Jesus: his way is not a path of triumph, power, and glory, but of humble obedience which involves rejection and crucifixion. However, as we noted above (p. 43) a more careful and critical study of the relevant Greek writings has shown that the 'divine man' concept was not known in the evangelist's day.

In any case, if we read Mark's story carefully from a literary-critical perspective, it becomes clear that the disciples are not consistently placed in a bad light. They are not characterized negatively in contrast to another group with whom the reader is intended to identify sympathetically. We have already noted that Jesus frequently seems to concentrate his teaching on them. In the opening scenes the disciples are firmly on Jesus' side. Simon, Andrew, James, and John all leave their fishing nets to follow Jesus. The latter two even employ hired servants, so they are leaving a flourishing fishing business, as well as their father Zebedee (1: 16–20). They then accompany Jesus throughout Galilee (1: 21, 29, 36–8). In the discussion about fasting in 2: 18–20, they are portrayed very positively. In contrast both to the Pharisees (who have already been marked out as critical opponents 2: 16–17) and also to the disciples of John, the disciples of Jesus do not fast. They are associated in the closest possible way with Jesus: he is the 'bridegroom' in whose presence the wedding guests (the disciples) cannot fast (2: 19).

In the dispute that follows concerning the plucking of ears of corn on the sabbath, the disciples are once again associated with Jesus in opposition to the Pharisees (2: 23–8). In the next chapter the twelve are given authority by Jesus to preach and to cast out demons—in other words to continue the ministry of Jesus. (In the gospel as a whole the twelve are not sharply differentiated from the larger group of disciples.) Similarly, in 6: 7–13 they are sent out as 'missionaries' to preach, heal, and exorcize demons; their 'success' is even underlined (6: 12–13).

The disciples are not only contrasted with the Pharisees, but also with the crowds: the latter are 'outsiders' for whom the parables of Jesus are just riddles. But the disciples have been given 'the secret of the kingdom of God' (4: 10–12).

The opening chapters establish such a strongly favourable portrait of the disciples that it is highly unlikely that Mark is writing polemically in order to denigrate a particular group or false views in his own day. If Mark is taken seriously as 'story' then the evangelist-narrator cannot allow a leading group of characters to 'change sides' without a most careful explanation—and that is never given to the reader. So how is the disciples' fear, anxiety, cowardice, and almost complete lack of understanding and faith to be explained?

There is little doubt that Mark is writing with more than half an eye on the needs of Christians in house-church communities with which he was in contact. Since his first listeners were well aware of their own weaknesses and failings, they would have had little difficulty in identifying with Mark's portrait of the disciples. By setting out so clearly the disciples' shortcomings, the evangelist is able to instruct his listeners on the nature of true discipleship. The weakness and self-centredness of the disciples is exposed ruthlessly in a number of passages, but the reader never finds it difficult to draw positive lessons. As we shall see, the faltering disciples are finally forgiven and their broken relationship with Jesus is restored.

The way of Jesus

In the important central section of Mark, from 8: 26 to 10: 52, the evangelist concentrates on the true nature of discipleship. In several passages the disciples are rebuked by Jesus, but in each case the reason for the apparent sternness of Jesus is clear. The disciples—and the listener—are being taught the full implications of what it means to be a follower of Jesus. The main point is stressed repeatedly: to be a disciple of Jesus involves being prepared to go *the way* of Jesus, and that means *the way* of humility, rejection, and suffering—*the way* of the Cross. The repetition of *ho hodos*, 'the way', and the associated themes would have made a powerful impact on the listeners to whom this gospel was read aloud.

In this part of Mark's story Jesus journeys inexorably towards Jerusalem. On the way Jesus explains to his disciples three times that 'The Son of man must suffer many things, and be rejected by the elders and the chief priests and the scribes, and be killed, and after three days rise again' (8: 33). The evangelist underlines the importance of this turning point in his story with the comment, 'And he said this plainly.' Almost identical words are used in predictions of the forthcoming death and resurrection of Jesus at 9: 31 and 10: 33–4. Since in each case the immediate context is important, we shall discuss all three passages briefly.

The journey to Jerusalem (which is a partly artificial framework for this section of the gospel) begins at 8: 27 where Jesus is 'on the way' to the villages of Caesarea Philippi. Jesus asks the disciples, 'Who do people say that I am?' and they answered him, 'John the Baptist; and others, Elijah; and still others, one of the prophets.' These answers are obviously incorrect, so when Jesus asks the disciples for their own opinion and Peter replies, 'You are the Messiah–Christ', the listener assumes that Peter's answer has correctly disclosed the identity of Jesus. While Peter is not told, as he is in Matthew's account of this incident (16: 17), that this insight has been revealed to him by God, in Mark Peter's response is not repudiated by Jesus, even though he is firmly rebuked in the verses which follow.

Jesus rounds on Peter, 'Get behind me Satan! For you are setting your mind not on divine things but on human things' (8: 33). Peter is rebuked not because of his acknowledgement that Jesus is the Messiah–Christ but because of his unwillingness to accept that the way of Jesus involves suffering, rejection, and death. Jesus then explains that true discipleship involves accepting the demanding way of Jesus: 'If any want to become my followers, let them deny themselves and take up their cross and follow me. For those who want to save their life will lose it: and those who lose their life for my sake, and for the sake of the gospel, will save it' (8: 34b–35). Since there is no immediate threat to the disciples, these words seem to be addressed to followers of Jesus in the evangelist's day who face persecution which may even include martyrdom. The passage as a whole teaches that the way of Jesus reverses completely any suggestion that his Messiahship is to be understood as that of a triumphant military leader. This understanding of Messiahship is found in Psalms of Solomon 17–18, written about a century earlier; it was probably still held by some Jews at the time of Jesus, but not by all.

The second forceful exposition of the way of Jesus, the so-called Passion prediction at 9: 33, is also not understood by the disciples. Once again there follows further important teaching on the nature of true discipleship. When Jesus was 'in the house' (the place where several important disclosures are made in Mark) he asks the disciples, 'What were you arguing about on the way?'. They are reduced to silence because they had been discussing with one another who was the greatest. As in the teaching which follows the first Passion prediction, the disciples' values are called into question: 'Whoever wants to be first must be last of all and servant of all' (9: 35).

The same pattern emerges with the third reference Jesus makes 'on the road, going up to Jerusalem' to the impending crisis (10: 32–3). This is followed by the request of James and John: 'Grant us to sit, one at your right hand and one at your left, in your glory.' Their misguided ambition embarrassed the later evangelists: Luke omits the whole incident even though he is following Mark at this point, and in Matthew it is the mother of James and John who is shown to be over-ambitious by pleading on their behalf (Matt. 20: 20). In Mark (and also in Matthew) Jesus explains that true disciples are called to follow his way and to accept the cup (of suffering) that he is about to drink and the baptism (of suffering) with which he is about to be baptized (10: 38–40). The point made at 9: 35 is repeated: 'Whoever wishes to become great among you must be your servant, and whoever wishes to be first among you must be slave of all' (10: 43b–44).

These three passages make the same points in different ways. Threefold repetition underlines their importance for Mark's story. The way of Jesus is not the expected path of triumph and glory; for Jesus Messiahship involves the way to Jerusalem. This teaching causes consternation among the disciples, but they are called to follow the same way of self-denial and suffering. Their apparently naive misunderstanding allows Mark to use the teaching of Jesus to set out even more fully the nature of true discipleship. This section of the gospel reaches its climax with a powerful exposition of the significance of the death of Jesus: 'For the Son of man also came not to be served but to serve, and to give his life as a ransom for many' (10: 45). Although parallels have been drawn several times between the way of Jesus—and the way his followers are called to follow, here there is a clear distinction. Disciples may well suffer rejection and even death, but only the death of Jesus is a 'ransom for many'. This saying alerts the reader to the deeper significance of the events which are about to be narrated. The final outcome of the story has already been anticipated in the threefold reference to the ultimate vindication of Jesus: 'after three days he will rise' (8: 31; 9: 31; 10: 34).

Confrontation with Jewish leaders

The final section of the gospel opens with the familiar accounts of the 'triumphal' entry of Jesus into Jerusalem and his 'cleansing' of the temple (11: 1–19). The latter (which will be discussed on pp. 284–6) provides an impressive example of the evangelist's narrative technique. Two separate incidents are interwoven in the following way; they are clearly intended to interpret one another:

- a. Jesus 'inspects' the Temple and departs (v. 11).
- b. Jesus 'inspects' the fig tree and curses it (vv. 12–14).
- A. Jesus 'cleanses' the Temple (vv. 15–19).
- B. The disciples discover that the fig tree has withered (vv. 20–3).

Like the fig tree, the temple is shown to be barren and is rejected. A solemn but rather enigmatic saying follows: 'Truly I tell you, if you say to this mountain, 'Be taken up and thrown into the sea', and if you do not doubt in your heart, but believe what you say will come to pass, it will be done for you' (11: 23).

The mountain which is about to be moved is the mountain of the temple. In the new era which Mark believes is dawning, the temple is rejected and its imminent destruction is expected. At the beginning of chapter 13 a similar point is made even more forcefully: not one stone of the temple will be left upon another.

In the incidents which follow the 'cleansing' of the temple, the confrontation of Jesus with Jewish leaders is set out even more starkly. Jesus is involved in a series of disputes with several groups of Jewish leaders (11: 27 to 12: 40). These incidents pave the way for the arrest, trial, and crucifixion of Jesus. They develop a theme for which the reader has been prepared in the opening chapters.

In the first set of controversy stories from 2: 1 to 3: 6, it becomes clear that the unconventional teaching and actions of Jesus will eventually lead to his downfall. A time will come when Jesus (the bridegroom) will be taken away from the disciples (2: 20). The sayings which follow stress that the new order (the coming of Jesus) cannot easily be merged with the old (from Mark's perspective, Judaism), just as new (unshrunk) cloth cannot be used to patch an old garment and new wine cannot be put into old wineskins (2: 21–2). This section ends on a dramatic and sombre note: 'The Pharisees went out, and immediately held counsel with the Herodians against him, how to destroy him' (3: 6).

The 'cleansing' of the temple leads to a similar plot to destroy Jesus, this time on the part of the chief priests and scribes (11: 18). John the Baptist's challenge to Herod Antipas (the Jewish ruler of Galilee on behalf of the Romans) leads eventually to his beheading. From this rather bizarre incident the reader learns what is likely to happen to those who challenge the conduct of the authorities. John's fate anticipates the fate of Jesus: John's disciples take away his body and place it in a tomb (6: 29).

As the story unfolds, controversy with various groups of religious leaders (the groups are not sharply distinguished by the evangelist) becomes more intense. In chapter 7 the disciples are criticized for their rejection of Pharisaic teaching concerning handwashing as an act of purification before meals. The disciples, as well as Jesus, are portrayed here (as they are also in 9: 14) as in dispute with the religious leaders of Judaism. Jesus' strong rejection of Pharisaic teaching on purity is underlined by the evangelist in an aside to the reader: 'Thus he declared all foods clean' (7: 19b).

The debates and disputes between Jesus and the religious leaders which are set in Jerusalem in chapters 11 and 12 form the climax of a theme which gradually becomes more prominent. Mark uses this material in order to explain why Jesus was put to death and also in order to distance his own Christian community from contemporary Judaism.

The same point is made in many of the accounts of exorcisms and healings, incidents which probably seem to modern readers to be quite unrelated to the disputes of Jesus (and Mark) with the Jewish leaders. Many of the individuals in Mark's drama were very much on the margins of contemporary Jewish society: those possessed by unclean spirits (1: 23–6 and several other passages and summaries); a leper (1: 40–5); tax collectors and sinners (2: 15–17); the physically handicapped (e.g. 2: 1–12 and 3: 1–6); a man who lived in a ritually unclean place, among the tombs (5: 1–20); a woman whose haemorrhage rendered her unclean (5: 24–34). These groups were all widely regarded as 'outsiders' and several were considered to be religiously impure. Yet Mark portrays Jesus as ignoring conventional attitudes.

A further related theme is developed both by hints and by explicit statements. The evangelist stresses that Jesus moves beyond the geographical boundaries of Israel and accepts the faith of some Gentiles. In the summary in 3: 7–8, the crowds who flock to Jesus come not only from various areas in Israel, but also from Idumaea, Transjordan, and the territories of the coastal cities of Tyre and Sidon. The presence of the pigs in the story of the Gerasene demoniac (5: 1–20) and the reference to the Decapolis confirm its setting in non-Jewish territory. Jesus himself visits the region of Tyre and Sidon and is approached by a Greek woman, 'a Syrophoenician by birth' (7: 26), whose plea for assistance is eventually accepted. The incident which follows is set in the Decapolis and implies that the deaf man who is healed is a Gentile.

In the final chapters the dispute between Jesus and Jewish leaders reaches its climax at the same time as the evangelist stresses that the Christian message is 'for all nations' (13: 10 and 14: 9). Both themes are juxtaposed in two verses which form the dramatic climax of Mark's whole story. In Mark's view the Jewish leaders are primarily responsible for the death of Jesus. They have rejected Jesus and he has rejected them. Yet in stark contrast, as Jesus 'breathes his last' a Gentile soldier confesses that he is God's Son (15: 39). In the preceding verse the evangelist notes that at the moment Jesus died the veil of the temple was torn in two, from top to bottom, thus symbolizing that access to God's presence is now open to non-Jews.

The final outcome

The ending of Mark's story puzzled his first readers and still teases readers today. In most early reliable manuscripts the women who discover the empty tomb flee, 'for trembling and astonishment had come upon them; and they said nothing to any one, for they were afraid' (16: 8). Some later scribes seem to have felt that it was inappropriate for the gospel to end on this enigmatic note—without even an account of an appearance of the risen Jesus. Various traditions, now usually printed in footnotes in modern translations, were added, some early in the second century.

A number of modern scholars have claimed that the last page of Mark's story must have been lost, since the evangelist could hardly have ended with the words 'for they were afraid'. While this solution of the puzzle is certainly possible, it is more probable that Mark intended to end on this note of awe and astonishment.

As we have seen, Mark emphasizes three times that after three days Jesus will rise (8: 31; 9: 31; 10: 34). The reader is prepared for the eventual outcome of the story in a further important passage immediately after the Last Supper. Jesus informs the disciples that though they will shortly all desert him and be scattered, they will be reunited with him: 'But after I am raised up, I will go before you to Galilee' (14: 28). Although the close relationship between Jesus and the disciples is about to be broken (in spite of their protestations to the contrary), it will be restored.

Following the discovery of the empty tomb the women are told by the messenger to tell the disciples and Peter that Jesus is going before them to Galilee. 'There you will see him, as he told you' (16: 7). The promise given by Jesus shortly before his arrest is about to be fulfilled. There is nothing more to be said. For the attentive reader the outcome of the story is clear, even though there is no explicit account of an appearance of Jesus and no formal commissioning of the disciples as in the resurrection traditions in the other three gospels.

The origin and purpose of Mark

Although there is now general agreement that Mark was the first gospel to be written, the date and place of its composition are still uncertain. If Matthew and Luke are seen as expansions and partial reinterpretations of Mark, then Mark must have been written perhaps a decade or so before the later gospels. But as we shall see in the chapters on Matthew and Luke that follow, these gospels can be dated only very tentatively at about AD 85.

There is one verse in Mark which may provide a clue. At 13: 14 there is a guarded reference to the 'desolating sacrilege' which was about to be set up 'where it ought not to be'. This is often taken as a dark hint (perhaps with hindsight) that the Jerusalem temple was about to be defiled by Roman soldiers. If so, then the gospel may have been written just before or just after the siege and fall of Jerusalem in AD 70. A number of other verses in chapter 13 refer to impending horrors; there is plenty of historical evidence which confirms that the years 68 and 69 were particularly turbulent, so the gospel may have been written at this time. If it was written much later, so the argument runs, then it is probable that the destruction of the temple would have been referred to more explicitly. A date just before or just after AD 70 is now widely accepted: it is difficult to choose between the two options.

This conclusion is supported by the comments of Irenaeus (c. AD 180) about the origin of our earliest gospel: 'Peter and Paul proclaimed the Gospel in Rome. After their death, Mark, the disciple and interpreter of Peter, transmitted his preaching to us in written form' (*Adv. Haer.* 3.1.1).

Peter almost certainly died during Nero's intense persecution of Christians in Rome in AD 64/5. So according to Irenaeus, Mark's gospel cannot have been written before this date. There is an alternative, slightly later, tradition which states that Mark was written *during* the lifetime of Peter. This sounds like an attempt to link Mark and Peter even more closely than the earlier tradition does. So Irenaeus, who admits that there was a gap between the death of Peter and the writing of Mark's gospel, is more likely to be correct.

The place of the composition of Mark is even more uncertain. At the end of the second century Clement of Alexandria believed that Mark was written in Rome. This tradition is still accepted by many scholars today who appeal to Mark's use of a handful of Latin loan-words and turns of phrase, and also to verses which seem to suggest that the gospel was written at a clear geographical distance from Palestine. But on any reckoning the evidence is slender: several other locations have been proposed, including Antioch (or somewhere else in Syria) and Alexandria in Egypt.

We have referred to the author by his traditional name, Mark, but who was he? In his history of the early church completed about AD 323 Eusebius of Caesarea refers to the views of Papias, bishop of Hierapolis in Asia Minor (who may have written 200 years earlier), on the origin of Mark.

And this is what the Elder said, 'Mark, who became Peter's interpreter, wrote accurately, but not in order, as many of the things said and done by the Lord as he had noted. For he neither heard the Lord nor followed him, but afterwards, as I said, he followed Peter, who adapted his teaching to the needs (of his hearers) but not as a complete work of the Lord's sayings. So Mark made no mistake in writing some things just as he had noted them. For he was careful of one thing, to leave nothing he had heard out and to say nothing falsely. (*Church History* 3. 39. 15)

Papias is citing an even older tradition, from the Elder. These words have been pored over many times. The precise nuance of several phrases is not entirely clear. Are the references to Mark's accuracy, carefulness, and honesty conventional rhetorical terms used to underline the general reliability of a writing, or are they to be taken literally? A decision is difficult.

Mark himself is not portrayed as an eyewitness: he is Peter's 'interpreter'. While this may mean 'translator' (from Peter's Aramaic into Greek), it probably refers to Mark's role as the person who transmitted and *explained* Peter's teaching. Perhaps the most interesting comment is that Mark wrote 'not in order'. While this may mean 'not in chronological order', it is more probably a rhetorical term which refers to Mark's lack of literary artistry. If this is the case, then Papias was mistaken. For recent studies have shown that Mark's gospel is not an unsophisticated anthology of Jesus traditions, but a work of considerable literary skill and theological subtlety.

How much weight should be given to these intriguing comments? My own view is that while they cannot be taken at face value, they do give us some insights into the origin of Mark's gospel. The reference to Mark as the author is surely an authentic tradition. The Mark named by Papias is probably the John Mark mentioned in Acts as an associate of Paul (12: 12,

25; 15: 37–9). John Mark was not a prominent leader in the early church; he was neither a disciple of Jesus nor an apostle. So why was his name chosen if there were not good grounds for naming him as the author of a gospel?

According to Papias, in his teaching Peter did not set out a full record of the actions and teaching of Jesus; he *adapted* the traditions to meet the needs of his hearers. At this point Papias partially anticipates some of the insights of modern scholarship: traditions about Jesus were shaped or redacted by the evangelists (and their predecessors) to meet the needs of specific groups of Christians.

Why was this gospel written? Many scholars have assumed that Mark is writing to *one* community of Christians, and have tried to reconstruct the make-up of the Marcan community and propose a quite specific historical or theological setting. For two reasons this general approach is implausible. It overlooks the genre of the gospel: Mark is not a letter like Paul's, addressed to one community with specific problems, but a *bios*, a biography. And this approach is usually able to make reasonable sense of only one or two of the many interrelated strands which the evangelist develops.

Richard Bauckham (1998) has taken these points even further and argued that Mark (and the other evangelists) was writing for Christians at large. He quite rightly insists that communication between Christian groups in different parts of the eastern Mediterranean was not difficult: Christian leaders such as Paul, Peter, and their co-workers travelled widely.

On the other hand, if Mark circulated very widely and very rapidly, why did it survive even though it was used extensively by Matthew and Luke? It seems likely that individual gospels circulated in certain restricted geographical areas. Mark's gospel includes several cryptic references which suggest that the author and the first recipients were known to one another. For example, the reference to the young man who ran away naked at the arrest of Jesus (14: 51–2) and the reference to Simon of Cyrene as 'the father of Alexander and Rufus' (15: 21). These references were deleted by Matthew and Luke, presumably because they were meaningless to readers in the communities for which they wrote.

So it seems preferable to assume that the evangelists wrote to groups of house-churches in close contact with one another. Since no more than about fifty people could meet in an individual house-church, the gospels were probably not written for a single community, but for a cluster of communities in a given geographical area. This is strongly suggested by the fact that Mark's purposes are many. He sets out in dramatic form the story of Jesus so that it will be meaningful for faltering and hard-pressed Christians in his own day.

4

MATTHEW'S GOSPEL: THE WAY OF RIGHTEOUSNESS

In the early church Matthew's gospel was used more widely and more extensively than any of the other gospels. The reasons for its popularity are not hard to find. Matthew has ordered his whole gospel most effectively. His prose is rhythmical and often poetic; individual sections contain carefully balanced and readily memorable phrases. Matthew's gospel is nearly half as long again as Mark and contains many more sayings of Jesus.

In the early church the evangelist was widely believed to have been one of the disciples of Jesus. It is probably for this reason that Matthew always heads lists and copies of the four gospels in the early church, even though there are some variations from the order familiar today.

There is a further reason for the popularity of Matthew in nearly all strands of early Christianity. The evangelist has been influenced strongly by the Old Testament and by contemporary Judaism, and his gospel has always been regarded as the most 'Jewish' of the four. But his gospel also includes in a number of passages clear universalist teaching: 'this good news of the kingdom will be proclaimed throughout the world, as a testimony to all the nations' (Matt. 24: 14; cf. 28: 20). Matthew's gospel is Jewish, anti-Jewish, and pro-Gentile: it is a comprehensive gospel with wide appeal.

Modern readers are often more ambivalent. They find many of the distinctive features of this gospel attractive and fascinating, but are puzzled by some of the evangelist's emphases. Matthew's Sermon on the Mount is widely respected and often referred to, even by non-Christians. It is his versions of the Beatitudes and of the Lord's Prayer, rather than Luke's, which are used universally. The evangelist's full and well-ordered account of the teaching of Jesus is appreciated. But his often awkward way of using the Old Testament as a set of proof texts puzzles modern readers, as does the severity of his anti-Jewish statements and his harsh comments on judgement.

The structure of Matthew's gospel

This gospel is dominated by five lengthy discourses of Jesus: chapters 5–7, the Sermon on the Mount; chapter 10, the mission discourse; chapter 13, a collection of parables; chapter 18, instructions for the community; chapters 24–5, teaching concerning the future. (The woes against scribes and Pharisees in chapter 23 should probably also be seen as part of the final discourse.) At the end of the first four discourses (7: 28; 11: 1; 13: 53; 19: 1) the same wording is used to mark the transition from the teaching of Jesus to the narratives which follow: 'When Jesus had finished these sayings . . .'. At the end of the fifth discourse the pattern recurs, but the word 'all' is added: once Jesus has finished *all* his discourses, the passion story unfolds.

The five discourses are interspersed with numerous narratives, and also with shorter collections of the sayings of Jesus at 12: 25–45; 16: 21–8; 19: 23–30; 21: 28 to 22: 14. The first discourse is preceded by a lengthy Prologue or introduction which is in two parts: chapters 1–2, the infancy narratives, and chapters 3–4, which record the preaching of John the Baptist and the temptations of Jesus. The fifth discourse is followed immediately by the passion narratives, chapters 26–8.

By giving such prominence to the five discourses, the evangelist stresses the continuing importance of the teaching of Jesus for his own day. This point is made explicitly in the final verse of the gospel where the disciples are sent by the Risen Lord to teach 'all nations' to observe all that Jesus has commanded them (28: 20). In other words, for Matthew's readers (or listeners) the teaching of Jesus lies at the heart of their missionary proclamation.

It has often been suggested that there is a parallel between Matthew's five discourses and the first five books of the Old Testament, the Pentateuch. On this view the first discourse, the Sermon on the Mount, is set on a mountain which recalls Mt Sinai and Jesus is portrayed as a greater lawgiver than Moses. Did Matthew intend to imitate the Pentateuch and to present Jesus as the new Moses who leads a new Exodus? Opinion is divided. While some scholars emphasize the 'New Moses' theme, others insist that although it can be traced in some of the traditions the evangelist has used, he does not in fact develop the theme himself. They also note that many Jewish and Graeco-Roman writings have five divisions or sections, so Matthew's decision to include *five* major collections of the sayings of Jesus may not have particular significance.

The five discourses have been composed most carefully. The first (chs. 5–7) and the last (chs. 24–5, and probably also ch. 23) are much longer than the other three and correspond to one another. The Sermon on the Mount is a full initial account of the teaching of Jesus; it contains many of the themes which the evangelist stresses in other parts of the gospel. The final discourse looks to the future and contains repeated warnings and exhortations to the disciples—and to Matthew's own community. The second and fourth are related. In chapter 10 Jesus instructs and encourages the disciples to continue his 'mission'—and warns them that they too will face rejection. Chapter 18 contains advice for the internal life of the Christian community which has responded to the missionary proclamation. The central discourse contains a cluster of parables, many of which are concerned with acceptance or rejection of Jesus. All five discourses have been constructed in a similar way. Sayings of Jesus from various sources have been gathered together into discourses which have thematic unity and some internal structure. In all of them the sayings of Jesus have been reshaped by the evangelist and often bear his own distinctive stamp.

Matthew's gospel contains one further major structural feature. The Sermon on the Mount has been juxtaposed with a set of narratives (most of them miracle stories) which are concerned with twin themes which dominate the gospel: the significance of Jesus (Christology) and the nature of discipleship. These five chapters are carefully marked off by the evangelist with an introduction (4: 23) and a conclusion (9: 35) which use almost identical words and which have both been composed by the evangelist himself: 'Jesus went throughout Galilee, teaching in their synagogues and proclaiming the good news of the kingdom and curing every disease and every sickness among the people.' The summaries stress that Jesus is a teacher and preacher, and also a healer. The first half of this long section, the Sermon on the Mount in chapters 5–7, presents Jesus as Messiah of Word; the second half, chapters 8 and 9, presents Jesus as Messiah of Deed.

Are there other major structural divisions in the gospel? Many attempts have been made to discern the evangelist's overall intention from the way he has arranged the traditions at his disposal. But there is no generally agreed conclusion. While it is clear that the evangelist has taken great care over the composition of the five major discourses and of numerous shorter sections, he does not seem to have developed a broad overall structure as a way of underlining his main purposes.

The extent of Matthew's Prologue provides a good example of differences of opinion on the overall structure of the gospel. Many have claimed that the infancy narratives in chapters 1 and 2 form the Prologue: the first major section begins at 3: 1 with the preaching of John the Baptist. Some exegetes have claimed that the Prologue ends at 4: 22, immediately before the summary at 4: 23 which introduces the major section from 4: 23 to 9: 35. Others have insisted that 4: 16 marks the end of the Prologue. On this view (which has been prominent in recent discussion) 4: 17 opens the second main section of the gospel with the words, 'From that time Jesus began . . .', and the same words at 16: 21 introduce the third main section. But 4: 17 does not seem to be a major turning point in the story, for it belongs with 4: 12–16: Matthew wishes to stress that after John was arrested, Jesus, on whom the Spirit had been bestowed, continued John's proclamation of repentance and of the Kingdom of Heaven. Matt. 4: 12, rather than 4: 17, marks the opening of the ministry of Jesus. The return of Jesus to *Galilee* (cf. 2: 22 and 3: 13) is especially important, as his citation of Isa. 9: 1–2 (with its reference to 'Galilee of the Gentiles') in 4: 15–16 confirms. After the lengthy introduction from 1: 1 to 4: 11, the story proper begins in Galilee—where it also ends (28: 7, 10, 16).

The evangelist is particularly fond of triads, i.e. short blocks containing three related traditions. For example, the genealogy is divided into three sections (1: 2–17). The so-called antitheses in the Sermon on the Mount are made up of two groups of three traditions, 5: 21–33 and 33–47, with 5: 48 as a pithy conclusion. In chapter 13 Matthew follows Mark's parable chapter fairly closely (Mark 4: 1–32); he then includes two groups of three short parables (13: 24–33 and 44–50). The three longer parables from 21: 28 to 22: 14 are closely related.

Perhaps this phenomenon (and many more examples could be given) is the outcome of the composition of this gospel for oral delivery. Since it would take about three hours to read the whole gospel aloud, it was probably read in shorter sections, the length of which varied from time to time.

Both readers and listeners would appreciate the care the evangelist took with the structure of shorter sections, but the division of the whole gospel into three, four, or five major sections was less important.

Sources and methods

Matthew's five discourses, his two chapters which narrate the birth of Jesus, and his more frequent quotations from the Old Testament all suggest that this is a very different gospel from Mark. But first impressions are sometimes misleading. Matthew is in fact so closely dependent on Mark that his gospel should be seen as a much expanded and revised second edition of Mark. Although some of Mark's rather verbose pericopae are abbreviated, very few are omitted. Only about 50 of Mark's 662 verses are not found in Matthew.

In the second half of his gospel Matthew follows Mark's order very closely indeed and makes hardly any significant alterations. Between 4: 12 and 11: 1 there are a number of changes from Mark's order, but they are not arbitrary alterations. Many of them are related to Matthew's carefully constructed presentation of Jesus as Messiah of Word and Deed from 4: 23 to 9: 35, to which we have just referred.

Matthew shares with Luke about 230 verses which are not found in Mark. This material, which consists almost entirely of sayings of Jesus, is usually called the Q source. The Q hypothesis (and its rivals) was discussed in Chapter 2 (pp. 23–7). If the Q hypothesis is accepted, then Matthew has gathered Q traditions and woven them together with other traditions to form the five great discourses, and several other shorter discourses. While Luke has retained the order of Q much more faithfully than Matthew, the wording of Q has often (but not always) been retained more accurately than by Luke.

In addition to Mark and Q, Matthew has used traditions not found elsewhere in the gospels. This material, which amounts to about one quarter of the gospel, consists of sayings of Jesus and a number of parables, the traditions behind Matthew 1 and 2, the so-called 'fulfilment' citations of the Old Testament, and some narratives, such as the accounts of the fate of Judas in 27: 3–10 and of Pilate's wife's dream in 27: 19. Although this material has sometimes been called the 'M' source, it is so diverse that it does not come from one written source. However, it is possible that the ten 'M' parables were collected together before the evangelist incorporated them into his gospel.

With the aid of a synopsis it is not difficult to study the methods Matthew has used in adapting his sources. He regularly removes from Marcan narratives redundant phrases so that what he takes to be the main point will stand out more clearly. His traditions are frequently linked together according to their subject matter, often in groups of three.

In addition to abbreviating and tidying his sources, Matthew sometimes expands them. There are a number of passages where he even seems to have 'created' words of Jesus. Almost without exception his intention is to expound and to clarify his traditions. Some examples were given in our discussion of Matthew's longer version of the Lord's Prayer (pp. 8–10) and further examples will be noted later in this chapter in our discussion of the Beatitudes. Matthew is rarely an innovator: nearly every one of his distinctive themes and emphases can be seen as his elaboration and elucidation of an earlier tradition.

In the previous chapter we referred to Mark as a dramatic story. In some ways it is also appropriate to read Matthew in this way. Some themes are developed more fully in narrative and in discourse as the story unfolds. As we shall see, several of Matthew's most prominent themes are already foreshadowed in his lengthy Prologue. But much of the dramatic drive of Mark's narrative is missing.

Matthew's handling of Mark 8: 27 to 10: 52 provides a good example of the difference between the two gospels. In this important section of Mark (see above pp. 48–50) Jesus journeys inexorably towards Jerusalem. Mark clarifies what it means to 'follow the way of Jesus'. Although Jesus is instructing his disciples, the storyline continues. With the exception of just three verses, Matthew retains all this Marcan material—and in exactly the same order! But his equivalent section (16: 13 to 20: 34) is 25 per cent longer. At 18: 1–35 he includes the fourth of his five major discourses, only a few verses of which are taken from Mark. And at 20: 1–16 he has inserted the parable of the labourers in the vineyard. As in many other parts of his gospel, Matthew's catechetical purposes have partly smothered Mark's lively, dramatic style. Whereas in Mark the teaching of Jesus is usually woven into the narratives (and is very much less extensive), in Matthew the storyline stops in the five major discourses and in the several other shorter discourses. No wonder that narrative critics have not been able to comment effectively on Matthew's great discourses in their expositions of Matthew's storyline, plot, and characterization!

Infancy narratives

In our chapter on Mark we saw how the evangelist introduces his main themes to his readers in his Prologue in 1: 1–13. Matthew's Prologue falls into two parts: the infancy narratives in chapters 1 and 2 (which do not have parallels elsewhere), and the accounts of the preaching of John the Baptist and the temptations of Jesus from 3: 1 to 4: 11 (which are taken from Mark and from Q). Both parts of the Prologue set out theological themes which will be prominent throughout the rest of the gospel, but simply for convenience we shall concentrate in this brief discussion on the infancy narratives.

Many modern readers of the gospels will be very familiar with the traditions about the birth and infancy of Jesus in the opening two chapters of both Matthew and Luke. But they would find it difficult to summarize accurately the infancy narratives found in either one of the two gospels; they would be surprised to learn that there is little overlap between Matthew and Luke. Countless nativity plays and Christmas card scenes have merged together traditions and themes from the two gospels. The result is that the distinctive features of Matthew 1 and 2 and of Luke 1 and 2 are rarely appreciated.

The origin and historicity of many of the details of the infancy narratives in Matthew and in Luke are much disputed. Since Part I of this book is primarily concerned with the teaching of the evangelists, these fascinating but difficult questions cannot be considered here. There would, however, be general agreement that the infancy narratives contain both history and poetry, as well as considerable literary and theological artistry, all of which are closely interwoven and cannot easily be disentangled.

In the paragraphs which follow we shall see how closely some of the most prominent themes in Matthew's infancy narratives are related to the major themes of the whole gospel. In both Matthew and Mark the opening verse makes an important Christological statement. Right at the outset of the story, both evangelists set out clearly for the reader the significance of

Jesus. Like Mark's opening verse, Matt. 1: 1 introduces the Prologue rather than the whole gospel. But there the similarity between the openings of Matthew and Mark ends.

The opening phrase of the gospel 'An account of the genealogy of Jesus the Messiah' is a traditional heading for a biblical genealogy. Jesus is then referred to as the 'son of David', the 'son of Abraham', phrases which hint at major concerns of the evangelist.

The term 'son of David' introduces the single most important point in the whole opening chapter: Jesus the Messiah–Christ comes from David's line. Joseph, who is a son of David, is not the father of Jesus, but Jesus is 'ingrafted' into David's line through his conception by the Holy Spirit (1: 20). As verse 17 stresses, the genealogy is divided into three groups of fourteen names: from Abraham to David, from David to the Babylonian exile, and from the exile to the Messiah. The number fourteen seems to have been chosen deliberately in order to underline the Davidic descent of Jesus, though surprisingly the third set contains only thirteen names. In Hebrew each letter of the alphabet has a numerical value; the Hebrew form of 'David' has a numerical value of fourteen. In five passages later in the gospel the evangelist adds 'son of David' to his sources (9: 27; 12: 23; 15: 22; 21: 9, 15). While Matthew is certainly stressing that Jesus as son of David is Israel's Messiah, it is not entirely clear why this title is of particular interest to the evangelist.

Jesus is also referred to right at the outset of the gospel as 'the son of Abraham'. Abraham was chosen partly because he was considered to be the father of every Jew and of the nation Israel, and partly in order to obtain the required fourteen generations before David. But there was probably a further reason for the use of this phrase. From Matthew's point of view, the promise given to Abraham at Gen. 22: 18 was extremely important: 'By your descendants shall all the nations of the earth bless themselves.' Although this promise was rarely stressed in Jewish circles, the evangelist emphasizes that following Israel's failure to produce the 'fruits of the king-dom' and her rejection of the Messiah, the Kingdom of God would be taken away from her and given to the Gentiles (21: 43).

As we shall see, Matt. 21: 43 with its double emphasis on God's rejection of Israel and his acceptance of Gentiles as part of his 'people' is one of the most important verses in the whole gospel. These twin themes are prominent in the infancy narratives. In chapter 2 the infant 'king' Jesus is hounded ruthlessly by the Jewish king Herod. In vivid and dramatic stories this chapter narrates the clash between the two kings. The note in 2: 3 that King Herod and all Jerusalem are troubled at the coming of King Jesus is echoed in 21: 10 in a phrase which Matthew adds to Mark's account of the triumphal entry of Jesus into Jerusalem: once again the city is shaken by the arrival of Jesus. In chapter 2 King Herod is apparently all-powerful, but he is unable to destroy Jesus. After Herod's death, the child Jesus, his mother, and Joseph travel safely to Nazareth in order to fulfil Scripture (2: 23). God's hand is upon them rather than on King Herod.

In the second half of the Prologue the rejection theme is developed further. John the Baptist warns the Pharisees and Sadducees (the parallel passage in Luke refers simply to 'crowds') that it is not enough to appeal (with all Jews) to Abraham as their father: they must bear fruit that befits repentance (3: 7–10). Just as the tree which does not bear good fruit is cut down, so will Israel be rejected if she fails to produce the fruits of the kingdom (3: 10).

Acceptance of the Gentiles (as well as Jews) is foreshadowed not only in the reference in 1: 1 to Jesus as 'the son of Abraham' but also in the genealogy itself. A first-century reader would be puzzled by the unexpected references in the genealogy to four women. Why were women referred to instead of men? One of the more likely explanations notes that the women are included because in some first-century Jewish circles they were all considered to be non-Jews. Matthew's point is then that even the genealogy of Jesus shows that with his coming Gentiles as well as Jews will be accepted. The same point is made in chapter 2: the wise men from the east who come to worship the young child are representatives of the Gentile world. Scripture is cited twice as divine sanction for a mission to the Gentiles (4: 15 and 12: 18–21). This theme is developed further in Jesus' acceptance of the faith of the Gentile centurion (8: 10), and in the broad hint that followers of Jesus will be rejected not only by Jewish households, but also by Gentiles (10: 18). Before the end comes, 'this gospel of the kingdom will be proclaimed throughout the earth as a witness to all nations' (24: 14; cf. also 26: 13). In the final command of the Risen Jesus (28: 18–20), which will be considered later in this chapter, earlier hints become a clarion call.

In the important section 1: 18–25 there are two further Christological themes which the evangelist develops later in his gospel. In a dream Joseph is told by the angel of the Lord to call the son whom Mary would bear Jesus, 'for he will save his people from their sins' (1: 21). Matthew refers to Israel in the traditional manner as God's people: Jesus is Israel's Messiah. In some contemporary Jewish circles the Messiah was expected to set aside or correct the sins of men and women. Later in the gospel Matthew returns to this theme, but develops it in a distinctively Christian (and especially Pauline) way. At 26: 28 Matthew adds an important phrase to the words of Jesus at the Last Supper. In Mark's account, which Matthew uses, Jesus says: 'This is my blood of the covenant, which is poured out for many' (Mark 14: 24). Matthew adds 'for the forgiveness of sins', thus stressing explicitly that the death of Jesus atones for sins.

At 1: 23 the evangelist cites the Greek translation of Isa. 7: 14 in order to show that the virginal conception and birth of Jesus are a fulfilment of Scripture. Matthew is also especially interested in the Hebrew name *Emmanuel* mentioned in this verse. He translates it 'God *with us*' in order to make sure that his readers understand the full significance of the coming of Jesus. Matthew returns to this theme in the final verse of his gospel. The Risen Lord promises the disciples, 'Remember, I am *with you* always' (28: 20). In a rather 'learned' way which is characteristic of the evangelist Matthew, the same major theological point is made at the beginning and at the end of his gospel: through Jesus people experience God's presence with them.

Although the infancy narratives are not referred to explicitly in later chapters, they are an integral part of the gospel. In Matthew 1 and 2 it is very difficult to isolate with any precision Matthew's redaction of his sources, but the evangelist's own methods and emphases are undoubtedly present.

The way of righteousness: the Beatitudes 5: 3–11

One of the evangelist's most important themes, however, is almost entirely absent from the infancy narratives. In numerous passages the evangelist gives prominence to the demands of Jesus for standards of ethical behaviour which conform to the will of God (in Scripture). In a key verse in the Sermon on the Mount which contains a cluster of Matthew's own favourite words, strong demands are made of followers of Jesus (in

Matthew's day): 'Unless your righteousness exceeds that of the scribes and the Pharisees, you will never enter the kingdom of heaven' (5: 20). As we shall see below (pp. 74–6), the communities to which Matthew wrote have almost certainly parted company rather painfully with contemporary Judaism. Like many other minority religious groups at different periods of history, Matthew's Christian communities are urged to adopt higher standards of ethical behaviour than those of the majority from whom they have separated.

The same point is made in 6: 1–18. The traditional Jewish religious practices of giving alms, prayer and fasting are not abandoned in the communities to which the evangelist wrote. They are to be carried out with sincere motives, 'not like the hypocrites' (6: 2, 5, 16). In the context, the opponents whose religious practices are being ridiculed are the scribes and Pharisees of 5: 20. In 6: 1 the 'superior' standards demanded of followers of Jesus are referred to as 'practising righteousness', though this is obscured by the NRSV translation 'beware of practising your piety'.

Matthew's strong ethical emphasis and repeated use of the term 'righteousness' is a feature of the Sermon on the Mount, and, as we shall see, of the Beatitudes in particular. This theme is foreshadowed in two verses in the Prologue. At 1: 19 Joseph is described as a 'just' or 'righteous' man. And in a difficult passage at 3: 15 Jesus and John the Baptist 'fulfil all righteousness'. By allowing himself to be baptized by John, even though he has no need to repent, Jesus carries out God's will and is 'righteous' in God's sight.

The noun 'righteousness' is not found in Mark and it occurs only once in Luke (1: 75). But in Matthew it is used seven times, and in every case the evangelist has almost certainly introduced the word himself. This is one of Matthew's most important and distinctive themes. Whereas Paul uses the word to refer to God's *gift* of grace or salvation by which man is enabled to stand in a right relationship with his Creator, in Matthew the word refers to the righteous conduct which God *demands* of disciples. It would be a mistake, however, to contrast Matthew and Paul too sharply. Like Paul, Matthew emphasizes the importance of baptism (28: 19) and relates forgiveness of sins to the death of Jesus (26: 28).

The evangelist's strongly ethical emphasis is particularly clear in the Beatitudes where 'righteousness' is mentioned twice (5: 6, 10). In Matthew there are nine Beatitudes, only four of which are found in Luke. Most scholars accept that both Matthew and Luke have taken over and reinterpreted the four Beatitudes found in Q which referred to the poor, the hungry, those who weep, and those who are persecuted. Matthew has added (in part from earlier oral traditions) five further Beatitudes which are found in his gospel alone: the blessings on the meek (5: 5), the merciful, the pure in heart, the peacemakers, and a second saying concerning persecution (5: 7–10).

Matthew's additional five Beatitudes and the changes he makes to the Q sayings confirm that he is particularly concerned with ethical conduct. In Luke those in desperate need—those who are literally poor, hungry, and weeping (6: 20–1)—are promised that their position will be reversed by God. In Matthew the dominant theme is one of encouragement to disciples—and to followers of Jesus in the evangelist's own day.

The two Beatitudes which refer to righteousness support this general conclusion. The saying at Luke 6: 21 which corresponds to Matthew's fourth Beatitude refers to those who are literally hungry: in their rather desperate state they will be blessed by God and their hunger satisfied. In Luke (but not in Matthew) there is a corresponding 'woe': 'woe to you that are rich, for you have received your consolation' (6: 24). As we shall see in the next chapter, Luke is particularly interested in poverty and riches. In Matthew, however, God's blessing is promised to a rather different group: to those who 'hunger and thirst for righteousness' (5: 6), i.e. to those who are 'hungry' to do God's will.

In 5: 10 those who are 'persecuted for righteousness' sake' are promised that the kingdom of heaven is theirs. This saying (like 5: 20, see pp. 67–8) contains so many of Matthew's favourite words that the evangelist may have created it himself. As in several other similar cases, Matthew does not introduce new ideas, but develops themes already present in the sources he is using. The second half of 5: 10, 'for theirs is the kingdom of heaven', echoes 5: 3 (Q); the first half of 5: 10 underlines the importance of the Q Beatitude which follows in 5: 11 where disciples are encouraged in the face of persecution. Matt. 5: 10 gives the reason for the fierce opposition which is being experienced: followers of Jesus are being pilloried on account of their righteous conduct. Presumably this is a reflection of the hostility being experienced by followers of Jesus in the evangelist's day. A few verses later a more positive note is struck: 'Let your light so shine before others, so that they may see your good works and give glory to your

Father in heaven' (5: 16). Here 'good works' seems to be synonymous with 'righteousness'.

We have now referred to four verses in the Sermon in which the word 'righteousness' is prominent: 5: 6, 10 and 20, and 6: 1. The fifth and final use of this word is instructive. At 6: 33 the Q clause 'strive for his kingdom' (Luke 12: 31) is expanded by Matthew: 'strive *first* for his kingdom *and his righteousness*'. Here the 'righteousness' which is demanded of followers of Jesus is linked explicitly with God's kingdom, or kingly rule. As we saw on p. 9, the same point is made in Matthew's expansion of the shorter Q version of the Lord's Prayer. Matthew explains, as it were, that the petition 'Thy kingdom come' involves 'doing the will of the Father'. A similar expansion of a terse Q saying is found at 7: 21. The Q saying 'Why do you call me "Lord, Lord," and not do what I tell you' (Luke 6: 46) becomes: 'Not every one who says to me, "Lord, Lord," will enter the kingdom of heaven, but *only the one who does the will of my Father who is in heaven.*' For Matthew, the 'way of righteousness' means 'doing the will of the Father'.

Use of the Old Testament

The Old Testament is cited and alluded to in many passages in Matthew in broadly similar ways to those found in the other three gospels. But in addition there is a set of ten quite distinctive 'fulfilment quotations' which have long intrigued scholars. In each case a citation from a passage in one of the prophets is introduced by a set formula: '(this took place) in order that what was declared (by the Lord, or through the prophet) might be fulfilled'. They all function as asides or comments of the evangelist on the significance of a preceding narrative.

For example, at 2: 15 the following comment is added to the brief account of the departure of the child Jesus, his mother, and Joseph to Egypt: 'This was to fulfil what had been spoken by the Lord through the prophet, "Out of Egypt have I called my son"'. At the end of a summary account of the healing ministry of Jesus we read: 'This was to fulfil what was spoken through the prophet Isaiah, "He took our infirmities and bore our diseases"' (8: 17).

Has Matthew himself chosen these passages? Or has he taken them from a source—perhaps from an early Christian collection of Old Testament passages which were considered to be especially valuable for Christians to use either in catechetical instruction or in debates with Jewish opponents? In order to settle this issue it is necessary to establish which text or translation of the Old Testament is used both within the fulfilment citations and elsewhere in the gospel. At times the passage quoted is closer to the original Hebrew than to the Greek translation of the Old Testament (= LXX, the Septuagint) which is usually used by early Christian writers. In some places the form of the citation seems to have been adapted by the evangelist to fit the narrative to which it is joined. In a few cases there even seem to be traces of the use of the Aramaic paraphrases of the Hebrew text which are known as the 'targums'.

The evangelist was a learned writer who almost certainly had access to the original Hebrew as well as to Aramaic and Greek translations. But it is often difficult to decide which textual tradition is being used since recent research has shown that both the Hebrew and the Greek textual traditions of the Old Testament were very much more fluid than used to be supposed. The form of any Aramaic targum known to Matthew is even more uncertain. Hence it is not surprising that scholarly opinion is divided and that discussion continues.

Perhaps the most likely solution is as follows: when the evangelist introduces as a fulfilment citation a passage that was already known in Christian usage, he is likely to have reproduced the familiar wording, but if Matthew himself was the first to have seen the possibilities of an Old Testament fulfilment, he is likely to have chosen or adapted a wording that would best suit his own purposes.

In some cases Matthew's choice of an Old Testament verse as a comment on a particular tradition about Jesus seems odd to modern readers. But he is not simply concerned to underline purely incidental agreements between an Old Testament passage and Jesus. His main intention is to use Old Testament prophecy to *interpret* the passage to which it is attached, for he is convinced that the story of Jesus is very much at one with God's purposes.

Matthew clearly believes in the continuing importance of the Old Testament for Christians. He strenuously resists the claim which may have been made by his Jewish opponents that Christians have abandoned the Old Testament. As the introduction to a lengthy collection of sayings on the attitude of Jesus to the Law (5: 21–48) he sets down this saying of Jesus: 'Do not think (as some do) that I have come to abolish the law and the prophets; I have not come to abolish, but to fulfil' (5: 17).

For Matthew the continuing validity of the Law is important, but even more important is its correct interpretation. The essence of the Law is summed up in two ways. In two Old Testament citations which do not include the fulfilment formula, Matthew appeals to the interpretation of the Law by the Old Testament prophets as the vantage point from which the Law is to be approached. At 9: 13 and again at 12: 7 Pharisaic attitudes to the Law are rejected with a quotation from Hosea 6: 6, 'I desire mercy, not sacrifice' (9: 13; 12: 7).

For Matthew the essence of the Law is also summed up by two sayings of Jesus. When asked to quote the greatest commandment in the Law, Jesus refers to the command to love God and then cites the command to love one's neighbour as oneself. 'On these two commandments hang all the law and the prophets' (22: 36–40).

In an equally important verse at the climax of the Sermon on the Mount the so-called 'golden rule' is cited: 'In everything do to others as you would have them do to you' (7: 12). These words are close to the original Q saying included by Luke at 6: 31, but Matthew adds a most important interpretative comment: 'for this is the law and the prophets'. In other words, for Matthew the Old Testament remains authoritative: it is neither to be discarded nor is it to be interpreted narrowly along the lines used by Matthew's Pharisaic and scribal opponents. The teaching of Jesus strengthens and fulfils the prophets, and it provides the correct criterion for interpretation of the Law.

How are 5: 18 and 5: 19 to be interpreted? At first sight they seem to fit awkwardly with the points made in the preceding paragraphs.

For truly, I tell you, until heaven and earth pass away, not one letter, not one stroke of a letter, will pass from the law until all is accomplished. (5.18)

Therefore, whoever breaks one of the least of these commandments, and teaches others to do the same, will be called least in the kingdom of heaven; but whoever does them and teaches them will be called great in the kingdom of heaven. (5.19)

These two verses seem to imply that even for Christians the Law continues without modification. Many scholars accept that a qualification is introduced (perhaps by the evangelist himself) with the phrase 'until all is accomplished'. On this view the coming of Jesus does mark the fulfilment of God's purposes and so provides a new perspective from which the Law is to be viewed.

If this explanation is at least plausible, how is 5: 19 to be interpreted? At this point many exegetes accept without further ado that the evangelist is inconsistent: he has taken over without modification a very conservative saying. But it is difficult to believe that Matthew has retained teaching with which he himself does not agree. So some scholars have suggested that the 'commandments' in 5: 19 which are not to be 'broken' are not the Old Testament commandments, but the sayings of Jesus recorded in Matthew's gospel. It is quite possible that this is how the evangelist understood this saying, for the final verse of the gospel insists that 'all nations' are to be taught to observe *all the commandments of Jesus* (28: 20).

The commissioning of the disciples: 28: 18–20

In the closing three verses of the gospel the evangelist both underlines and develops his earlier themes. These verses have been described as the key to the understanding of the whole book. The evangelist seems to have used the word 'all' to draw together into one unit three originally separate sayings. Although this is often obscured in modern translations, the passage refers to 'all authority', 'all nations', 'all the commandments', and 'all the days'.

Both in this passage and in the gospel as a whole, the evangelist's primary concern is to spell out what he takes to be the full significance of Jesus. In several passages, and most notably in 9: 8 and 11: 27, the evangelist has drawn attention to the authority given to Jesus in his earthly ministry. But now that authority is extended to include heaven as well as earth. In what sense does the exalted Jesus exercise authority in heaven? The evangelist seems to be alluding to Daniel 7: 13–14 where 'one like a son of man' enters the presence of the Ancient of Days (God), 'and to him was given dominion and glory and kingship, that all peoples, nations and languages should serve him'.

This striking interpretation of the significance of Jesus has been anticipated earlier in the gospel. The evangelist has extended considerably

Mark's strong emphasis on Jesus as the Son of God. And whereas in Mark Jesus is referred to by the disciples as 'teacher' and in Luke as 'master', both simply terms of respect, in Matthew the disciples (but not others) use the much more profound term 'Lord'.

As we have seen, the command to 'make disciples of all nations' is indeed a key to the understanding of this gospel. Israel's rejection of her Messiah has led to God's acceptance of Gentiles (cf. 21: 43). Although the evangelist includes fierce denunciations of the Jewish leaders which most Christians find embarrassing, he does not seem to accept that Israel's rejection is final. 'All the nations' who are to be evangelized include Israel.

The command to the disciples to baptize 'in the name of the Father and of the Son and of the Holy Spirit' is quite without parallel in the New Testament. Elsewhere baptism is spoken of as being in or through the name of Jesus (for example, see Acts 2: 38; 10: 48; Rom. 6: 3; 1 Cor. 1: 13, 15 and 6: 11). Matthew's use of the threefold name in baptism is a later development which quickly became the standard Christian formulation.

In the very last verse the continuing importance of the teaching of Jesus is emphasized. If 'making disciples' includes teaching disciples to observe all the commandments of Jesus, it is no surprise to find that Matthew has set out that teaching in systematic fashion in five lengthy discourses. In the final phrases the evangelist returns to Christology, the theme with which this concluding section, and the whole gospel, began.

The setting and purpose of the gospel

Why did Matthew write his gospel? We have stressed the extent to which the evangelist has been influenced by Mark. One of his primary purposes is similar to Mark's: to set out fully his own understanding of the story and significance of Jesus. Like Mark, Matthew is not writing a historical record, but addressing followers of Jesus in his own day. As we have seen, Matthew stresses the ethical conduct demanded of disciples. At the end of the Sermon on the Mount, for example, Matthew's readers and listeners are urged by Jesus to do the will of their heavenly Father and to hear and obey his words 'like a wise man who built his house upon the rock' (7: 21, 24–7).

Throughout the gospel Matthew's Christian communities are clearly in view. Only in Matthew is the word 'church' used (16: 18; 18: 17). Whereas in

Luke 15: 3–7 the parable of the lost sheep speaks of God's love for those on the margins of society, the tax collectors and sinners, in Matt. 18: 12–14 the parable is used to encourage Christians to care for the 'straying' members of their communities. In the same chapter 'regulations' for settling disputes among Christians are set out (18: 15–18).

Matthew has chosen and 'shaped' his traditions with the needs and concerns of Christians in his own day in mind. Matthew writes as a pastor. But can we be more specific about the circumstances for which he wrote? One of the most distinctive features of Matthew is the ferocity of anti-Jewish polemic and this seems to be related to the evangelist's original purposes. Polemical sayings are found already in Mark and in Q, but Matthew has sharpened and extended these traditions considerably.

In chapter 23 seven strongly worded woes are addressed to the scribes and Pharisees. In the final woe Matthew claims much more explicitly than in the underlying Q tradition that the scribes and Pharisees are the sons of those who murdered the prophets: they, too, are murderers (23: 31). They are then addressed as 'You serpents, you brood of vipers'—the very phrases John the Baptist addresses to the crowds in general at Luke 3: 7, but specifically to the Pharisees and Sadducees in Matt. 3: 7. Then follows a reference to the 'Christian' prophets, wise men and scribes whom Jesus is sending to the Jewish leaders, some of whom will be killed and crucified just like Jesus himself. Some will be scourged in the synagogues of the Pharisees and scribes and persecuted from town to town. As a result, God's judgement will come upon those who have persecuted and murdered the followers of Jesus (23: 34–5).

The final verses of this chapter take this point further: 'Jerusalem, Jerusalem, the city that kills the prophets and stones those sent to it . . . See, your house is left to you, desolate' (23: 37–8). At 21: 43, in a verse Matthew adds to the Marcan parable of the wicked husbandmen (Mark 12: 1–12), the reader is told that God's kingdom will be taken away from Israel and 'given to a people that produces the fruits of the kingdom'.

Perhaps the most plausible explanation of Matthew's intensified anti-Jewish polemic is that Matthew's communities have recently parted company with Judaism after a period of prolonged hostility. Opposition, rejection, and persecution from some Jewish quarters is not just a matter of past experience: for the evangelist and his readers the threat is still felt strongly and keenly. Matthew is puzzled—indeed pained—by Israel's continued rejection of Jesus and of Christian messengers who have pro-claimed Jesus as the fulfilment of Israel's hopes. Hence the anger and frustration.

Like many a minority group which feels itself (rightly or wrongly) to be under threat from a dominant group from which it has parted company, Matthew uses polemical denunciations to justify his own stance. This sug-gested setting for the evangelist's anti-Jewish polemic perhaps explains the harshness of his words, but it does not excuse them. Christians today rightly feel acutely embarrassed by them and by the way they have been used by some in earlier generations to fuel anti-Semitism.

I have defended in some detail the view sketched in the preceding para-graphs (see the Bibliography). But an alternative way of reading the evi-dence has been proposed by J. A. Overman (1990), A. J. Saldarini (1994), and David C. Sim (1998). Overman insists that many of the issues which are prominent in Matthew were also of great concern to other first-century Jewish groups and 'sects'. Matthew takes his stand *within* Judaism, for Matthew 'does not allow formative Judaism to go one way and his com-munity to go another' (p. 157). Sim claims that the evangelist and his readers observed the law in full: 'the Matthean community was therefore Jewish ... its religious tradition is most aptly described as Christian Judaism' (p. 299).

There are no easy answers. I have sometimes encouraged my students to take sides and to debate the issues in class. Invariably those who take a different view from my own have prevailed!

On some key points nearly all are agreed. The evangelist Matthew is a Jew, and not a Gentile. Matthew's listeners and readers are closely related to Judaism, and yet in some tension with at least some of the strands of the Judaism of their day.

Although it is fashionable to read between the lines of this gospel in order to discern points at which Matthew is at odds with some contempor-ary Christian or Jewish groups, this will always be a speculative endeavour. We should not lose sight of Matthew's primary purpose: he is primarily concerned to set out the story, the teaching, and the significance of Jesus in order to encourage and exhort followers of Jesus in his own day.

The origin of Matthew's gospel

If Mark was written just before or just after the traumatic events of AD 70, then Matthew's carefully revised and considerably extended edition of Mark must have been written some time later. Most scholars accept that Matthew's version of the parable of the wedding feast reflects the destruction of Jerusalem in AD 70 (22: 1–14). The parable tells how the king (God) has repeatedly sent his servants (the prophets) with an invitation to a marriage feast. Those who are invited spurn the invitation; some reject and kill the servants. At this point Matthew adds a verse which is not found in the similar parable in Luke 14: 16–24: 'The king was enraged. He sent his troops, destroyed those murderers, and burned their city' (22: 7). Here the destruction of Jerusalem is almost certainly linked with Israel's rejection of Jesus.

The gospel seems to have been written at some point between about AD 80 and 100, earlier rather than later, but it is impossible to be precise. A date well before AD 115 is probable because at that point Matt. 3: 15 is cited by Ignatius, bishop of Antioch, in his letter to the Smyrneans.

Since Matthew was known and used in Antioch by AD 115, it has often been suggested that it was written in that city. This may well have been the case. Although there is no conclusive evidence, there are other factors which are often used to support this suggestion. The central part played by Peter in Matt. 16: 16–19 may point to Antioch, for this city may have come under the influence of Peter after his dispute with Paul in Antioch (Gal 2: 11–14). Matthew's gospel is used by the Didache, a Christian writing which may have originated in Syria, not far from Antioch, by about AD 100. Antioch was a Greek-speaking city which contained several Jewish synagogues; Christianity was very firmly established there by AD 80. So it is not hard to envisage in Antioch the tensions which seem to be reflected in Matthew between dominant Jewish synagogues and Matthew's smaller mixed Jewish and Gentile Christian communities. But Antioch was by no means the only city with well-established Jewish and Christian communities. So our considerable knowledge of Antioch in the final decades of the first century should be used only with caution in the interpretation of this gospel.

Who wrote Matthew's gospel? Like all four gospels, Matthew was originally anonymous. Early in the second century the name Matthew was attached to the gospel, perhaps in order to differentiate it from other gospels known in the area. In Matt. 10: 3 one of the disciples is named 'Matthew the tax collector', thus identifying him with the tax collector Matthew who, according to Matt. 9: 9, became a follower of Jesus. But this disciple and eyewitness is unlikely to have been the author of our gospel: an eyewitness would not need to depend so heavily on Mark's gospel.

The name Matthew was known to Papias, whom we met in Chapter 3 (see pp. 55–6). In about AD 110 Papias wrote as follows: 'Matthew collected the sayings (or records) in the Hebrew (or Aramaic) language and every person interpreted (or translated) them as he was able.' Unfortunately this comment raises more questions than it answers. The origin and date of the tradition are not entirely clear and the interpretation of almost every word is much disputed. Papias probably believed that Matthew wrote the gospel we now have and not a collection of sayings of Jesus (Q), nor a collection of Old Testament proof texts, nor an early forerunner of the gospel. But our Matthew never did exist in Hebrew or Aramaic; the evangelist wrote in Greek and used both Mark and Q in Greek.

There is one further puzzling fact. The tax collector Matthew referred to in Matt. 9: 9 is called Levi in the original account in Mark! Why was Levi changed to Matthew? And why does this gospel alone refer to the disciple Matthew as a tax collector (10: 3)? Perhaps Matthew the tax collector eventually became a Christian leader and was thought (at first) to have had a hand in collecting some traditions (which can no longer be singled out) of the sayings and actions of Jesus. At a later stage he came to be known as the author of the whole gospel. Since Matthew was not a prominent leader in the early church, it is difficult to believe that his name was linked with this gospel without good reason.

5

LUKE'S GOSPEL:
GOD'S WAY TRIUMPHS

Although Luke's gospel was not as popular as Matthew's in the early church, for many readers today it is the most attractive of the four gospels. It seems to lack the harsh severity of some parts of Matthew, the terseness and the enigmatic features of Mark, and the 'other-worldliness' of John. Luke's portrait of Jesus seems to stress his human qualities. Even more than Matthew and Mark, Luke emphasizes the concern of Jesus for women, for tax collectors and sinners, and for those on the fringes of society. Several of the most universally popular parables, such as the parables of the Good Samaritan and the Prodigal Son, are found only in this gospel. And Luke's keen interest in the gap between riches and poverty strikes a modern note. Three of the 'hymns' from his infancy narratives, now known as the Magnificat (1: 46–55), the Benedictus (1: 68–79), and the Nunc Dimittis (2: 29–32), are widely used in worship.

While these features of Luke's gospel are undeniably important, there are, as we shall see, several equally striking aspects of his work. Some of the themes just mentioned are present (if less prominently) in the other gospels. Some are present in Luke primarily because they are found in the traditions to which the evangelist alone seems to have had access: these so-called 'L' traditions amount to about one third of the gospel.

In order to appreciate fully Luke's distinctive interpretation of the story of Jesus, we need to note that Luke was the only one of the four evangelists who wrote a sequel to his gospel. Luke's gospel and Acts are the two longest writings in the New Testament. They would each have filled a standard-sized papyrus roll of 31 or 32 feet in length; no doubt this is one of the reasons why Luke–Acts was written in two volumes instead of one. By writing a second volume, the evangelist has given his gospel one of its most striking features: he has set out the story of Jesus as the prelude to the story of the origin and growth of the early church. The evangelist's story ends not with appearances and words of the Risen Jesus, but in Rome. In spite of numerous temporary reversals, God's plan of salvation triumphs and the 'word of the Lord' reaches the very heart of the Roman Empire.

Since the same literary style and theological emphases are found in both volumes, ideally they should be studied together. This is not always practicable, since Luke–Acts makes up very nearly one quarter of the New Testament writings! In the second century Luke's gospel came to be linked with the other three gospels and Acts was somewhat neglected. Acts was eventually placed rather awkwardly between the four gospels and the epistles. The separation of the gospel from Acts in the collections of early Christian writings which became the New Testament was most unfortunate since the interrelationship of the two writings is still not always fully appreciated. Like Matthew, Luke places his own stamp on the traditions about Jesus which he has used, but his concerns are often related to those which emerge more clearly and more fully in Acts. Repeatedly the main themes of Acts are foreshadowed in the gospel.

As several examples of the close links between Luke's gospel and Acts will be given in this chapter, at this point we shall note just one Lucan theme which is important in both writings. As the dedication of his two volumes to 'most excellent Theophilus' confirms, Luke writes with an eye on intelligent Gentile readers—people whom we now call the 'opinion formers' in society. He takes pains to stress that the story of Jesus is related to contemporary events and culture.

At Acts 26: 26 Paul is confident that King Herod Agrippa II, the Jewish 'puppet' king acting for the Romans, will know all about the 'story of Jesus', for 'this was not done in a corner'. The same theme is found in three passages in Luke's gospel. In Luke 2: 1–2 the birth of Jesus is linked to the decree of the Roman emperor Augustus 'that all the world should be registered'. The evangelist tells his readers that John the Baptist began to preach in the fifteenth year of the reign of the emperor Tiberius—and he goes on to list six local rulers of various kinds who held office at that time (Luke 3: 1–2). In the final chapter of the gospel, which is set on the road to Emmaus, Cleopas says to the stranger who has joined him: 'Are you the only stranger in Jerusalem who does not know the things that have taken place there in these days?' (24: 18). One of Luke's primary concerns in the gospel as well as in Acts is to show that God has worked out his purposes in and through secular history.

Luke's Prologue: 1: 1–4

To Theophilus: Many writers have undertaken to draw up an account of the events that have taken place among us, following the traditions handed down to us by the original eyewitnesses and servants of the gospel. And so I in my turn, as one who has investigated the whole course of these events in detail, have decided to write a connected narrative for you, your excellency, so as to give you authentic knowledge about the matters of which you have been informed. (REB)

The first four verses of Luke's gospel are taken up with one impressive Greek sentence. (The verse divisions in the New Testament were in fact introduced only in 1551.) Like the short opening sentences of both Mark and Matthew, Luke's first sentence sets out for the reader some of his main concerns. But there the similarity ends. Luke 1: 1–4 is probably the most carefully honed sentence in the New Testament: many classical Greek writers would have been proud of Luke's elegant style. Its two parts, each with three carefully balanced phrases, cannot easily be preserved in a translation. Like many Greek historians and medical writers, Luke has provided a formal prologue which sets out in some detail the origin and purpose of his work. His sophisticated literary introduction indicates that his two volumes are intended to be 'up-market', i.e. part of the literature of his day.

The Prologue to the second volume, Acts 1: 1–2, and two other single sentences, Luke 3: 1–2 and Acts 15: 24–6, resemble but do not quite match the style of his opening sentence. But Luke's literary abilities can be discerned throughout the two volumes, even where he is closely dependent on written sources or oral traditions. His range of vocabulary, polished style, and literary artistry differ as much from Mark as today's quality newspaper differs from its mass-circulation counterpart.

In his Prologue Luke acknowledges his dependence on sources. He does not intend to disparage his predecessors: the sense is rather, 'because others have written, I may also write'. Luke sets his contribution alongside that of the 'many' who have compiled narrative accounts of the 'events that have taken place among us'. In this latter phrase he implies that he himself has witnessed some of the events he narrates. Since he is introducing both volumes, this seems to be a reference to some of the events of Acts: he is not himself an eyewitness of the story of Jesus since he states that he depends on those who were 'the original eyewitnesses and servants of the gospel'.

In verse 3 Luke states that he has investigated 'the events' and the work of his predecessors. He makes three particular claims. He has striven for completeness, for accuracy, and to produce an 'orderly account'. The latter expression does not refer to chronological order. Perhaps surprisingly, Luke is even less interested in precise chronology than Mark. Only once does he include a chronological reference which has no equivalent in Mark (Luke 22: 59), but in some eight passages Luke either does not have an equivalent chronological note or has a less precise expression. By 'orderly' Luke means 'in a systematic way'; there is probably a hint here at his understanding of the successive stages of salvation history which we shall discuss below (pp. 92–4).

Although many of the words and phrases of the Prologue are found in numerous secular Greek literary prologues, two have a 'Christian' nuance. In verse 1 Luke refers to 'the events that have taken place among us'. This rather bland REB translation hides the fact that Luke uses this verb elsewhere with the sense 'the things promised and performed by God, i.e. 'fulfilled', the verb used in the NRSV.

The REB translation quoted above accurately catches the sense with its translation 'servants of the gospel', although the Greek means literally 'servants of the word'. This phrase is striking. In numerous passages in Acts Luke sums up the content of the Christian proclamation as 'the word', 'the word of God', or 'the word of the Lord', and in one verse (15: 7) as 'the word of the gospel'. Luke has not merely received records of *past* events, but the 'word of God', the Christian Gospel, and it is this which he intends to transmit to Theophilus.

In the final verse of the Prologue Luke sets out his primary purpose in writing. He states that he is setting out his own narrative account so that Theophilus will realize that the information he has received about the story of Jesus (and its sequel) is solidly based. At a crucial point in Acts the Roman centurion Cornelius enters the story. Peter proclaims to him the story of Jesus and its significance (Acts 10: 36–44). Peter's message is referred to as 'the word' (10: 44, cf. 10: 36; 11: 1) and as the 'word of the Gospel' (15: 7). Theophilus and Cornelius seem to be in the same position. Both Roman officials have heard something about Jesus and the Christian message and need to be assured of its basis. Luke is not attempting to provide either historical proof for Christian claims about Jesus (for Luke, this is the role of the Spirit), or an accurate historical record. The carefully placed final word in the original Greek of this remarkable opening sentence, the 'truth' or 'authentic knowledge' (REB) (of the Christian message), indicates Luke's primary concern in his two volumes.

Unfortunately we know much less about Theophilus than we do about Cornelius. Theophilus is mentioned again in Acts 1: 1, but otherwise we we are told nothing more about him. Like Cornelius (and the Roman centurion at Capernaum (Luke 7: 1–10)) he may have been a 'Godfearer': a Gentile loosely attached to a Jewish synagogue. He may in fact have first heard about the story of Jesus and its sequel via friends or contacts in the synagogue. But this is merely a plausible reconstruction. There is no reason to doubt that Theophilus was a real person: only at a much later period was the name interpreted symbolically and taken to mean 'beloved of God'. Luke addresses him as 'your excellency', a term of respect for a very distinguished member of society. Sometimes (but not always) the person to whom a Prologue was dedicated was expected to take responsibility for its publication, but there is no indication that Theophilus was expected to do this.

Luke and his sources

Whereas Matthew incorporates very nearly the whole of Mark's gospel, Luke uses only half of his major written source; Marcan traditions make up just over one third of this gospel. Mark is used in three large blocks: (a) Luke 3: 1 to 6: 19; (b) Luke 8: 4 to 9: 50; (c) Luke 18: 15 to 24: 11. Some non-Marcan material is incorporated within these three blocks, but up until the passion narrative, Mark's sequence and content is followed closely. Between the first and second blocks of Marcan material (i.e. 6: 20 and 8: 3), the so-called lesser interpolation is made up of traditions shared with Matthew (i.e. Q) and traditions found only in Luke (usually called 'L' material). Similarly, Q and 'L' traditions make up the so-called greater interpolation between 9: 51 and 18: 14.

Often the introductions and conclusions to pericopae (or paragraphs) betray Luke's superior stylistic abilities, but Mark's content is usually retained carefully. With very few exceptions Luke does not make changes to Mark's order. Luke's modifications of Mark can often be related to his wider concerns; some examples will be given later in this chapter. However, the reasons for Luke's omission of about half of Mark remain a mystery. In some cases he seems to have preferred similar 'L' traditions, but this is only a partial explanation.

Traditions found only in Luke, usually referred to as 'L' traditions, make up over one third of the gospel. Some have been composed by the evangelist himself: for example, Luke 1: 1–4; 3: 1–2. Others were taken by Luke from the oral traditions to which he had access. In some it is difficult to decide whether or not Luke had composed a tradition himself. The Magnificat (1: 46–55), for example, is thoroughly Lucan in most of its emphases and steeped in scriptural phraseology. Did Luke compose Mary's song himself? Did he utilize an earlier source, perhaps with some of his own modifications? Even the most sophisticated analyses have failed to settle the issue.

Some of Luke's 'L' traditions have baffling links with John's gospel. For example, Luke's account of the woman who anointed Jesus' feet (Luke 7: 36–50) has many similarities with John 12: 1–8. There are similar accounts of remarkable catches of fish in Luke 5: 1–11 and John 21: 1–14. And Luke's and John's gospels both mention the role Satan played in Judas' betrayal of Jesus (cf. Luke 22: 3 and John 13: 2, 27a). However, the similarities are not sufficiently close to suggest direct literary dependence. Luke and John seem to be drawing independently on similar oral traditions.

Q traditions (i.e. traditions shared with Matthew, see pp. 23–7) make up about one fifth of Luke's gospel. Whereas Matthew has woven together Q and other traditions into his five great discourses, it is generally agreed that Luke has retained the order of Q faithfully, as he did with Mark. Hence in more advanced studies of Q, Luke's chapter and verse references are now often used. While this system is convenient, it does suggest that the order and wording of Q can be reconstructed readily from Luke. As we noted on p. 25, this not the case.

It has often been claimed that Luke may have written a first draft of his gospel before he became acquainted with Mark. On this view, known as the Proto-Luke hypothesis, Q and L traditions formed the basis of Luke's gospel; Marcan traditions were added later as supplementary material.

Luke's Passion narrative forms the mainstay of this suggestion. Of the 163 verses between Luke 22: 14 and 23: 53, only twenty are clearly dependent on Mark. If they are removed we still seem to have a coherent non-Marcan Passion narrative. And if the Marcan blocks are removed from the rest of the gospel, Proto-Luke, made up of Q and L traditions, may have begun with the formal words of Luke 3: 1: 'In the fifteenth year of the reign of Tiberius Caesar . . .'.

This proposal has been widely canvassed. More recently it has fallen out of favour, though there is still weighty support for the view that in Luke 22 and 23 Marcan material has been added to a pre-Lucan (and often historically reliable) passion narrative.

The arguments adduced in favour of the full Proto-Luke hypothesis are not compelling. At many points, only two of which can be mentioned here, Luke's gospel seems to betray its Marcan basis. (i) As we saw in Chapter 2 (p. 24), Luke contains a number of doublets. Normally the tradition derived from Mark precedes its counterpart from Q; this suggests that Q material has been added to Mark rather than the reverse.

(ii) If Luke has added Marcan material at a later stage, then his handling of the three Marcan passion predictions is decidedly odd. In Mark they occur at brief intervals (Mark 8: 31; 9: 30–1; 10: 32–4). In Luke the first two correspond closely (9: 22; 9: 43b–45), but there is then an enormous gap until the third prediction at 18: 31–4. On the assumption that Marcan material has been *added* to Proto-Luke it is difficult to account for the delay. But if Luke has inserted Q and L traditions into his Marcan base, then we can more easily understand why the third passion prediction is separated from the other two.

Luke has used and reshaped his sources with great skill. While it is often possible to trace the modifications he has made to his sources, especially Mark, there are obvious limitations to what is referred to as the first phase of redaction criticism. So it is not surprising that 'composition criticism' and in particular narrative criticism have been more prominent in recent study of Luke's gospel.

Lucan theology and artistry: 4: 16–30

As we saw in Chapter 4, Matthew deliberately chose to open his account of the teaching of Jesus with an interpretation of the Beatitudes which introduced some of his most characteristic concerns. Although Luke's account of the opening of the ministry of Jesus is very different, it has also been carefully designed in order to set out the evangelist's own major emphases. In fact all the major theological themes of this passage are developed further by Luke in his two volumes: these verses are indeed programmatic. This passage is typically Lucan in another sense: few passages in Luke–Acts betray more clearly Luke's literary artistry. So for these two reasons we shall consider this passage in some detail.

Mark 6: 1–6 contains an account of a visit of Jesus to the synagogue in his home town Nazareth towards the end of the Galilean ministry. Luke omits the Marcan tradition at that point—so he clearly considers his own partly similar account in 4: 16–30 to be an equivalent passage. Luke makes very few changes to Mark's order, but in this case he has deliberately placed this incident at the very outset of the ministry of Jesus. He has done this even though 4: 23 refers awkwardly to an earlier ministry in Capernaum which is recorded in Mark but which has not yet been mentioned in Luke!

Luke has probably used part of Mark's account in verses 16, 22, and 24, but the origin of the other verses is much disputed. Some exegetes argue that although Luke has drawn on some earlier traditions, he is largely responsible for the passage himself. Other scholars insist that it has come almost entirely from a non-Marcan source (i.e. L) or even from Q. But whatever may have been their origin, in their present form these verses clearly betray the stamp of Luke's own hand. By concentrating on four of the themes in this passage which are prominent elsewhere in Luke–Acts, we shall gain an introduction to some of the evangelist's most characteristic concerns.

(i) The declaration of Jesus that he has been anointed with God's Spirit (4: 18,21) is one of a series of important references Luke makes to the Spirit at the outset of his account of the ministry of Jesus. Just a few verses earlier at 4: 14a Luke has added a reference to the Spirit ('Jesus returned, filled with the power of the Spirit') to the Marcan summary he uses. At the beginning of this chapter there are two further important references to the Spirit: 'Jesus, full of the Holy Spirit, returned from the Jordan (where he was baptized and where the Spirit descended upon him) and was led by the Spirit in the wilderness for forty days . . .' (4: 1). In this latter verse Luke abandons Mark's essentially Old Testament view of the Spirit ('the Spirit *drove* him out into the wilderness', 1: 12). From Luke's distinctive perspective, Jesus, the One born of the Spirit (1: 35), is 'full of the Spirit'.

At the very end of the gospel the Risen Jesus dispenses the Spirit to the disciples (Luke 24: 49). The same point is made at Acts 2: 33: it is through the exalted Jesus that the Spirit is given to the community. Later in Acts there are so many references to the Spirit that it has very properly been suggested that Luke's second volume would be better entitled 'The Acts of the Holy Spirit'.

The repeated references to the Spirit in Luke 4 form part of a carefully drawn parallel between the opening of the gospel and the opening of Acts. In the gospel God's Spirit is active at the birth of Jesus and also as Jesus embarks on his ministry, 'full of the Spirit'. In Acts, at the 'birth' of the Christian community, God's Spirit is bestowed by Jesus (Acts 2: 33).

(ii) In the synagogue service in Nazareth Jesus reads from Isaiah 61: 1–2. This reading would almost certainly have been preceded by a reading from the Torah (Pentateuch). Our knowledge of synagogue services at this time is limited: in fact this passage forms an important part of the evidence. In the quotation there are some changes from the Greek translation of the Old Testament, the most interesting of which is Luke's omission in verse 19 of the reference in Isa. 61: 2b to 'the day of vengeance of our God', probably because he wishes to stress here the grace rather than the judgement of God.

Luke skilfully underlines the drama of the scene in his comments immediately after the reading from the Isaiah scroll: 'And he rolled up the scroll, gave it back to the attendant, and sat down. The eyes of all in the synagogue were fixed on him' (v. 20). Then follows the brief but powerful declaration of Jesus: 'Today this scripture has been fulfilled in your hearing' (v. 21). This is Luke's equivalent to the opening declaration of Jesus in Mark 1: 15: 'The time is fulfilled, and the kingdom of God has come near.' In Mark the stress is on the imminence of God's kingly rule; in Luke it is the coming of Jesus himself which is seen as the dawn of a new age when God's promises will be fulfilled. But too much should not be made of the difference. Although Luke's wording seems to reflect a post-Easter Christian understanding of the significance of Jesus, in sayings such as Luke 11:

20 (Q) Jesus himself hints that his own actions are to be seen as 'signs' that God's kingly rule is breaking in.

Some scholars have claimed that Luke's 'today' is in marked contrast with Paul's teaching in 2 Cor. 6: 2: 'Behold, now is the day of salvation.' Whereas Paul is stressing that his own day marks the realization of the 'day of salvation' promised in Scripture (Isa. 49: 8), Luke associates the fulfilment of God's promises with the 'past time' of the life of Jesus. This is partly true, though elsewhere Paul's teaching is closer to Luke's. In Gal. 4: 4 Paul looks back to the earthly life of Jesus and states that 'when the time had fully come', Jesus was sent by God 'born of a woman, born under the law' in order to provide redemption or salvation. In any case Luke associates the fulfilment of God's promises in Scripture not only with the life of Jesus, as in Luke 4: 21, but also with the life of the Christian community (Acts 1: 16; 3: 18).

The announcement in Luke 4: 21 that 'Today this scripture has been fulfilled in your hearing' is the first pronouncement made by Jesus in Luke's gospel. This theme is developed considerably further by Luke in the closing words of the gospel. In 24: 44–7 the Risen Jesus reminds the disciples that in his earthly life he had taught them that everything written about him in Scripture must be fulfilled. His death and resurrection, and also the preaching of 'repentance and forgiveness of sins in his name to all nations, beginning from Jerusalem', have all been foretold in Scripture.

(iii) This passage at the very end of the gospel marks the transition to Acts, but the reference to proclamation to 'all nations' (24: 47) is already foreshadowed in the scene set in the synagogue at Nazareth. In the second half of this passage the initial positive response ('all spoke well of him', v. 22) turns sour. Jesus hints at his rejection by his own people by quoting the proverb 'No prophet is accepted in the prophet's hometown' (v. 24). In the verses which follow he implies that he is a prophet who may be compared with the great prophets of Israel, Elijah and Elisha. They both bypassed those in need in Israel in favour of non-Jews. Here Luke hints at what becomes one of the major themes of his two volumes: as a result of Israel's rejection of Jesus, God's word is taken to the Gentiles.

This theme is stated most fully in Acts 13: 46, where Paul and Barnabas declare to the Jews in Antioch in Pisidia: 'It was necessary that the word of God should be spoken first to you. Since you reject it ... we are now turning to the Gentiles.' The Jews stir up persecution against Paul and

Barnabas and drive them out of their district, but they go safely on their way to Iconium (Acts 13: 50–1).

The parallels with Luke 4 are interesting. In both cases persecution is unsuccessful; after an amazing escape 'the word of God' continues to be proclaimed (cf. Luke 5: 1 and Acts 14: 1 ff.). There is a further significant parallel. Luke has quite deliberately placed a synagogue scene at the beginning of his account of the ministry of Jesus: the 'word of God' is first announced in the synagogue in Nazareth. This passage, where the word 'synagogue' is used three times, is preceded by a general reference (from Luke's own hand): 'Jesus began to teach in their synagogues' (4: 15). In Acts 13 the passage just quoted is preceded by Paul's speech in the synagogue, immediately after the reading of Scripture (13: 15). In Luke 4 and Acts 13 (cf. also Acts 9: 20 and 13: 5) Luke takes pains to stress that 'the word' is spoken first in the synagogue to Jews; following rejection, it is taken to Gentiles.

(iv) The final verse of our passage is phrased with two delicate touches which again betray Luke's skill as literary artist and as theologian: 'But he passed through the midst of them and went on his way' (4: 30). As Luke unfolds his story the reader will be told repeatedly that the machinations of men are unable to do more than halt temporarily the progress of God's plan. The resurrection of Jesus is seen by Luke as God's reversal of human wickedness. On the day of Pentecost Peter announces to the 'men of Judaea and all who dwell in Jerusalem' (Acts 2: 14): 'This Jesus, delivered up according to the definite plan and foreknowledge of God, you crucified and killed by the hands of lawless men. But God raised him up . . . ' (2: 23 f.; cf. 3: 14 f.). The martyrdom of Stephen and the subsequent persecution against the church in Jerusalem fail to thwart the 'word of God', they lead directly and quickly to further and more widespread missionary activity (Acts 8: 1 ff.). At the end of Acts Paul is brought as a prisoner to Rome. Even though he is under house arrest waiting for his appeal to Caesar to be heard, the very last words of Luke's two volumes note that Paul preaches and teaches in Rome 'with all boldness and without hindrance' (Acts 28: 31).

A related Lucan theme is also touched on for the first time in 4: 30. Jesus passes through the midst of those who attempt to kill him and 'proceeds on his way'. The Greek verb *ekporeuomai* is often used in a general sense 'go away', but Luke also uses it in several key passages in a more specific sense: Jesus 'proceeds' on his way—a way that will eventually lead to

Jerusalem. At the beginning of an important section of the gospel to which we shall turn in a moment, Luke uses this verb five times in seven verses (9: 51–7)! In a verse found only in Luke Jesus declares: 'I must be on my way, because it is impossible for a prophet to be killed outside of Jerusalem' (Luke 13: 33 and cf. also 17: 11 and 22: 22).

For Luke 'beginnings' and 'endings' are particularly important. The evangelist has constructed his account of the opening scene of the ministry of Jesus most carefully. In Luke 4: 16–30 he uses his considerable literary skill to introduce the reader to several of the theological themes which he will develop in his two volumes.

Luke's central section: 9: 51–19: 27

At this point in his story Luke parts company with Mark for nearly nine chapters; only in the final paragraphs between 18: 15 and 19: 27 is there once again close correspondence with Mark. In this lengthy section, which takes up more than one third of the whole gospel, Q and 'L' traditions have been combined. What are the main concerns of the evangelist?

At this point in their gospels both Mark and Matthew note the departure of Jesus from Galilee. Only Luke mentions Jerusalem explicitly as the goal: 'When the days drew near for him to be taken up, he set his face to go to Jerusalem' (9: 51). The importance of Jerusalem as the goal is underlined in 13: 32–4 and 17: 11.

Shortly before the major turning point in the story at 9: 51, Luke has given his readers an inkling of what is in store for Jesus in Jerusalem. In Luke's account of the Transfiguration of Jesus, but not in the parallel passages in Mark and Matthew, Moses and Elijah speak of the 'departure of Jesus, which he was about to accomplish in Jerusalem' (9: 31). The meaning of the word 'departure' (*exodos*) in this verse is not entirely clear: perhaps Luke is being deliberately allusive. While the reader can hardly miss a hint at the impending death of Jesus in Jerusalem, Luke also seems to have in mind that Jerusalem is the place where the resurrection and ascension of Jesus to the Father take place. This certainly becomes explicit at 9: 51. The REB translation conveys Luke's intention more precisely than the NRSV which was quoted above. 'As the time approached when he was to be taken up *to heaven*, he set his face *resolutely* towards Jerusalem.' For

Luke, Jerusalem is not only the place of rejection, but also the place of eventual triumph.

Following the dramatic reminder to the reader in 9: 51 that Jerusalem is the goal of the story, Jesus sends an 'advance party' to a Samaritan village to make preparations for his arrival. But Jesus is rejected by the villagers 'because his face was set toward Jerusalem' (9: 53)! The reader who recalls what happened immediately after the rejection of Jesus at Nazareth (4: 30) knows what to expect: Jesus proceeds on his way (9: 56–7). It is no coincidence that Luke chooses the same verb in both passages. While the verb normally means simply 'to go', Luke alludes to a deeper purpose behind the movements of Jesus: in spite of opposition and rejection, Jesus proceeds on the way marked out for him by God.

Luke might have been expected to continue the lengthy central section of his gospel with repeated references to the journey of Jesus to Jerusalem, the place of rejection—and triumph. But in the non-Marcan chapters which follow up until 18: 14, the journey theme is not developed. While there are occasional references to the movements of Jesus, it is impossible to construct an itinerary. Luke is not interested in setting out a record of the travels of Jesus. Although this central section of Luke's gospel is often referred to as Luke's 'travel narrative', this term is a misnomer.

In these chapters there is a rather baffling mixture of short narratives and accounts of the teaching of Jesus. At times Jesus speaks to opponents or to the crowds in general, at times to his disciples. It is frequently difficult to see how short sections of the teaching of Jesus are related to one another. Scholars have made numerous attempts to uncover careful design in these chapters, but with limited success.

Within the framework of the journey of Jesus to Jerusalem, Luke is primarily interested in the way Jesus equips his disciples for carrying on his preaching and teaching after his death. This broad intention is underlined in 9: 60; 10: 3, 16; 17: 22–5. After the dramatic reference to Jerusalem at 9: 51, Luke holds his readers in suspense, as it were, with just a few allusions to the goal of Jesus. In the meantime attention is focused beyond Jerusalem to the future responsibilities of the disciples.

The same theme is emphasized in Luke's account of the Last Supper. In Mark no further teaching follows the words of Jesus over the bread and the cup (14: 22–6). In Luke, however, before Jesus leaves the upper room and goes to the Mount of Olives, he prepares the disciples for the future with final words of instruction (22: 21–38). This section begins, as does the lengthy central section, with one of Luke's themes to which we have repeatedly drawn attention: 'The Son of Man is going his appointed way' (22: 22, REB). The verb used is the same verb used at 4: 30, at 9: 51, and at 9: 56–7. In the central section and again at the Last Supper the disciples are prepared for the future in the context of teaching concerning the 'way' Jesus is going.

Salvation history

In the previous section we saw that in his emphasis on the journey of Jesus to Jerusalem Luke's interest is theological rather than geographical. This theme becomes even more pronounced in Acts, where the 'programme' of the whole book is set out at 1: 8: the disciples are told by their Risen Lord, 'You will be my witnesses in Jerusalem and in all Judaea and Samaria and to the end of the earth.' Luke's geography is theological geography.

Similarly, Luke's interest in history turns out to have a strong theological dimension. As we have seen, Luke is convinced that God is working out his purposes in and through secular history (pp. 80–1). In recent decades there has been considerable interest in the 'salvation historical' interpretation of Luke's theology first developed by Hans Conzelmann in 1953. On this view Luke divides history into three epochs or periods. The time of the Old Testament which came to an end with John the Baptist is followed by the life of Jesus as the mid-point in God's dealings with humanity. The third epoch is the period of the church under stress.

Luke looks back to the life of Jesus as the 'middle of time', the central period of 'salvation history', the 'sacred time' which is 'Satan-free' (cf. Luke 4: 13 and 22: 3). The acts and words of Jesus during his lifetime become 'normative' and exercise their influence in the present. The church can endure in the world because it possesses an account of the life of Jesus. In the life of Jesus—the time of salvation *par excellence*—a picture is given of the future time of salvation, a picture that is now the ground of the church's hope.

This general exposition of Luke's theology is now widely accepted, though detailed points are difficult to resolve. Luke's presentation of John the Baptist is an interesting example. Using redaction-critical methods, some have claimed that Luke has carefully revised his traditions in order to separate Jesus from the Baptist: John belongs to the era of the law and the prophets, not to the new era inaugurated by Jesus.

In support, attention is drawn to Luke 16: 16 (Q): 'The law and the prophets were in effect until John came; *since then* the good news of the kingdom of God is proclaimed . . . '. However, the further claim that Luke deliberately places a much-abbreviated account of the imprisonment of John immediately before the baptism of Jesus is less convincing. John's era is said to be 'over' before the opening of the ministry of Jesus (Luke 3: 18–22). This revision of Mark's chronology is said to be part of Luke's way of setting out three carefully defined periods of salvation history.

But in chapter 3 Luke sketches out the roles of Jesus and John separately for literary and dramatic reasons, rather as part of a precisely drawn theological pattern. In chapters 3, 4, and 5 Luke takes pains to focus attention on Jesus, allowing the disciples to enter the scene only gradually. Jesus dominates the stage: at first there is no room for Simon, Andrew, James, and John as in Mark. In Luke 5: 1–11 Andrew disappears completely and James and John are kept in the background while attention is focused on Jesus and Simon Peter. Similarly, in chapter 22 Luke carefully presents the preparations for the Last Supper as initiated, sustained, and dominated by Jesus; the disciples are kept firmly in the background, whereas in Mark they are repeatedly linked with Jesus.

Luke's separation of Jesus and John in chapter 3 turns out to be part of a literary pattern whereby Luke frequently separates Jesus from those around him in order to focus attention on Jesus more sharply. From Luke's perspective, as the infancy narratives make clear repeatedly, the coming of both Jesus and John marks the beginning of the time of God's fulfilment of his promises.

In Luke 1 and 2 a carefully drawn sustained set of comparisons between John and Jesus is drawn, and the reader is left in no doubt that Jesus is greater. Two annunciations of the conception of John and Jesus (cf. 1: 5–25 and 1: 26–45, 56) are followed by two birth narratives, including the naming of John and Jesus (cf 1: 57–66, 80 and 2: 1–12: 15–27, 34–40). These traditions are often compared to a diptych, a medieval altarpiece in which two painted wooden panels closely correspond to one another. This comparison is apt, for Luke is a literary artist rather than a theologian. While he certainly insists that God's saving purposes for humankind are fulfilled in the life, death, and resurrection of Jesus, and continue in the era of the church, he has less interest in detailed, schematic patterns of salvation history than some of his modern interpreters.

The date and authorship of Luke–Acts

Unfortunately we have no idea where Luke wrote his two volumes. Intelligent guesses in ancient and modern times have included Rome, Asia Minor, and Caesarea. A late second-century prologue suggests Achaia (southern mainland Greece), and this tradition may well be correct.

Dates as far apart as AD 60 and AD 130 have been proposed. Supporters of a very early date note that Luke does not mention Paul's death or, indeed, any events after AD 61–3. Surely, they argue, Luke could hardly portray Rome and the Roman Empire in such a favourable light after Nero's persecution of Christians in Rome in AD 64, and the fall of Jerusalem and the temple to the Romans in AD 70.

But one might equally well argue that Luke wrote long after this date when memories of these two traumatic events had faded. Acts does end rather abruptly if it is read as a historical record, but that is not Luke's intention. Luke ends his story on a triumphant note: the word of God has reached the heart of the Roman Empire.

A date as late as 130 has been suggested on the grounds that Justin Martyr (who wrote a couple of decades later) does not seem to know Luke–Acts. Luke and Justin are both apologists who share a similar theological outlook, so they are said to belong to a similar period in the development of early Christianity. But it is by no means certain that Justin does not know Luke's writings. In any case writers who share similar theological emphases do not necessarily belong to the same era.

Luke was certainly written after Mark. But how much later? The saying of Jesus in Mark 13: 14 about the desecration of the temple becomes in Luke 21: 20 a saying about 'Jerusalem surrounded by armies'; this seems to reflect the siege and capture of Jerusalem in AD 70. The phrases used in Jesus' prophetic words over Jerusalem at 19: 43 (which do not have a parallel in Mark) also seem to betray knowledge of these events: 'Your enemies will cast up a bank about you and surround you, and hem you in on every side.'

Most scholars accept that these two passages do reflect the fall of Jerusalem in AD 70. If so, then Luke–Acts may have been written about AD 80–5. But it is worth noting once again that the evidence for the dating of all four gospels is scanty.

We have been referring to the evangelist as 'Luke'. But who was he? He is usually assumed to have been a well-educated Gentile Christian. His polished Greek style, his avoidance of most of Mark's Semitic words such as 'rabbi' (four times) and 'Talitha cumi' (Mark 5: 41), and some of Jesus' more 'technical' controversies with the Pharisees all suggest this. On the other hand the evangelist is so steeped in the phraseology of the Septuagint (the Old Testament in Greek) that some have suggested that the author of Luke–Acts was a Jew who became a Christian. In his major commentary J. A. Fitzmyer (1981) sets out a strong case for concluding that Luke was a Gentile Christian, not a Greek, but a non-Jewish Semite, a native of Antioch, where he was well educated in a Hellenistic atmosphere and culture. This is plausible, though I doubt whether we have enough evidence to be quite so specific.

Although the name 'Luke' does not occur in either the gospel or Acts, there are three references to a Luke elsewhere in the New Testament. In Philemon, verse 24, Paul refers to a Luke as one of his 'fellow workers'. In Col. 4: 14 there is a reference to Luke as 'the beloved physician' who is one of Paul's companions, and in 2 Tim. 4: 11 there is a further reference to Luke as a companion of Paul's. Is this Luke the author of the gospel and Acts? That was the conclusion drawn at the end of the second century on the basis of the three references just noted. It rapidly became the universal view in the early church. The traditional view has been supported in modern times, but there are good grounds for caution.

Was Luke a physician? Although it has been held that the evangelist uses numerous technical medical terms, closer study has shown that these words are also used by contemporary Greek writers who were not doctors. There is no compelling evidence either for or against the view that Luke was a doctor, so this question remains unresolved.

Was Luke a companion of Paul's? In Acts there are four passages which are narrated in the first-person plural and often referred to as the 'we' sections: 16: 10–17; 20: 5–15; 21: 1–18; and 27: 1 to 28: 16. Many believe that in these passages the author of Acts indicates that he himself participated in the events referred to. Although this is a reasonable assumption, it is not a necessary one; Luke may have been using an extended source or a diary for parts of the second half of Acts.

This latter view has been supported by some scholars who deny that the author of Luke–Acts could have been a companion of Paul. Luke's presentation of Paul's views, it is claimed, cannot have been written by a companion of Paul's since it differs so markedly from Paul's own letters. This question is still keenly debated; since passages in Acts rather than in the gospel are involved, we cannot pursue the discussion here. But two points may be mentioned briefly. On the traditional view Luke was not necessarily a close companion of Paul's over a long period—and even if he was a companion he may not have grasped some of the more difficult aspects of Paul's teaching.

Those who reject the traditional view find it hard to explain how the name 'Luke' came to be attached in the second century to the two volumes. Luke was not the only companion of Paul's; there are several others who might have been deduced from the 'we' sections to be the author of the gospel and Acts. So although the traditional view is not without difficulties, it may be the most satisfactory solution of an intriguing puzzle.

6

JOHN'S GOSPEL: 'I AM THE WAY'

John's gospel is like a stream in which children can wade and elephants swim. For many readers this gospel's main themes are simple and clear, and the evangelist's dramatic presentation of the story of Jesus is compelling. The first half of the gospel is dominated by dialogues between Jesus and a handful of individuals who do not appear in the other gospels but whose portraits are finely drawn: Nicodemus, the leading Pharisee who came to Jesus by night (ch. 3); the Samaritan woman by the well at Sychar (ch. 4) who turns out to have had five husbands; the man who had been ill for 38 years, lying beside the pool with five porticoes (ch. 5); the man born blind whose sight is restored and who gradually understands who Jesus is (ch. 9).

The gospel is full of poignant and dramatic moments not mentioned in the synoptic gospels, as the following four examples illustrate. At the marriage feast at Cana in Galilee, Jesus says to his mother, 'Woman, what concern is that to you and to me? My hour has not yet come' (2: 4). At the tomb of Lazarus Jesus weeps (11: 35). During his final meal with his disciples, Jesus washes the feet of his disciples and then says, 'You also ought to wash one another's feet' (13: 1–20). Among those standing by the cross of Jesus are his mother and 'the disciple whom Jesus loved'. Jesus says to his mother, 'Woman, here is your son!' He then says to the disciple, 'Here is your mother.' 'And from that hour', the evangelist notes, 'the disciple took her into his own home' (19: 25–7).

Many of the sayings of Jesus found only in John's gospel are among the best-known passages in the New Testament. They often seem to have the power of a much-loved poem: 'For God so loved the world that he gave his only Son, so that everyone who believes in him may not perish but have eternal life' (3: 16); 'You will know the truth and the truth will make you free' (8: 32); 'I am the way, and the truth, and the life' (14: 6).

The evangelist develops a small range of themes with great skill. His central theological points are repeated and explained in different ways. Indeed it has been said that the evangelist is his own best interpreter or commentator. If readers bury themselves in the gospel they often find that passages which at first seem obscure later become clear.

The structure of John's gospel is both simple and impressive. The Prologue is in two parts: 1: 1–18 (to which we shall turn in a moment) and 1: 19–51. In the latter part John (who is not called the Baptist in this gospel) bears testimony to Jesus as 'the Lamb of God' (1: 29, 36) and as 'the Son of God' (1: 34). Andrew tells Simon Peter (and the reader) that Jesus is the Messiah–Christ (1: 41). Nathanael confesses that Jesus is 'the Son of God, the king of Israel' (1: 49). At the end of the Prologue Jesus refers to himself as the Son of Man; heaven will be opened and the angels of God will ascend and descend upon him as they did upon Jacob's ladder, for like the ladder he is the link between heaven and earth (1: 51).

Like a great medieval cathedral, the main body of the gospel is in two sections. Chapters 2–12 with narratives, dialogues, and discourses with individuals and groups of opponents, is the 'public' part of the gospel, rather like a cathedral nave. In chapters 13–20, with the accounts of the last meal and the discourses with the disciples, and then the passion narratives, we move into the choir and on to the high altar. As we shall see, chapter 21 forms an appendix or epilogue.

This gospel can be appreciated (at least in part) by untutored readers, but it also engages minds well versed in the philosophical and religious ideas of the ancient world. Behind a veneer of simplicity lies profundity. The evangelist draws on two thought-worlds which partly overlapped one another in the first century: the Hellenistic, on the one hand, and the Jewish (and Old Testament) on the other. As we shall see later in this chapter, John's presentation of Jesus as the Word (*logos*) provides a good illustration of this point.

Fifty years and more ago it was customary to link John's gospel more firmly with Greek than with Jewish religious thought. But the publication of the Dead Sea Scrolls discovered at Qumran in 1947 has tilted the balance in the other direction. They have confirmed the extent to which John's gospel is indebted to some currents within first-century Judaism.

John's gospel is not only thoroughly Jewish, it is also profoundly anti-Jewish. The opponents of Jesus are repeatedly referred to as 'the Jews'. In his discussions with them, Jesus appears at times to be argumentative and even to quibble. The polemic is, if anything, even stronger than in Matthew's gospel.

One example will suffice. We quoted above the words of Jesus: 'You will know the truth and the truth will make you free' (8: 32). But in its context this is not, as it is often taken to be, an aphorism of universal validity for people of goodwill. These words occur in the middle of a lengthy and ferocious dispute between Jesus and 'the Jews'. At its climax there is some rather unpleasant name-calling. Jesus says, 'Why do you not understand what I say? It is because you cannot accept my word. You are from your father the devil, and you choose to do your father's desires. He was a murderer from the beginning, and does not stand in the truth' (8: 43–4). The Jews retort, 'Are we not right in saying that you are a Samaritan and have a demon?' (v. 48). Bemused and outraged by what they take to be provocative and blasphemous claims, the Jews take up stones to throw at Jesus. But he 'hid himself, and went out of the temple' (v. 59). Why did Jesus and the Jews exchange such harsh words? We shall suggest a possible answer to this question below (pp. 117–18).

We have quickly discovered some of the reasons why this gospel is something of an enigma. But so far we have hardly touched on one of the most puzzling questions of all: why is this gospel in some ways similar to Matthew, Mark, and Luke (the synoptic gospels) and yet is in so many ways very different?

John and the synoptic gospels

In Mark's gospel Jesus spends most of his ministry (which seems to last about a year) in Galilee. He does not reach Jerusalem until 11: 1 and meets his death there a week later. In Matthew and Luke the overall pattern is similar. In John, on the other hand, Jesus begins his ministry in Judaea and Jerusalem and spends more time there than in Galilee. He makes at least three journeys to Jerusalem (2: 13; 5: 1; 7: 10) and his ministry lasts two or three years.

The synoptic gospels contain short traditions of the teaching and actions of Jesus which are loosely linked together. Even longer discourses such as Matthew's Sermon on the Mount are built up from a series of shorter elements. In Chapter 2 we likened Mark's gospel to a block of chocolate which can easily be broken up into separate pieces. John's gospel, on the other hand, has been likened to a seamless robe! Both its thought and its structure are much more unified than the synoptic gospels.

John contains a series of extended discourses with the result that at times it reads more like a treatise than a 'story'. The second half of the gospel is dominated by the discourses of Jesus with his disciples in chapters 13–17. In the first half of the gospel there are a series of lengthy scenes which have a similar structure. An incident (often a miracle) leads into dialogue with an individual or a group of opponents; the dialogue is followed by a long monologue. Essentially the same pattern can be found in 3: 1–36 (Nicodemus); 4: 1–42 (the Samaritan woman); 5: 1–47 (the man lying ill by the pool called Bethzatha); 6: 1–71 (the feeding of the five thousand); 7: 1 to 8: 59 (Jesus at the feast of tabernacles); 9: 1–41 (the man born blind).

Many words which are prominent in the synoptic gospels rarely appear in John. In the synoptic gospels Jesus' proclamation of God's kingdom lies at the heart of his teaching. But in John the word 'kingdom' is found in only two passages, 3: 3, 5 and 18: 36, 38. The word 'power' (*dunamis*) is used ten times in Mark, thirteen in Matthew, fifteen in Luke, but never in John. 'Tax collector' occurs twenty-one times in the synoptic gospels, but not at all in John. These are just a few of many examples which could be given.

On the other hand, John's favourite vocabulary is largely absent from the synoptic gospels: 'life', 'light', 'the world', 'the Jews', 'to witness' (and the related nouns), 'love' (as noun and verb) are all used very frequently in John, but no more than a handful of times in the synoptic gospels. John's vocabulary is much more limited in extent than Mark's. His Greek style is very simple but not uncouth.

While several miracle stories in John are not unlike synoptic miracle stories (e.g. 4: 46–54; 5: 1–9; 9: 1–7), exorcisms are entirely absent. In the synoptic gospels parables of Jesus are prominent. In John, although there are a few parabolic sayings, there are no parables comparable with the synoptic tradition. The extended allegories of the sheepfold and the door in 10: 1–18 and of the vine in 15: 1–11 are hardly even partial exceptions.

In the synoptic gospels Jesus rarely makes overt claims about his own significance: his teaching focuses on God. In John, on the other hand, Jesus repeatedly makes explicit claims about himself. The 'I am' sayings (which have no direct synoptic counterparts) provide a clear illustration: 'I am the bread of life' (6: 35); 'I am the light of the world' (8: 12); 'I am the door' (10: 9); 'I am the good shepherd' (10: 11); 'I am the resurrection and the life' (11: 25); 'I am the way, the truth and the life' (14: 6); 'I am the true vine' (15: 1). In four further passages, 'I am' is used without a predicate (8: 24; 8: 28; 8: 58; 13: 19; cf. also 18: 5). Jesus is presented as speaking in the same manner in which God speaks in many Old Testament passages: 'I am Yahweh'. Exodus 3: 14 is particularly important; here God reveals himself as 'I am'. (Note also Isa. 41: 4.) No wonder, then, that when Jesus says 'Before Abraham was, I am', this claim was considered to be blasphemous, an offence worthy of death by stoning (8: 58–9).

The synoptic and Johannine portraits of Jesus differ markedly. In the synoptic gospels the 'glory' of Jesus is, as it were, glimpsed by Peter, James, and John only temporarily at the Transfiguration (Mark 9: 1–8 and parallels), and even then they fail to grasp the significance of this disclosure. In John the 'glory' of Jesus is revealed openly at the very outset of his ministry at the wedding in Cana in Galilee: this is the first of the 'signs' which Jesus does and in his concluding comment the evangelist notes that its outcome was that 'his disciples believed in him' (2: 11).

As a further example, we may compare the scenes which immediately precede the arrest and trial of Jesus. In Mark's account of the last meal of Jesus with the disciples, Jesus institutes what Christians later called 'the Lord's supper' or 'the eucharist'. Jesus then goes with them to Gethsemane to pray. He is 'distressed and agitated' and says, 'I am deeply grieved, even to death.' He then prays, 'Father, for you all things are possible; remove this cup (of suffering) from me; yet not what I want, but what you want' (14: 32–6).

In John, however, four chapters of discourses with the disciples are set in the context of their final meal with Jesus (chapters 13–17) and there is no account of the institution of the Lord's supper, though 6: 53–8 is generally considered to be 'eucharistic'. Nor is there an account of the 'agony' of Jesus at Gethsemane. Full of serene confidence, Jesus takes the initiative and moves forward to meet his captors. When they state that they are seeking Jesus of Nazareth, he replies 'I am he'. This phrase is related to the 'I am' sayings to which we have just referred. At this allusion to his divine status his captors 'stepped back and fell to the ground' (18: 6). At the conclusion of this scene Jesus says confidently to Peter, 'Am I not to drink the cup that the Father has given me?' (18: 11) Thereafter throughout the passion narratives

Jesus remains in control of events: there is no distress or sadness. In the synoptic gospels Jesus is on trial; in John it is his captors who are on trial. In John Jesus is not so much 'the man of sorrows' as 'the king of glory'.

Alongside these examples (and more could be added) of the differences between John and the synoptics must be set numerous striking similarities. There are some ten passages which occur *in the same order* in John and Mark. And in numerous passages there is very close verbal similarity over several lines of Greek text. Compare, for example, Mark 1: 7–11 with John 1: 26–34; in very different accounts of the preaching of John and of the baptism of Jesus a number of identical phrases are found.

The accounts of the anointing of Jesus with ointment at Bethany in Mark 14: 3–9 and John 12: 1–8 contain many differences, but also several particularly striking points of agreement in phraseology. In Mark 14: 3 and in John 12: 3 the nard ointment used is said in several modern translations to be 'pure' . But this is no more than an intelligent guess at the meaning; the adjective *pistikos* is so rare that we simply do not know what it means! It is found nowhere else in the New Testament and in only a handful of passages in the whole of ancient Greek literature. The occurrence of such an unusual word in these two verses (taken with the many other similarities) suggests that there is a relationship between Mark and John.

But precisely what kind of relationship? Does the fourth evangelist know Mark, and perhaps Luke, and use them and revise them very freely and extensively? If so, does he intend to 'correct' them? Or does he know the synoptic gospels, use them from time to time, but also frequently ignore them, preferring to develop his own independent traditions from his own distinctive viewpoint? Or is the fourth gospel not dependent at all on any of the synoptic gospels in their final form? If so, from where did he obtain the traditions he has welded together and developed into his gospel? Why are some of these 'pre-Johannine' traditions similar to synoptic traditions, but some not? These questions are still being keenly debated: there are no agreed answers.

In the early decades of the twentieth century the dominant view was that John knew and used at least Mark, perhaps also Luke. The similarities were so striking that this seemed the obvious solution. In 1938 P. Gardner-Smith challenged this consensus by claiming that the similarities could be accounted for by use of common or related oral tradition. (In the preceding decades the development of form criticism had placed more weight on the importance of oral traditions in early Christianity.) Gardner-Smith also insisted that the differences between John and the synoptics were so considerable that John could not possibly have used any one of the synoptic gospels. On this view, which is now widely accepted, some of the traditions which lie behind parts of the fourth gospel are closely related to traditions on which the synoptic evangelists drew, but they have been developed independently and in quite distinctive ways within the Johannine 'wing' of early Christianity. Other scholars (most notably C. K. Barrett and F. Neirynck) continue to believe that John knew and used (at least from time to time) Mark's gospel and perhaps Luke's.

At the end of the second century Clement of Alexandria referred to John as 'the spiritual gospel', and since then it has been universally accepted that John contains a profound theological portrait of Jesus. If so, must we conclude that John is historically unreliable? While some scholars have drawn that conclusion, it is now generally recognized that in some respects John's gospel may be at least as *historically* reliable as the synoptic traditions and sometimes more so! Historical reconstructions of the life and teaching of Jesus now rarely ignore John's gospel. Examples will be given in several chapters in Part II of this book.

As we saw in Chapter 2 (pp. 29–32), the advent of redaction criticism has led to a new appreciation of the distinctive theological emphases of the synoptic evangelists. The older view that one went to the synoptic gospels for history and to John for theology has completely broken down. All four gospels contain both history and theology. All four gospels are a subset of Graeco-Roman biographies (see pp. 14–18). All four evangelists are concerned to tell the story of Jesus and to spell out his significance, though it can hardly be denied that there is much more 'significance' (Christology, to use the technical term) than 'story' in John's gospel.

The composition of the fourth gospel

We referred earlier to John's gospel as a 'seamless robe'. So in many ways it is, but there is a large number of loose threads! Chapter 21 is almost certainly a later appendix added by another hand. The main part of the gospel ends impressively at 20: 30–1: 'Now Jesus did many other signs in the presence of his disciples, which are not written in this book. But these are written that you may come to believe that Jesus is the Messiah, the Son of God, and that through believing you may have life in his name.'

After that grand finale addressed to the reader, one doesn't expect further material. Chapter 21, set in Galilee rather than Jerusalem (the setting for chapter 20), fits awkwardly, and ends with a 'finale' in verse 25 which reads like a pale imitation of the passage just quoted.

The verse immediately before the conclusion just quoted implies that there will not be any more appearances of the Risen Jesus: Jesus says to Thomas, 'Blessed are those who have not seen and have yet come to believe.' And yet in chapter 21 there *is* a further appearance. Close analysis of the vocabulary and style strongly suggests (but not quite conclusively) that this chapter was not written by the author of the main part of the gospel.

Why was this appendix added? The closing verses are concerned with the relationship of Peter and the 'beloved disciple'. In the second half of the gospel the 'beloved disciple' plays a prominent role (13: 23–5; 19: 26 f.; 20: 2–8; and, according to some, 18: 15 f. and 19: 35; see also below, p. 114). Both Peter and 'the beloved disciple' have died (21: 18–19 and 21: 23). Peter's pastoral authority is clarified, as is the unique authority of the 'beloved disciple'. The natural death of the latter does not make him less important than Peter who dies a martyr's death. So perhaps chapter 21 marks an acceptance of Peter's authority as long as the special authority of the 'beloved disciple' is not denigrated.

If chapter 21 is a later addition, then perhaps other stages in the composition of the gospel can be traced. There are in fact several other awkward breaks in sequence, known as aporias. At the final meal with his disciples, Jesus' discourse seems to reach a conclusion at 14: 31. After the disciples have been carefully prepared for the 'departure' of Jesus to the Father, Jesus says, 'Rise, let us go hence.' But no one goes anywhere until 18: 1! In chapter 15 Jesus continues to address the disciples and starts with a quite new theme. Similarly, chapter 16 reaches a conclusion at verse 33; chapter 17, in which Jesus addresses the Father (in prayer) rather than the disciples, contains quite different material and may have been added. So even the so-called 'farewell discourses' may once have existed as three originally independent discourses: chapter 14; chapters 15–16; chapter 17.

The turning of water into wine at the wedding feast at Cana in Galilee is referred to as 'the first of the signs which Jesus did' (2: 11). The healing of the son of the official from Capernaum is 'the second sign that Jesus did after coming from Judea to Galilee' (4: 54). Between the first and second signs there is a reference in a summary to 'the signs' which Jesus did in Jerusalem (2: 23). This suggests immediately that the 'signs' carefully numbered 'first' and 'second' may once have belonged together. In his influential commentary Rudolf Bultmann went considerably further and claimed that these two 'signs', along with five further miracle stories (and some other material) from the first half of the gospel, once belonged together in a 'signs source' which ended with 20: 30–1. In this source, Bultmann suggested, Jesus is portrayed as a semi-divine miracle-worker. Although this hypothesis has been refined further more recently, it is no more than a possibility. The word 'signs' is used several times in the so-called 'signs source', but after the 'first' and 'second' signs there is no further enumeration and some of the miracle stories are not referred to as 'signs' at all.

If the miracle traditions may once have belonged to a source, what about the discourses which are such a prominent feature of this gospel? Bultmann proposed that they too once belonged to a separate source. On his view the discourses and signs (along with passion narratives) were brought together by the evangelist to form the gospel as we now have it. Some of the 'signs' are loosely related to the discourses to which they are now attached. The discourse recorded in chapter 5, for example, starts with a dialogue between Jesus and the Jews concerning healing on the sabbath (5: 10–47). However, the account of the healing of the man ill for thirty-eight years to which it is attached makes no reference to the sabbath. Only after we are told that the man was healed, took up his pallet, and walked, is there the rather unexpected note, 'Now that day was a sabbath' (5: 9b).

If all the 'signs' and discourses were linked together as awkwardly as this, then the case for a separate discourse source would be strengthened. But this is not so. The 'bread of life' discourse in chapter 6, for example, is very closely related to the 'sign' of the feeding of the five thousand. And in some chapters (for example, chs. 4, 9, and 11) narrative and discourse are woven together so closely that it is difficult to envisage that the discourse element was ever a separate tradition. The vocabulary and style of the miracle traditions, and of the narratives and the discourses, has been analysed very closely, but this evidence neither confirms nor denies that there was ever a separate discourse source. So we seem to be left with an open question.

Several rather abrupt transitions have now been noted. There are more. In the discourse which follows Jesus' dialogue with Nicodemus, a quite separate short section concerned with John's baptism and his relationship to Jesus starts at 3: 22. At verse 31, however, the discourse addressed to Nicodemus seems to resume. If 3: 22–30 is removed, the order of chapter 3 is improved; if these verses are placed between 2: 12 and 13, the itinerary in chapter 2 becomes more natural.

It has often been suggested that chapters 5 and 6 should be reversed. In the present order of the gospel chapter 5 is set in Jerusalem, but in 6: 1 Jesus goes to the 'other side of the Sea of Galilee' without any indication that he has left Jerusalem! And 7: 1 is even more awkward: 'After this Jesus went about in Galilee; he would not go about in Judaea, because the Jews sought to kill him.' This verse implies that Jesus has just been in Judea but for his own security he has decided to go to Galilee. But chapter 6 is set in Galilee and Jesus hasn't been in Judaea since 5: 47! If chapters 5 and 6 are reversed these oddities are removed.

There are other less striking awkward transitions. How are they all to be accounted for? Some claim that the evangelist has composed the gospel over a long period and has simply overlooked the awkward transitions. Others suggest that after the gospel was written, the original papyrus sheets were displaced; anyone who has dropped an unnumbered manuscript or typescript of fifty or more pages will readily concede that this suggestion is by no means absurd! Still others claim that the awkward transitions have arisen as the result of later insertions into the gospel.

In the final decades of the twentieth century several scholars developed further Bultmann's theories concerning the composition of this gospel. For example, Robert Fortna (1988) restated and elaborated Bultmann's theory concerning a 'signs' source. With differences in some details, Raymond Brown (1979) and J. L. Martyn (1968) distinguished separate stages in the evolution of the gospel and linked them to stages in the history of the Johannine community. John Ashton (1991) published a sophisticated interpretation of this gospel from a similar perspective. (See the Bibliography for details.)

However, in these same decades a very different approach began to attract support. This was closely allied to the literary approaches to the gospels referred to in Chapter 2 (pp. 32–6). It was claimed that students of John's gospel had paid too much attention to its loose threads, at the expense of the 'seamless robe'. Questions were raised about the speculative nature of the reconstructions of both the stages in the composition of the gospel itself and of the history of the Johannine community. Attention was focused on the final form of the text: this is the only text we have, and it is this text which profoundly influenced later Christian thought and devotion. Detailed studies confirmed that the same stylistic features, the same literary devices such as irony and double-meanings, and the same theological motifs are found in all parts of the text. In spite of the awkward transitions, this gospel is a unity and its basic design and structure are simple and clear.

These two ways of approaching John's gospel are not quite like chalk and cheese. It is possible to adopt and appreciate the merits of both, as this chapter attempts to do. (In the first edition of this book, however, the balance was tilted towards 'reconstructions' rather than 'final form'.) It is time now to turn to the text itself, and to focus on three key passages, 1: 1–18; 12: 44–50; 18: 1–40.

The Prologue: 1: 1–18

In our earlier chapters we have seen the importance of the opening verses of Mark, Matthew, and Luke. Like the opening lines of the synoptic gospels, John's Prologue is a lens through which the reader is intended to view the narratives and discourses which follow. But there the similarity ends. John's Prologue is the most sustained and profound exposition of the significance of Jesus found in the New Testament.

The Prologue functions rather like the chorus at the opening of a Greek drama: the reader or observer is not only introduced to the themes which will follow, but given the correct perspective from which to view them. The sending of Jesus the Word into the world was no afterthought: in the beginning was the Word (v. 1). The Word was associated with God in creation: all things were made through him (v. 3). He is the light of life for men (v. 4), a light which those who rejected Jesus were unable to master (vv. 5 and 10 f.). Those who receive him and believe in his name are given the ability by God's grace (v. 16) to become 'children of God', to stand in a right relationship with God (v. 12). The Prologue ends on the same note on which it begins: Jesus Christ the only Son has made known, or—as the

Greek suggests—*interpreted*, the Father, for he is God's Word to all people. In short, Christ as the Word is associated both with creation and with redemption.

As with great poetry, the depths and riches of the Prologue can never be fathomed, and yet we can hardly miss the author's main concerns. The evangelist takes pains to spell out in the main body of his gospel nearly all the themes which are stated so succinctly in the Prologue.

There is one partial exception. In his later chapters the evangelist does not refer to Jesus as the Word of God. There are, however, some related passages which are relevant. The spoken words of Jesus (i.e. his teaching) are referred to as 'the word'. The one who hears the word of Jesus has eternal life (5: 24; and see also 6: 63, 68; 7: 31). At 5: 37 ff. the evangelist stresses that although the opponents of Jesus know the actual words of the Scriptures, God's message to men (which the written words embody) does not 'abide in them'. God's word can be discerned in the Old Testament, but it is to be found supremely in the word of Christ. 'And the word that you hear', says Jesus, 'is not mine, but is from the Father who sent me' (14: 24). For the evangelist the spoken words of Jesus are in a specific sense a life-giving power by means of which he gives himself to men.

Why does the evangelist open his gospel by referring to Jesus as the Word or *Logos* of God? There are several reasons. *Logos* was used in Greek as a way of referring both to inward thought, and to the outward expression of thought in speech. For the Stoic philosophers the 'word' was the rational principle in accordance with which the universe existed.

Jewish readers steeped in the Old Testament were also familiar with the term. In numerous Old Testament passages 'the word of God' refers to God's communication with men, especially through the prophets. God's word is effective; it is full of life and power. In some passages God's word almost has an independent existence of its own. 'God sent forth his *word*, and healed them' (Psalm 107: 20). 'My *word* goes out from my mouth; it shall not return to me empty, but it shall accomplish that which I purpose' (Isa. 55: 11).

A second Old Testament theme lies behind the Prologue. In Prov. 8: 22–31 Wisdom is associated closely with God in creation and almost seems to be an independent entity. God's Wisdom says, 'The Lord created me at the beginning of his work, the first of his acts of long ago . . . When he established the heavens I was there . . . When he marked out the foundations of the earth, then I was beside him, like a master worker.' This theme is taken further in several later Jewish writings which are related to Proverbs. In Wisdom of Solomon 7: 22, for example, Wisdom is spoken of as 'the fashioner of all things' (Wisdom 7: 22). In 1 Enoch 42 Wisdom is sent forth by God to find a dwelling place among all the people. Many of the phrases of John's Prologue are strikingly similar to passages in these writings. The evangelist (and his Greek-speaking Jewish readers) would almost certainly have been familiar with them.

Old Testament and later Jewish writings which speak about God's Wisdom almost certainly lie behind the Prologue. But why do these verses speak of Jesus as God's *Word* rather than as God's *Wisdom*? Although Paul dared to refer to Jesus as the Wisdom of God (1 Cor. 1: 24), John may have been reluctant to do so because 'Wisdom' is a feminine noun in both Greek and Hebrew. In any case in earlier Christian usage 'the word' had been used to refer to the Christian message, with Christ as its focal point. (See, for example, 1 Thess. 2: 13; Col. 3: 16; Acts 10: 36; 13: 26; 15: 35, 36.)

The evangelist took an unprecedented step in referring to Jesus as the Word associated with God in creation and as the Word made flesh. He may well have been influenced not only by Greek thought and by passages in Old Testament and Jewish writings, but also by early Christian usage of 'the word'.

In the opening lines of the Prologue the relationship of the Word to God is presented in a paradoxical way, just as is the relationship of the Son to the Father throughout the gospel. The evangelist echoes the opening line of the Old Testament, 'in the beginning', but he does not start, as does Genesis 1: 1, with *God*; instead, we read, 'in the beginning was the *Word*'. This is indeed a bold opening line. But the evangelist emphasizes that the Word was not *independent* of God, for he was 'with God', or, we might translate, 'in God's presence'. The Word is dependent on God, and is not simply to be equated with God; this important point is brought out in the REB translation: 'what God was, the Word was' (1: 2). In the gospel itself Jesus claims, 'The Father and I are one' (10: 30), but he also insists, paradoxically, that his relationship with the Father is one of *dependence*. He refers to himself repeatedly as the one sent by the Father, and, as if to rebut any suggestion that he is a 'second God', he states, 'the Father is greater than I' (14: 28).

Many scholars accept that the Prologue originated as a hymn or poem into which the reference to John's testimony to the light (vv. 6–8) was added at a later stage. Verses 1–5 and 9–12 (and parts of 13–18) can be set out as short lines of poetry. Many lines begin by repeating the end of the previous line, so that there is 'step-stair' parallelism; this is still partly visible in a translation of vv. 1–5:

> In the beginning was the *Word*
> And the *Word* was with *God*
> And what *God* was, the *Word* was.
> The *Word* was in the beginning with *God*.
>
> All things *came into being* through *him*,
> And without *him not one thing came into being*.
> What *came into being* in him was *life*
> And the *life* was the *light* of all people.
> And the *light* shines in the *darkness*
> And the *darkness* did not master it.

However the 'step-stair' parallelism is less clear in vv. 10–12 and not present at all in vv. 14 and 16, verses which are usually taken to be part of the original hymn or poem. And there is no general agreement on precisely which verses or phrases were inserted into the hymn.

Not surprisingly some (notably C. K. Barrett, 1978) have questioned whether this hypothesis is plausible. They reject the claim that the Prologue is (or was at an earlier stage) a hymn or poem, and insist that the evangelist himself wrote the whole Prologue in highly rhythmical prose.

As with the gospel as a whole, it is impossible to be certain about earlier stages of composition. Some would say that this is a matter of no consequence. We are faced with the two possible approaches mentioned above: reconstruction or final form. However, all would affirm the effectiveness of this opening chorus-like statement about the significance of the drama which is about to unfold.

Johannine themes: 12: 44–50

At the end of the first main section of the gospel the evangelist sums up nearly all the themes which have been developed in the preceding chapters.

In some ways this 'summary' is attached rather awkwardly to the preceding verses. In 12: 36 Jesus goes into hiding; in the verses which follow the evangelist comments on the unbelief of those who have seen his many signs. The summary at the end of the chapter opens without any indication of the context or of the audience: 'And Jesus cried aloud and said . . . ' (12: 44).

But the present position of these verses is appropriate. They not only summarize neatly the whole of the first half of the gospel; they also turn out, on closer inspection, to be related to the immediately preceding verses. There the evangelist has noted that 'many even of the authorities believed in Jesus, but for fear of the Pharisees they did not confess it, lest they should be put out of the synagogue' (12: 42). Two other verses in the gospel, 9: 22 and 16: 2, refer to expulsion from the synagogue of those who believe in Jesus. There is some Jewish evidence (though its dating and interpretation are disputed) that suggests that in about AD 85 a clause (the so-called benediction against heretics) was added to the synagogue liturgy which may have led to the expulsion of Christians.

So 12: 42 may well reflect strong tensions between Jews who accepted Christian claims about Jesus and others who did not. Several passages in the preceding chapters refer to the accusations made against Christians by Jews. Their most bitter complaint was that Christians had made Jesus equal to God. At 5: 18 we read that the Jews sought to kill Jesus 'because he was not only breaking the sabbath, but was also calling God his Father, thereby making himself equal with God'. As we saw above, when Jesus refers to himself as 'I am' at 8: 58, this is taken by his opponents as a claim to divine status, and they immediately seek to stone him. In 10: 33 we read of a further attempt to stone Jesus for blasphemy, because, the Jews say to Jesus, 'you, though only a human being, are making yourself God'.

The evangelist responds to these accusations by stressing repeatedly that Jesus acts and speaks in complete dependence on the Father. Christians do not claim that Jesus is a 'second God'. This response is prominent both at the beginning and at the end of the summary with which the evangelist ends this section of the gospel. Verses 44 and 45 stress the close relationship between Jesus and God: *belief* in Jesus is belief in him who sent Jesus; *seeing* Jesus is seeing him who sent Jesus. These two verses contain the evangelist's characteristic way of referring to God: he is the one who has sent Jesus. Seventeen times in the preceding chapters Jesus refers to God as 'the one who has sent me', thus stressing his complete dependence on the Father. At the end of this summary this point is underlined again. Jesus does not speak on his own authority. 'The Father who sent me has himself given me a commandment about what to say and what to speak . . . What I speak, therefore, I speak just as the Father has told me' (12: 49–50).

Verses 44 and 45 are closely related to 13: 20b: 'Whoever receives me receives him who sent me.' Believing, seeing, and receiving Jesus, are, for the evangelist, virtually synonymous. John 13: 20 recalls clearly Matt. 10: 40: this is one of several points at which the synoptic and Johannine accounts of the sayings of Jesus are closely related. There are two further examples in this summary. 'I do not judge anyone who hears my words and does not keep them' (12: 47a) recalls Matt. 7: 26; 12: 48, 'the one who rejects me . . . ', recalls Luke 10: 16.

Verse 46 refers in summary form to the light–darkness theme which is so prominent in chapters 3, 8, and 9. In 8: 12 Jesus says, 'I am the light of the world. Whoever follows me will never walk in darkness but will have the light of life.' In the verses which follow (8: 15–16), as also in 3: 17–19 and 9: 38–41, the light–darkness theme is closely linked to judgement. So it is no surprise to find that verses 47 and 48 summarize the teaching on judgement found in earlier chapters. Whoever rejects Jesus and does not accept his words is judged by the word that Jesus has spoken. Jesus has not come to judge the world but to save the world (3: 17 and 12: 47). Those who do not respond to Jesus as the light sent into the world remain in darkness and, in effect, judge themselves (3: 18–19 and 12: 46). For the fourth evangelist judgement takes place in the present as people respond or fail to respond to the light sent into the world. Although the evangelist emphasizes strongly that judgement is a present reality, for him, as for other New Testament writers, there is also a future judgement 'on the last day' (12: 48 and 5: 27–9).

In the final verse of this summary there is a reference to 'eternal life' which is the gift of the Father through Jesus. This phrase is used fourteen times in the preceding chapters. For the fourth evangelist, those who believe in Jesus are given now, in this life, an anticipation of the life of the age to come. Perhaps the most striking passage is 5: 24: 'Very truly I tell you, anyone who hears my word and believes him who sent me has eternal life, and does not come under judgement, but *has passed from death to life.*' 'Eternal life', then, is not just 'life after death' (as it became in the later Christian tradition); in Jesus future blessing becomes present reality.

Finally, it is worth noting how many of the themes of this summary are already found in the Prologue: light and darkness (cf. 1: 4–5, 9 and 12: 46); life (cf. 1: 4–5 and 12: 50); the coming of Jesus leads to his rejection (by some) (cf. 1: 10 f. and 12: 47–8); to believe in Jesus is to believe in God (cf. 1: 12 and 12: 44); seeing the Father (cf. 1: 18 and 12: 45). Some of these parallels are closer than others, but taken together they support our contention that the evangelist develops a small range of themes in his gospel and expounds them from many angles. He sets them out briefly in his Prologue and sums them up in these verses which close the first main part of his gospel.

The opening of the passion narrative: John 18

John 18 will seem to many modern readers to be similar to the synoptic gospels. Judas' betrayal and the arrest of Jesus are narrated (18: 1–12; cf. Mark 14: 43–6). The ear of the slave of the High Priest is cut off in an impulsive act (18: 10–11; cf. Mark 14: 47). Peter denies Jesus more than once (18: 15–18, 25–7; cf. Mark 14: 66–72). Jesus is taken to the High Priest (18: 12–14, 19–24; cf. Mark 14: 53–65). Jesus is brought before Pilate who asks, 'Are you the King of the Jews?' (18: 28–33; cf. Mark 15: 1–10). A reference to the custom of the release of a prisoner at Passover is followed by the crowd's insistence before Pilate that Barabbas, not Jesus, should be released (18: 38–40; cf. Mark 15: 11–15).

The similarities are striking, but a close reading of the narratives soon reveals many differences, some of which concern historical details. Several examples will be referred to in a moment. But first of all we must note the extent to which John 18, apparently so similar to narratives of the same events in the synoptic gospels, is impregnated with distinctive Johannine themes.

When Judas brings soldiers and police to arrest Jesus, Jesus 'knows all that was to happen to him' and takes the initiative by identifying himself to the arresting party (18: 1–5). In the Johannine passion narratives Jesus is in control of events and others react to him (cf. 18: 6–8, 11, 20–1, 22–3, 34–7). There is no agony or tragedy (as in Mark), no pathos (as in Luke), and no sadness (as in all three synoptic gospels). Jesus is the true Judge and the true King (18: 33–8; cf. 19: 14).

In vv. 15–16 there are references to 'another disciple' who is with Simon Peter. This is the 'beloved disciple' who is associated with Peter in 13: 23–4; 20: 2–10; 21: 20–4. A careful reading of this narrative is very revealing. Whereas Peter enters the courtyard only to deny Jesus, the 'beloved disciple' enters with Jesus and does *not* deny Jesus.

The significance of this becomes clear in the narrative of the discovery of the empty tomb (20: 2–8). The 'beloved disciple' outruns Peter and reaches the tomb 'first' (vv. 4, 8). Although Peter enters the tomb first, he does not believe. However, when the 'beloved disciple' enters the tomb, 'he saw and believed' (v. 8).

These two narratives (along with other evidence) strongly suggest that the 'beloved disiciple' is carefully being given precedence over Peter. Perhaps John's gospel is counteracting claims made on behalf of Peter in certain circles. What is clear is that this gospel is drawing attention to the claims of its founder and chief authority, the 'beloved disciple' (whose identity will be discussed below). So there is more to the apparently straightforward narratives in John 18 and 20 than meets the eye.

We turn now to two further examples of distinctively Johannine themes in chapter 18. In John 18: 9 and 32 the evangelist addresses the reader directly in an aside in order to make sure that the deeper significance of the incident just recorded is fully appreciated. At his arrest Jesus urges the arresting party to let his disciples go. The evangelist comments: 'This was to fulfil the word that Jesus had spoken, "I did not lose a single one of those whom you gave me"' (cf. John 6: 39; 10: 28; 17: 12). When 'the Jews' tell Pilate that they are not permitted to put anyone to death, the evangelist informs the reader that 'this was to fulfil what Jesus had said when he indicated the kind of death he was to die' (18: 32; cf. 12: 33; 3: 14; 21: 19). (The evangelist's aside is placed in brackets in the NRSV in order to assist modern readers!) From the evangelist's perspective, the 'lifting up' of Jesus on a Roman cross (cf. 3: 14; 12: 32) rather than death by the Jewish mode of stoning was God's will. The reader is being reminded that Jesus' prophetic foretelling of the mode of his own death is now being fulfilled. Just like the Scriptures, the words of Jesus are authoritative and are fulfilled.

In John 18 there are eight references to 'the Jews'. In the gospel as a whole there are about seventy! In stark contrast, in Matthew and Luke there are only five such references, and in Mark, six. The only derogatory reference in the synoptic tradition is Matt. 28: 15. In John, nearly all the references to 'the Jews' are negative; some are neutral (e.g. 2: 6, 13; 3: 1; 5: 1; 6: 4) and only a very few can be considered to be positive (e.g. 4: 22).

The repeated use of this term has been studied intensively. Although various explanations have been proposed, several of the examples in John 18 confirm that in this gospel the phrase 'the Jews' has become almost a technical term for the religious authorities, especially in Jerusalem, who were hostile to Jesus. In John 18: 3 we are told that the arresting party moved against Jesus at the behest of the chief priests and the Pharisees; later in the chapter the arresting party becomes 'the Jews' (cf. vv. 14, 31). Similarly in chapter 8: in 8: 13, 19, and 21 there are references to the Pharisees; later in the same chapter they become 'the Jews' (cf. vv. 22, 48, 52, 57).

The evangelist's use of the phrase 'the Jews' keeps sounding like a gong right through the gospel. The term has undoubtedly fuelled Christian anti-Semitism down through the centuries, and this fact continues to embarrass Christians. However a careful reading of the text of the gospel confirms that it was not part of the evangelist's intention to pillory all Jews of all time. The evangelist depicts 'the Jews' as belonging to 'the world'—the terms are virtually synonymous; he has in mind Jewish leaders who expressed overt hostility to Jesus and his disciples. It is important to note that a positive note is also sounded. Some Jews do believe (8: 30; 10: 19), even 'many of the authorities' (12: 42). So if 'anti-Semitism' is taken to mean 'unremitting racial hatred', then the evangelist is not guilty, however much this gospel has been misused.

There are several historical puzzles in John 18. Who arrested Jesus? A 'detachment' of soldiers, a cohort (*speira*) of about 200 Roman soldiers (18: 3a; cf. 18: 12), together with Jewish temple police ('from the chief priests and the Pharisees', 18: 3b). So this gospel (unlike the synoptics) states that there was both Roman and Jewish involvement in the arrest of Jesus. Is this plausible historically? Or is the evangelist emphasizing that representatives of both the Roman and the Jewish authorities, i.e. all the forces of darkness, are arrayed against Jesus? It is possible that the Jewish authorities did request the support of some Roman soldiers who were stationed nearby in the Antonia garrison in order to quell disturbances. In that case, John's gospel preserves accurately a detail not found in the synoptic gospels. The evangelist, however, is primarily concerned with the deeper significance of the opposition to Jesus: the world which does not know the Father who has sent Jesus into the world (17: 25–6).

Was Judas in charge of the arresting party (18. 3)? The REB (and some other translations) leaves the question open: 'Judas *made his way there* with a detachment of soldiers, and with the temple police.' One can visualize Judas mingling with the arresting party. The NRSV (and other translations) reflect the Greek much more accurately: 'Judas *brought* a detachment of soldiers.' Judas takes the initiative, leads the way, and hence is fully culpable.

John 18: 13 records that Jesus was taken first of all 'to Annas, who was the father-in-law of Caiaphas, the high priest that year'. Annas is then referred to twice as 'high priest' (18: 19, 22). Since there could only be one high priest in post at any one time, is the evangelist's reference to both Annas and Caiaphas as 'high priest' hopelessly muddled? Probably not. It is likely that the title 'high priest' continued to be used for Annas even after his departure from office: he held a 'patriarchal' position in high-priestly circles (cf. Luke 3: 2; Acts 4: 6), and still enjoyed the courtesy title, 'high priest', as did some other respected high priests (Josephus, *Antiquities* §34). The comment that Caiaphas was high priest 'that year' does not necessarily imply that the evangelist believed (wrongly) that the office was held for only one year: most scholars accept that the sense is 'that particularly memorable year'.

The preceding discussion of some of the issues raised by a close reading of John 18 confirms that this gospel is like a stream in which children can wade and elephants swim. My hope is that my readers will want to become elephants and wade further into other parts of this fascinating but enigmatic gospel.

Purpose and setting

In the final verse of the gospel proper, the evangelist seems to state his purpose very clearly: the signs written in this book are recorded 'so that you may believe that Jesus is the Christ, the Son of God' (20: 31). But does the evangelist mean that these are written 'so that you may continue to believe' or 'in order that you may come to believe'? Is the gospel written to strengthen faith or is it intended to be a missionary tract? Unfortunately the Greek is ambiguous. And to make matters worse two forms of the verb are found in the early manuscripts.

Most scholars accept that the evangelist writes with his own Christian readers and listeners primarily in mind. In 6: 68–9 Peter speaks for the reader: 'Lord . . . you have the words of eternal life. *We* have come to believe and know that you are the Holy One of God.' Passages such as 8: 31 ('If you continue in my word, you are truly my disciples') and 15: 4 ff. ('Abide in me . . . those who abide in me, and I in them bear much fruit') are addressed to believers. At the climax of the Prologue in 1: 14, the faith not only of the evangelist himself, but also of Christians associated with him, is confessed in the words: '*we* have beheld his glory, glory as of the only Son from the Father' (cf. also 1: 16).

What do we know about the recipients of this gospel? We have already noted passages which indicate that they are involved in fierce controversy with the Jewish synagogue. (See pp. 99 and 111.) This is a pervasive theme. The rejection of Jesus by 'his own people' is noted in the Prologue (1: 11). In the dialogue with Nicodemus there is a dramatic change at 3: 11. Up until that point Jesus and Nicodemus have been speaking as individuals. But suddenly the evangelist switches to plural pronouns: this change cannot be brought out in English translations unless we resort to 'thee' and 'thou' in the preceding verses. In 3: 11 we move to John's day and to discussion between Christians and Jews: '*We* (Christians) speak of what we know, and testify to what we have seen; but *you* (Jews) do not receive our testimony.' In chapters 5–9 there are repeated references to the theological disputes between Christians and Jews. The evangelist's readers are undoubtedly at loggerheads with their Jewish neighbours.

At least some members of the evangelist's communities have parted company painfully with local synagogues. Down through history minority religious groups which have parted with the 'parent' group have tended to become inward-looking and isolated from the world 'outside'. This attitude is often said to be 'sectarian', though that term begs questions of definition. What is hardly in doubt is that the evangelist and his readers are at odds not only with Judaism but with the world in general. This is reflected clearly in the farewell discourses addressed by Jesus to the disciples—but on another level the evangelist is speaking to his own readers and listeners. In 15: 18–19 Jesus says: 'If the world hates you, be aware that it hated me before it hated you. If you belonged to the world, the world would love you as its own. But because you do not belong to the world, but I have chosen you out of the world—therefore the world hates you.'

This isolation from the world is also expressed clearly at the climax of the farewell discourses in chapter 17. Jesus does not pray for the world, but 'on behalf of those whom you gave me' (v. 9). The disciples are 'not of the world, just as I am not of the world' (vv. 14, 16).

Not surprisingly, the ethical teaching in this gospel is directed almost entirely to Christians. The 'new commandment' which Jesus gives his disciples is 'love one another' (13: 34). This is the central ethical principle in John: it is love for one's fellow-Christian which is being expressed, not love for one's neighbour or enemy. This is in strong contrast to Matt. 5: 44, 'I say to you, Love your enemies and pray for those who persecute you', and to the parable of the good Samaritan which is the reply to the lawyer's question, 'Who is my neighbour?' (Luke 10: 25–37; cf. also Mark 12: 31 ff.). The sayings of Jesus in the synoptic gospels on marriage, divorce, property, and the state are all missing in John. There is no sign of Luke's insistence that the story of Jesus is related in any way to world history (see above, pp. 80–1).

The recipients of this gospel, then, do seem to be decidedly at odds both with their Jewish neighbours and also with the world in general. What was their relationship to other strands of early Christianity? This is an interesting but difficult question: it raises numerous issues which we cannot pursue here. In his influential commentary Rudolf Bultmann (1971) argued that some passages in John were added by an 'ecclesiastical redactor' after its composition in order to bring it into line with 'mainstream' Christianity at the end of the first century. He claimed that in genuine Johannine thought there is no room for the sacraments; the passages which seem to allude to them most clearly were later additions. Similarly, the passages which refer to future judgement 'at the last day' (5: 28–9; 6: 39–40, 44, 54; 12: 48) are taken as additions. Bultmann insisted that the evangelist's primary emphasis was on the judgement which takes place in the present when people are confronted with the claims of Jesus, so there can be no room for future judgement.

If Bultmann's analysis is correct, then this gospel does represent a form of Christianity which is very different from most of the strands we can trace in the closing decades of the first century. But even if, with most scholars, we judge his case for later additions 'not proven', his insistence that many of the evangelist's central emphases are quite distinctive is not refuted. John's attitude to the sacraments is, at best, ambivalent. And his emphasis is undoubtedly on judgement and eternal life as present realities.

Ernst Käsemann (1968) took Bultmann's approach still further, with special reference to the evangelist's portrait of Jesus. On Käsemann's view the climax of the Prologue comes at 1: 14b, 'we beheld his glory'. Jesus is a semi-divine being whose feet hardly touch the earth. The result is that John's portrait of Jesus is docetic: Jesus only *appears* to be fully human. John prepares for the later development of Gnosticism and is perhaps already influenced by it. This highly provocative interpretation has won few supporters. Most would agree that it is based on a small range of passages (especially 1: 14b and ch. 17).

But Käsemann's work does raise once again the question of the relationship of John to Gnostic thought. It is now clear that in the second century John's gospel was used extensively in Gnostic circles. (There are a number of parallels in the *Gospel of Truth*, for example.) This probably explains why it was used hardly at all in 'mainstream' Christian circles until the closing decades of the second century. Although some of John's distinctive vocabulary (e.g. light, life, knowledge, truth) is prominent in Gnostic writings, it is often used in different ways. And John's gospel is certainly far removed from the full-blown Gnosticism which the later church fathers attacked as heretical.

Finally, we must consider briefly the relationship of John's gospel to the three Johannine letters and the book of Revelation. There are sufficient similarities to suggest that all these writings come from the same circles. John's gospel and Revelation are such different writings that common authorship has rarely been proposed. The letters, however, do seem to be related much more closely to the gospel. However, most scholars now accept that the vocabulary, style, and ideas of the epistles all suggest that they were not written by the author of the gospel.

1 John 2: 19 informs us that there has been a split in the Johannine community: 'They went out from us, but they did not belong to us; for if they had belonged to us, they would have remained with us.' 1 John 4: 5 strikes such a pessimistic note that it may suggest that the secessionists are having greater numerical success: 'They are from the world—and the world listens to them.' Most scholars accept that the letters were written

after the gospel: the split reflected in 1 John was caused by differing interpretations of the gospel. The group associated with the author of 1 John remained in touch with 'mainstream' Christianity, but the successors of the secessionists are to be traced to the Gnostic circles which valued the gospel so highly.

Date and authorship

As we saw in our chapters on Mark, Matthew, and Luke, the date of their composition is uncertain. So even if we could be confident that John has used one or more of the synoptic gospels, we would still find it difficult to date John. If John does reflect steps taken to exclude Christians from the synagogue then it may have been written about AD 90; however, as we saw on p. 111, this is disputed. Perhaps c. AD 90 is the most probable date, but it is important to note that this view is based on rather general assumptions concerning the length of time it would have taken for John's profound and sophisticated thought to have emerged in early Christianity.

We can, however, be reasonably certain that John was not written much after AD 100. The very earliest papyrus fragment of any part of the New Testament (P52, also known as Rylands Papyrus 457) contains a few verses from John 18; by analysing closely the writing, ink and layout, papyrologists date it at about AD 130. The 'Unknown Gospel' (Papyrus Egerton 2), which we shall consider briefly in Chapter 7 (pp. 132–3), depends (partly) on John and strongly suggests that John was circulating in Egypt well before the middle of the second century. So perhaps we can conclude that John was written between AD 80 and 100; it would be rash to be more precise.

At the end of the second century Irenaeus states that John the son of Zebedee lived to a great age in Ephesus and there wrote the gospel. Similar statements are found in other writers from this period and it quickly became an established tradition. However, it is difficult to accept its accuracy. There is no evidence in earlier writers that John resided in Ephesus; if he did so, this silence is surprising. The gospel itself does not make any explicit statement about its author.

In the second half of the gospel we meet the 'beloved disciple' (13: 23–5; 19: 26f.; 20: 2–8; and, according to some, 18: 15f. and 19: 35). Although numerous attempts have been made to equate the beloved disciple with

John the son of Zebedee, on the basis of chapters 1–20 the best that can be said is that this is a possible inference. In 21: 7 (a later appendix) the beloved disciple is identified as one of the group of disciples mentioned in 21: 2: Peter, Thomas, Nathanael, the sons of Zebedee, and two other disciples who are not named. Once again the beloved disciple *may* be linked with John son of Zebedee, but this is not a necessary conclusion. It is in fact unlikely. If the beloved disciple belonged to the circle of the disciples of Jesus from the beginning, why does the first reference to the beloved disciple come only at 13: 23?

The beloved disciple appears finally in 21: 24. 'This is the disciple who is testifying to these things and has written them, and we know that his testimony is true.' At first sight this verse suggests that the beloved disciple wrote the gospel. But does 'these things' refer to the whole gospel, to the whole of chapter 21, or just to the immediately preceding incident? And even if 21: 24 does refer to the whole gospel, it may well be no more than an attempt from the time when the appendix was added to identify the beloved disciple as the author of the gospel. So we are left with a number of unresolved problems.

Nor can we be more confident about the place in which the gospel was written. Those who accept the reliability of the late second-century tradition propose Ephesus; some scholars do so on other grounds. Alexandria has been suggested, as has Antioch, but this issue too is best left open.

7

WHY FOUR GOSPELS?

Some thirty Christian writings which date from before *c.* AD 600 refer to themselves as 'gospels', or have been so described by others. In later centuries from time to time further gospels which were certainly hoaxes or forgeries appeared. The thirty or so earlier gospels are a very diverse set of writings. Some have survived only in very fragmentary form; some are related (at least partly) to the four New Testament gospels, but others are not remotely comparable to these.

In addition to the thirty or so 'gospels', there are a number of other early Christian writings which are in some ways similar to the four New Testament gospels. Some contain sayings of Jesus; a smaller number contain accounts of his actions.

The writings which were not accepted as authoritative or canonical are known as the 'apocryphal gospels'. This term was first used towards the end of the second century by Irenaeus, the influential bishop of Lyons, who was referring to the esoteric or secret writings of Gnostic sects which he deemed to be heretical. The term has come to be used more widely to refer to gospels outside the New Testament, many of which were originally intended to take the place of the four New Testament gospels or to offer supplementary traditions.

The existence of such a large number of early Christian writings with at least some similarities to the four New Testament gospels raises a number of important questions. Do any of these writings contain material which adds to our knowledge of the life and teaching of Jesus? Why did the early church not accept at least some of these writings as authoritative, and, eventually, as part of the New Testament? Paul insists that there is only one 'gospel of Christ' (Gal. 1: 7), so why did later Christians accept as 'Scripture' four written gospels? Would they not have been wiser to choose only one gospel? In short, why did the early church settle on four gospels, no more, no less?

From time to time sensational claims have been based on some these writings. Some have been said to reveal (at last) the hidden years of Jesus. These writings raise a whole set of interesting and complicated textual problems which have teased scholars for a long time. But in many cases our knowledge of their origin is so limited that conclusions should be both cautious and tentative.

In recent years these writings have attracted renewed scholarly attention, partly as the result of new discoveries. New editions of the texts in the original languages and new translations have been published. The Gospel of Thomas and the Gospel of Peter are major pillars in J. D. Crossan's widely discussed reconstruction of the historical Jesus (1991). Crossan's work has deeply influenced the North American Jesus Seminar led by R. W. Funk. In 1993 the Jesus Seminar attracted considerable media attention with the publication of *The Five Gospels: the Search for the Authentic Words of Jesus*. The fifth gospel is Thomas.

The apocryphal gospels and the non-canonical sayings of Jesus were not overlooked in the first edition of this book. However, in the light of the renewed attention that has recently been given to them they will be discussed fully in this chapter. We shall then consider how and why towards the end of the second century the early church accepted as authoritative the four New Testament gospels. The Bibliography includes further information and suggestions for further study.

The Gospel of Thomas

At the beginning of the twentieth century three papyrus fragments in Greek known as P. Oxy. (= Papyri Oxyrhynchi) 1, 654, and 655 were discovered separately. These papyri do not come from the same manuscript; the earliest (P. Oxy. 1) dates from *c.* AD 200, the other two from the third century AD. Since they contain some fourteen sayings of Jesus, their publication at the beginning of the twentieth century attracted considerable attention. Numerous unsuccessful attempts were made to link them with one or more of the Jewish Christian gospels referred to below. But a definite solution to the puzzle did not emerge until the publication of the Coptic Gospel of Thomas in 1957.

The fragmentary Greek sayings turned out to be closely related to sayings in the Coptic Gospel of Thomas which was discovered in 1945 among a large collection of writings known as the Nag Hammadi Library. Two years later the first Dead Sea Scrolls began to appear, and they have featured regularly in newspaper colour supplements and in radio and television programmes ever since. In contrast, until recently, the Nag Hammadi Library has remained the preserve of specialists, but for the student of early Christianity its writings are almost as important as the Dead Sea Scrolls (see pp. 152–4).

Fifty-two tractates were discovered at Nag Hammadi in Upper Egypt. Six of the tractates are duplicates; six were already known. Forty are previously unknown writings. Nearly all the writings come from Gnostic circles which flourished in the second and third centuries and which were vigorously attacked as 'heretical' by the leading 'orthodox' Christian writers of the period.

The most important Nag Hammadi tractate is the Gospel of Thomas. It contains a collection of 114 sayings of Jesus, almost all introduced by 'Jesus says'. There are hardly any indications of the 'setting' of the saying or even of the audience to whom Jesus is speaking. There is almost no trace either of the opponents of Jesus, or of the very varied types of people with whom Jesus associates in the canonical gospels, or of the healing actions of Jesus. Occasionally the disciples ask a question, but this is patently a literary device designed to break up the string of sayings of Jesus. The sayings are in the form of proverbs, parables, aphorisms, and exhortations. A few sayings are grouped by theme, but it is very hard to find any structure or overall design in the collection.

In its present form, Thomas is a Gnostic writing, as are most of the writings in the Nag Hammadi Library. Gnosticism was one of the main threats to 'orthodox' Christianity in the second and third centuries. Although Gnosticism flourished in several different forms, there were some common features. For Gnostics, the world is an evil place, created by an evil God, Yahweh, who had turned away from the one true God. Gnostics saw themselves as descendants of the one true God, as sparks of divine light trapped in this evil world. Christ the Redeemer was sent to remind Gnostics of their true nature. He shares with them secret knowledge (*gnōsis*) which enables them to break free from this evil world and return to the true God. In such a schema neither the first-century Jewish context of Jesus, nor his death and resurrection, is of importance. Although Thomas does not set out a Gnostic myth along these lines, it is now generally agreed that in its present form this collection of sayings of Jesus presupposes such a myth, especially the structure of the Gnostic myth in the Hymn of the Pearl. (See further, Bentley Layton, 1987, p. 376.)

The opening and closing words of any writing are particularly important. In the preceding chapters we emphasized the importance of the beginnings and ending of the canonical gospels. So too with Thomas: its first and last sayings make clear its link with a Gnostic world view.

The opening logion of Thomas functioned as a title or key to the whole collection: 'These are the hidden words which the living Jesus spoke, and Didymos Judas Thomas wrote them down. And he (Jesus) said: "Whoever finds the explanation of these words will not taste death."'

The sayings which follow are words of the 'living' Jesus, not Jesus of Nazareth, a first-century Jewish prophet. For the readers of Thomas, it is the esoteric, timeless *words* of the living Jesus, not his actions, his death and resurrection, which are the key to salvation. These sayings convey to the reader crucial secret wisdom or knowledge.

Thomas closes with this baffling logion (114):

Simon Peter said to them:
'Let Mary go away from us, for women are not worthy of life.' Jesus said, 'Look, I will drag her in order to make her male, so that she too may become a living male spirit being similar to you.
(But I say to you): 'Every woman who makes herself male will enter the kingdom of heaven.'

This is hardly a good example of political correctness! Mary is to undergo transformation from her present 'worldly' nature to a higher spiritual nature. As in many Gnostic writings, there is a misogynist streak: the female role in bearing more 'imprisoned spirits' is deprecated.

Several other sayings show Gnostic influence and many more are amenable to Gnostic interpretation, so it is generally agreed that the Coptic version of Thomas which has survived has a Gnostic veneer. Logion 80, for example, expresses typical Gnostic radical rejection of the created world: Jesus says: 'Whoever has come to know the world has found the dead body, of him the world is not worthy.' (See also logia 18, 29, 50.)

Logion 52 differentiates sharply Gnostic Christianity from the forms found in the New Testament writings: 'His disciples said to him,

"Twenty-four prophets have spoken in Israel, and all (of them) have spoken through you." He said to them, "You have pushed away the living (one) from yourselves, and you have begun to speak of those who are dead." '

The number twenty-four is the key to this dialogue. In Jewish tradition the Scriptures contained twenty-four books, so here we have polemic against Christians who claim that Jesus is the fulfilment of the Scriptures. This sharp rejection of the Scriptures is reminiscent of Marcion, whose influential views were rejected as heretical in AD 144. Although Marcion was not himself a Gnostic, like many Gnostics he believed that the God of Jesus was not the creator God of the Scriptures. The dialogue in logion 52 underlines just how far Thomas is from 'mainstream' first- and second-century Christianity.

The following are examples of sayings not found in the canonical gospels:

Jesus said, 'Become passers-by.' (logion 42)

Jesus said, 'Whoever has become rich should reign. And the one who has power should renounce [it].' (logion 81)

Jesus says, 'The person who is near me is near the fire, and the person who is far from me is far from the kingdom.' (logion 82)

Jesus says, 'The kingdom of the [father] is like a woman who is carrying a [jar] filled with flour. While she was walking on [the] way, very distant (from home), the handle of the jar broke (and) the flour leaked out [on] the path. (But) she did not know (it); she had not noticed a problem. When she reached her house, she put the jar down on the floor (and) found it empty.' (logion 97)

Jesus said, 'The kingdom of the father is like a person who wanted to kill a powerful person. He drew the sword in his house (and) stabbed it into the wall to test whether his hand would be strong (enough). Then he killed the powerful one.' (logion 98).

Now two examples of sayings similar to those included in the canonical gospels:

Jesus says, 'A city built upon a high mountain (and) fortified cannot fall, nor can it be hidden.' (logion 32; cf. Matt. 5: 14)

Jesus says, 'Blessed are the poor, the kingdom of heaven belongs to you.' (logion 54; cf. Matt. 5.3 = Luke 6: 20).

Some sayings are more developed versions of sayings found in the synoptic gospels. Compare, for example, logion 47 with Matt. 6: 24 and Luke 16: 13: 'Jesus says, "It is impossible for a person to mount two horses and to stretch two bows. It is impossible for a servant to serve two masters. Or he will honour the one and insult the other . . ."'.

Some are more terse than their synoptic counterparts. The parable of the rich fool in Luke 12: 16–21 is found in logion 63 in a much more concise form: 'Jesus says: "There was a rich man who had many possessions. He said, 'I will use my possessions so that I may sow and reap and plant (and) fill my storehouses with fruit so that I will not lack anything.' This was what he was thinking in his heart. And in that night he died."'

Once Thomas's Gnostic 'overlay' is removed, what is left? Do the sayings not found elsewhere go back to Jesus? Are the sayings which have synoptic counterparts earlier, more authentic versions? These questions are keenly contested.

Many of the sayings in Thomas which have parallels in the canonical gospels are shorter. Since they often lack the theological elaborations and interpretations found in the New Testament gospels, some scholars claim that many of them are earlier and more likely to go back to Jesus of Nazareth. However, 'short' does not necessarily mean 'earlier'. In passage after passage Matthew abbreviates Mark's traditions in order to set out his own rather different portrait of Jesus. Perhaps Thomas has similarly abbreviated and adapted passages in the gospels.

Scholars who claim that Thomas contains independent and therefore invaluable traditions note that there is hardly a trace of the order of the sayings of Jesus found in the synoptic gospels. Surely Thomas did not dismember the order of the canonical gospels; hence it must be independent of the canonical gospels. This argument would be strong if we could be certain that there is no order at all in Thomas. If there are some signs of groupings of sayings according to catchwords or themes, then Thomas would had had a motive for abandoning the order of sayings in the canonical gospels. In fact there are some such links between sayings in Thomas. And elsewhere the sayings may well have been arranged according to a logic which is not clear to us, in view of our ignorance of Gnostic patterns of thought. Christopher Tuckett (1988) has made a further important point: since it is clear that Thomas has revised the wording of many sayings which have parallels in the gospels, why should the order not also have been changed radically?

The final bone of contention is whether or not it is possible to discern in Thomas traces of the evangelists' own shaping or redaction of sayings of Jesus. If it is, Thomas would seem to have drawn on the gospels in their final form—not simply on earlier oral traditions which found their way into the gospels. Both sides agree that there are some phrases which fall into this category, though they differ in their explanations.

Those who maintain that Thomas is basically independent of the canonical gospels insist that such sayings are few in number and most readily accounted for as late assimilations of some sayings to the canonical text. They envisage that the original Greek version of Thomas incorporated sayings of Jesus on the basis of oral tradition rather than the written gospels. At the point when Thomas was translated into Coptic, or during the transmission of the Coptic text of Thomas, some sayings were modified, perhaps unconsciously, in the light of the phraseology of the written gospels.

This is a strong point. However it is not a knock-down argument. There are a number of such phrases—perhaps too many to be accounted for as later assimilations. And there is one piece of evidence which is particularly striking. Logion 5 (2) reads, 'For there is nothing hidden which will not become manifest.' This saying is preserved in the Greek fragment P. Oxy. 1, where it closely parallels the verbal changes Luke 8: 17 makes to Mark 4: 22. As several scholars have noted, Thomas seems to presuppose Luke's finished gospel here: the link with Luke pre-dates the translation into Coptic and cannot be laid at the door of the Coptic translator.

One more general point is relevant. Sayings of Jesus in Thomas have counterparts in all four gospels, in Q, in 'M', and in 'L' traditions. While it is just possible that Thomas drew solely on many strands of oral traditions from diverse branches of earliest Christianity, it is perhaps more likely that some traditions have been drawn from the canonical gospels.

The arguments are complex. The evidence does not all point clearly in one direction. Perhaps Thomas drew on an early harmony of the gospels; this would largely account for the absence of the synoptic order of sayings of Jesus in Thomas. We know that shortly after AD 150 Tatian composed a harmony of the four gospels (see p. 136). It now seems probable that there were even earlier harmonies.

At least some of the sayings included in Thomas were drawn (but perhaps only indirectly via a harmony) from the written gospels. Other sayings may be independent of the canonical gospels and have come from oral tradition: it did not die out once the gospels were written. This conclusion sounds like a classic compromise between two extremes. Nonetheless, it may be closer to the truth than either of the alternatives.

Thomas does not provide a new royal path back to the historical Jesus. We have only one copy of the full text, written in Coptic about AD 350. Since there are differences in wording and order between the second-century Greek and the fourth-century Coptic versions, the text of Thomas was fluid. We know that an earlier Greek version was composed no later than the end of the second century. How much earlier must remain an open question. In addition, there is a further major obstacle in the path of those who wish to use Thomas to reconstruct the teaching of Jesus. In its present form, Thomas is a Gnostic writing: removal of the Gnostic veneer will never be easy.

How many of the 'new' logia may possibly go back to Jesus of Nazareth? The Jesus Seminar is enthusiastic in its advocacy of the value of Thomas for students of the teaching of Jesus, but after critical scrutiny, only five of Thomas' logia are deemed to have good claims to be authentic. The five logia are the five listed above on p. 126. While the historian must always be grateful for new scraps of evidence, these five sayings hardly mark a dramatic advance.

But what about the sayings of Jesus in Thomas which do have counterparts in the New Testament gospels? Are the versions in Thomas more likely to be original? If they are not simply revised versions of sayings from the canonical gospels, then this is possible. In the case of the parables of Jesus in particular, this possibility must be considered.

Enough has been said already to confirm that there are no easy answers. Reconstruction of a non-Gnostic Greek version of Thomas behind the present Coptic text is problematic, to say the least—and even then we may still be at least a hundred years after the time of Jesus. In the quest for historical evidence for the life and teaching of Jesus, Thomas must not be ignored, but the obstacles are much more formidable than in the case of the four canonical gospels. Hence to dub Thomas a 'fifth gospel' is surely misleading.

Five writings from the Nag Hammadi Library are called 'gospels', but the Gospel of Thomas is the only one which contains a collection of sayings of Jesus. The Gospel of Truth and the Gospel of Philip, for example, are theological treatises, not remotely comparable in form with the New Testament gospels. On the other hand, several writings which are not called gospels do contain sayings of Jesus. The Dialogue of the Saviour, for example, preserves traditions of the sayings of Jesus in the form of a dialogue between Jesus and three of his disciples, Judas, Matthew, and Mariam. This writing seems to be related to the Gospel of Thomas. Several writings, like Thomas, contain 'revelations' of the Risen Jesus. In the Apocryphon of John and the Sophia Jesu Christi, for example, it is not the historical Jesus who teaches his disciples but the exalted Revealer who discloses secret knowledge.

The Gospel of Peter

Until the discovery in 1886–7 in Akhmîm in Egypt of a single eighth- or ninth-century Greek manuscript, the text of the Gospel of Peter was unknown. The manuscript contains sixty verses which are broadly similar to parts of the passion and resurrection traditions of the New Testament gospels. The fragment starts in mid-sentence with a reference to the trial of Jesus. Following an account of the discovery of the empty tomb, the Gospel of Peter ends with these words (14: 60): 'But *I, Simon Peter*, and my brother Andrew took our nets and went to the sea. And Levi, the son of Alphaeus was with us, whom the Lord . . .' Here the author identifies himself as Peter. An account of a resurrection appearance of Jesus to Peter and other disciples probably followed.

We do have references to the Gospel of Peter in early Christian writings, but no quotations. However, one, or possibly two, pieces of further evidence have come to light. In 1972 a papyrus fragment (P. Oxy. 2949) from the end of the second century, or early in the third, was published; it contains some sixteen words which correspond with the Gospel of Peter 2: 3–5. The differences in wording are so marked that it is clear that the text of the Gospel of Peter changed considerably between the second and the eighth centuries. In 1993 a possible further small fragment (P. Oxy. 4009) was published. Like 14: 60 quoted above, it uses the first-person singular ('I said to him . . . he said to me'), but since it does not overlap with the main fragment, certainty is not possible. This minimal and mainly very late textual evidence is in sharp contrast to the plentiful manuscript evidence for the canonical gospels.

In some places the traditions in the Gospel of Peter correspond closely with the comparable traditions in the canonical gospels; in places there are significant variations and additions, and some omissions. Unlike any New Testament writing, the resurrection of Jesus is *described* in legendary fashion with a strong emphasis on the eyewitness character of the report. The soldiers guarding the tomb of Jesus

saw three men coming out of the tomb, with the two supporting the other one, and a cross following them, and the head of the two reached up to heaven, but that of the one being led out by the hand surpassed the heavens. And they heard a voice from the heavens saying, 'Have you preached to those who have fallen asleep?' And from the cross there was heard an answer, 'Yes.'   (10: 39–42)

Several passages seem to be later developments of traditions in Matthew's gospel; there are less extensive echoes of traditions in Luke and John, and probably none at all of Mark. As examples of later developments, the following may be noted: Herod is described (inaccurately) as having jurisdiction in Jerusalem, and as the one whom Pilate must ask for the body of Jesus; when crucified, 'the Lord was silent as having no pain'; the darkness at midday caused many to go around with lamps, thinking it was night; the centurion sent to guard the tomb receives a name, Petronius; the stone rolls away from the tomb itself; two references to Sunday as 'the Lord's Day' (9: 35; 12: 50) seem to reflect early second-century developments. These features (and others) strongly suggest that the Gospel of Peter was composed after the New Testament gospels by someone who knew at least three of them. The author may not have had a copy of Matthew in front of him as he wrote, but he knew this gospel very well.

J. D. Crossan has put forward with great ingenuity a very different account of the origin and importance of the Gospel of Peter. Crossan claims that once the later traditions have been removed, the earliest stratum (which he calls the Cross Gospel) is in fact the only source used by Mark, and then by Matthew and Luke, and finally John. In *The Historical Jesus* (1991) Crossan lists the 'Cross Gospel' as a primary historical source, composed by the 50s AD, possibly in Sepphoris in Galilee.

An attempt to find very early historical traditions in a fragmentary writing which has survived almost exclusively in one eighth-century manuscript is rash, to say the least. At the one point where comparison of the second-century and the later form of the text is possible, there are major variations. So it is very unlikely that the textual traditions remained stable over such a long period. This is in sharp contrast to the much greater stability of the canonical gospel traditions over this period.

Crossan's views have been severely criticized for further reasons. If the canonical evangelists used the 'Cross Gospel' as their major source, why did they make so little use of its vocabulary and word order? And why did they leave out so many details which would have added colour to the passion narratives? For example, if Mark copied from the 'Cross Gospel' the reference to the centurion at 15: 44–5, why did he not include his name, Petronius? Several scholars have shown that the traditions isolated as the earliest stratum of the Gospel of Peter show clear knowledge of Matthew's gospel.

The Gospel of Peter gives us fascinating insights into the ways passion and resurrection traditions developed in the second century, but as a historical source for Jesus of Nazareth it is valueless.

The Egerton Gospel

In 1935 the publication of the four papyrus fragments known as Papyrus Egerton 2, or *The Egerton Gospel*, created a considerable stir. The editors dated them to the middle of the second century. In 1987 an additional few lines, known as PKöln 255, were published. Since the new fragment fits neatly on to the bottom of Fragment One, it is from the same manuscript. Suddenly it became possible to fit together two pieces of a large jigsaw puzzle, most of whose pieces are still missing.

In Fragment One phrases in John 5: 39, 45, 46, and John 9: 29 are echoed. The correspondence is striking, but the text of John's gospel is not being quoted carefully. A story of the leper cleansed by Jesus has close links to Mark 1: 40–5, but some of the phraseology is reminiscent of Matthew's and Luke's accounts of this incident. The final phrase 'sin no more' recalls John 5: 14, where it concludes a quite different miracle tradition. This mixture of synoptic and Johannine phraseology is baffling.

What is to be made of these fragments? Ever since their initial publication, most scholars have concluded that the Egerton Gospel is later than the New Testament gospels, and dependent on them: the author seems to have drawn on his memory of a number of passages in all four gospels.

In recent years several scholars have challenged this consensus and insisted that Papyrus Egerton 2 is independent and earlier than the canonical gospels, and perhaps even used by them. J. D. Crossan champions Egerton's cause and suggests that it could be as early as the 50s AD. However, at numerous points its phraseology seems to be either dependent on or secondary to the comparable traditions in the canonical gospels. It is very difficult to imagine how traditions in the canonical gospels could have developed from these fragments. It is less difficult to envisage their author writing down Jesus traditions from memory on the basis of knowledge of the canonical gospels.

Fragmentary 'gospels' and isolated sayings of Jesus

Several Church Fathers refer to or cite gospels used by Christian groups or sects of which they disapproved. Most (but not all) of these groups saw themselves as more closely related to Judaism than did the 'mainstream' Christianity of the Church Fathers, so their writings are often referred to as the Jewish Christian gospels. Since in some cases two or more names are given to what seems to be the same gospel, it is not certain just how many Jewish Christian gospels there were. Many scholars distinguish three: the Gospel of the Nazaraeans, a gospel which existed in Aramaic or Syriac and which was closely related to Matthew; the Gospel of the Ebionites, again related to Matthew; and the Gospel of the Hebrews, which is referred to more frequently than the others and which seems to have differed considerably from the synoptic gospels.

In view of our discussion of the Lord's Prayer on pp. 6–12, one reference to the Gospel of the Hebrews is of particular interest. In his commentary on Matt. 6: 11, Jerome, who lived in the second half of the fourth century and the first two decades of the fifth, included the following note on the puzzling petition for bread: 'In the so-called Gospel according to the Hebrews, instead of "essential to existence" I found *mahar*, which means "of tomorrow", so that the sense is: Our bread of tomorrow—that is, of the future—give us this day.'

Only a handful of quotations from the Gospel of the Hebrews have survived, but some of them—like the one just quoted—are very important. This interpretation may well reflect accurately the original intention of Jesus. If so, then the sense of the petition would be 'Give us bread today as an anticipation of the feast of heaven.'

In addition to a number of 'gospels' of which only fragments have survived, a large number of isolated sayings of Jesus are cited in various early Christian writings, and some are found in Jewish and Islamic sources. They are often known as the *agrapha*, the 'unwritten' sayings—i.e. the sayings not written in Scripture. It is generally agreed that only a dozen or so have good claims to be considered on a level with sayings included in the New Testament gospels. Only three examples can be included here. At Acts 20: 35 Paul says to the Ephesian elders: 'Remember the words of the Lord Jesus, how he said, "It is more blessed to give than to receive".' Clement of Alexandria records the following saying which may be an adaptation of Matt. 6: 33: 'Ask for great things, and God will add to you what is small.' In an important fifth-century manuscript (Codex Bezae) an additional intriguing saying of Jesus is included at Luke 6: 4: 'When on the same day he (Jesus) saw a man doing work on the Sabbath, he said to him: "Man! if thou knowest what thou doest, blessed art thou! But if thou knowest not, thou art cursed and a transgressor of the law".'

Infancy gospels

We have noted above that several Gnostic writings are post-resurrection discourses or dialogues. In other circles attention focused on the infancy narratives in Matthew and Luke: they were 'filled out' with numerous legends, some of which strongly influenced popular piety and Christian art in later centuries. The Protevangelium of James, which probably dates from the second half of the second century, gives an account of the birth of Mary to her parents, Joachim and Anna. The rather restrained accounts of the birth of Jesus in Matthew and Luke are woven together and expanded considerably. There is a strong interest in the glorification of Mary.

The Infancy Gospel of Thomas (which is quite unrelated to the Nag Hammadi Gospel of Thomas) contains accounts of seventeen miracles worked by the child Jesus between the ages of five and twelve. One example will indicate just how markedly this cycle of miracle stories differs from miracle traditions in the New Testament gospels.

When he was six years old, his mother gave him a pitcher and sent him to draw water and bring it into the house. But in the crowd he stumbled, and the pitcher was broken. But Jesus spread out the garment he was wearing, filled it with water and brought it to his mother. And when his mother saw the miracle, she kissed him, and kept within herself the mysteries which she had seen him do.   (ch. 11: 1–2)

The 'gospel' ends with a version of Luke 2: 40–52 in which Luke's rather restrained account of the twelve-year-old Jesus in the temple becomes a tale of an infant prodigy.

In the preceding pages of this chapter the more important Jesus traditions outside the New Testament gospels have been considered. They are of considerable importance for our understanding of the development of Christianity in the early centuries. But how valuable are they for the student of the life and teaching of Jesus? Renewed attention given to them in recent decades has produced meagre results. Thomas, however, will remain at the centre of discussion.

The fourfold gospel

By the end of the second century the four New Testament gospels were widely accepted as authoritative. There was very rarely any suggestion that any other should be put on a par with them. How did the early church come to accept as authoritative four gospels, no more, no less? As we have seen, there were plenty of rivals. No more than a brief sketch can be given here. Even a full discussion would be tentative at numerous points, since there are still large gaps in our knowledge. Indeed it has been said that the fourfold canon slid into existence almost furtively.

Early in the second century several Christian writers refer to 'the words of the Lord Jesus' or 'the Gospel' as of equal importance to 'the Scripture' (i.e. the Old Testament), but we do not know whether they are referring to written or to oral traditions. Although writers such as Clement of Rome and Ignatius of Antioch cite words of Jesus, scholars still discuss whether they knew one or more of the New Testament gospels.

In the middle decades of the second century several different attitudes can be traced. Some Christian writers continue to use oral traditions. Papias, who knew and valued at least Matthew, Mark, and John, preferred 'the living voice' to written words: 'For I did not suppose that information from books would help me so much as the word of a living and surviving voice.' Justin Martyr almost certainly quotes from several of the gospels, but he also seems to quote from the continuing oral tradition.

Although Marcion probably knew several gospels, he accepted as authoritative only *one* gospel—his own truncated and revised version of Luke. Why did he do this? Marcion saw himself as a true follower of Paul. He understood phrases in Paul's epistles such as 'my gospel' and 'the gospel of Christ' to be referring to *one* written book. And so he revised Luke to make it consistent with his interpretation of Paul's epistles. Marcion may also have been aware of the claims of opponents of Christianity that the gospels were self-contradictory.

Tatian was certainly aware of such accusations. But the solution he adopted, perhaps in opposition to Marcion's use of only one gospel, was very different. He used all four gospels (and, possibly, an apocryphal gospel) and composed from them one gospel—a harmony which was widely influential in some parts of the early church. In Syria Tatian's harmony was regarded as 'the gospel' until the fifth century. Tatian's concerns were primarily historical: he believed that the church would be better equipped to meet the barbs of her critics with one 'foundation document' rather than with four writings which did not always agree with one another.

By the end of the second century oral traditions had died out and neither Marcion's nor Tatian's solution was generally accepted. The view of Irenaeus, the influential bishop of Lyons, prevailed. He insisted that there may be neither a greater nor a lesser number of gospels than the four which the church accepts. Irenaeus almost always uses the word 'gospel' in the singular. For him it is still a question of *the* gospel which has taken literary shape in fourfold written form: *one gospel according to* Matthew, Mark, Luke, and John.

By the time Irenaeus mounted his defence of the fourfold gospel *c.* AD 180 he may have known examples of the four gospels bound together in one codex (i.e. book). It has now been established beyond reasonable doubt that papyrus fragments of Matthew and Luke located in Paris, Oxford, and Barcelona come from a four-gospel codex which can be dated to *c.* AD 200. This codex was a most handsome literary production; the formal handwriting style and the meticulously planned layout of each page suggest that it will have had ancestors earlier in the second century.

In the second and third centuries non-Christians continued to use the customary roll for their writings. While Christians did not invent the codex format, they used it for almost all their writings. One of the reasons for their marked preference for the codex was that one codex could contain all four gospels, or all Paul's letters; no roll could do this. The development of the four-gospel codex and the acceptance of four authoritative gospels are like chicken and egg: the need to encourage the use of four gospels was related to Christian preference for the codex; binding four gospels into one codex discouraged the use of rivals.

Irenaeus accepted four gospels even though he was very well aware that 'false teachers' alleged that the gospels were not authoritative because they contradicted one another. He claims that 'the gospel has been given in four forms but united in one spirit'. As he puts it,

It is not possible that the gospels can be either more or fewer in number than they are, since there are four directions of the world in which we live, and there are four principal winds. The Church has been sown thickly over all the earth; the pillar and prop of the Church is the gospel and the Spirit of life, so it is only reasonable that she has four pillars ... The four living creatures (of Rev. 4: 9) symbolize the four gospels ... and there were four principal covenants made with humanity, through Noah, Abraham, Moses, and Christ.   (*Adv. Haer.* III. 11. 8)

This defence of the fourfold gospel seems quaint to us. But Irenaeus' readers would have been more impressed: for them the number four would have evoked solidity and harmonious proportion.

There were in fact several reasons why four gospels came to be accepted. Shortly after the middle of the second century Justin Martyr reports that the 'memoirs of the apostles' are read in Sunday worship. He uses this phrase several times and in his Dialogue (108: 3) explicitly emphasizes that these memoirs were written 'by the apostles or by those who were their disciples'. Here he seems to reflect the view which soon became universally accepted: Matthew and John were written by apostles, Mark and Luke by close followers of the apostles. The four gospels came to be regarded as 'apostolic' and therefore as authoritative.

But as we have seen, the names of other apostles such as Peter, Philip, and Thomas were attached to several other gospels. Why were they not accepted as Scripture? They were rejected because they were considered to differ in content from the four 'apostolic' gospels. In this connection the Gospel of Peter is particularly interesting. About AD 200 Serapion, bishop of Antioch, had sanctioned use of the Gospel of Peter without reading it himself. Subsequently he discovered that while the greater part of it was 'in accordance with the true teaching of the Saviour', there were numerous heretical additions. So he issued a treatise entitled 'The so-called Gospel of Peter' in which he made it clear that this gospel should be rejected. In other words a gospel should not be accepted just because it had the name of an apostle attached to it. Continuity with apostolic faith was more important.

Was the eventual decision to accept Matthew, Mark, Luke, and John correct? Today it is generally agreed that neither Matthew nor John was written by an apostle. And Mark and Luke may not have been associates of the apostles. But modern historical study does provide a conclusion of some importance. While some early (and perhaps authentic) traditions about the life and teaching of Jesus may have found their way into later Christian writings, the four New Testament gospels were written earlier than any of the other 'gospels'. As we have seen, J. D. Crossan's attempt to challenge this consensus has been unsuccessful.

In our four chapters on the individual New Testament gospels we stressed their distinctive literary and theological features. However, when the four gospels are set alongside all the other 'gospels' and related writings which flourished for a time in some circles in the early church, it is the similarities of the four rather than their differences which are striking. Unlike some of the apocryphal gospels, they largely lack purely legendary or novelistic traditions, or an interest in the miraculous for its own sake. Unlike Marcion who rejected the Old Testament, they all portray Jesus as the fulfilment of the hopes of Israel. They all focus on the actions and teaching of Jesus rather than solely on his sayings (as does Thomas) or on post-resurrection 'revelation' discourses or dialogues. They all insist that the significance of the story of Jesus can be understood only in the light of the Cross and Resurrection.

The early church retained four gospels in spite of regular embarrassment over the differences in which opponents took particular delight. Most people would agree that, taken together, four distinctive portraits of, say, Luther, Churchill, or John Kennedy are more revealing than one. So too with the four evangelists' portraits of Jesus of Nazareth.

Historians are happy to have four sources available for reconstruction of the actions, words, and intentions of Jesus. In principle, the more sources the better—though they must all be assessed critically. For Christians matters are not so clear-cut. Why do they need four accounts of the story and significance of Jesus, all of which are in some way normative for Christian faith? As we have seen, in the second century there were strong tides running in favour of acceptance of only one gospel, one of the four (Marcion), or one harmonized gospel (Tatian). Only with difficulty did the crucial conviction win the day: the four are all witnesses to the one gospel. It is for this reason that the earliest titles for the gospels (which may date to the beginning of the second century) take the form 'the gospel *according to* Matthew', 'Mark', 'Luke', 'John'.

Palestine from AD 6 to AD 44

PART II

JESUS IN GOSPEL TRADITION

8

WHAT DO WE KNOW ABOUT
JESUS OF NAZARETH?

In the opening pages of this book we sketched out some of the reasons why Christians and non-Christians alike continue to be fascinated by the life and teaching of Jesus of Nazareth. But we resisted the temptation to go searching for the historical Jesus until we had gained an appreciation of the evangelists' individual ways of setting out both the story and the significance of Jesus. In Chapter 9 we shall discuss some of the methods which can be used to recover the teaching and actions of Jesus. In this chapter we shall consider whether or not Jesus existed, and then turn to literary and archaeological evidence from outside the gospels which may help us in our quest.

Did Jesus exist?

Many readers will be surprised to learn that the very existence of Jesus has been challenged. From time to time since the eighteenth century a number of writers have claimed that our gospels were written *c*. AD 100 (or later) and that only then did the early Christians 'invent' Jesus as a historical person. During the communist era Soviet encyclopaedias and reference books consistently made that claim. In recent years the existence of Jesus has been debated heatedly on the Internet.

The most thoroughgoing and sophisticated statement of this theory has been set out in five books by G. A. Wells; the most recent is *The Jesus Legend* (1996). His case is quite simple: until the beginning of the second century AD Christians worshipped Jesus as a mythical 'Saviour' figure; only at that point did they make their 'Saviour' a historical person who lived and taught in Galilee.

This intriguing theory rests on several pillars, all of which are shaky. Nonetheless it is worth taking it seriously, for it raises important issues for the student of the gospels.

Wells argues that before c. AD 150 there is no independent non-Christian evidence for the existence of Jesus. The slender Jewish and pagan references to Jesus all echo Christian insistence that Jesus died under Pontius Pilate—and Christians began to make this claim only at the end of the first century. Why did Roman writers such as Tacitus, Suetonius, and Pliny say hardly anything about Jesus and his followers? As Wells himself concedes, from their point of view Jesus and earliest Christianity were no more important than the many other charismatic religious leaders and movements which were two a penny all over the Roman empire—and Palestine was a remote corner of the empire!

Wells stresses that in the earlier New Testament letters there is a strange silence about the life of Jesus and his crucifixion under Pontius Pilate. Wells notes (correctly) that the very earliest Christian credal statements and hymns quoted by Paul in his letters in the 50s do not mention either the crucifixion or Pilate, or in fact any events in the life of Jesus. But as every student of ancient history is aware, it is an elementary error to suppose that the unmentioned did not exist or was not accepted. Precise historical and chronological references are few and far between in the numerous Jewish writings discovered in the caves around the Dead Sea near Qumran. So we should hardly expect to find such references in very terse early creeds or hymns, or even in letters sent by Paul to individual Christian communities to deal with particular problems.

Wells claims that the four gospels were written c. AD 100 and that the evangelists largely invented their traditions about the life of Jesus. But by this date Christianity was flourishing in many parts of the Roman Empire: it had hardly survived at all in Palestine and the four gospels were almost certainly not written there. If, as Wells claims, they were largely invented in a Roman and Hellenistic cultural setting, it becomes much harder than he supposes to account for the numerous details, many of which are purely incidental to the purposes of the evangelists, which do fit into our knowledge of first-century Palestine.

As we have stressed repeatedly in the preceding chapters, traditions about Jesus were preserved and to a certain extent modified in the light of the convictions about his significance held by his followers in the period after Easter. But indications of modification do not (as Wells supposes) necessarily imply invention. If the gospel traditions were invented about AD 100, why is it far from easy (with the exception of John's gospel) to find in them traces of the convictions, emphases, and problems of the Christians of that period?

Why would proclamation of Jesus as a historical person assist Christian evangelism more than proclamation of a mythical figure? If the historical existence of Jesus was invented only in about AD 100, why was it necessary to create so many detailed traditions?

We have a good deal of information about the polemical and often bitter arguments Christians, Jews, and pagans had with one another in the early centuries. But the early Christians' opponents *all* accepted that Jesus existed, taught, had disciples, worked miracles, and was put to death on a Roman cross. As in our own day, debate and disagreement centred largely not on the story but on the significance of Jesus.

Today nearly all historians, whether Christians or not, accept that Jesus existed and that the gospels contain plenty of valuable evidence which has to be weighed and assessed critically. There is general agreement that with the possible exception of Paul, we know far more about Jesus of Nazareth than about any first- or second-century Jewish or pagan religious teacher.

Literary evidence from outside the gospels

Since the evangelists wrote from their own distinctive Christian perspectives, any evidence from outside the gospels is bound to be of special interest to the historian. In Chapter 7 we referred to traditions about Jesus which are found in early Christian writings, some of which are independent of the New Testament gospels (see pp. 123–35). But what about evidence in non-Christian writings?

The Roman historian Tacitus was born *c.* AD 56; we do not know when he died. His *Annals* were intended to cover the history of Rome from AD 14 to 68. Only about half of this ambitious history has survived. Unfortunately the section of the *Annals* which covered AD 29 to 32, and which might have referred to the trial and crucifixion of Jesus, has not survived. The earliest manuscript dates from the eleventh century—in marked contrast with the early strong evidence for the text of the gospels.

In his account of the outbreak of the great fire of Rome in AD 64, Tacitus tells us—all too briefly—about the Christians who were blamed by the emperor Nero for the fire in order to squash rumours that he himself was responsible. 'They got their name from Christ, who was executed by sentence of the procurator Pontius Pilate in the reign of Tiberius. The pernicious superstition, suppressed for the moment, broke out again, not only throughout Judaea, the birthplace of the plague, but also in the city of Rome' (*Annals* 15: 44).

There is no reason to doubt the genuineness of these negative comments. Although they are brief, they are invaluable. Tacitus does not say that Jesus was *crucified* by Pilate, but his readers would naturally assume this, for crucifixion was a standard Roman method of capital punishment. He states that the execution of Christ was only a temporary setback and implies that the Christ-movement began before his execution.

The reference to Pilate as 'procurator' is important. In an inscription discovered in 1961 at Caesarea Maritima (on the coast; see the map on p. 140), Pilate is referred to as 'prefect' not 'procurator' during his term of duty in Judaea. Tacitus may have slipped in his reference to Pilate as 'procurator', or it is possible that that the two terms were almost interchangeable.

Tacitus was a close friend of Pliny the Younger, governor of Bithynia in Asia Minor from AD 111 to 113. One of Pliny's letters written to the emperor Trajan in about AD 111 is of special interest. He passes on to the emperor information he has gleaned about Christians: 'They meet on a certain fixed day before sunrise and sing an antiphonal hymn to Christ as a god, and bind themselves with an oath: not to commit any crime, but to abstain from all acts of theft, robbery and adultery, and from breaches of trust' (*Letters* 10: 96).

Pliny's references to early Christian worship, and to Christ as a god, are striking, but neither in this letter nor in Trajan's reply is there any reference to the life and teaching of Jesus.

Writing about AD 120 Suetonius may refer briefly to Christians in his life of the emperor Claudius: 'He [Claudius] expelled the Jews from Rome, because of the riots they were causing at the instigation of Chrestus.' 'Chrestus' is probably a spelling variant for 'Christus'. If so, then Suetonius (or an earlier source) states that 'Christ' encouraged (directly or indirectly) Jews or Jewish Christians to riot in Rome in AD 49. While this comment is of great interest to students of earliest Christianity in Rome, we are not much further forward in our quest for information about Jesus of Nazareth.

Later in the second century the satirist Lucian of Samosata mentions that Christians worshipped 'that great man who was crucified in Palestine because he introduced this new cult into the world'. Lucian also notes that Christians 'worship that crucified sage of theirs and live according to his laws' (*Peregrinus* 11). So by the latter part of the second century at least some educated pagans knew a little about Christianity: Jesus a 'sophist' or sage was crucified in Palestine.

There is one further often overlooked piece of evidence. In a poignant letter written in Syriac from prison to his son, Mara bar Serapion points out that those who persecuted wise men were overtaken by misfortune. He gives as examples the deaths of Socrates, Pythagoras, and the 'wise King of the Jews'.

What advantage did the Jews gain from executing their wise King? It was just after that that their kingdom was abolished. . . . But Socrates did not die altogether; he lived on in the teaching of Plato. Pythagoras did not die altogether; he lived on in the statue of Hera. Nor did the wise King die altogether; he lived on in the teaching which he had given.

The only manuscript which has survived dates from the seventh century, but the letter was probably written shortly before the middle of the second century. Was the writer a Christian? Almost certainly not, for a Christian would have wanted to name the 'wise King', and to say rather more than that he lived on in his teaching. On the other hand, the writer seems to have been influenced by Christians: he makes the usual Christian claim that 'the Jews' (not the Romans) were responsible for the execution of Jesus. Here we have an intriguing cameo from a Stoic writer who lived right outside the Roman empire.

These extremely meagre comments are all that we have from pagan writers. Why are we not told more? As it happens, few Roman writers provide information on the history of the Roman empire in the east in the first century AD. From the point of view of a Roman historian, Jesus of Nazareth and his followers were of no interest. Judaea was an obscure corner of the empire and the execution there of a troublemaker was of no consequence.

Josephus

The most important references to Jesus outside the New Testament are found in the writings of the Jewish historian Josephus (born in Jerusalem in AD 37, died *c.* 100). In AD 66 he was prominent in the Jewish resistance against the advancing Roman armies in Galilee and was taken prisoner. He later changed sides and supported the Roman cause. The Flavian Roman emperors Vespasian and his sons Titus and Domitian became his patrons. Hence he is often known by his Roman name, Flavius Josephus. His most extensive work, *Jewish Antiquities*, was written in AD 93–4. Since it includes a brief reference to Jesus as the brother of James, a long paragraph about Jesus, and an extended account of the life and death of John the Baptist, it is of considerable importance in any quest for the life and teaching of Jesus of Nazareth. We shall defer discussion of Josephus' comments on John the Baptist until Chapter 10 (pp. 184–5).

In one respect, Josephus is not unlike the New Testament evangelists: he also wrote from a distinctive biased point of view which has to be kept constantly in mind. Josephus wrote in an apartment in the emperor's house in Rome, so naturally he sets out a pro-Roman point of view. He hoped that fellow Jews would read his writings and be more sympathetic both to Roman conduct during the Jewish war, and to his own decision to switch sides. However, his writings were later largely ignored by his fellow Jews who considered him to be a traitor. They were preserved through the centuries by Christians who recognized the importance of the comments of a Jewish historian on Jesus and John the Baptist. As we shall see, at some point Josephus' comments on Jesus were interpolated by Christians.

Josephus refers in passing to Jesus in a comment on the stoning of James in AD 62. He notes that Ananus the high priest, a Sadducee, acted rashly: 'He convened the judges of the Sanhedrin, and brought before it the brother of Jesus the so-called Messiah, James by name, and also some others. When he had accused them of transgressing the law, he handed them over to be stoned' (*Antiquities* xx. 200).

This brief comment is most unlikely to be a later Christian interpolation. A Christian would have referred to James as 'the brother *of the Lord*' (as in Gal. 1: 19; cf. 1 Cor. 9: 5), and would not have referred to Jesus as 'the *so-called* Messiah'. James is a common name, so some further identification would be expected, normally in the form, 'James, son of X'. Here, however,

James is identified with reference to his better-known brother, Jesus. This single Greek sentence does not tell us very much, but it provides further confirmation from outside the gospels that James was known as the brother of Jesus, and that Jesus was recognized by some as the Messiah.

Josephus implies that Jesus is well-known: he probably intends his readers to recall that he had earlier said rather more about Jesus. There is in fact an earlier extended, but rather problematic, reference to Jesus in *Antiquities* xviii. 63–4. Although this passage is found in all the Greek manuscripts of the writings of Josephus which have survived, and although it is quoted in full by the Christian historian Eusebius early in the fourth century, in its present form it cannot be attributed to the pro-Roman Jewish historian. The passage refers to Jesus as a wise man, but adds a comment which can only have been written by a Christian, 'if one ought to call him a man'. Jesus is referred to as 'the Christ' and he is said to have 'appeared alive again on the third day' to his followers in fulfilment of the prophets.

Although in the past many scholars have written the whole paragraph off as a later interpolation by a pious Christian scribe, opinion has changed recently. Once the obviously Christian additions are removed, the remaining comments are consistent with Josephus' vocabulary and style. It is possible that later Christians not only interpolated this statement, but also removed some negative comments about Jesus of which they disapproved. This paragraph is preceded by a reference to two riots during Pilate's term of office, so there may well originally have been a reference to the trouble Jesus caused. Perhaps Josephus referred to Jesus as 'the so-called Christ', as he did in his comment on the death of James, the brother of Jesus.

The whole paragraph reads as follows in the Greek manuscripts which have survived; words and phrases I take to be Christian additions are placed in square brackets:

About this time lived Jesus, a wise man [if indeed one ought to refer to him as a man]. For he was one who did surprising deeds, a teacher of those who delight in accepting the unusual. He brought trouble to many Jews, and also many from the Greek world. [He was the Messiah–Christ]. On the accusation of our leading men Pilate condemned him to the cross, but those who had loved him from the first did not cease to do so. [For on the third day he appeared to them again alive, just as the divine prophets had spoken about these and countless other marvellous things about him.] And to this day the tribe of Christians, named after him, has not died out. (Josephus, *Antiquities* xviii. 63–4)

Once the obvious interpolations are removed, this paragraph gives an ambivalent or even a mildly hostile assessment of Jesus—one which can be attributed to Josephus with confidence. Jesus is portrayed as a 'wise man', a teacher and a miracle-worker who impressed rather gullible people. The gospels suggest that Jesus accepted the faith of non-Jews only with great reluctance, but for the benefit of his Roman patrons Josephus might well have exaggerated the numbers of Gentiles who were attracted to Jesus. The extent to which Jewish leaders were involved in the arrest and trial of Jesus is a much-disputed issue to which we shall return in Chapter 17 (pp. 279–81).

Further Jewish evidence

The handful of scattered references to Jesus in the rabbinic writings are even more difficult to assess. The earliest document in written form is the Mishnah, which was compiled from earlier traditions about AD 200. It does not contain any references to Jesus, though this is hardly surprising since it contains sixty-three tractates of religious law. Commentaries or supplements to the Mishnaic traditions (known as *Gemaras*) were set alongside the Mishnah itself in the Palestinian and Babylonian Talmuds, which were completed in *c.* AD 350 and 500. In this supplementary material there are two passages which may reflect a fairly widespread rabbinic assessment of Jesus. In *b. Sanh. 43a* an anonymous tradition is introduced with the formula, 'It is said', an indication that it is a *baraitha*, an old tradition:

On the eve of Passover Yeshu was hanged. For forty days before the execution took place, a herald went forth and cried, 'He is going forth to be stoned because *he has practised sorcery and enticed and led Israel astray.* Anyone who can say anything in his favour, let him come forward and plead on his behalf.' But since nothing was brought forward in his favour, he was hanged on the eve of Passover. Ulla retorted: 'Do you suppose that he was one for whom a defence could be made? Was he not *a deceiver,* concerning whom scripture says (Deut. 13: 8), "Neither shalt thou spare neither shalt thou conceal him?" With Yeshu however, it was different, for he was connected with the government.'

Two possible links with John's gospel are worth noting. According to the synoptic gospels Jesus shared a Passover meal with his disciples and was crucified the following day. But John 19: 14 (and the passage above) locate the crucifixion on the eve of Passover. John's gospel also implies more clearly than the synoptics that formal moves against Jesus were made some time before his eventual downfall (cf. John 7: 1, 10–13, 30, 32, 44–7).

In *b. Sanh. 107b* a similar accusation against Jesus is noted:

One day he (R. Joshua) was reciting the Shema when Jesus came before him. He intended to receive him and made a sign to him. He (Jesus) thinking it was to repel him, went, put up a brick and worshipped it.
'Repent', said he (R. Joshua) to him. He replied, 'I have thus learned from thee: He who sins and causes others to sin is not afforded the means of repentance.'
And a Master has said, 'Jesus the Nazarene *practised magic and led Israel astray.*'

The reference to 'worshipping a brick' has baffled interpreters and there is no satisfactory explanation. These lines are noteworthy for the initial welcome which seems to have been extended to Jesus: only after a misunderstanding is Jesus criticized. These two rabbinic traditions are very difficult to interpret in detail, and even more difficult to date with any confidence.

The accusation in the final sentence is also prominent in the preceding passage. Since it is found in a wide range of early anti-Christian polemical writings, it may be an early stock criticism of Jesus, even though this form of the tradition was not committed to writing until *c.* AD 500. I shall discuss its significance further in Chapter 11 (p. 235).

In the Middle Ages a Jewish polemical writing known as *Toledoth Jeshu* was popular and existed in many different versions. It probably goes back to the end of the third century, and it may have even earlier roots. Although some of its traditions about Jesus are polemical versions of traditions in the gospels, some may well be independent. Unfortunately a modern critical edition of the texts in English is not available, so it is difficult for non-specialists to make an assessment of this material.

With the exception of Josephus, why do Jewish writings say so little about Jesus? The earliest rabbinic writing, the Mishnah, contains religious law; it does not include explicit polemic against 'heretical' Jewish groups, let alone an apostate daughter religion, Christianity. The later rabbinic writings stem from a period when Christianity had become dominant, so it is not surprising to find scattered polemical references to Jesus and his followers. But by and large the later rabbis ignored Christianity, perceiving it to be an alien Gentile religion. They were more concerned with pressing internal matters.

The literary evidence we have just referred to briefly is limited in extent, but it is of great value. It would be a mistake to suppose that, unlike the gospels, it is unbiased and that it therefore gives us direct access to the historical Jesus. This evidence from outside the gospels, as well as evidence of the gospels themselves, has to be sifted critically and assessed carefully with sound historical methods.

The Dead Sea Scrolls

In 1947 a Bedouin shepherd found some manuscripts in a cave near the north-western shores of the Dead Sea. Further discoveries in eleven caves quickly followed. For students of the Bible and of early Judaism, this discovery turned out to be the archaeological find of the twentieth century.

The discoveries encouraged the first full-scale archaeological study (1951–6) of ruined buildings nearby at Khirbet Qumran. The oldest part of the buildings may date from c. 700–600 BC. In the second century BC there seems to have been an influx of new occupants and expansion of the buildings. The discovery of two inkwells and a plastered table and bench strongly suggested that one of the rooms was a scriptorium, a room set apart for writing or copying manuscripts. Pottery of the same type provided a further probable link between the buildings and the caves nearby in which the manuscripts were discovered. The buildings and the nearby cemetery suggest that about 200 people lived there.

Most scholars accept that the new arrivals in the second century BC were Essenes, perhaps following a rift within that movement. Shortly before the arrival of the Romans in AD 68, the writings were hidden in eleven nearby caves by the members of the 'Essene' sectarian community whose ruined buildings have been excavated at Qumran. Analysis of the handwriting styles of the manuscripts suggests that most of them were written in the last two centuries BC, results which were confirmed in 1991 by carbon 14 analysis of tiny samples of manuscripts undertaken with new techniques.

About 800 manuscripts have been recovered; 225 are copies of biblical books, the remainder are religious writings. The finds in Cave 4 are mind-boggling: about 15,000 fragments from about 550 different manuscripts. Some of the scrolls are remarkably complete, but there are thousands of tiny fragments.

As early as 1948 came the dramatic announcement that a complete copy of the Hebrew text of Isaiah had been discovered: a scroll one thousand years older than any other complete manuscript of this writing which Jews and Christians have always valued so highly. At first publication of the finds proceeded apace, but in the 1970s and 1980s progress was much slower. This led to quite unwarranted allegations of a Vatican conspiracy to hide evidence which would undermine Christianity. The truth is more prosaic: in several cases the delays were exacerbated by personal tragedies; in other cases scholarly reluctance to publish editions which were less than perfect led to procrastination. This storm has now blown over, for since 1993 all the material has been readily available for scholarly study.

The Dead Sea Scrolls do not refer or allude to Jesus, John the Baptist, James, Mary Magdalene, or any early Christians. Nearly all of the scrolls were written during the two centuries *before* Jesus was born. Rigorous new carbon 14 analysis is confirming the dating based on analysis of handwriting styles. None of the writings tested so far has been dated to the first century AD, necessary if they are to contain references to Jesus or his followers. The claim that a tiny fragment of Mark's gospel known as 7Q5 has been found in Cave 7 has now been discredited.

Attempts to link the scrolls directly to Jesus and early Christianity will continue to be made by scholars with a penchant for speculation and media attention. But scholars of all persuasions agree that the importance of the scrolls lies elsewhere. Detailed study will continue for several more decades—and debate for even longer. Nonetheless, it has been clear for some time now that the scrolls (and to a lesser extent, the ruined buildings at Qumran) are revolutionizing our understanding of Judaism from about 200 BC to AD 68 when the scrolls were hidden at the approach of Roman armies.

The scrolls provide an immense amount of information about Judaism at the time of Jesus. But what kind of Judaism do the scrolls reveal? Until recently the consensus was that the writings were the product of a sectarian group identical or closely related to the Essenes described by Josephus and the Jewish philosopher Philo (*c.* 20 BC to *c.* AD 50). Members of the Qumran community had isolated themselves from other Jews (whom they considered to be 'doomed'), in order carry out the requirements of the law more faithfully than they believed was possible in 'corrupt' and 'impure' Jerusalem. They rejected the sacrificial worship of the temple and replaced it with their own rituals; they believed that in the forthcoming eschatological war they would regain control over the temple and its worship. They believed that the renewal of Israel would come through their scrupulous observance of the law in a monastic-like community.

If the scrolls are the product of an Essene or Essene-like sectarian community somewhat isolated from other strands of contemporary Judaism, then they must not be used without further ado to reconstruct Jewish beliefs and practices at the time of Jesus. However, the Essene hypothesis is being vigorously challenged by several scholars. On the basis of analysis of handwriting styles they claim that the texts have been written by hundreds of different people—and very few scribes seem to have copied more than one text. Norman Golb (1995) claims that the scrolls are the library of the Jerusalem temple, no less, brought to Qumran during the revolt against Rome.

While Golb's theory is not widely accepted, it is becoming increasingly clear that only a proportion of the scrolls can be considered 'sectarian'. A very important corollary follows: the scrolls may put us in touch, not solely with an isolated sectarian community in the Judaean desert, but with much wider sections of first-century Judaism.

Archaeological evidence

Archaeological discoveries fascinate most people and regularly attract media attention. Archaeology seems to offer an easier path for the historian than literary evidence, but this is an illusion. Artefacts or foundations of buildings uncovered by the archaeologist's spade, brush, and vacuum cleaner have to be dated, interpreted, and set in a social context. And these tasks are no easier than assessment of literary evidence.

Many of the most important recent discoveries from the time of Jesus have been unspectacular and have not caught the attention of the media. Discoveries of some first-century pottery and a handful of coins from

Galilee or Jerusalem are not likely to feature in newspaper colour supplements, but they can often bring a fresh perspective on aspects of the political, cultural, economic, and religious world in which Jesus lived and taught.

In recent years important steps forward have been taken by archaeologists working in Galilee and Judaea. In the past the key question has often been, 'Does this or that discovery prove (or disprove) the reliability of the gospels?' Archaeologists now hope that their work may lead to a better appreciation of the social world of Jesus and his followers. So archaeologists often work hand in hand with social anthropologists. This development is full of promise for the future.

Until recently archaeologists and specialists working with literary evidence managed to live largely separate lives. Now they both realize that they need one another's expertise. No longer will scholars writing major books on Jesus of Nazareth ignore the site reports of archaeologists working in Galilee. No longer will archaeologists attempt to interpret their finds without considering the relevant literary evidence most carefully. In exploring the social and religious world of Jesus, one needs a spade in one hand and relevant texts in the other.

Galilee

What was life like in Nazareth where Jesus grew up? Were the villagers simple peasants dependent both economically and culturally on the neighbouring capital city of Sepphoris? (See the map on p. 140.) To what extent were the inhabitants of Nazareth aware of the heavy hand of Rome? And how close were the religious ties with Jerusalem and its temple to the south? These questions are high on the current agenda of archaeologists working in Galilee. Steady progress has been made in recent years, and further advances can be expected.

Today tourists to Israel will almost certainly be taken to Nazareth, even though there are very few significant first-century remains to be seen. In spite of intensive searches, there is as yet no trace of the synagogue at Nazareth to which so much importance is attached in Luke 4: 16–30. Recent estimates put the population of Nazareth at the time of Jesus at about 500. Nazareth was a satellite village of Sepphoris, about 5 kilometres to the north-west—less than an hour's walk away.

Archaeological work in Sepphoris has been gathering pace in recent years. Sepphoris has a Roman theatre, an extensive Jewish quarter, a superb large Roman villa with a mosaic which depicts the 'Mona Lisa of Galilee', several streets almost as fascinating as the streets of Pompeii, and a number of eye-catching mosaics. Digging still continues; perhaps only a quarter of the city has been excavated. Dating and interpreting the rich finds will continue for decades.

Did Jesus visit Sepphoris? How would Sepphoris have been perceived from Nazareth—as a cosmopolitan city to be avoided by a loyal Jew, as a fortified Roman base to be despised, or as a market town with a largely Jewish population and deep Jewish roots?

When Joseph took Mary and the child Jesus to Nazareth, Herod Antipas (the Rome-sponsored tetrarch or ruler of Galilee and Perea from 4 BC to AD 39) was recruiting workmen from villages all over Galilee to rebuild and expand his capital Sepphoris. Some of the workmen may well have come from Nazareth. When Josephus mentions that Herod fortified Sepphoris as 'the ornament of all Galilee' and 'the strongest city in Galilee' (*Antiquities* xviii. 27), he may have had in mind both the splendour and the size of its buildings, as well as its hilltop location with extensive views over fertile Galilee.

The well-preserved Roman theatre seated about 5,000 people. In his excellent guide *The Holy Land* (3rd edn. 1992, p. 413), Jerome Murphy-O'Connor writes: 'The most natural explanation of Jesus' use of *hypokritēs* ("stage actor") in criticism of the religious leaders of his day (e.g. Mark 7: 6) is that he went to this theatre, the nearest one to Nazareth. The word, which has no Semitic equivalent, would not have been part of the vocabulary of a village artisan.'

If this is correct, perhaps some sayings of Jesus should be interpreted against a Graeco-Roman rather than a Jewish background, and an urban rather than a village setting. A great deal hangs on the dating of the theatre, but unfortunately archaeological opinion is divided. Several specialists believe that the theatre was built in time for possible visits by Jesus; others date it up to one hundred years later. The latter view seems to be gaining ground.

Excavations have uncovered nearly thirty Jewish ritual baths (*miqva'ot*) in a number of houses in the upper part of the city. Some of them date from the time of Jesus. This evidence, as well as evidence for strict burial outside the city precincts, strongly suggests that at the time of Jesus there was a substantial Jewish community in Sepphoris which sought to observe the Jewish law faithfully.

In AD 20 Herod Antipas moved his capital to a site on the Sea of Galilee and named it Tiberias after the Roman emperor (cf. Luke 3: 1; see the map on p. 140.). Archaeological work continues there, but very little of it has yet been published. We do know that there was a mixed Jewish and Gentile population in Tiberias.

The gospels do not record that Jesus ever taught or healed in Sepphoris or Tiberias, the two leading Galilean cities of his day. Since Matthew 11: 20–4 = Luke 10: 12–15 (Q) refers to unsuccessful visits to places in Galilee, the failure of the gospels to mention visits to Sepphoris and Tiberias is not likely to be due to Jesus' lack of success there. Both cities were the power bases of the despised Herodian family and the ruling elite of the day, and suspected of holding pro-Roman views. So Jesus and his followers almost certainly deliberately avoided both cities, perceiving them as a threat.

Mark records that Jesus moved from Nazareth and set up base in Capernaum (1: 9, 21; see the map on p. 140). Capernaum is mentioned in several other passages in the gospels (e.g. Mark 2: 1; 9: 33; Matt. 4: 13; 8: 5 = Luke 7: 1–10, and in John 2: 12; 4: 46; 6: 17, 24, 59). This large fishing village was used by Jesus as his headquarters in Galilee.

Excavations there have unearthed a splendid fourth-century white lime-stone synagogue. The remains are so substantial that they are unlikely ever to be removed in order to allow full excavations of the black basalt foundations and walls of a first-century synagogue, the one visited by Jesus (Mark 1: 21; Luke 7: 5; John 6: 59).

Rather extensive remains of houses have been uncovered. Capernaum was planned carefully with 40 × 40 metre blocks, each with three or four one-story houses with rooms opening onto common courtyards. About 100 metres from the synagogue is a first-century house which since 1968 has been claimed by some to be Simon Peter's house in which Jesus healed the fever which had struck Peter's mother-in-law (Mark 1: 29). Early Roman pottery and coins under the floor confirm that it existed in the first century. From the graffiti scratched by Christians on the plaster walls of the house after it was rebuilt as a church in the middle of the fifth century, it is clear that in the fourth century, if not earlier, this house was revered as Peter's. Was this wishful thinking by Christian pilgrims? Or is it possible that the graffiti reflect an accurate tradition which survived from the first century? Once again caution is called for: the graffiti are fragmentary and very difficult to interpret and to date.

There is new archaeological evidence which indicates that Romans lived in Capernaum in the first century, so it was not isolated from the presence of the occupying power. The centurion who asked Jesus to heal his very ill servant was a Roman, but neither Matthew (8: 5–13) nor Luke (7: 1–10) tells us why he was there.

Plenty of archaeological evidence confirms that at the time of Jesus Capernaum was a thriving commercial and agricultural centre, partially supported by fishing. About 1,000 people lived there, not the 12,000 to 15,000 suggested by some earlier scholars. Capernaum was on an important trade route, only 5 kilometres from the border between Herod Antipas' territory of Galilee, and the territories on the other side of the Jordan ruled as tetrarch by his brother Philip from 4 BC to AD 34. As Mark 2: 14 notes, there was a customs office there. Capernaum would have been a natural place for Jesus to choose as the base for an itinerant preaching and healing ministry.

Jerusalem

Between 1969 and 1983 extensive archaeological excavations were carried out in the part of Jerusalem known as the Herodian quarter, just to the south and east of the Temple mount. These were the first excavations of a first-century AD residential area in Jerusalem. The remains of six luxurious houses, as well as a large number of artefacts, were discovered. Coins found there, as well as signs of destruction by fire when Jerusalem fell to the Romans in AD 70, confirm that these buildings near the Temple existed at the time of Jesus. The everyday life of wealthy Jerusalem families, probably aristocratic priestly families, was revealed for the first time.

At least one and often two or more ritual baths (*miqva'ot*) existed in each house for purification from uncleanness, so the owners obviously kept the Jewish law meticulously. The houses contain numerous floor mosaics and decorated wall frescoes which are very similar in design to those found in many parts of the Graeco-Roman world, especially in houses in Pompeii. Geometric and floral patterns abound: biblical commands against images led the owners of the houses to avoid mosaics depicting people or animals (and, of course, gods and goddesses). So right in the heart of Jerusalem the cultural influence of the Graeco-Roman world made a strong impact, even among families which maintained their distinctive Jewish way of life.

The lifestyle of the wealthy priests who lived in these houses may well have caused outrage to the Galilean prophet Jesus when he visited Jerusalem. The contrast between these houses and the tiny houses in Capernaum from the time of Jesus could hardly be more stark. At this point archaeology forces one to return to the literary evidence with two key questions in mind. Did Jesus challenge the elite religious and political establishment in Jerusalem and call in God's name for the renewal of Israel? If so, did this confrontation cause his downfall? I shall return to these questions in Chapter 17.

Mark 14: 3–9 records that in the house of Simon the leper in Bethany (a village very close to Jerusalem) a woman poured very costly perfume over the head of Jesus. Mark attaches great significance to this action: Jesus is reported to have said, 'she has anointed my body beforehand for burial. Truly I tell you, wherever the good news is proclaimed in the whole world, what she has done will be told in remembrance of her' (14: 8–9). The Greek verb used to describe the way the woman opened the small bottle of perfume has long puzzled readers, for it means 'smash' or 'break'. If she 'smashed' the alabaster jar, then surely fragments would have fallen into the costly ointment.

Archaeologists now seem to have solved this particular puzzle. Small perfume flasks with very long narrow necks have been discovered in first-century tombs on the edge of the Valley of Hinnom, Jerusalem's refuse tip. They would have been ideal for storing expensive perfume; inexpensive pottery jars were normally used for storing perfume for everyday use. The woman in Simon's house may have snapped off the long narrow neck of an alabaster jar cleanly before pouring the valuable perfumed ointment over the head of Jesus.

In 1990 on the southern outskirts of Jerusalem a spectacular discovery of twelve burial boxes for bones of deceased persons (ossuaries) was found. One bears an inscription on the long side of the ossuary, 'Yehosef bar Qayafa', Joseph son of Caiaphas; on the shorter side is an apparently abbreviated form, 'Yehosef bar Qafa'. Was this the burial box which contained the bones of the high priest Caiaphas who handed Jesus over to the Romans (cf. Matt. 26: 3, 57; John 18: 13–14)? The ossuary contains the bones from six different people, including a male aged about sixty. The unusually elaborate decoration on the ossuary and the inscriptions both suggest that the bones of Caiaphas may have been placed in this very ossuary. Josephus refers to a 'Joseph who was called Caiaphas of the high priesthood' (*Antiquities* xviii. 35), so Caiaphas may have been a family name or a nickname. The inscription 'Joseph son of Caiaphas' does not necessarily mean that Caiaphas was Joseph's father; it may well refer to Joseph of the family of Caiaphas, as the reference in Josephus suggests.

However, doubts have recently been raised about the interpretation of the inscriptions on the ossuaries. On the linguistic evidence now available, the identification with the high priest Caiaphas cannot be classed as probable.

The gospels do not give detailed information on the precise way in which Jesus was crucified. But Luke 24: 39 implies that the hands and feet of Jesus were nailed to the cross, and John 20: 25, 27 refers explicitly to the nailprints in his hands. These two references were combined in later Christian piety in which devotion to the 'five wounds of Jesus' (his two hands, two feet and side) became popular. Since there was no archaeological evidence for the custom of nailing hands or feet to a cross, some doubted the accuracy of the gospels at this point.

In 1970 a first-century ossuary from Jerusalem was discovered. It contained the bones of a young man who, as the inscription on the ossuary stated, was named Yehohanan and had been crucified. The right heel bone had been pierced by an iron nail and there was said to be evidence of nails piercing the wrist or forearm. The bones of the lower leg had been broken by a blow. According to John 19: 32 this was done to the fellow-victims of Jesus, but not to Jesus himself. Traces of wood were found on either side of the bones and it was a natural inference that the nail had secured the victim to a cross.

This discovery provided for the first time archaeological evidence for the crucifixion in Palestine of a near-contemporary of Jesus. Two details found in John's gospel—the very gospel which was widely thought to be the least likely of the four to contain accurate historical information—seemed to be confirmed: the breaking of the bones of a crucifixion victim and nailing to a cross. Needless to say this evidence was used to refute the view that the gospel narratives are irresponsible fabrications. Some earlier writers had suggested that the evangelist John had invented the reference to the breaking of the bones of the two crucified with Jesus, but not the bones of Jesus himself, in order to make the death of Jesus conform precisely to Old Testament passages such as Exodus 12: 46 or Psalm 34: 20.

In 1985 much more rigorous investigation uncovered a number of errors in the original report. The leg bones do not seem to have been deliberately broken while the young man was alive on the cross; bone-breaking may have occurred much later during the course of putting the bones into the ossuary. There is clear evidence that Yehohanan's feet were nailed to the upright, with an olive wood plaque between the head of each nail and the foot. However, there is no evidence for nailing the arms or wrists, which would have been tied to the crossbar.

In spite of the need to revise aspects of the original report, this discovery provides important archaeological evidence for crucifixion at the time of Jesus. It should remove scepticism about the accuracy of Luke's and John's references to the nailing of Jesus to the cross.

This reference to the crucifixion of Jesus brings us finally to the Turin Shroud. All four gospels record that Joseph of Arimathea asked Pilate for the body of Jesus and wrapped it in linen. Ever since the Middle Ages some have claimed that a 4-metre-long piece of linen in the cathedral at Turin is in fact the very cloth in which the body of Jesus was wrapped. The history of the shroud can be traced from the middle of the fourteenth century, but nothing certain is known about any earlier history.

Does this cloth date from the first century? For many Christians the shroud offered tangible proof of the reliability of the gospels. Those who were doubtful about the cloth's authenticity stressed that even if scientific study could confirm beyond reasonable doubt that the cloth dates from the first century, how could we ever be sure that it provided a link with Jesus of Nazareth? Many others who died violently in the first century would have been wrapped in linen for burial.

'Believers' in the shroud pointed to two pieces of evidence. Traces of pollen grains from plants which grow in and near Palestine have been found on it; however, one of the pollens common there, that of the olive tree, is missing. Much more puzzling is the startling image which appears when the shroud is photographed, a phenomenon noticed when the shroud was first photographed in 1898.

The church authorities in Turin finally granted scientists permission to submit very small sections of the cloth to three different laboratories in order to test radioactive carbon 14 particles. This is a well-tried method for dating fragments of living material. In order to carry out 'blind' testing, other small pieces of cloth known to belong to the first century and to the Middle Ages were sent to the laboratories along with the fragments of the Shroud. In 1988 the results were announced. All three laboratories gave the same answer: the cloth was made between AD 1260 and 1390, to a 95 per cent degree of certainty.

The story of the Turin Shroud confirms the attachment many people have to objects said to be associated with Jesus. For them seeing is believing. At the end of the first century readers of John's gospel were reminded that this is a false trail: 'Blessed are those who have not seen and yet have come to believe' (John 20: 29).

The examples of archaeological discoveries I have discussed sound warning bells. Extravagant media claims may be undermined by more careful patient research. Even cautious conclusions may well have to be revised in the light of further research. For every two steps forward, there may be one backwards.

However, in the past fifty years there have been a series of discoveries which have withstood critical appraisal and revolutionized our understanding of the religious, cultural, and political world of Jesus. In recent years, the pace of genuine advance, especially in Galilee, has undoubtedly quickened. Aided by technological developments and further interdisciplinary co-operation, it will continue to do so.

We now know far more about the economic, ethnic, and political make-up of pre-AD 70 Galilee than we knew even twenty years ago. The numerous villages of Galilee were linked economically to the urban centres of Sepphoris and Tiberias with their substantial non-Jewish Greek-speaking populations. Not far away, just beyond the borders of Galilee, were the major Graeco-Roman trading cities of Scythopolis (the capital of the Decapolis) and Caesarea Maritima (with its fine harbour), both of which had a considerable minority Jewish population (see the map on p. 140). So even though Jesus steered well clear of these cities, the Galilean villages which were the focus of his ministry were not hermetically sealed Jewish islands cut off from the neighbouring Graeco-Roman urban centres, for trade was essential for survival. Jesus and his followers are likely to have spoken some Greek as a second language to Aramaic, for we now know that Greek was spoken widely in Galilee.

The shadow of Roman control lay heavily over Galilee. It certainly fomented political tensions and incidents during the lifetime of Jesus, but it is hard to judge the extent of political unrest in the early 30s. We do know that it increased sharply in the three following decades.

The Jewish ritual baths (*miqva'ot*) uncovered in Sepphoris have encouraged renewed interest in the literary evidence for Galilean Judaism at the time of Jesus. There is no evidence that Galilean Jews were less observant than Jews who lived in Jerusalem and Judaea. We do know that the Galileans were fiercely loyal to Jerusalem and the temple.

Most of the recent archaeological discoveries in Galilee and Judaea have been unspectacular, but they have led to fresh appraisals of the literary evidence. From both quarters new light is being shed on the political, economic, social, and religious worlds of Jesus and his followers.

A very wide range of literary and archaeological evidence has been considered in this chapter. Important questions of method have emerged. It is often suggested that since evidence from outside the gospels comes from 'unbiased' sources, it should be given preference over the New Testament gospels. But the historian and the archaeologist rarely have access to 'neutral' evidence. Evidence of all kinds from outside the gospels has to be assessed critically for it is rarely unambiguous. As we shall see in the following chapter, it is a mistake to suppose that the evangelists' convictions about the significance of Jesus make their accounts worthless for the historian.

9

ASSESSING THE EVIDENCE

The four gospels contain a large number of traditions about the actions and teaching of Jesus. But how does the historian engaged in a quest for the historical Jesus assess that evidence? The evangelists set out the significance of Jesus for readers some forty to fifty years after his lifetime. The traditions on which they drew were used for several decades in oral form in Christian communities. So to what extent have the traditions about Jesus been shaped and developed, or even created, in the course of this transmission? What do we know about Jesus? What were his aims and intentions? Are historians' reconstructions at odds with the faith affirmations made by his followers following his crucifixion?

These questions are not new. In the early centuries many attempts were made to resolve discrepancies and contradictions in the gospels, but historical inquiry as we know it developed only in the latter part of the eighteenth century.

It is customary to differentiate three quests for the historical Jesus. H. S. Reimarus is usually said to have started the 'old' or 'first' quest', and to be the father of modern historical inquiry into Jesus and the origins of Christianity. The first of his provocative *Wolfenbüttel Fragments* were published anonymously in 1774, six years after his death. Although Reimarus had predecessors in his attempt to discredit orthodox Christianity, there is no doubt about the importance of his work. He was the first person to ask about the intentions of Jesus, and one of the first to raise serious questions about the relationship of John's gospel to the synoptics. He claimed that Jesus did not intend to abolish the Jewish religion and put another in its place: his intention was reversed completely after his death by his followers.

In 1835 D. F. Strauss (1808–74), an admirer of Reimarus, published the first edition of his *Life of Jesus*. In subsequent editions he changed his mind more than once about the historical value of John's gospel. In contrast to Reimarus, he believed that Jesus was at odds with the religious leaders of his day. He attempted to remove the layers of 'mythical' veneer from the gospels in order to expose the timeless truths of the non-miraculous core traditions.

The 'old' or 'first' quest is usually considered to have been brought to an end by the polymath Albert Schweitzer, whose *The Quest of the Historical Jesus* was first published in German in 1906. Schweitzer assessed critically a whole series of nineteenth-century 'lives of Jesus'. He set out his own view of Jesus who died as a failed apocalyptic prophet; nonetheless 'a mighty spiritual force streams from him and flows through our time also.'

The so-called 'new quest' was sparked off in 1953 by Ernst Käsemann in reaction to the overemphasis by Karl Barth and Rudolf Bultmann on the 'Christ of faith' and their denial of the importance of the 'Jesus of history' both for the early church and for their own day. The term 'third quest' was coined by N. T. Wright in 1988 to refer to what was then seen as a resurgence of interest in the historical Jesus, especially in the work of B. F. Meyer (1979), A. E. Harvey (1982), and E. P. Sanders (1985).

I am doubtful about the customary divisions myself, for although fashions have changed several times over during the last two centuries, quests for the life and teaching of Jesus have never faltered. There are so many lines of continuity between the so-called 'old quest', the 'new quest', and now the current 'third quest' that the usual divisions are somewhat misleading. For example, N. T. Wright links the Jesus Seminar, which began in 1985, to the 'new quest'; arguably it has more in common with some strands of the 'old quest', and some of the 'third quest'.

Jesus of Nazareth is as fascinating a figure in the twenty-first century as he was in the first. So it is natural that both non-believers and believers will want to sift the historical evidence carefully. For Christians there is a further issue at stake. While historical research can never *prove* the validity of Christian faith, it is at least theoretically possible that historians' results might undermine faith. If historians were able to show conclusively that Jesus of Nazareth did not exist, or that he was utterly unlike the portraits of the evangelists, then Christian faith as it is usually understood would be called in question.

In order to make this important point clear, let us take an extreme example. If historians were able to confirm that Jesus was in fact a selfish rogue who practised violence, then it would surely be impossible to affirm with Paul, 'I live by faith in the Son of God who loved me and gave himself for me' (Gal. 2: 20). While Christian faith does not depend on the accuracy of every detail in the gospels, Christians do need to know whether or not the evangelists' differing portraits are misleading.

In recent decades two extreme positions have been defended. In some conservative circles the accuracy of every last detail has been defended on the assumption that the credibility of Christianity is at stake. If the gospels are inaccurate on historical and geographical matters (so the argument has run), how can the reader accept the faith the evangelists proclaim? This approach has sometimes led to bizarre results. One attempt to explain the variations in the accounts of Peter's denials proposes six cock crowings! Did Jesus heal a blind beggar as he was *leaving* Jericho (Mark 10: 46)? Or was the blind man healed as Jesus *approached* Jericho (Luke 18: 35)? Since he is named Bartimaeus in Mark, but is unnamed in Luke, some have supposed that Jesus healed two blind men near Jericho—one blind man on the way into the city and Bartimaeus on the way out! This fanciful explanation ignores the fact that close comparison of the accounts in Mark and Luke confirms that the *same* tradition is being used by both evangelists. It is probable that Luke has altered Mark's chronology for his own purposes.

At the other extreme some writers claim that since the gospels reflect the interests of the evangelists and since the traditions used by the evangelists have been shaped and developed very considerably in the course of their transmission, the historian can say very little at all about the life and teaching of Jesus. On this view we must remain content with the gospels as we have them and spurn any attempt to dig behind the gospels for historical nuggets, for they will turn out to be fools' gold.

But this is an unnecessarily sceptical view. Historians constantly have to assess evidence which has been written from a distinctive political, social, or even religious stance. And if they were to confine themselves to sources written *immediately* after the events recorded, they would have very little to say! Every shred of evidence from the ancient world is valuable: it has to be assessed carefully and used critically. The key question is, 'What is this piece of evidence valuable for?' It may well turn out, as in the case of the gospels, to shed light both on the writers' interests and concerns and also on the events they purport to record.

So what are the appropriate methods to use in reconstruction of the actions, teaching, and intention of Jesus? The first step is to recognize that the gospels contain three layers: the level of the teaching of the evangelists; the level of the early church which transmitted the traditions; the level of the life of Jesus himself. As we have done in the first half of this book, we must start with the top layer, with the gospels as we have them, and assess the extent to which the evangelists themselves have shaped the traditions on which they have drawn.

We may then turn to the second layer, the 'tunnel period' between Jesus and the gospels. Here we must consider how oral traditions about Jesus were transmitted and used before they were committed to writing in our gospels, and consider the extent to which they may have been modified in transmission.

Only once authentic traditions concerning the teachings and actions of Jesus have been identified, may we attempt to reconstruct his intention. Did Jesus have an overriding aim which accounts for all or most of the traditions about him which have survived? What was his 'mission'? Was it primarily a 'ministry' to individuals in need? Or did Jesus attempt to convey God's challenge to the whole of Israel to fulfil its calling? Why was Jesus put to death on a Roman cross?

In this chapter we shall assess the evidence of the first two layers. The chapters which follow take up the questions just posed.

The evangelists' redaction

In the opening chapters of this book we set out a number of examples of the modifications the evangelists made to earlier traditions (i.e. redaction criticism). Once we accept that Matthew and Luke have both used Mark, it is not difficult with the use of a synopsis of the gospels to trace the changes the two later evangelists have made.

In addition to such modifications, the evangelists often reinterpret their traditions by placing them in a particular context. In Luke 15: 3–7, for example, the parable of the lost sheep is the first of a trilogy of parables used to explain why Jesus 'welcomes sinners [and tax collectors] and eats with them' (Luke 15: 1–2): they are the 'lost sheep'. Luke himself is probably responsible for bringing these three parables together as a reply to the complaint of the scribes and Pharisees about the outrageous conduct of

Jesus. Matthew, on the other hand, has placed the same parable of the lost sheep in a very different setting and so given it a quite different interpretation. In Matt. 18: 12–14 the parable is used to encourage Christians in the evangelist's day to search out the 'lost sheep' who has strayed from the community. In Matthew the 'lost sheep' is not a sinner or a tax collector but a Christian disciple.

In Matt. 11: 2–6 John's disciples are told by Jesus to go and tell their imprisoned leader that they have seen evidence of the fulfilment of Scripture: the blind are regaining their sight, the lame are walking again, the lepers are being made clean, the deaf are hearing, the dead are being raised to life, the poor are hearing the good news proclaimed to them. So it is no surprise to find that in the preceding two chapters Matthew has reordered Marcan (and other) traditions to make sure that examples of all these actions of Jesus have been given. In their original context in Mark and Q these traditions were not necessarily set out as the fulfilment of Scripture, but they are in Matthew. This is stated explicitly in 8: 17: 'This (i.e. the healing activity of Jesus) was to fulfil what had been spoken by the prophet Isaiah, "He took our infirmities and bore our diseases."'

Mark's account of the death of John the Baptist (6: 17–29) provides a further example of a tradition which is reinterpreted by being set in a wider context. Mark probably knew from oral tradition the account of the beheading of John at the instigation of Herodias. The evangelist does not seem to have altered the tradition, but the context in which he has set it is significant. The disciples of Jesus have just been sent out on a mission to further Jesus' proclamation of repentance (6: 12), the very theme central in the preaching of John (1: 4). In the introduction to the account of the beheading the reader is told that Jesus and John are so similar that Herod has confused them (6: 14–16)! So as the story of the fate of John proceeds, the reader is almost bound to ask whether or not the fearless preaching of Jesus will also lead to his downfall. Mark makes the parallel between Jesus and John explicit in his own final comment at 6: 29: 'When his disciples heard about it [i.e. the beheading of John], they came and took his body, and laid it in a tomb.' In its present context as part of the story of Jesus, the account of the death of John is set in a different light: it is now an anticipation of the ultimate fate of Jesus.

Even as recently as the middle of the twentieth century it was customary to suggest that Peter's confession of Jesus as the Messiah at Caesarea

Philippi marked a watershed in his ministry. On this view, at first Jesus appealed openly to the crowds, but their failure to respond led him to change his tactics and concentrate his teaching on the disciples. There were many such explanations of the life and intention of Jesus, some of which were along elaborate psychological lines. But form criticism and redaction criticism have shown that Mark is largely responsible for the ordering of the traditions in his gospel. We have to concede that we do not have evidence which allows us to construct in any detail the course of the ministry of Jesus and certainly not of any change in his tactics or intentions.

The evangelists have quite often added their own explanatory comments to the traditions they are using. On p. 9 we suggested that Matthew has added two additional petitions to the original version of the Lord's Prayer. The Beatitudes provide further examples; see pp. 67–70.

There is also a handful of sayings in the gospels which presuppose a setting after the lifetime of Jesus and which are attached only loosely to the adjacent traditions. In Matt. 10: 18 Jesus warns the disciples whom he is sending out on their mission that they will be persecuted both by Jewish and by Gentile authorities. There is no evidence that such persecution took place in the lifetime of Jesus, though it certainly did in later decades. In Matt. 18: 20 we read: 'For where two or three are gathered in my name, I am there among them.' This saying can hardly come from the historical Jesus, but it does make sense in a post-Easter setting in which disciples gather in the name of Jesus and, as the Risen Jesus promises in Matt. 28: 20, experience his continuing presence with them.

In reconstructing the teaching of Jesus one must first provisionally set aside modifications and additions which stem from the evangelists, and verses which presuppose a setting in the evangelists' own day. In particular, traditions both of the teaching and of the actions of Jesus must be detached, again at least provisionally, from the contexts in which they have been placed by the evangelists. The word 'provisionally' is chosen deliberately, since at least some of the changes, additions, and contexts provided by the evangelists may turn out after further investigation to reflect accurately the original teaching and intention of Jesus.

Between the gospels and Jesus

Where did the traditions which found their way into Mark and Q come from? What can we say about the origin of the traditions found only in Matthew and Luke often known as 'M' and 'L' material? Before the emergence of form criticism (which is discussed on pp. 27–9) it was generally assumed that the evangelists were able to draw on the eyewitness testimony of some of the disciples. But the form critics were able to show convincingly that the traditions lacked the characteristics which are usually found in accounts given by eyewitnesses. They rarely include memorable details or exact biographical or topographical precision. The form critics claimed that the traditions behind the gospels look much more like oral traditions preserved and transmitted by communities than the eyewitness testimony of individuals. The gospel traditions played an important part in the faith and life of the early Christian communities which preserved them.

The debate over the extent to which eyewitnesses may have exercised control over the development of the traditions has reached a stalemate. Some claim that eyewitnesses must have been responsible for the vivid details in the gospels. For example, in Mark's account of the feeding of the multitudes the grass is 'green' (6: 39). And at the arrest of Jesus (Mark 14: 51–2) 'a certain young man was following him, wearing nothing but a linen cloth. They caught hold of him, but he left the linen cloth and ran off naked.' But others point out that even if eyewitnesses are ultimately responsible for the *origin* of the gospel traditions, their historicity is by no means assured since eyewitnesses do not always agree. The appeal to vivid details by no means settles the matter since such details proliferate in the later apocryphal gospels, whose historicity no one wishes to defend.

Given this impasse, attention has naturally turned to the transmission of oral traditions. Once again opinions are divided. Some scholars insist that since the gospel traditions were preserved and used in the life of early Christian communities, they must have been shaped to a considerable extent by the needs and faith of those communities. In other words, the traditions tell us a good deal about early Christianity in the post-Easter period, but very little about the life of Jesus.

But others point out that our knowledge of those earliest

communities is so sketchy that the case for extensive development of the traditions is not proven. In any case, where we *do* have knowledge of the central concerns of Christians in the post-Easter period, it is often possible to show that those concerns have not been 'read back' into the traditions. For example, we know that the early church quickly made bold claims about the significance of Jesus (i.e. developed a Christology), but the traditions in the synoptic gospels frequently portray a Jesus who was very reticent about his own person; he claimed to be Messiah reluctantly, if at all. As we saw in Chapter 1, the Lord's Prayer does not contain a trace of post-Easter Christian faith. We know from Acts and Galatians that there were fierce controversies in the early church over acceptance of Gentiles. Should non-Jews be required to be circumcised before being accepted into Christian communities? And should Gentiles be welcomed at table? But in the gospels the issue of circumcision is not referred to and Jesus himself is portrayed as accepting non-Jews only grudgingly. The traditions on which the evangelists drew often fail to reflect the needs and interests of the post-Easter period at the very points at which they might have been expected to do so.

The Swedish scholar Birger Gerhardsson (1961) has pressed still further the case against the more radical claims of some form critics by insisting that the gospel traditions were transmitted orally with great care in the period between Jesus and the emergence of the written gospels. Gerhardsson claimed that the followers of Jesus used the traditional techniques devised within Judaism in order to ensure the accurate transmission of oral traditions. Some of his critics claimed that while those techniques were developed within Judaism in the second century and later, evidence for their use at the time of Jesus is slender.

In several recent writings Gerhardsson has responded to his critics and set out his case more cautiously and more fully. He now concedes that in the course of transmission of traditions about Jesus there was ongoing interpretation; attempts were made to understand the words and deeds of Jesus more fully and to discover their importance for the problems and questions which faced Christians in the post-Easter period. But he still insists that this process of alteration and reinterpretation is entirely consistent with his claim that early Christianity has handed down the gospel material as 'memorized text', for a similar process can be observed in the transmission of Jewish oral traditions. The influential Jewish scholar Jacob

Neusner has given weighty support in an extended preface to a new edition of the original study (1998).

Although Gerhardsson has correctly reminded us that Jesus was a teacher whose disciples would have valued his words highly and transmitted them carefully, questions remain. There is still uncertainty about the precise methods of instruction used by Jewish teachers at the time of Jesus. As we shall see in Chapter 11 (p. 200), the relationship between Jesus and his disciples is not precisely the same as that of a rabbinic teacher and his pupils. And parts of the teaching of Jesus were not directed at the disciples at all, but at crowds; in that setting techniques of careful memorization used in a teacher–pupil relationship would hardly have been applicable.

Debate about the origin and transmission of gospel traditions has also been vigorous in a quite different area. In his influential form-critical study, *The History of the Synoptic Tradition* (1921), Rudolf Bultmann claimed that some sayings attributed to Jesus in the gospels originated in the post-Easter period as utterances of the Spirit speaking through Christian prophets to the church. Verses such as Rev. 3: 20 and 16: 15, in which the Risen Christ speaks to the church, show one stage of this development. There is no doubt that the earliest Christian communities were acutely conscious of the presence of the Spirit. There is also evidence that Christian prophets were active in many congregations. But did such prophets play an active role in the creation of sayings of the earthly Jesus?

There are good grounds for caution. In the Old Testament and in early Judaism we frequently find a deep-rooted suspicion of anonymous prophetic oracles: the name of the prophet is normally included. Rev. 1: 1–2 is a good example: the book is introduced as 'the revelation given by God to Jesus Christ'. The exalted Christ has 'made known the words of this prophecy'; the recipient is not an anonymous prophet but is named as 'his servant John'. It is unlikely that important prophetic oracles would have been accepted in early Christianity from anonymous prophets. False prophecy was well known, so criteria (which differed from place to place) were worked out whereby true prophetic words could be distinguished from false. So widespread acceptance of a large number of oracles from prophets who claimed to speak in the name of the exalted Christ is unlikely. And if sayings of the earthly Jesus were created in this way on a large scale, we should expect to find examples not only in the gospels but in other early Christian writings. But as we saw in Chapter 7, only a small number of sayings attributed to the earthly Jesus are found outside the gospels.

While Christian prophets may have been less influential in the development of sayings of Jesus than some have supposed, the possibility that some new sayings of Jesus were created in this way cannot be ruled out. Matt. 10: 18 and Matt. 18: 20 were noted above on p. 169 as examples.

The preceding paragraphs show that on the one hand good reasons can be advanced for accepting the general reliability of the gospel traditions on which the evangelists drew; yet on the other hand reinterpretation and even the creation of traditions in the post-Easter period cannot be ruled out. How does one isolate traditions which can be used confidently as evidence for the teaching and actions of Jesus of Nazareth?

Several criteria were proposed during the so-called 'new quest' initiated by Ernst Käsemann in 1953. First, the 'criterion of dissimilarity'. If a gospel tradition is *dissimilar* to the teaching and practices of early Judaism, then it can hardly have been taken over by the disciples or later followers of Jesus and attributed to him. And if a tradition runs counter to Christian teaching in the post-Easter period, it can hardly have been created then. So if traditions of either the sayings or the actions of Jesus are dissimilar from *both* early Jewish *and* early Christian teaching or practice, then we may accept them with confidence as solid historical evidence.

The attitude of Jesus to fasting is a good example. In Mark 2: 18 we read that while John's disciples and the Pharisees did fast (as was the general custom), the fact that the disciples of Jesus did not fast caused offence. We know that many very early Christian circles continued to fast. This is simply assumed to be a normal Christian religious observance in Matt. 6: 16–18 and in the Didache, chapter 8, which may date from about AD 100. In both cases Christians are told not to fast 'like the hypocrites', but the practice is not called in question. Since the failure of Jesus to fast cannot have been 'taken over' either from contemporary Jewish teaching or 'created' by Christians in the immediate post-Easter period, this must be an authentic tradition.

However, this criterion is not as helpful as we might at first suppose. Since our knowledge both of first-century Judaism and of early Christianity is limited, we can never be absolutely certain that a saying of Jesus is 'dissimilar' to both. This criterion undermines the Jewishness of Jesus, since everything which Jesus shared with his fellow-Jews is rejected as suspect. It can even lead to an anti-Jewish Jesus. And it assumes that the early church never understood Jesus. If we are seeking to understand an individual, we do not normally concentrate *solely* on those views and attitudes which are not shared by his contemporaries and which are not accepted by his successors. If we were to do so, we would gain a very distorted impression.

By using the 'criterion of coherence' some have sought to extend the amount of material which can be considered authentic. Traditions which are broadly coherent with traditions isolated by means of the criterion of dissimilarity are accepted as authentic. But some uncertainty is inevitable: opinions will differ on which traditions can be considered coherent with others.

The 'criterion of multiple attestation' has also been prominent in attempts to isolate authentic traditions. If we find a saying of Jesus in Mark, in Q, and perhaps in the 'M' or 'L' traditions as well, or even in the Johannine traditions, then its widespread attestation is noteworthy. The same saying or character trait is unlikely to have been 'invented' within several independent Christian communities which were preserving parts of the gospel traditions. As an example, we may note that three independent passages record that Jesus' acceptance of tax collectors drew critical questioning: Mark 2: 13–17; Matt. 11: 19 = Luke 7: 34 (Q); and the partly pre-Lucan tradition at Luke 15: 1–2. While almost all scholars accept without hesitation the authenticity of these and the related traditions by appealing to the criterion of multiple attestation, it is worth noting that rigorous use of the criterion of dissimilarity does not allow us to be certain. From Luke 3: 12 and 7: 29 we learn that John the Baptist also associated with tax collectors. So it must remain at least possible that something which was characteristic of the teacher-prophet John was transfered to Jesus.

Embarrassment, historical plausibility, and aftermath

The traditional criteria for authenticity discussed above need not be discarded without further ado, but they undoubtedly have their limitations. Are there other appropriate ways of determining authentic evidence for the actions and teaching of Jesus? Three further considerations are important.

Traditions which would have been an embarrassment to followers of Jesus in the post-Easter period are unlikely to have been invented. There are rather more such traditions than one might suppose. For example, the criticism of Jesus that 'he has gone out of his mind' is not refuted, and thus is likely to be authentic (Mark 3: 21). Mark 1: 41 refers to the anger of Jesus; Matthew and Luke omit the reference and scribes quickly changed 'moved with anger' into 'moved with compassion' in many copies of Mark. The reference on the lips of Jesus to his ignorance of the time when the end would come (Mark 13: 32) is not included by Luke.

We shall see in the next chapter that a number of traditions concerning John the Baptist and Jesus have been retained even though they draw attention to John's similarities to Jesus. Traditions which portray Jesus at odds with his own family must also have been an embarrassment (see especially Mark 3: 20–1, 31–5; 6: 1–6a). The traditions of the betrayal by Judas and the desertion of Jesus by the inner circle of his followers were hardly a matter of pride in the post-Easter period. The crucifixion of Jesus was an acute embarrassment to his followers: they were proclaiming as Messiah–Christ and God's Son one who had died an ignominious death on a Roman cross.

A more general consideration, known as 'historical plausibility', is particularly important. As we saw in the previous chapter, our knowledge of first-century Judaism has increased rapidly in recent decades. Since it is now possible to place Jesus within that context with much more confidence, Jesus traditions which can plausibly be linked to that context may be accepted.

Gerd Theissen makes this point strongly. He emphasizes that Jesus can only have said and done what a first-century Jewish charismatic could have said and done (1998, p. 118). He accepts that Jesus can come into conflict with his environment, for first-century Judaism is full of sharp criticism of individual charismatic figures and of polemic between Jewish groups.

Whereas the criterion of dissimilarity *separates* Jesus from his first-century context and produces a handful of 'authentic' sayings, an appeal to 'historical plausibility' does the opposite. It takes as seriously as possible the Galilean and Judaean context of the actions and sayings of Jesus. When that is done, it is surprising how many of the Jesus traditions in the gospels fit neatly into that context. As we have seen, relatively few betray traces of post-Easter influence or of a setting beyond Galilee and Judaea.

Scholars who appeal to 'historical plausibility' sometimes place undue weight on sayings of Jesus which can be translated 'backwards' from the Greek of the evangelists to the Aramaic of Jesus: only they are held to be authentic. There are several difficulties with this line of argument. Even when sayings of Jesus can be translated from the Greek of the gospels back into Aramaic (and this is never easy), we are not necessarily in touch with the original words of Jesus. For some of the very earliest post-Easter communities were Aramaic-speaking; so it must remain at least possible that they were responsible for sayings of Jesus which can be translated readily into Aramaic.

Fresh evidence, especially from inscriptions on ossuaries, confirms that Greek was widely spoken in Judaea and Galilee at the time of Jesus. So some of the gospel traditions may have been translated into Greek at a very early stage, perhaps even in the lifetime of Jesus. Jesus traditions probably coexisted in Aramaic and in Greek from a very early point.

The final and perhaps most important consideration of all is the *aftermath* of Jesus. It is greatly to the credit of E. P. Sanders (1985, p. 3 and pp. 18–19) to have drawn attention to the question posed in 1925 by the distinguished Jewish scholar Joseph Klausner: 'How was it that Jesus lived totally within Judaism, and yet was the origin of a movement that separated from Judaism, since *ex nihilo nihil fit*, nothing comes from nothing, or more idiomatically, where there is smoke there is fire.'

Sanders notes that in our quest for the historical Jesus we must always bear in mind that the end result of his actions and words was crucifixion by the Romans. After his death followers of Jesus continued as an identifiable movement, and at least some Jews persecuted at least parts of the new movement.

I would add a further point to which I shall return in Chapter 18. Shortly after the crucifixion, followers of Jesus began to worship him as Lord and to proclaim him as God's Son, and to accept into their fellowship non-Jews. Where is the fire behind this smoke?

It is time to sum up. The evangelists' adaptation and reinterpretation of the traditions they incorporated into their gospels must always be the first step towards recovery of authentic traditions. Their oral transmission over three or four decades must be considered carefully. Although there are good reasons for accepting their general reliability, reinterpretation and even the creation of traditions in the post-Easter period cannot be ruled out.

Traditions which were an embarrassment in the post-Easter period and traditions which pass the test of 'historical plausibility' are likely to be authentic. And finally, the aftermath of Jesus is a consideration of prime importance. These considerations provide valuable guidelines, but by their very nature they do not allow us to produce a list of traditions which are undeniably authentic.

To some this general approach will seem to be too cautious. Some have proposed that unless gospel traditions can be *shown* to stem from Jesus rather than the early church, they should not be considered to be authentic. But we do not have criteria which enable us to make such judgements. Scholars who have tried to reconstruct the intention of Jesus on this basis have not been particularly successful. Their use of apparently rigorous methods turns out to be illusory. More often than not, it is possible to raise serious doubts about the validity of the starting point adopted. The single strand of evidence that is accepted as authentic often turns out to fit all too neatly a particular theory which is being advanced; inconvenient evidence is set aside as unauthentic.

10

JOHN THE BAPTIST

John the Baptist is referred to some ninety times in the New Testament writings. Only Jesus, Peter, and Paul are referred to in more passages. The four evangelists all give a prominent role to John the Baptist. Why is John referred to so frequently? As we shall see, it is not easy to answer this simple question, especially since some passages underline his importance, while others stress his inferiority to Jesus. In this chapter we shall see that an examination of the traditions concerning John is an important first step in our attempt to uncover the main features of the teaching and actions of Jesus.

The evangelists all take pains to spell out carefully the relationship between Jesus and John. As we shall see, in effect they 'Christianize' John. They do not attempt to set out a historical record of the ministry of John: they are primarily interested in his significance for the story of Jesus. And yet the evangelists retain with little modification a number of traditions about John which are not related to their own 'Christian' portraits of him. Since many of those traditions were deeply embarrassing to followers of Jesus, they have very strong claims to authenticity (see p. 175). As in the case of Jesus, we have historical evidence of considerable value even though it does not come to us in 'neutral' traditions and some of it is difficult to interpret.

John 'the witness' in the fourth gospel

Several features of the portrait of John in the synoptic gospels are also found in the fourth gospel: he is a prophetic figure who baptizes in water in order to prepare the way for the coming of Jesus (1: 23–7). But John's role as baptizer is subordinate to his main task, which is to bear witness to

Jesus. In this gospel John is never called 'the Baptist' and his message of impending judgement, which is prominent in the synoptic gospels, has disappeared. In the fourth gospel there are so many references to John's witness that it is more accurate to refer to him as 'John the witness' than as John the Baptist. John has become a 'Christian evangelist'. And yet we shall see that in spite of this carefully drawn Christian portrait, this gospel contains some traditions of considerable importance for historical reconstruction.

After the powerful and dramatic references to the Word in the opening five verses of the Prologue, John is introduced rather unexpectedly: 'There was a man sent from God whose name was John. He came *as a witness* to testify to the light, so that all might believe *through him*. He himself was not the light, but he came to testify to the light' (1: 6–8). Through John's witness all will believe in Jesus as the Son of God. This theme is underlined at 1: 15 and elaborated at length in 1: 19–42. John's witness to Jesus as 'the Lamb of God' encourages two of his own disciples to follow Jesus (1: 35–7). One of the two disciples who hears John's witness is Andrew; he brings his brother Simon Peter to Jesus with the words, 'We have found the Christ' (1: 40–2). So the very first disciples of Jesus follow him not as a result of Jesus' call to them (as in Mark 1: 16–20 and parallels) but in response to John's witness.

In John 5: 31–5 Jesus himself refers to the importance of John's witness. He states that he cannot bear witness to himself, thus alluding to the legal principle set out in Deut. 19: 15 whereby a man cannot be convicted of a crime on the testimony of one witness. 'There is another who testifies on my behalf, and I know that his testimony to me is true. . . . I say these things so that you may be saved.' This same point is emphasized further at 10: 40–2, the final reference to John in this gospel. Many of John's followers go to Jesus and say, 'Everything that John said about this man [i.e. Jesus] was true.' The evangelist then states that many believed in Jesus as a result of John's witness. It is surely no coincidence that this final comment recalls the opening comment in the Prologue: John came that many might believe (in Jesus) through him (1: 7). Here we have a well-established literary technique whereby opening and closing comments are linked in order to underline their importance.

This strongly positive portrait of John as a 'Christian evangelist' is counterbalanced by several 'negative' references to John which have led some scholars to conclude that the evangelist is indulging in anti-John polemic. John emphasizes that he is *not* the light (1: 8), *not* the Christ (1: 20 and 3: 28), *not* Elijah who was expected by some to return as the forerunner of the Messiah (1: 21), and *not* the Prophet like Moses expected by some (1: 21). There is even a hint of rivalry: following the reference to 'people who kept coming and were being baptized' by John (3: 23) we read that a report reached the Pharisees that Jesus was winning and baptizing more disciples than John (4: 1). In John's own final words about Jesus he stresses that Jesus must increase, but he must decrease (3: 30). Do these passages suggest that the evangelist is trying to repudiate extravagant claims by followers of John in his own day?

There is slender evidence that towards the end of the second century some claimed that John, not Jesus, was the Messiah (Pseudo-Clementines, *Recognitions* I. 60). Was such a claim made a century earlier? In Acts 19: 1–7 Luke refers to a group whom Paul met in Ephesus who knew only John's baptism of repentance. But since they are said explicitly to be 'disciples' (a term Luke always uses to refer to followers of Jesus) this passage provides little or no support for the existence in the first century of groups who saw John rather than Jesus as the Messiah. While a polemical intention cannot be ruled out, the fourth evangelist's primary concern lies elsewhere: supremely important though John is, Jesus has priority in every sense (1: 30).

Does John baptize Jesus? Perhaps this is the most enigmatic aspect of the traditions concerning John in the fourth gospel. John bears witness that he saw the Spirit descend as a dove from heaven and remain on Jesus (1: 32–4). A reader familiar with the accounts of the baptism of Jesus in the synoptic gospels will naturally assume from this passage that John baptized Jesus. But the fourth evangelist does not state this explicitly. He does not wish to suggest that Jesus, the Lamb of God who takes away the sin of the world (1: 29) and who himself baptizes with the Holy Spirit (1: 33), needed to go to John for baptism. As we shall see in a moment, a similar hesitation can be discerned in Matthew and Luke.

In one important respect the fourth gospel gives a fuller and historically more accurate account of John's relationship to Jesus than do the synoptic gospels. The latter state that the beginning of Jesus' ministry was quite distinct from John's: Jesus began to teach and to heal in Galilee 'after John was arrested' (Mark 1: 14; Matt. 4: 12; Luke 3: 21–3). Matthew even reminds the reader that John was 'in prison' (a phrase he adds to his source at 11: 2) during the first part of the ministry of Jesus (see also 14: 3). But in several passages the fourth gospel states that Jesus and John were active at the same time (1: 29; 1: 35–42; 3: 22–4; 4: 1–3). Two of the disciples of Jesus (and perhaps Jesus himself) were originally disciples of John (1: 35–7). In other words, Jesus' ministry overlapped with John's.

An important passage in Q also suggests that the ministries of Jesus and John may have overlapped. In Matt. 11: 2–6 = Luke 7: 19–23 John sends disciples to Jesus to ask, 'Are you the one who is to come, or are we to wait for another?' Jesus says to them, 'Go and tell John what you hear and see.' Jesus then refers to his healing activity and 'preaching of the good news' as fulfilment of Scripture (especially Isa. 35: 5–6 and 61: 1). In the verses in Q which follow Jesus speaks about John positively and in some detail. This lengthy Q passage implies, just as the fourth gospel does, that there was a very close relationship between Jesus and John.

The synoptic evangelists portray John as the forerunner of Jesus whose baptizing and preaching ministry was over (or nearly over) before Jesus appeared on the scene. This portrait has strongly influenced later Christian tradition. But the fourth gospel and Q suggest that the ministries of Jesus and John overlapped. And the fourth gospel states unambiguously that two of the disciples of Jesus originally belonged to John's circle. Since these 'alternative' traditions run counter to the tendency to 'separate' Jesus and John and to stress John's inferior role, they are likely to be historical. They pass the 'embarrassment' test discussed in Chapter 9 with flying colours (pp. 174–5). If so, John may well have influenced Jesus. Hence the student of the life and teaching of Jesus will do well to consider carefully the traditions concerning John the Baptist.

John the Baptist in Mark, Matthew, and Luke

We have already detected some ambivalence on the part of the evangelists concerning the precise relationship of Jesus and John to one another. Nowhere is this clearer than in the accounts of the baptism of Jesus. Mark's account is terse and seems straightforward: 'in those days Jesus came from Nazareth of Galilee and was baptized by John in the Jordan' (1: 9). But on reflection the reader may well ask why Jesus needed to be baptized by John.

John preached 'a baptism of repentance for the forgiveness of sins' (Mark 1: 4), so was Jesus sinful? In one of a handful of fragments which has survived from the apocryphal Gospel of the Hebrews (perhaps written early in the second century) this question becomes explicit. The mother of the Lord and his brothers say to Jesus, 'John the Baptist is baptizing for the remission of sins. Let us go and be baptized by him.' Jesus replies, '*In what way have I sinned* that I should need to go and be baptized by him?'

This question seems to lie behind the comment in Matthew that when Jesus came to the Jordan to be baptized by him, John would have prevented him, saying, 'I need to be baptized by you, and do you come to me?' (3: 14). Jesus does not need to be baptized by John—indeed the reverse is the case. In Matthew John agrees to baptize Jesus only after Jesus has indicated to him that he should proceed in order 'to fulfil all righteousness' (i.e. to carry out God's will) (3: 14–15).

A similar hesitation over the baptism of Jesus by John can be discerned in Luke's rehandling of Mark's account of the baptism of Jesus. Luke does not include Mark's account of the beheading of John by Herod Antipas at the instigation of Herodias, his wife (Mark 6: 17–29; Matt. 14: 3–12). But immediately before his account of the baptism of Jesus he does include a very brief account of John's entanglement with Herod (3: 19–20): Herod the ruler, who had been rebuked by him because of Herodias, his brother's wife, and because of all the evil things that Herod had done, added to them all by shutting up John in prison.

In the account of the baptism of Jesus which follows there is no reference at all to John's role. Luke simply notes that when Jesus also had been baptized and was praying, heaven was opened, and the Holy Spirit descended upon him in bodily form, like a dove (3: 21–2). As in the fourth gospel, the reader unfamiliar with Mark or Matthew will not necessarily assume that John baptized Jesus.

A very different Q passage probably reflects further ambivalence over John in the early church. The original form of Matt. 11: 11 = Luke 7: 28 probably ran as follows: 'Among those born of women no one has arisen greater than John; yet the least in the kingdom of God is greater than he.' In the first half of this saying John is acclaimed highly by Jesus. Without the modification of the second half of the verse, these words would have been an embarrassment to the early church since they imply that John is even more important than Jesus. So it is at least possible that the second half is a later addition which makes it clear that important though John is, he belongs to the old order and is not to be reckoned as 'in the kingdom'.

In Mark John's role is very much that of the forerunner of the coming one. Mark is hardly interested in John apart from his role as the one who prepares the way for Jesus. John's own message is reported briefly in only two verses, both of which look forward to the coming of Jesus. 'The one who is more powerful than I is coming after me . . . I have baptized you with water, but he will baptize you with the Holy Spirit' (Mark 1: 7–8). John's suffering anticipates the fate of Jesus: they are both treated with utter contempt (cf. 9: 12–13), just as Christians are in the evangelist's own day (13: 9).

Matthew's portrait is much fuller. He shares with Luke an extended account of the preaching of John (3: 1–12 = Luke 3: 2–17) taken from Q. In this gospel the proclamation of John and of Jesus is summed up in identical words: 'Repent, for the kingdom of heaven has come near' (3: 2; 4: 17). We have seen examples of the ways the early church took pains to distinguish John and Jesus. So why does Matthew state that their preaching was identical? From the evangelist's point of view there is no question of confusion between John and Jesus; the reader has been told at length of the full significance of Jesus as Son of God before John is introduced. So Matthew is able to draw attention to some similarities between John and Jesus. Jesus and John together are carrying out God's saving plan (3: 15). From Matthew's point of view John's activity starts the new order of the kingdom of heaven (11: 11–12). Like Jesus, John came to Israel 'in the way of righteousness' (21: 32). Their rejection by Israel is all of a piece with the fate of the prophets of old, a fate shared by Christian prophets in the evangelist's own day (5: 10–12; 23: 34, 37). One further aspect of Matthew's portrait of John is worth noting. He drops Mark's association of 'the forgiveness of sins' (1: 4) with John's baptism. Matthew links forgiveness of sins with the death of Jesus (26: 28), as does Paul in numerous passages.

Whereas Matthew links John with Jesus as a herald of the new era of the kingdom, Luke places John firmly in the 'old' era of the law and the prophets: the good news of the kingdom of God is preached only after John's day (Luke 16: 16; cf. Acts 10: 36–7). Matthew does not refer to John in his infancy narratives, but in Luke 1 and 2 a great deal of space is devoted to John's birth. Detailed traditions about the births of John and Jesus are carefully juxtaposed, but at every point the subordination of John to the one for whom he is preparing is clear.

What do we know about John the Baptist?

In addition to the evidence found in the four gospels there is an important paragraph in Josephus, *Antiquities* xviii. 116–19. Unlike the paragraph on Jesus referred to on pp. 149–50, this passage does not seem to have been modified or interpolated by Christians. Although the Jewish historian was not free of prejudice or historical bias, there is no reason to set aside his comments on John. They follow Josephus' account of the defeat in AD 36 of the army of Herod Antipas by the Nabataean king Aretas IV, whose kingdom is marked on the map on p. 140. Herod Antipas governed Galilee and Perea in dependence on Rome from 4 BC to AD 39.

116. But to some of the Jews it seemed that Herod's army was destroyed by God, indeed as a just act of vengeance for his treatment of John, surnamed the Baptist.

117. For Herod had put him to death, even though he was a good man and had encouraged the Jews to lead righteous lives, to practise justice towards one another and piety towards God, and so doing to join in baptism. For only thus would the baptism be acceptable to God: they must not use it to gain pardon for whatever sins they committed, but rather for the purification of their bodies, implying that their souls had already been thoroughly cleansed by right behaviour.

118. When others too joined the crowds about him, because they were roused to fever pitch by his words, Herod became alarmed. He feared that John's ability to sway people might lead to some form of sedition, for it looked as if they would act on John's advice in everything that they did. Herod therefore decided that it would be much better to strike first and be rid of him before his work led to an uprising . . .

119. And so John, because of Herod's suspicions, was brought in chains to Machaerus . . . and there put to death. But the verdict of the Jews was that the destruction of Herod's army was a punishment of Herod, since God saw fit to inflict harm on Herod. (*Antiquities* xviii. 116–19)

A close study of the significant similarities and differences between the

John the Baptist traditions in Josephus and in the gospels is a valuable exercise. Josephus is silent about John's proclamation of God's imminent eschatological judgement, portraying John as 'a Hellenistic teacher of virtue' (Theissen 1998, p. 200). Theissen goes on to note that elsewhere Josephus tends to keep quiet about the eschatological aspects of Judaism, which were suspect in the eyes of the Romans; so there is a suspicion that here such traditions are being suppressed. Josephus has an agenda, as do the evangelists.

Josephus implies that Herod Antipas put John to death c. AD 32. Luke indicates that John began to preach in the fifteenth year of the reign of the emperor Tiberius (Luke 3: 1). Although we cannot be certain about the accuracy of these chronological references, John may well have been active for about four years. Josephus certainly stresses more strongly than do the gospels that John's call for baptism and repentance was welcomed enthusiastically by large numbers of people: John attracted such a large following that Herod feared an uprising.

Although Josephus does not refer to John as a prophet, his twofold comment that the military defeat of Herod was seen by many as a vindication of John is in stark contrast to the scorn he pours on several 'false prophets' who led abortive uprisings. The evangelists have no hesitation in referring to John as a prophet (Mark 11: 32 and par.; Matt. 14: 5; Luke 1: 76; John 1: 21, 25). In Matt. 11: 9 = Luke 7: 26 Jesus refers to John as 'a prophet, indeed more than a prophet'.

Some passages describe the call, appearance, and preaching of John in ways which link him firmly to the Old Testament prophets. The phraseology of Luke 3: 1–2, 'In the fifteenth year of the reign of emperor Tiberius ... the word of God came to John son of Zechariah in the wilderness' recalls the call of Jeremiah (Jer. 1: 1–3). Mark's description of the physical appearance of John is intended to recall Elijah (2 Kings 1: 8). His declaration of God's impending judgement, his call for repentance, and his fearless denunciation of Herod (Mark 6: 18) recall the words and actions of many Old Testament prophets.

In a difficult but important set of sayings in Q, Jesus differentiates John from the Old Testament prophets (Matt. 11: 11–13 = Luke 7: 28 and 16: 16). These sayings have been modified by Matthew and Luke, who both tone down the very high estimate of John they contain. In their original form they are so striking and in such sharp contrast to the later Christian tendency to confine John's role to that of the forerunner to Jesus that they are undoubtedly authentic. Jesus states that 'among those born of women no one has arisen greater than John the Baptist'. 'The law and the prophets prophesied *until John.*' John is not merely the prophet who points to the One who comes after him (Mark 1: 7 par.), he himself ushers in the new era.

John's baptism

We have now found a number of ways in which careful historical probing suggests that John was a far more influential and striking figure than most Christians have supposed. His call for baptism must be added to the list, for it differs from other forms of baptism and lustration rites known in his day. All the evidence in early Judaism points to Jewish ritual bathing practices being self-administered. John's baptism was performed 'by him' (Mark 1: 5, 9), and John himself states, 'I baptize . . . ' (Mark 1: 8; cf. also Matt. 3: 11 = Luke 3: 16 (Q)).

Some scholars have linked John's baptism to the 'proselyte baptism' by which Gentile converts to Judaism were received. But even if this practice was known in John's day (and this is doubtful) there are important differences: in proselyte baptism there was no baptizer and it was strictly for non-Jews, whereas John announced a baptism of repentance for Jews.

Others have pointed to the ritual baths taken by the highpriest on the Day of Atonement (Lev. 16: 24) and to the lustration rites for purification of priests which are referred to in Lev. 22: 5. It is probable that these practices were followed by some non-priestly Jewish groups in the first century. Lustration rites were certainly practised by members of the Qumran community. But these rites were all repeated, in some cases perhaps daily. In contrast, John's baptism was a once-for-all action for those who accepted his call for repentance.

There are so many gaps in our knowledge of first-century Judaism that it is rash to label any belief or practice 'unique'. But as far as we know John's once-for-all baptism was unique, as was his call to all sections of society. Proselyte baptism was confined to small numbers of non-Jews; the various self-administered lustration rites we have just referred to were practised by groups of law-observant Jews. In contrast, large crowds went to be baptized by John (Mark 1: 5; Luke 3: 7; Josephus—see above), including tax collectors (Luke 3: 12; 7: 29), soldiers (Luke 3: 14), and harlots (Matt. 21: 32).

John and Jesus: similarities and differences

Both John and Jesus were seen as prophets. Both called for radical repentance. Both attracted crowds. Both had an inner group of disciples (for John, see Mark 2: 18; Matt. 11: 2 = Luke 7: 19; Luke 11: 1). Both taught their disciples to pray in a distinctive fashion (Luke 11: 1). Jesus links himself closely with John: John and Jesus are both sent by God—'God's wisdom is proved right by *both her children*' (the original Q wording of Matt. 11: 19 = Luke 7: 35). Both were written off by opponents who claimed that their prophetic words were spoken not on God's authority but as a result of their possession by a demon (see Matt. 11: 18 for John; Mark 3: 22 for Jesus). Some confused John and Jesus (Mark 8: 28 and cf. 6: 14). Matthew even suggests that, like Jesus, John was rejected by the religious leaders (21: 32).

Both Jesus and John were opposed to the temple establishment. This is a conclusion which needs some explanation. We shall see in Chapter 17 that Jesus' actions in the temple 'triggered' his downfall. What was John's attitude to the temple? As noted above, whereas all the various Jewish lustration rites were self-administered, John carried out baptism himself. This probably led to his nickname, the 'baptizer'. The gospels and Josephus both emphasize that John called people to repentance. In his role as baptizer, John himself mediated God's forgiveness. As Robert Webb has recently stressed (1994, p. 192), his role was 'parallel to the mediatorial role of a priest performing a sacrifice to mediate forgiveness in the sacrificial system (e.g. Lev. 5: 5–10)'. Webb goes even further (I think correctly) and suggests that John's acts of baptism functioned at least implicitly as a protest against the temple establishment.

At first sight the causes of the deaths of John and Jesus seem to have been very different. John was the victim of a grudge-killing at the instigation of Herodias, Herod Antipas' 'wife' (Mark 6: 19). But the comments of Josephus suggest that John and his followers were seen as a possible threat to political stability. As we shall see in Chapter 16, Jesus may have been put to death for similar reasons, as least as far as the Romans were concerned.

So much for the similarities. What were the main differences? Several scholars have suggested that while John the Baptist still remains in the realm of the law, with Jesus the good news of the gospel begins. While this seems to have been Luke's view (16: 16 and cf. Matt. 11: 11b), it is undoubtedly an exaggeration—and not only because it wrongly implies that Jesus repudiated the law of Moses. As we noted above, Jesus himself saw John's coming as the dawn of the new era (Matt. 11: 11a and 13). And we must also recall that John's baptism was linked with the forgiveness of sins (Mark 1: 4; Luke 3: 3; and see Josephus above). John's prophetic denunciations contain harsh language (see especially Matt. 3: 7–10 = Luke 3: 7–9), but announcement of hope of forgiveness of sins is good news.

Unlike John, Jesus was not an ascetic (Matt. 9: 19; 11: 18 = Luke 7: 33–4). Unlike John's disciples, the disciples of Jesus did not fast (Mark 2: 18). Unlike John, Jesus stopped baptizing (John 3: 22; 4: 2). Unlike John, who remained in the wilderness, Jesus travelled from village to village. Unlike John, who confronted Herod Antipas, the Roman puppet, Jesus avoided Herod's power bases, the cities of Sepphoris and Tiberias (see above, p. 157). Unlike John, 'who performed no miracle' (John 10: 41), Jesus performed numerous healings and exorcisms. Unlike John, Jesus shared table fellowship with tax collectors and sinners. Unlike John, whose prophetic preaching focused on the future, Jesus announced that God's kingly rule was breaking into the present *now*, through his own actions and words (e.g. Matt. 11: 2–5 = Luke 7: 18–23 [Q]; Matt. 12: 28 = Luke 11: 20 [Q]).

Some scholars have suggested that John (and perhaps some of his disciples) may have had links with the Qumran community (see pp. 152–4). Although there is no evidence of a direct link, this is an interesting suggestion: both John and the Qumran community withdrew from 'corrupt' and 'impure' Jerusalem into the wilderness in order to seek the renewal of Israel. Unlike John, Jesus was no 'wilderness prophet'.

How are these differences to be accounted for? Paul Hollenbach (1982) discerns a shift in Jesus' ministry from baptizer to healer, and accounts for the change by referring to Jesus' experience of the kingdom of God in his power to heal and exorcize. Robert Webb (1994, pp. 225–6) accepts this explanation and adds a further observation: as a prophet, Jesus experienced God's call at the time of his baptism by John, and only gradually understood the full significance of that call. 'Jesus' shift from baptizer to healer and exorcist implies a shift to an increased experience and intimacy with the divine realm.'

Such appeals to the personal religious experience of Jesus are not fashionable: they are said to involve 'psychologizing', for which the sources do not provide evidence. But surely a profound awareness of God's call and commissioning is fundamental to the experience of the Old Testament prophets. We need not doubt Jesus' own experience of God's call; this may well have led to a shift in focus in his actions and proclamation.

Whereas profound theological significance came to be attached to the death and resurrection of Jesus, this was not the case with John. A rumour that John had been resuscitated from the dead did reach Herod (Mark 6: 14, 16). The followers of Jesus, however, did not claim that he had been resuscitated back to life, only to die again at some later point.

In this chapter we have noted some of the similarities between John and Jesus which embarrassed later Christians, and hence are likely to be authentic. Two of the leading disciples of Jesus, and perhaps even Jesus himself, may originally have belonged to the circle of disciples around John (see p. 181). So John almost certainly influenced Jesus.

Like John, Jesus led a renewal movement within Judaism. The traditions concerning John pass the 'historical plausibility' test discussed in Chapter 9 (pp. 175–6): they can be located within first-century Judaism, even though in several respects John was no conventional prophet.

Following John's death at the hands of Herod Antipas, there was no significant aftermath, as with Jesus. In later generations John was known, but not worshipped: this is obvious, but nonetheless important. We have sketched above some of the other differences: most of them will be discussed more fully in the chapters which follow. In particular, in Chapter 12 we shall discuss the central theme of the proclamation of Jesus, the kingdom of God, a phrase John does not seem to have used.

11

PROPHET AND TEACHER

For most people today 'prophet' and 'teacher' are quite distinct terms. A prophet is a rugged individualist whose message shatters complacency or even subverts generally held views. Today a prophet is not normally considered to be the sort of person who would gather a group of disciples and instruct them carefully in a teacher–pupil setting.

In the first century, however, 'prophets' and 'teachers' were much more closely related. The Teacher of Righteousness who founded the community at Qumran around the middle of the second century BC was perceived by his followers to be both a prophet and a teacher. A Qumran scroll refers to David as both prophet and teacher: he was a wise man and a scribe who was inspired by God and who taught prophetically (11Q5, column xxvii).

In the preceding chapter we saw that John the Baptist was considered by many who heard him to be a prophet. Nonetheless, he is called 'teacher' in one passage (Luke 3: 12) and there are several references to his circle of disciples (Mark 2: 18; 6: 29; Matt. 11: 2 = Luke 7: 18; Luke 11: 1). If, as we suggested, Jesus originally belonged to the circle of John's disciples, then it will not be surprising to discover that he too was thought to be a prophet–teacher who gathered around him a group of disciples.

Once again we shall start our discussion with a brief examination of the views of the evangelists before we set out Jesus' own self-understanding as 'prophet' and 'teacher', and discuss the nature of his call to discipleship.

According to the evangelists

Mark records that when Jesus taught in the synagogue in Nazareth, eyebrows were raised, questions asked, and jibes were thrown at him (6: 1–3). In response Jesus the teacher quotes a proverb: 'Prophets are not without honour, except in their home town' (6: 4). This passage not only confirms the close relationship between prophets and teachers, it also marks out clearly some of the main lines of the evangelist's portrait of Jesus.

Two passages in Mark record that Jesus was thought either to be John the Baptist brought back to life, or Elijah the prophet (whose return was expected by some), or 'a prophet, like one of the prophets of old' (6: 15 and 8: 28). In Mark's account of the Transfiguration (9: 2–8) Jesus is set along-side the great prophets, Moses (cf. Deut. 18: 15) and Elijah. At the end of the hearing before the high priest Jesus is blindfolded, struck, and taunted: 'Prophesy' (14: 65). Whereas Jesus is perceived by his opponents to be a false prophet, Mark's readers know that Jesus is indeed a prophet. This is underlined in the immediately following verses which record the fulfilment of Jesus' prophecy of Peter's denial (14: 66–72).

Matthew retains and extends these features of Mark's portrait of Jesus. In his adaptation of Mark's account of the entry of Jesus into Jerusalem, Matthew adds a notable reference to Jesus as a prophet. The crowds shout 'Hosanna to the Son of David! Blessed is he who comes in the name of the Lord!' and then exclaim, 'This is the prophet Jesus from Nazareth of Gali-lee' (21: 9–11). In a summary passage the evangelist notes that although the authorities wanted to arrest Jesus, they were unable to do so, 'because the crowds regarded Jesus as a prophet' (21: 46). Matthew may be echoing the view found also in John's gospel (1: 21, 25; 6: 14 and 7: 40) and in Acts (3: 22–6 and 7: 37) that Jesus is not simply *a* prophet: he is *the* prophet like Moses whom God promised to raise up for his people in Deut. 18: 15, 18.

Luke has a special interest in portraying Jesus as a prophet. In the important opening scene of the ministry of Jesus which is set in the syna-gogue in Nazareth (4: 16–30; see above pp. 86–90) Jesus refers to himself as a prophet (v. 24) who has been anointed with the Spirit of God (v. 18). At the climax of the scene Luke records that the prophet Elijah was sent to a widow in Sidon, outside Israel; the prophet Elisha cleansed Namaan the Syrian. Like them, the prophet Jesus will not be acceptable in his own country but will (eventually) find acceptance outside Israel (4: 24–8). Here Luke anticipates a major theme of his second volume: the 'word of God' will be taken first of all to Jewish synagogues, but following its rejection there it will be taken to the Gentiles.

Luke alone records that Jesus restored to life the widow's son at Nain. When the man who was dead began to speak, the crowd said, 'A great prophet has arisen among us!' and 'God has looked favourably on his people' (7: 16). The account (found only in Luke) of the anointing of Jesus in a Pharisee's house by 'a woman of the city' also portrays Jesus as a prophet (7: 36–50). In the dramatic scene at the close of the gospel Cleopas and his companion refer to Jesus as 'a prophet mighty in deed and word' (Luke 24: 19).

Jesus is referred to as a prophet in John's gospel by the Samaritan woman (4: 19) and the man born blind (9: 17; see also John 4: 44 and 7: 52). In both passages the evangelist indicates that this is a positive but partial assessment of the significance of Jesus. The Samaritan woman and her acquaintances eventually confess that Jesus is the Christ, the Saviour of the world (4: 25, 29, 42). The man born blind finally confesses his faith in Jesus as the Son of man and worships him (9: 35, 38).

The evangelist insists that John is definitely not to be understood as *the* expected eschatological prophet like Moses (1: 21, 25; Deut. 18: 15). The firm denial may suggest that some did view John in this way. But what about Jesus? The claim by crowds that Jesus is *the* prophet is not repudiated, but from the evangelist's perspective this is not a wholly satisfactory way of expressing the significance of Jesus (6: 14; 7: 40).

So all four evangelists note that Jesus was considered to be a prophet. As was the case generally in early Christianity, the evangelists themselves prefer to spell out the significance of Jesus in other ways; 'prophet' did not become a title for Jesus in the post-Easter period, perhaps partly because it would not have differentiated Jesus and John the Baptist sufficiently sharply. Hence there is no reason to doubt that the references to Jesus as a prophet put us in touch with the views of many of those who heard him. This may be an obvious conclusion, but it is a significant one. In many circles at the time the appearance of a prophet 'like the prophets of old' was seen to herald the dawn of the promised new era in God's dealings with his people.

The evangelists also all portray Jesus as a teacher. In his first comment on the teaching of Jesus Mark notes that Jesus taught in the synagogue at Capernaum 'as one who had authority, and not as the scribes' (1: 22). In key summary passages Mark notes that Jesus went about among the villages of Galilee teaching (6: 6b); later, in Judaea he again taught the crowds (10: 1), as he also did in the temple in Jerusalem (10: 49).

Mark shows that unlike that of the scribes, the teaching of Jesus did not centre on learned interpretation of the law (though he could and did dispute with scribes, e.g. 7: 1, 5; 9: 11). The teaching of Jesus was 'a new teaching, with authority' (Mark 1: 27). The Greek word translated as 'authority' includes (in this context) the notion of power which comes from God. So in Mark 1: 22 and 27 we may translate: 'Jesus *taught* with *prophetic* authority'. The other passages in Mark in which reference is made to the 'authority' of Jesus confirm this interpretation. (See especially Mark 11: 27–33; also 2: 10; 3: 15; and 6: 7.)

Mark emphasizes the teaching activity of Jesus, but it has often been observed that he includes comparatively few examples of the actual teaching of Jesus. Some scholars have claimed that since Mark expected the end-time quite soon, he was not interested in the content of the teaching of Jesus. But it is only by comparison with Matthew's and Luke's much longer gospels that Mark seems to have so few examples of the teaching of Jesus; in fact about 40 per cent of Mark consists of words of Jesus which are 'didactic'.

Twelve times in all in Mark in a variety of settings both disciples and 'outsiders' refer to Jesus as 'teacher'. There is a very different pattern in Matthew and in Luke, where disciples are *not* allowed to call Jesus 'teacher', though other people do so (six times in Matthew, twelve in Luke). In several passages in Matthew disciples call Jesus 'Lord' (e.g. 8: 25; 17: 4, 15), and in six places in Luke Jesus is addressed as 'master', a word not found in the other gospels. These variations seem to reflect concern to underline the special relationship between Jesus and the disciples.

The term 'rabbi' has led to much scholarly discussion. Both Matthew and John indicate that it is the Aramaic equivalent of *didaskalos*, 'teacher' (Matt 23: 8; John 1: 38). Some have claimed that since the term is not found in Jewish traditions which can be dated before AD 70, its use in the gospels is anachronistic. However, it has been found written on two ossuaries (small boxes in which the bones of the deceased were placed) which come from the Jerusalem area before AD 70. The evidence from rabbinic writings is complex and difficult to assess. 'Rabbi' (or an earlier form *rab*) seems to have originated shortly before the time of Jesus as a general term of respect for various leading figures, and especially for teachers. 'Rabbi' then became limited to teachers before AD 70; at the time Matt. 23: 8 and John 1: 38 were written towards the end of the first century 'rabbi' could be translated into

Greek as 'teacher'. In the second century 'rabbi' came to be used as a formal title for an ordained scribe.

'Rabbi' is used twice by Peter in Mark, both in contexts which indicate its inadequacy (9: 5; 11: 21). At the moment of his betrayal of Jesus, Judas addresses Jesus as 'rabbi' (Mark 14: 45). Matthew goes further: he reserves 'rabbi' for Judas alone (26: 25, 49). Not surprisingly Luke avoids 'rabbi', an Aramaic term not likely to be known to his readers. In John's gospel, on the other hand, 'rabbi' is used eight times, generally by disciples, but once by Nicodemus (3: 2), and once by John's disciples who address him as 'rabbi' (3: 26).

Although the evangelists all attach continuing significance to the sayings of Jesus, they do not use the terms 'prophet' or 'teacher' as *titles* for Jesus—and neither do other early Christian writings. For the evangelists Jesus was greater than a prophet; he was the one through whom God had spoken anew to Jew and Gentile—the Messiah–Christ, the Son (of God), Lord. Although it was not part of their intention to elicit confession of Jesus as prophet–teacher, the evangelists have retained traditions which do portray him in these ways. Hence we need not doubt that this part of their portraits of Jesus is authentic.

Jesus as prophet and teacher

In only two of his sayings does Jesus refer explicitly to himself as a prophet. But a number of other sayings and several of his actions confirm that he saw himself as a prophet. Mark records that Jesus rounded on his critics in the synagogue in his home town with these words: 'Prophets are not without honour, except in their home town, and among their own kin, and in their own house' (6: 4). While Jesus seems to be quoting a common proverb (there are also versions of it in Luke 4: 24 and John 4: 44), he accepts not only that it applies to him but also that a prophet must expect to be rejected.

In an incident recorded only by Luke, Jesus asked some Pharisees to go and tell Herod Antipas ('that fox'): 'I must be on my way, because it is impossible for a prophet to be killed outside of Jerusalem' (Luke 13: 33). This is not a proverb since there is no sign of an expectation in early Judaism that a prophet should expect to perish in Jerusalem. Luke then immediately adds from Q the lament of Jesus:

Jerusalem, Jerusalem, the city that kills the prophets and stones those who are sent to it! How often have I desired to gather your children together as a hen gathers her brood under her wings, and you were not willing! See, your house is left to you. And I tell you, you will not see me until the time comes when you say, 'Blessed is the one who comes in the name of the Lord!' (13: 34–35; cf. Matt. 23: 37–39)

With these words Jesus links himself with the tradition (which was strong in many circles in his day) that the prophets of old were not only opposed but killed. Since Jesus is himself a prophet, he expects to die a martyr's death in Jerusalem (Matt. 23: 37 = Luke 13: 34; see also Matt. 23: 34 = Luke 11: 49; Matt. 5: 11–12 = Luke 6: 22–3; Matt. 23: 29–32, 34–6 = Luke 11: 47–51; Acts 7: 52; 1 Thess 2: 15). At this point we are in touch with one of the most important ways Jesus understood his own mission.

The same theme is found in one of the parables of Jesus. In the parable of the vineyard (Mark 12: 1–12 and parallels) the owner lets out his vineyard to tenants and goes off to another country. He sends a servant to the tenants 'to collect from them his share of the produce of the vineyard'. The servant is beaten and sent away empty-handed, as is a second servant. A third servant is sent, but killed; 'and so it was with many others; some they beat, and others they killed.' Finally the owner sends 'his beloved son', confident that the tenants will respect his son. Hoping to gain the heir's inheritance, the tenants killed him, and cast him out of the vineyard. 'What will the owner of the vineyard do? He will come and destroy the tenants, and give the vineyard to others.'

In Mark the parable is understood allegorically. The series of servants represents the prophets sent to Israel, only to be persecuted and killed. The beloved son is Jesus, but he too is rejected and killed. Some of the allegorical features may have been elaborated in the early church before Mark's day, and some by Mark the evangelist. But since in several other passages Jesus aligns himself with the 'rejected prophets of old', the original version of this parable was almost certainly told by Jesus himself.

It is striking that in the three passages in which Jesus most clearly refers to himself as a prophet, he refers to the ultimate rejection a prophet must expect to face. We shall return to this point.

Jesus refers to himself as a 'teacher' in three passages: Mark 14: 14 and parallels; Matt. 23: 8 (cf. also John 13: 14) and Matt. 10: 24–5 = Luke 6: 40.

The latter passage is particularly interesting. The underlying Q tradition may have been as follows: 'A disciple is not above his teacher; it is enough for the disciple to be like his teacher.' It is impossible to reconstruct the original context of this saying, but its main thrust is clear. A disciple should aim to appropriate as much of his master's teaching as possible, but teacher and disciple will always be distinct, for a disciple is dependent on his teacher.

In the final section of this chapter, Jesus' action in calling twelve disciples and his teaching on discipleship will be discussed. In Chapter 12 the central theme in Jesus' teaching (or, prophetic proclamation) of the kingdom of God will be considered. Chapter 13 focuses on the parables and aphorisms of Jesus and examines the recent claim that the historical Jesus was primarily a wisdom teacher, closely related to Cynic philosopher–teachers.

Prophetic sayings and actions

In numerous Old Testament passages we read of a prophet's conviction that he has been called and commissioned by God to speak to his people. For the evangelists the baptism of Jesus by John functions in a partly similar way: Jesus has a visionary experience ('he saw the heavens opened') and hears a voice from heaven: 'You are my Son, the Beloved; with you I am well pleased' (Mark 1: 10–11 and parallels). But the accounts of the baptism of Jesus are not closely similar in structure to Old Testament 'call' narratives. In any case it is impossible to know what this experience meant to Jesus, as distinct from the theological significance attached to the traditions by the early church and the evangelists.

There are, however, a number of sayings of Jesus which do reflect his conviction that he had been sent by God: sayings introduced by 'I came' or 'I was sent' (e.g. Mark 1: 38 and parallels; 2: 17 and parallels; 10.45 and parallel; Matt. 5: 17; Matt. 10: 34–6; Luke 12: 49; Matt. 11: 19 = Luke 7: 34; Mark 9: 37; Luke 10: 16; Matt. 15: 24). The authenticity of some of these sayings has been disputed, but it is unlikely that they were all formed in the early church since they are deeply embedded in the various strands of the synoptic traditions.

The Old Testament prophets frequently introduce their proclamation with 'Thus says the Lord'. Although this formula is not found in the gospels, 'I say to you' is very common on the lips of Jesus and has been seen by some writers as a parallel expression. However it is now clear that at the time of Jesus 'I say to you' was used in a wide variety of contexts. Although Jesus certainly used the formula as an expression of his authority, it is not necessarily an indication of his prophetic consciousness.

In some passages in the gospels 'I say to you' is preceded by *amēn*, a transliteration of the Hebrew (which is usually translated as 'truly' in the NRSV). It has often been claimed that whereas *amēn* is widely used in early Judaism and early Christianity as a response (as amen is normally used today), its use as a preface is unique to Jesus and reflects his conviction that he speaks with the authority of God. If this is so, it would have the same force as the Old Testament prophets' claim to speak in the name of God: 'Thus says the Lord.' However, recent careful study has undermined this claim: *amēn* as an introduction is attested (though it is rare) in Judaism; the 'Amen, I say to you' sayings of Jesus do not differ significantly from the more frequent sayings introduced by 'I say to you'.

In one important Q saying Jesus indicates (very much in the manner of some Old Testament prophets) that it is by the inspiration of God that he has been granted a 'special revelation': 'At that time Jesus rejoiced in the Spirit and said: I thank you, Father, Lord of heaven and earth, because you have hidden these things from the wise and the intelligent and revealed them to infants.' (The Q saying behind Matt. 11: 25–6 = Luke 10: 21.)

Visionary experiences are frequently associated with Old Testament prophets. One rather enigmatic saying of Jesus seems to record a visionary experience, though its content is not paralleled in the Old Testament: 'I watched Satan fall from heaven like a flash of lightning' (Luke 10: 18). The vision records the final conquest of Satan by God. It forms part of the reaction of Jesus to the triumphant return of the disciples from the mission on which they were sent: as representatives of Jesus they have confronted evil in its various manifestations. In the Old Testament (and in early Judaism) the visions of prophets were often connected closely with their proclamation. Similarly with Jesus: there is a set of sayings of Jesus which seem to be closely related to this vision. In Matt. 12: 27–9 = Luke 11: 19–22 Jesus claims that his exorcisms are an indication of the partial presence of the kingly rule of God and that Satan's power is being assaulted.

There are several passages in the gospels in which Jesus prophesies the destruction of Jerusalem and the temple. While some of the phraseology in these passages seems to reflect what happened some forty years later when the Romans destroyed Jerusalem in AD 70, Jesus almost certainly predicted impending disaster. In several Old Testament passages there is prophetic criticism of the temple and its worship, and even some predictions of its destruction along with Jerusalem. (See, for example, Hos. 6: 6; Amos 5: 4–7, 21–3; Isa. 1: 10–12; Jer. 7: 14; 26: 4–9, 12; Dan. 9: 26; 11: 31). Josephus records several prophecies of the fall of Jerusalem and the temple. So it is quite possible that Jesus aligned himself with such criticisms of the temple and of Jerusalem.

Three oracles, which in their structure are not unlike oracles of some Old Testament prophets, suggest that he did so. We quoted above the words of Jesus 'Jerusalem, Jerusalem, the city that kills the prophets and stones those who are sent to it', with its climax: 'See, your house is left to you' (Matt. 23: 37–9 = Luke 13: 34–5). A structurally similar oracle is recorded in Luke 19: 41–4: 'If you, even you, had only recognized on this day the things that make for peace! . . . Your enemies will not leave within you one stone upon another; because you did not recognize the time of your visitation from God.'

As he is led to the place of crucifixion Jesus addresses the women who 'were beating their breasts and wailing for him':

Daughters of Jerusalem, do not weep for me, but weep for yourselves and for your children. For behold the days are surely coming when they will say, 'Blessed are the barren, and the wombs which never bore, and the breasts that never nursed!' Then they will begin to say to the mountains, 'Fall on us'; and to the hills, 'Cover us.' For if they do this when the wood is green, what will happen when it is dry? (Luke 23: 27–31)

The final enigmatic sentence suggests that if Jesus who is innocent is about to crucified, those who are guilty can expect even greater catastrophe. The lack of specific details in this prophecy of the impending disaster suggests that it is authentic.

In Mark's account of the trial of Jesus 'false witnesses' allege that Jesus said: 'I will destroy this temple that is made with hands, and in three days I will build another, not made with hands' (14: 58). (Versions of a similar prophecy are found in Mark 13: 2; John 2: 19–21; Acts 6: 13–14.) Mark correctly dubs this as a false statement since Jesus did not predict that *he himself* would destroy the temple. However, behind this saying may well lie a more general prediction of an impending disaster for the temple which was looming. In view of the political tension between Jews and Romans Jesus may well have spoken along these lines.

As was the case with Old Testament prophets, at the time of Jesus prophetic *actions* were highly dramatic ways of conveying God's will and purpose. The actions of Jesus which are most clearly those of a prophet are the 'cleansing' of the temple (Mark 11: 15–17 and parallels) and the cursing of the fig tree (Mark 11: 12–14, 20–5 and parallels). They are related to his prophetic *sayings* which refer to the crisis and disaster which Jerusalem and the temple faced. By his actions in the temple Jesus may well have intended to indicate that the temple would soon be overthrown (see further pp. 284–5). The cursing of the fig tree was also a sign of the imminent judgement of God on Israel.

Morna Hooker (1997, pp. 38–54) has drawn attention to several further prophetic actions of Jesus: for example, his choice of twelve disciples who clearly symbolize the twelve tribes of Israel; his eating with tax collectors and sinners; his actions at the Last Supper. These actions will all be discussed further below (see pp. 201–2; 215–17; 274–9).

The renaming of Simon as 'Cephas' or 'Rock' is noted by Hooker as an often overlooked prophetic sign (p. 39). A name meaning 'rock' is hardly appropriate for someone with Peter's character, so the renaming is an indication of the role Peter was going to play in the new community. 'This renaming reminds us of the way in which Hosea (1: 3–9) and Isaiah (8: 1–4) deliberately gave prophetic names to some of their children.'

Disciples and discipleship

Mark's account of Jesus' call of the first disciples is disarmingly simple: 'As Jesus passed along the Sea of Galilee, he saw Simon and his brother Andrew casting a net into the sea—for they were fishermen. And Jesus said to them, "Follow me and I will make you fish for people." And immediately they left their nets and followed him' (1: 16–18). Modern readers of the gospels usually assume that the disciples were poor and uneducated. In first-century Galilee, fishermen were in fact the businessmen of their community; James and John (whose 'call' is recorded in the next two verses) were affluent enough to have hired servants. The disciples were reasonably well-educated; as well as their local Galilean Aramaic dialect, they almost certainly used some Greek in order to trade.

It is striking that Jesus himself takes the initiative and 'calls' the disciples. In a teacher–pupil relationship in early Judaism the pupil himself usually requested permission to join the 'school'; he would then carefully learn his master's teaching (often referred to as 'learning Torah') and seek to imitate his pattern of behaviour. All this is missing in the gospels. 'Following Jesus' involved sharing his itinerant ministry, with all its uncertainties. Above all it involved commitment to proclamation of 'the kingdom of God', to which we shall turn in our next chapter.

For Simon and Andrew 'following Jesus' also meant 'leaving their nets' and for James and John it also meant 'leaving their father Zebedee in the boat' (Mark 1: 18 and 20). Other passages in the gospels confirm that these comments are more than casual reminiscences. Disciples called by Jesus were expected to be prepared to abandon their family ties and also their property and livelihood. In Mark 10: 28–30 we read:

Peter began to say to Jesus, 'Look, we have left everything and followed you.' Jesus said, 'Truly, I say to you, there is no one who has left house or brothers or sisters or mother or father or children or fields, for my sake and for the sake of the good news, who will not receive a hundredfold . . .'

The hundredfold reward promised for this age ('houses and brothers and sisters and mothers and children and fields', v. 30) refers to the reshaping of relationships within the community of disciples: the 'new family' takes precedence over normal family ties.

This is confirmed by Mark 3: 31–5. In this passage Jesus is told that his mother and brothers have come to visit him, but he is quite indifferent. Looking around the circle of disciples Jesus said, 'Here are my mother and my brothers. Whoever does the will of God is my brother and sister and mother'.

The radical nature of discipleship is underlined even more sharply in a Q saying which is universally considered to be authentic because it cuts across respect for parents and for proper burial for the dead, both of which are deep-seated in the Old Testament and in early Judaism. The Q saying which underlies Matt. 8: 21–2 = Luke 9: 59–60 may be reconstructed as follows: 'Another [disciple] said to him: teacher, let me first go and bury my father. But Jesus said to him, "Follow me, and let the dead bury their own dead."' Those who are 'spiritually dead' may carry out the customary burial rites, but the would-be disciple of Jesus has an even higher priority.

There is good evidence for concluding that Jesus had an inner group of disciples and spoke frequently of 'the twelve'. The fact that the names of the twelve vary, especially towards the end of the lists (Mark 3: 16–19; Matt. 10: 2–4; Luke 6: 14–16; Acts 1: 13), suggests that the early church did not 'invent' the twelve, for in that case greater trouble would have been taken to produce a fixed list of names.

Writing at least twenty years before Mark, Paul refers to a tradition he received which recorded a resurrection appearance of Jesus to Cephas (i.e. Peter) and 'then to the twelve' (1 Cor. 15: 5). The number twelve is firmly fixed in this early pre-Pauline tradition. Only a century or so later did some scribes who were copying this verse realize that the betrayal of Jesus by Judas meant that at the time of the resurrection appearances there could only have been eleven disciples, and so they changed 'twelve' to 'eleven'.

What is the significance of the number twelve? Jesus' choice of this number provides an important clue to his intentions: the twelve were chosen by Jesus as the nucleus of the 'true' or 'restored' twelve tribes of Israel which he sought to establish. This is suggested by the Q saying behind Matt. 19: 28 = Luke 22: 28–30: 'You who have followed me will also sit in the kingdom on twelve thrones [i.e. one throne for each of the twelve] judging the twelve tribes of Israel'. The importance of the call of the twelve can scarcely be exaggerated. In this prophetic action Jesus is calling for the renewal of Israel. He is also expressing the conviction that God is now beginning to establish anew his people—and will bring this promise to fulfilment.

The number twelve also provides an important clue to the self-understanding of Jesus. We might have expected Jesus to choose eleven to make up, with himself, a symbolic 'true Israel'. But Jesus stands, as it were, above and outside the group. We are reminded of his saying, 'a disciple is not above his teacher; it is enough for the disciple to be like his teacher' (Matt. 10: 24–5a = Luke 6: 40).

Both Mark and Q record that Jesus sent out his disciples on a mission (Mark 6: 1–6; Matt. 9: 37–8; 10: 1–16; 11: 20–4; 10: 40 = Luke 10: 1–20). They were given authority both to preach and to heal; for both Jesus and the disciples preaching and healing were interrelated. An important Q saying confirms that the disciples were sent as formal representatives of Jesus himself—an unusual step for Jesus to take: 'Whoever listens to you listens to me, and whoever rejects you rejects me, and he who rejects me rejects him who sent me' (Matt. 10: 40 = Luke 10: 16; cf. also John 13: 20). This saying reflects a well-attested Jewish principle: 'one sent is as the sender himself'. It not only underlines the closeness of the relationship of Jesus and his disciples, but points to Jesus' self-understanding as a prophet sent by God.

In this chapter an answer to the question 'Who was Jesus of Nazareth?' has begun to emerge, though it will need to be explored further in the chapters which follow. Jesus, like John the Baptist, was a prophet–teacher who gathered around him a group of disciples. Unlike John (as far as we know) Jesus was keenly aware that as a prophet he would be rejected. Jesus warned of an impending catastrophe for Jerusalem and the temple, and called for the renewal of Israel. His call to radical discipleship contained several unexpected and striking features, the most notable of which was the choice of twelve disciples as the nucleus of a renewed Israel.

12

THE KINGDOM OF GOD

Mark, Matthew, and Luke all stress that Jesus the 'prophet–teacher' referred to the kingdom of God frequently. The opening verses of Mark's gospel are terse but dramatic. Mark's account of John the baptizer, of the baptism of Jesus, and of the temptation of Jesus by Satan pave the way for the first words of Jesus himself: 'Now after John was arrested, Jesus came to Galilee, proclaiming the good news of God, and saying, "The time is fulfilled, and the kingdom of God has come near; repent and believe in the good news"' (Mark 1: 14–15). For Mark the evangelist the central theme of the preaching of Jesus is "the kingdom of God has come near".

In his much expanded version of that summary Matthew includes his characteristic phrase 'the kingdom of heaven' (Matt. 4: 12–17). Matthew's phrase (which is never found in the other gospels) reflects a Jewish writer's avoidance of direct reference to 'God', though Matthew does in fact use the phrase 'the kingdom of God' four times (12: 28; 19: 24; 21: 31, 43). In two important passages Matthew summarizes the ministry of Jesus in Galilee as 'proclaiming the good news of the kingdom and curing every disease and every sickness among the people' (4: 23 and 9: 35). Matthew stresses that the disciples are sent out by Jesus with exactly the same message: they are to heal and to proclaim the kingdom of heaven (Matt. 11: 1, 7–8); Luke makes the same point, but uses 'kingdom of God' (Luke 9: 2; cf. 10: 9).

In three summary passages Luke also emphasizes that the kingdom of God was central in the proclamation of Jesus (4: 43; 8: 1; 9: 11). In the important opening scene in Luke's account of the ministry of Jesus (Luke 4: 16–30, see above, pp. 86–90) the evangelist stresses that the coming of Jesus marked the fulfilment of the promises of Isa. 61: 1–2. The word 'kingdom' is not used, though many of the main points of this passage are related to 'kingdom' sayings which Luke includes elsewhere. In the very last verse of Acts (28: 31) Luke summarizes the preaching of Paul as 'proclaiming the kingdom of God'; in this way he draws attention to the continuity between the message of Jesus and the preaching of the early church. (See also Acts 8: 12; 14: 22; 19: 8; 20: 25; 28: 23.)

In John's gospel, however, matters are very different, as they are in so many other respects. Whereas the synoptic gospels contain numerous references of various kinds to the kingdom of God, in John 'kingdom' occurs in only two passages. In his reply to Nicodemus Jesus says, 'Unless one is born anew, he cannot enter the kingdom of God' (3: 5; cf. also 3: 3). This saying is closely related to Matt. 18: 3 and to other 'entering the kingdom' sayings in the synoptic gospels to which we shall refer in a moment. In the other passage, which is quite unrelated to the synoptic 'kingdom' sayings, Jesus explains to Pilate that his kingdom (or, better, 'kingship') is not of this world (18: 36); in the synoptic gospels the kingdom or kingship belongs to God, not Jesus. It has sometimes been suggested that the fourth evangelist has transposed the 'kingdom' sayings of the synoptic gospels into another key and has used as an equivalent phrase his own favourite term 'eternal life'. This is only partly true; the differences in the ways these two phrases are used are more striking than the similarities.

The synoptic evangelists not only use the term 'kingdom of God' (or 'of heaven') in their summaries of the proclamation of Jesus, they reinterpret 'kingdom' sayings of Jesus partly by setting them in particular contexts and partly by rewording them in their attempts to clarify them. In so doing they have made it very difficult for the modern student of the gospels to reconstruct with confidence this central strand in the teaching of Jesus. Later in this chapter we shall consider in some detail two striking examples.

Jesus and the kingdom

There is almost universal agreement that Jesus taught frequently about the kingdom of God. Most scholars would go further and claim that the 'kingdom' sayings give us vital clues to the overall intention of Jesus. But at that point unanimity stops. The teaching of Jesus on the kingdom of God has been understood in a wide variety of ways.

Why has there been such diversity of scholarly opinion? There are two main reasons. First, Jesus left no clear explanation of his precise meaning.

And even if we assume that his listeners would have known immediately just what Jesus meant when he referred to the 'kingdom of God', we are no further ahead, for it is not at all easy to work out how villagers in Galilee would have understood the phrase. And secondly, as we shall see, Jesus seems to have used 'kingdom of God' in several different senses. For more than a hundred years now, individual scholars have tended to fasten onto one strand of the sayings as 'central' or 'dominant' and then either ignore the other strands or claim that they go back to the early church, not Jesus. In many cases it is possible to see that theological concerns have won out over careful attention to the evidence in all its variety.

In the last two or three decades of the nineteenth century A. Ritschl's views were very influential: he saw the kingdom of God as human society organized through action inspired by love. This approach, which emphasizes human initiative and the gradual permeation of society by the kingdom, is still reflected in phrases such as 'extending' or 'building' the kingdom which are often used by Christians today. In 1892 J. Weiss vigorously repudiated such views. Weiss believed that Jesus was strongly influenced by the apocalyptic thought of his day. The kingdom was no moral cause, but a reality to be initiated by God in the immediate future, 'the breaking out of an overpowering divine storm which erupts into history to destroy and to renew, and which man can neither further nor influence'.

Was Jesus, as Weiss suggested, an apocalyptic prophet who expected God to bring the present age to an end within his lifetime? Or was C. H. Dodd correct in his insistence in his *Parables of the Kingdom* (1935) that for Jesus the kingdom had actually come with his own actions and words? Dodd claimed that in contrast to the speculations on the future found in the apocalyptic writers, Jesus declared that 'the eschaton [end-time] has moved from the future to the present, from the sphere of expectation into that of realized experience.' Over the past fifty years some scholars have rejected or modified radically both these approaches. Others have tried to plot a middle path: Jesus proclaimed that the kingdom was in some ways partly present in his actions and teaching (or was already making its impact felt in the present), though its full and final disclosure still lay in the future.

What did Jesus mean? We must start with the use of the phrase in the Scriptures and in later Jewish writings. For this was the backdrop for both Jesus himself and his listeners. Rather surprisingly, however, the precise phrase 'the kingdom of God' is not found in the Old Testament, and it is not as prominent in later Jewish writings as one might have expected. Nonetheless, the phrase encapsulates the declarations of God's beneficent kingship, and his sovereign, dynamic rule which are embedded in the Old Testament—especially in some Psalms and in some passages in Isaiah. We shall discuss briefly representative passages.

Psalm 145: 8–13 is one of many passages in the Psalms which provide the backdrop to the message of Jesus concerning God's kingly rule. The Psalmist speaks of God's mercy, steadfast love, and compassion (vv. 8–9). He then announces a threefold assignment for the Lord's faithful people: 'They shall speak of the glory of your kingdom, and tell of your power, to make known to all people your mighty deeds, and the glorious splendour of your kingdom' (vv. 11–12). Here 'kingdom' and 'power' are almost synonymous. The Lord's kingdom is an everlasting kingdom (v. 13a); in the passage as a whole it is both a present experience and a future hope.

Isaiah 52: 7 also announces God's kingly rule, but in the more specific context of a promise to the exiles. 'How beautiful upon the mountains are the feet of the messenger who announces peace, who brings good news, who announces salvation, who says to Zion, "Your God reigns".' The four tasks given to the messenger are closely related: they are intended to interpret one another. God is mercifully forgiving and redeeming his people, and will bring them out of exile in a new exodus as they return to a purified Jerusalem. There is no doubt that this and related passages provided a script for Jesus.

Some later Jewish writings contain similar themes. Some of the Psalms of Solomon express the hope that God will soon reverse the disaster brought by the capture of Jerusalem by the Roman general Pompey in 63 BC. Several passages speak about God as king, and express the hope that his kingly rule will be made manifest. Psalm of Solomon 17 opens and closes with a declaration of the everlasting kingship of the Lord (v. 1 and v. 46), and uses the phrase 'kingdom of God' in verse 3.

The central section of Psalm of Solomon 17 is even more significant, though its theme has few parallels in Jewish writings from this period. Here the Lord God is urged to raise up a king, 'the son of David, to rule over your servant Israel in the time known to you, O God' (v. 21). The hoped-for human, Davidic king will be the Lord Messiah (v. 32), who will purge Jerusalem from the Gentiles who trample her to destruction (v. 22).

The Messiah's kingly role as the one who will put the Romans to flight is clearly subordinate to the Lord God (v. 34).

Once again God's kingly rule is a deep-seated hope, but for the Psalmist in the middle of the first century BC it is not yet realized. In Psalms of Solomon 17–18 there are unusually explicit references to the means God will use to manifest his kingly rule: the Davidic Messiah will exercise a political and military role on behalf of God's hard-pressed people. Although it was an option for Jesus to fulfil this particular expectation, it is clear that he eschewed violence (Matt. 5: 38–9 = Luke 6: 29–30; cf. also Luke 22: 38) and urged his followers to love their enemies (Matt 5: 44 = Luke 6: 27). Did Jesus see himself as the Davidic Messiah, albeit with a very different role from the one set out in Psalms of Solomon 17–18? If so, Jesus was reluctant to spell out the nature of his messiahship, but his actions and words provided plenty of hints for his followers to reach this conclusion for themselves. We shall return to this point in Chapter 15.

These three passages (and other similar ones) affirm God's kingly rule and express the hope that he will soon act powerfully on behalf of his beleaguered people. The kingdom of God is his sovereign, dynamic rule. More often than not, there is a clearly temporal sense: the kingdom is referred to in the context of hope for the future.

The importance of this latter point becomes clear as soon as we turn to Jesus' teaching about the kingdom of God. Jesus uses such varied phraseology in his kingdom sayings that they cannot be readily analysed, though they do fall into two main groups. Many sayings refer to the kingdom in the temporal sense just mentioned. In some of these sayings Jesus announces that the kingdom will come in the future; in others, the kingdom is near, or has already come. In the other main group there are a number of sayings which have a spatial rather than a temporal reference: the kingdom is a place (or realm) to be entered, to be inherited, to be received, or to be 'in'.

Is the kingdom temporal or spatial?

In the relevant passages in Old Testament and later Jewish writings, as well as in the sayings of Jesus themselves, the temporal sense is not only more common than the spatial, but primary. God's kingdom is his dynamic, kingly rule, not a geographical location with boundaries. If the primary sense is temporal, it is possible to explain the 'spatial' sayings as an implication of God's kingly rule. God's sovereign rule is not exercised in a vacuum, but among his people: so, to 'enter', to 'inherit', or to be 'in' the kingdom means to be among the people who experience God's kingly rule. However, if the spatial sense is primary, it is not easy to explain why so many sayings have a clearly temporal sense.

In Mark 10: 23–5, for example, the phrase 'enter the kingdom of God' occurs three times. Jesus says twice over, 'How hard it is [for the wealthy] to enter the kingdom', and then illustrates his point with the graphic comparison: 'It is easier for a camel to go through the eye of a needle than for someone who is rich to enter the kingdom of God.' The context concerns discipleship, so the kingdom to be entered is not a realm with boundaries, but the people among whom God exercises his kingly rule, whether now or in the future.

Does Jesus claim that God's kingly rule is being experienced 'in the here and now' in his own message and miracles, or is the kingdom a wholly future hope? There are a clutch of kingdom sayings which refer to a future coming. Once again only a few representative passages can be noted. The second petition of the Lord's Prayer asks, 'Your kingdom come' (Matt. 6: 10 = Luke 11: 2); the coming of the kingdom is a future hope. A Q tradition (Matt. 8: 11–12 = Luke 13: 28–9) declares that people will come from the east and west and eat in the kingdom with Abraham, Isaac, and Jacob. In the eschatological banquet in heaven Gentiles (or, perhaps, diaspora Jews) will join the patriarchs, but in the final judgement, those who reject Jesus will be rejected by God—and there will be weeping and gnashing of teeth. Here Jesus subverts the expectations of his listeners. He draws on graphic apocalyptic motifs, though in other sayings Jesus distances himself from the apocalyptic traditions popular in some circles which spelt out detailed timetables and scenarios for the future (Mark 13: 32–3; Luke 17: 20).

In the opening beatitudes the poor, the mourners, and the hungry are declared to be 'happy' or 'blessed' (Matt. 5: 3–6 = Luke 6: 20b–21). Why? Because the kingly rule of God reverses their present state. It is not often noted that in the first beatitude the kingdom is a present reality, while in the two following beatitudes the promise is that God *will* act on behalf of those in need. A present and a future temporal sense are juxtaposed.

Several sayings express the presence or the nearness of the kingdom, though in each case their precise temporal sense is difficult to determine. In Mark 1: 15, for example, is the sense, 'the kingdom of God has come' or, 'is at hand', or 'is upon you'? Protracted discussion has led to the widely accepted conclusion that this verse announces the nearness of the kingdom: it is so near that a response is imperative.

The presence of the kingdom is clear in Matt. 12: 28 = Luke 11: 20, Jesus' declaration that his exorcisms are confirmation of the presence of God's kingly rule. Luke 17: 20–1, which we shall discuss shortly, also states that the kingdom is a present reality.

Several important sayings declare that God's promises are being fulfilled *now* in the words and actions of Jesus, even though the phrase 'kingdom of God' is not used. When the imprisoned John the Baptist sent his disciples to ask Jesus about his role and his intention, Jesus told them to tell John what they had heard and what they had seen. He then elaborated by couching his reply with phrases taken from Isaiah which link together the message and miracles of Jesus: 'The blind receive their sight, the lame walk, the lepers are cleansed, the deaf hear, the dead are raised, and the poor have good news brought to them' (Matt. 11: 4–5 = Luke 7: 22–3; cf. Luke 4: 16–18).

A beatitude not included in the Sermon on the Mount runs as follows in its original form: 'Happy are the eyes that see what you see, for I tell you that many prophets and kings longed to see what you see and did not see it, and to hear what you hear and did not hear it' (Matt. 13: 16–17 = Luke 10: 23–4). Jesus' contemporaries are in a specially privileged position, for they have heard the words and seen the actions which are in fulfilment of ancient hopes. Once again message and miracles are inextricably linked. And once again Jesus claims that his ministry is the fulfilment of Scripture's promises and hopes.

Enough has been said to confirm that there are very varied emphases in the kingdom of God sayings. They should not be squeezed into one mould. Both the future and the present (or nearness) sayings have good claims to authenticity, though their precise relationship to one another is unclear.

We turn now to discuss two kingdom sayings which are particularly important and interesting; in both cases, however, they are difficult to interpret.

The kingdom of God is among you:
Luke 17: 20–1

Once Jesus was asked by the Pharisees when the kingdom of God was coming, and he answered, 'The kingdom of God is not coming with things that can be observed; nor will they say, "Look, here it is!" or "There it is!" For, in fact, the kingdom of God is among you.'

This passage is found only in Luke's gospel. As there is no direct link with either the preceding or the following material, it is a detached saying. It is possible that Luke himself has included the reference to the Pharisees' question. The first saying about the kingdom raises few problems; 'things [or signs] that can be observed' refers to careful observation of premonitions or other indications that the future kingdom is near. Jesus refuses to speculate about the time or the place of the coming of the kingdom and thus parts company with apocalyptic prophets who set out timetables for the signs which would precede the end-time.

What did Jesus mean when he said that the kingdom was 'among you'? The traditional interpretation which was common in the early church is reflected in the translation used in the Authorized or King James Version (1611), and also the NIV (1978): the kingdom is 'within you'; it is referred to in a footnote in the NRSV as a possible alternative translation. On this view the kingdom is an inward power or reality 'within you', 'within your hearts'.

But Jesus can hardly have suggested to the Pharisees that the kingdom was within them. So the scholars who defend this interpretation have to assume that Luke has added the reference to the Pharisees rather awkwardly. Elsewhere in the gospels the kingdom is never 'in the hearts' of individuals, so this is unlikely to be the correct interpretation of this saying, even though it has been prominent in Christian thought over many centuries.

The NRSV (quoted above) reads 'among you'. The REB also translates 'the kingdom of God is among you' (though the notes suggest three other possibilities, including 'within your grasp'). On this view the kingdom is related to the things Jesus is saying and doing. If so, then this is a rare hint from Jesus that although the kingdom is God's, his own actions and words are 'signs' of its presence among men. The Greek phrase *entos humōn* may possibly mean 'among you', but we have very few examples of the phrase. But since there is a common phrase (*en mesō*) which could have been used to express 'among you', its absence here is puzzling if this was the intended meaning.

Several scholars have proposed a third possibility. The saying may mean 'the kingdom of God is within your reach', 'it can be shared in by you, if you want it'. Supporters of this interpretation appeal to several examples of the rare phrase *entos humōn* found in recently discovered papyri in everyday (i.e. non-literary) Greek from the first century. This interpretation makes excellent sense in the context: the Pharisees are invited by Jesus to participate in God's kingdom. But although this is an attractive solution, it is no more than a good possibility since the precise sense of the examples in the papyri is not clear!

Most exegetes and translators conclude that the second interpretation is the most likely but readily admit that certainty is not possible. This saying raises a further dilemma. One of the alternatives listed in the REB notes is, 'for suddenly the kingdom of God will be among you'. On this view, the kingdom is not present but future. Although this interpretation would allow Luke 17: 20–1 to be linked closely to the verses which follow in verses 22–37, 'suddenly' is not found in the Greek at all. Hence most scholars accept that although the precise sense of *entos humōn* must be left as an open question, the saying confirms that in some sense the kingdom is already a present reality.

The kingdom under attack? Matthew 11: 12–13 = Luke 16: 16

From the days of John the Baptist until now the kingdom of heaven has suffered violence, and the violent take it by force. For all the prophets and the law prophesied until John came. (Matthew)

The law and the prophets were in effect until John came; since then the good news of the kingdom of God is proclaimed, and everyone tries to enter it by force. (Luke)

This saying has teased scholars for a very long time. It raises immediately the relationship between Jesus and John the Baptist. In Chapter 10 we tried to underline the importance of this question for our understanding of Jesus. Luke's version of this saying seems to separate Jesus and John, as was the case generally in early Christianity: John belongs to the old order of law and prophets. Matthew's version, however, links John and Jesus closely together, and in this respect at least it is almost certainly the more original version of the saying.

Luke's version is the more straightforward. 'Everyone tries to enter the kingdom by force' must refer to the enthusiastic response to the preaching of the good news; the REB translates, 'everyone forces a way in'. The word 'everyone' may be something of an exaggeration; this part of the saying may be referring to the response of tax collectors and sinners, the poor, women, and others on the fringe of society who elbow their way into the kingdom ahead of the Pharisees and scribes. Or, alternatively, the correct translation may be 'everyone is pressed to enter the kingdom'; the saying would then refer to the urgent invitation of Jesus and would correspond to Luke 14: 23: 'Go out into the roads and lanes, and compel people to come in.'

Matthew's version of the saying bristles with difficulties. The NRSV translation we have quoted suggests that the appearance of John has sparked off opposition to God's kingdom which has persisted up to Jesus' day. Who are the violent people who are taking the kingdom by force? In Matthew the saying follows shortly after a reference to the imprisonment of John the Baptist (11: 2), so the evangelist may well envisage that Herod Antipas (who imprisoned John) is the leading man of violence who has taken the kingdom by force.

The Greek verb *biazetai*, which the NRSV translates as 'has suffered violence', is found elsewhere in the New Testament only in Luke 16: 16. It may be translated with an active sense: 'the kingdom has been forcing its way forward'. The related noun 'the violent' is then likely to have a 'good' sense: tax collectors and sinners storm the kingdom. If so, then the meaning of Matt. 11: 12–13 is similar to Luke 16: 16. Many scholars have supported this general approach—though with differences in details.

However, careful attention to other examples of the three key words in this saying ('has suffered violence', 'the violent', and 'take it by force') in Greek writings from this period has recently tipped the scales in favour of taking the whole saying in a 'bad' sense. 'The kingdom of God is being opposed with violence'. This is almost certainly the original sense intended by Jesus. If so, then we are in a world far removed from the 'gentle Jesus, meek and mild' of much popular Christian piety.

Whether the original Q version of Matt. 11: 12–13 has a 'good' or a 'bad' sense, it links Jesus and John closely together. Both interpretations imply that the kingdom is in some sense already present in the proclamation of Jesus.

What did Jesus mean?

At this point we must sum up this discussion of the 'kingdom' sayings. The primary intention of these sayings is to declare the reality and power of God's presence and the response this demands. It was as difficult to speak meaningfully about God in the first century as it is today. Hence it is not surprising to find that the sayings are very diverse: they may be seen as varied ways of speaking about the 'sphere' of God's kingly rule and power.

A careful comparison of the kingdom sayings in the gospels with references to the kingdom in Jewish writings which come from the first century does not enable us to speak confidently about ways in which the proclamation of Jesus about God's kingdom was unique. But such a comparison does lead to a significant conclusion: the extent and diversity of the kingdom sayings in the gospels is surprising. As far as we know (and our knowledge is certainly far from complete), no other first-century prophet or teacher spoke so frequently or in such diverse ways about God's kingdom.

As we have seen, a number of sayings of Jesus declare that the kingdom of God is now present in his own actions and proclamation. They are undoubtedly among the most striking sayings in the gospels, but if they are singled out for special attention the richness and diversity of all the kingdom sayings is missed. Since they are congenial to later Christian theology, which claims that in the life (and death and resurrection) of Jesus God intervened in a new way in human history, some scholars believe that they may have been 'shaped' or even created in the early church. But there are strong counter-arguments: many of them are so difficult to interpret with precision that they are unlikely to have been created in the early church; very few of them bear clear traces of later Christian thought. The two sayings we have discussed in some detail provide good illustrations of this important point.

How may we sum up Jesus' meaning? The following summary is not intended to be a definition of the phrase 'kingdom of God', but it does attempt to do justice to the diversity of the sayings and to the dominant nuances which are found in the Old Testament and in Jewish writings from the time of Jesus. *The kingdom of God is God's kingly rule, the time and place where God's power and will hold sway.* Jesus is primarily concerned with God's initiative. We do not need to decide whether the 'present' or the 'future' sense is dominant.

In the sayings of Jesus 'the kingdom of God' is above all a series of ways of speaking about the reality of God. Jewish thought rarely speculated on the 'nature' of God (as did Greek thought); to speak about God was to speak about his relationship to his people, and vice versa. In other words, 'the kingdom of God' always carried ethical implications. This is clearly implied in the sayings which refer to the individual's response—sayings which refer to entry into the kingdom, or to the kingdom as something to be possessed or sought after. Even in the sayings about the 'reality of God's presence' which stress God's initiative, human response is expected. Mark underlines this point in his summary verse in 1: 15: 'the kingdom of God is at hand, *repent* . . .'.

The kingdom is always *God's* kingdom. Later Christian thought often associated the kingdom with Jesus rather than with God. In the second century Marcion claimed that the kingdom of God was 'Christ himself'; in the third century Origen wrote similarly. But Jesus did not link himself explicitly with the kingdom. Only a very few sayings suggest this—and they almost certainly do not go back to Jesus himself. For example, Matt. 16: 28, which refers to the Son of man's kingdom, is Matthew's redaction of Mark's 'kingdom *of God*' (Mark 9: 1). (See also Luke 23: 42; John 18: 36.)

The kingdom of God is yours

To whom did Jesus proclaim his distinctive message about the power and presence of God? In the first of the beatitudes Jesus announces that the poor are blessed, 'for yours is the kingdom of God' (Matt. 5: 3 = Luke 6: 20 (Q)). The word translated 'blessed' has rich connotations: it means 'God's favour now rests upon . . .'. But who are the poor to whom Jesus declares God's favour or blessing? Matthew modifies the first beatitude to 'blessed are the poor in spirit'; the words are now addressed to the spiritually poor—those who are poor before God. Luke has in mind those who live in poverty (this is confirmed by the woe addressed in 6: 24 to those who are rich and Luke's emphasis elsewhere on those who are literally poor). So Luke and Matthew have rather different understandings of 'the poor'.

How did Jesus use the term? In Matt. 11: 5–6 = Luke 7: 22–3 'the poor' have good news preached to them—and this causes offence. Who took offence at Jesus and on what grounds? There are several passages in the gospels which record criticism levelled at Jesus. In a Q saying Jesus refers to the taunt thrown at him by his unspecified opponents: 'Look, a glutton and a drunkard, a friend of tax collectors and sinners!' (Matt. 11: 19 = Luke 7: 34). Mark 2: 16–17 records the critical questioning of the scribes of the Pharisees: 'Why does Jesus eat with tax collectors and sinners?' In Luke 7: 36–50 we read that Jesus accepted the devotion and faith of 'a woman of the city who was a sinner' (v. 37); this also led to critical comment from a Pharisee (v. 39). Luke 15: 1–2 (which in its present form comes from the evangelist himself) also refers to the complaints Pharisees and scribes levelled against Jesus as a result of his table fellowship with tax collectors and sinners.

Jesus' acceptance of tax collectors and sinners is well attested: the examples just cited come from three strands of the gospel traditions: Q, Mark, and 'L' (Luke's special traditions), as well as from Luke the evangelist. A specific link between Jesus' proclamation of the kingdom and his acceptance of tax collectors and sinners is made in Matt. 21: 31: 'Truly I tell you, the tax collectors and the prostitutes are going into the kingdom of God ahead of you.' Hence we may be confident that 'the poor' to whom the kingdom is promised include the tax collectors and sinners. In extending table fellowship to tax collectors and sinners Jesus acted out his proclamation of the kingly rule of God; this is an example of a prophetic action referred to in Chapter 11.

Sharing a meal with a friend today is often no more than a convenient way of consuming food. In the Graeco-Roman and Jewish worlds of the first century, however, eating food with another person was far more significant socially: it indicated that the invited person was being accepted into a relationship in which the bonds were as close as in family relationships. One normally invited to meals only people whom one considered social and religious equals.

Some of the first-century conventions associated with table fellowship are sketched vividly in Luke 14: 7–14. This passage concludes with a surprising reversal of the customary expectations of reciprocity in hospitality: 'But when you give a banquet, invite the poor, the crippled, the lame, and the blind. And you will be blessed, because they cannot repay you, for you will be repaid at the resurrection of the righteous.' Followers of Jesus are urged to do exactly what he himself did: to extend table fellowship to those whom most would shun.

'Why does Jesus eat with tax collectors and sinners?' (Mark 2: 16). This criticism is levelled at Jesus by the scribes of the Pharisees when they see whom Jesus has invited to share meals with him. In his reply Jesus insists that he has not come to invite to table fellowship those who consider themselves to be law-abiding ('righteous') but 'sinners' (Mark 2: 17). In an independent tradition, Luke records similar indignant criticism (15: 1–2) and links to it the reply of Jesus in the form of the parables of the lost sheep, the lost coin, and the prodigal son (15: 3–32).

The Q tradition in which Jesus himself quotes a jibe thrown at him is even more important: 'Look, a glutton and a drunkard, a friend of tax collectors and sinners!' (Matt. 11: 18–19 = Luke 7: 34). Jesus accepts the legitimacy of this accusation, so his actions are quite deliberate. The accusation is the finale of a lengthy set of sayings of Jesus (Matt. 11: 2–19 = Luke 7: 18–35; 16: 16) in which one of the central issues is the coming of God's kingly rule. When the jibe is read in context it becomes clear that the opponents of Jesus failed to see that his table fellowship with tax collectors and sinners was an implication of the coming of the kingdom.

Who were the tax collectors and sinners? The tax collectors in Galilee were despised not because they were colluding directly with the Romans (though that would have been the case in Judaea), but because in their abuse of a long-standing system of collecting tolls and duties they were blatantly dishonest. Strictly speaking they were toll collectors or tax farmers; they were not collecting direct taxes. As E. P. Sanders (1985) has stressed, the 'sinners' were not simply apathetic about religious observance, they were those who intentionally ignored God's commandments. So Jesus insisted on accepting openly in intimate table fellowship those who were notorious for their dishonesty or their high-handed rejection of the law.

Those who were physically disabled, lepers, and those possessed by demons were also considered to be on the fringe of society. In some circles they were shunned because they were considered to be ritually impure. Numerous traditions in the gospels confirm that Jesus took a special interest in such socially and religiously marginalized people. We shall return to the miracle traditions in the next chapter, but for the moment we may note that those who were sick in body or mind are closely related to 'the poor', and to the tax collectors and sinners. To them all, both by actions and by proclamation, Jesus declared, 'the kingly rule of God is yours'.

13

PARABLES AND APHORISMS

The parables are one of the most distinctive features of the teaching of Jesus. The synoptic evangelists all record that Jesus used parables extensively. Mark claims (no doubt with some exaggeration) that Jesus did not speak to the crowds without a parable (4: 34). Mark includes six parables, Matthew twenty-one, and Luke twenty-nine; nine parables can be traced to Q, nine to the special traditions found only in Matthew ('M'), and eighteen to Luke's special traditions ('L'). In each gospel *some* of the parables are linked explicitly to Jesus' proclamation of the kingdom of God.

While parables were not unknown in the Graeco-Roman world, they were not usually part of the stock in trade of religious teachers or philosophers, and most of them were fables or allegories. Aesop's fables were well-known, but they are very different from the parables of Jesus.

In the Old Testament there are only five extended (or 'narrative') parables, so it hardly offers a strong precedent for Jesus' use of parables. Unlike any of the parables in the gospels, three of them are fables in which plants or animals act and speak like human beings (Judges 9: 7–15; 2 Kings 14: 8–10; Ezek. 17: 1–10). Only Nathan's parable of the poor man and his lamb (2 Sam. 12: 1–10) is usually accepted as a close parallel to the parables of Jesus.

While other first-century Jewish prophet-teachers did use parables, very few have survived which are even broadly comparable with those in the gospels. Although there are a number of parables in later rabbinic writings, no more than a handful are said to have been told by any one rabbi. In most cases the parables of later Jewish teachers were used to illustrate or expound Scripture. While the parables of Jesus do contain some Scriptural images, very few are exegetical. It would be rash to claim that the parables of Jesus are unique, but in his extensive use of them Jesus was not following the conventions of the day.

What is a parable? In the gospels the Greek word *parabolē* (which is usually translated 'parable') is used in a wide variety of ways. In Luke 4: 23 just three words are said to be a *parabolē*: 'Physician, heal yourself.' This is obviously a proverb, as is the *parabolē* in Luke 6: 39: 'Can a blind man lead a blind man? Will they not both fall into a pit?' In Mark 7: 17 *parabolē* refers to a riddle; in Luke 14: 7 it refers to some general advice about proper behaviour at a feast. This wide range of meanings for *parabolē* can be attributed to its use in the Greek translation of the Old Testament (LXX) for the Hebrew word *māshal,* which means 'maxim' or 'aphorism' (especially in Proverbs), 'proverb', 'parable', 'riddle', and 'allegory'.

In this chapter we shall focus first of all on the 'parables proper' in the gospels. They are comparisons which use storytelling techniques and details drawn from everyday life in order to present religious truth in a way which attracts the attention of the listener or reader by its vividness or strangeness, and thus provokes further reflection and appropriate action. As we shall see in a moment, there are different kinds of 'parables proper' in the gospels. In the latter part of the chapter we shall turn to the aphorisms of Jesus (i.e. his short pithy sayings); they are closely related to the 'parables proper' and have been prominent in some recent reconstructions of the historical Jesus.

The evangelists and the parables

As in the other chapters in Part II of this book, we shall start by considering the evangelists' own understanding of the parables before we discuss Jesus' use. In the course of their transmission in the early church and their use by the evangelists, the parables have undergone more extensive adaptation and reinterpretation than any other part of the traditions about the actions and teaching of Jesus. The reasons for this are easy to understand. A parable is an extended metaphor or comparison. A metaphor such as 'John is a lion' can be understood in different ways: it may mean that John is strong, or that he is tenacious or even ruthless, or, perhaps, that he has an enormous appetite. The metaphor's meaning is determined by the context in which it is used. So too with the parables.

For example, what is meant when the disciples are said to be 'the salt of the earth' in Matt. 5: 13? In the first century salt was used in a variety of ways—as a preservative, as a purifying agent, as seasoning, and even as a fertilizer. Clearly 'you are the salt of the earth' is a very open comparison which can be applied to followers of Jesus in several ways. Context is all-important.

The evangelists have frequently reinterpreted the parables by placing them in the contexts in which they are now found in the gospels. As we saw on pp. 167–8, the parable of the lost sheep is set in different contexts and interpreted in quite different ways by Matthew and Luke.

The evangelists have also added 'endings' or applications to many of the parables. The first two parables in Luke's trilogy in chapter 15 end with a similar refrain: 'Just so, I tell you, there will be more joy in heaven over one sinner who repents than over ninety-nine righteous persons who need no repentance' (15: 7; cf. v. 10). The third parable in this group, the parable of the prodigal son, has a double 'rounding-off' refrain: 'for this son of mine was dead, and is alive again; he was lost, and is found!' (15: 23; cf. v. 32) Luke himself may well have added these four refrains to bring out what he took to be the meaning of these parables.

Similarly, Matthew has added a refrain to the parable of the lost sheep with many of his own distinctive turns of phrase: 'So it is not the will of your Father in heaven that one of these little ones should be lost' (18: 14). For further examples of endings to parables which make their meaning explicit, see Matt. 18: 35; 20: 16; 21: 31–2; 21: 43; 22: 14; 24: 44; 25: 13; Luke 12: 40; 12: 59; 14: 11; 14: 24; 18: 14b. Some of the endings may have been supplied by the evangelists, some added at an earlier stage, and some may have belonged to the parable in its earliest form; unless the same parable is found in another gospel with different wording, it is not always easy to be sure at what point an ending has been added.

The evangelists have often also provided introductions and set individual parables in groups. In chapter 13 Matthew has expanded considerably Mark's chapter of parables (ch. 4) with four further parables. In this chapter Matthew includes no fewer than six pithy parables, all of which open with the phrase, 'the kingdom of heaven is like . . .'. The kingdom is compared to a mustard seed, yeast, hidden treasure, a merchant in search of fine pearls, a net thrown into the sea, a master who brings out of his treasure what is new and what is old (Matt. 13: 31–3, 44–7, 52). Matthew has grouped together three parables in 21: 28–32; 33–43, and 22: 1–14; the parables partly interpret one another.

Although it is often difficult to determine the extent to which Mark has reshaped and developed the earlier traditions on which he draws, he himself is largely responsible for the collection of parables in chapter 4. In Mark 4: 2 the evangelist has added the introduction to the trilogy of parables he has included in this chapter: 'And Jesus began to teach them many things in parables, and in his teaching he said to them: "Listen! A sower went out to sow . . ." '. Mark himself is probably responsible for the extended allegorical explanation of the parable of the sower in vv. 13–20; in v. 17 a reference to the 'persecution which arises on account of the word' anticipates a theme Mark develops later in his gospel (e.g. 8: 34–5; 13: 9–13).

Mark's own hand can be detected at other points in this chapter. In vv. 10–12 and 33–4 he has added explanations of the parables and of their purpose. In v. 33 he refers to the parables as 'the word' spoken by Jesus to the crowds. The evangelist Mark has in mind his own summary of the proclamation of Jesus in 1: 14–15: 'the word' is 'the gospel of God', i.e. 'the kingdom of God is at hand'. In the explanation of the parable of the sower, 'the word' is used several times to refer to the seed sown by the sower as the proclamation of Jesus, and (especially in v. 17) to the Christian gospel on account of which the post-Easter church faced persecution.

In his conclusion to the trilogy of parables (4: 34), Mark emphasizes that Jesus explained the parables privately to his disciples. So for Mark at least, the parables of Jesus are anything but simple and clear. In v. 10 some of the crowds who heard the parables ('those who were about him') and the disciples come to Jesus for further information. They are told that 'the secret of the kingdom of God' has been given to them. Mark seems to imply that this group does have at least a partial understanding of who Jesus is. This puzzling comment follows: 'But for those outside everything comes in parables; in order that "they may indeed look, but not perceive, and may indeed listen, but not understand; so that they may not turn again, and be forgiven"' (Mark 4: 10–12).

'Those outside' is a strong term which refers to a group in sharp contrast to the crowd and the disciples who respond positively, i.e. opponents of Jesus. In 12: 12 the opponents of Jesus do 'see' the parable of the wicked husbandman at one level, but they do not 'understand' in the sense of ending their opposition to Jesus; they remain 'blind'. This seems to be the point Mark is making in 4: 10–12 with its reference to Isa. 6: 9–10. The parables are 'heard' by opponents of Jesus but 'not understood'.

Mark makes it clear later in the same chapter that the parables were not intended to provide insight for insiders and to confirm blindness to outsiders: 'for there is nothing hidden except to be disclosed; nor is anything secret, except to come to light' (Mark 4: 22). The ultimate purpose of the parables is not to hide, but to reveal. 'Is a lamp brought in to be put under the bushel basket, or under the bed, and not on the lampstand?' (Mark 4: 21; cf. also 4: 33)

Parables are conspicuous by their absence from John's gospel. The word *parabolē* is not found at all, but the synonymous word *paroimia* is used in two passages; 10: 6 and 16: 25, 29. The former refers to the preceding verses about the shepherd, the thief, and the doorkeeper which are explained by Jesus in vv. 7–21: 'I am the door of the sheepfold . . . I am the good shepherd.' Several scholars have suggested plausibly that in 10: 1–5 two parables have been fused together.

In John 16: 25, 29 Jesus says that the hour is coming when he will no longer speak to the disciples in 'figures of speech'. Just a few verses earlier (16: 21) the evangelist has included the aphorism or maxim of the woman in childbirth which is not unlike Luke 11: 21–2 and Mark 4: 26–9. There are many passages in John which are 'parabolic' in a broad sense, and still more which are symbolic. But there is hardly a trace of parables comparable with narrative parables in the synoptic gospels such as the sower (Mark 4: 3–9) or the lost sheep (Luke 15: 3–7).

Similitudes, narrative parables, and allegories

At this point we must differentiate between three kinds of 'parables proper' (i.e. not aphorisms) in the gospels. The term 'similitude' is used to refer to an extended comparison which refers to a familiar everyday scene. Many are in the form of a simile: John fought *like* a lion; 'The kingdom of God is like a mustard seed' (Mark 4: 31); 'the kingdom of heaven is like a treasure hidden in a field, which a man found and covered up; then in his joy he goes and sells all that he has and buys that field' (Matt. 13: 44); 'the kingdom of heaven is like a merchant in search of fine pearls, who on finding one pearl of great value, went and sold all that he had and bought it' (Matt. 13: 45). In each case the similitude gives instruction about or illustrates an aspect of the kingdom.

A narrative parable does not have an introductory formula such as 'the kingdom is like'; it is not a simile. Like a metaphor ('John *is* a lion') it offers a direct comparison. Its narrative form distinguishes it from a metaphor. A narrative parable goes straight to the point and narrates something which happened just once. 'Listen! A sower went out to sow. And as he sowed, some seed fell on the path, and the birds came and ate it up . . .' (Mark 4: 3–4). 'Which one of you, having a hundred sheep, and losing one of them, does not leave the ninety-nine in the wilderness, and go after the one that is lost until he finds it?' (Luke 15: 4). 'There was a rich man who had a manager . . .' (Luke 16: 1). These parables are not giving instruction about the kingdom; they are teasing the listener or reader into reflection. Why is such a story being told at this point? What is going on in this story?

In some ways narrative parables are like poetry. They communicate in unexpected ways and often at a deeper level than prose. Narrative parables may also be likened to a good political cartoon. At first sight a slightly curious and unexpected picture and caption catch one's attention, but then one is forced to respond. Is it really so? Perhaps my views need to be reconsidered. So with the parables of Jesus. There is an element of surprise which forces one to think again about God and his will for humankind. As we shall see, narrative parables are generally considered to be the most distinctive form of parabolic teaching used by Jesus.

In an allegory, on the other hand, each detail in the narrative has a significance of its own. Matt. 13: 36–43 provides a good example. Here the significance of each detail of the parable of the tares (13: 24–30) is explained:

> The one who sows the good seed is the Son of Man;
> the field is the world,
> and the good seed are the children of the kingdom;
> the weeds are the children of the evil one;
> and the enemy who sowed them is the devil;
> the harvest is the end of the age,
> and the reapers are angels.   (13: 37–39)

In its present form the parable of the vineyard in Mark 12: 1–12 is an allegory. The careful reader of Mark's gospel eventually realizes that the vineyard stands for Israel. The servants who are sent to the tenants but are rejected are the Old Testament prophets; the 'beloved son' who is finally sent to the tenants is Jesus, but he too is killed and cast out of the vineyard. In order to understand this parable one needs to know Mark's full story of Jesus. An allegory communicates to the reader what is already known—though it does this in story form and in symbolic fashion. In contrast, the parables encourage the listener or reader to consider new possibilities.

Since the gospels themselves contain allegories which set out the Christian message in vivid story form, it was not surprising that the early church assumed that most of the parables in the gospels were allegories. At the end of the second century Tertullian interpreted the parable of the prodigal son (Luke 15: 11–32) allegorically. The father represents God; the younger son represents the Christian; the elder son is the Jew who is envious of the divine offer of salvation to Gentiles; the citizens in the far country represent the devil; the pigs whom the prodigal feeds are the demons; the ring given to the prodigal on his return represents Christian baptism; the feast is, of course, the Eucharist; and the fatted calf killed for the feast represents Christ present at the Eucharist.

In the early church the parable of the Good Samaritan (Luke 10: 29–37) was interpreted allegorically in a wide variety of ways. Towards the end of the second century Irenaeus set out a limited allegorical interpretation. Early in the third century Clement of Alexandria developed this approach further. By the time Augustine wrote about two centuries later elaborate allegorical explanations had become customary. The man who goes down from Jerusalem (paradise) to Jericho (the world) is Adam or everyman. The priest and the Levite who pass by unconcerned are the Old Testament law and prophets. The Good Samaritan is, of course, Christ, and the inn is the church. The two pence paid to the innkeeper (Peter or Paul) gave plenty of scope to keen imaginations. Some interpreters claimed that they stood for the sacraments of baptism and eucharist, others the Old and New Testaments, or love of God and love of neighbour; still others claimed that the two pence referred to reward in this life and the next (Matt. 19: 29), the preaching of the law and the gospel, or knowledge of the Father and the Son.

Once one begins to use allegorical interpretation imaginatively, the possibilities are almost endless. The varied interpretations just noted all presuppose an acquaintance with the main lines of Christian teaching. Often by means of vivid and lively stories, allegories confirm *what the reader or listener already knows*. The various details of the parables are like a set of pegs on which favourite doctrines are hung. Allegorical interpretation presupposes that the parables are for insiders who have the 'key' to their meaning; for outsiders they are meaningless tales.

In the sixteenth century Luther protested against arbitrary allegorical interpretation of the parables, but he did not always practise what he preached. Calvin was more consistent. 'How silly it is to want to interpret each detail in the parables', he wrote. In his comments on the parable of the Good Samaritan, he rejected several allegorical interpretations as implausible and then noted that 'we ought to have a deeper reverence for Scripture than to reckon ourselves at liberty to disguise its natural meaning.' But Calvin's approach did not win the day. Until the end of the nineteenth century, almost without exception the parables were considered to have a 'hidden', 'deeper', or 'spiritual' meaning and were therefore interpreted allegorically.

Modern interpretation of the parables

In two large volumes published in 1888 and 1889 (but never translated from German into English) Adolf Jülicher mounted a full-scale attack on allegorical interpretation of the parables. He insisted that the parables of Jesus were not allegories in which every single item had an esoteric meaning. Each parable was intended to make only *one* point; this single point was almost invariably a general ethical or religious principle. The parable of the talents (Matt. 25: 14–30 = Luke 19: 12–27) encourages us to be faithful with all that God has entrusted to us. The prodigal son (Luke 15: 11–32) teaches thriftiness.

C. H. Dodd accepted that there could be no return to allegorical interpretation. In his influential book *Parables of the Kingdom* (1935) Dodd insisted that the parables must be understood in terms of the proclamation of Jesus that the kingdom had come with his teaching and actions. Partly under the influence of form criticism, Dodd claimed that the parables must be interpreted in the light of their setting in the life of Jesus: some were a general challenge to his hearers in view of the coming of the kingdom; some were concerned with the relationship of disciples to the kingdom, while others were expressions of the presence of the kingdom as 'unprecedented concern for the "lost"'. While it is now generally recognized that it is not possible to relate parables to an original specific setting in the life of Jesus, Dodd's further point about the way parables make their impact has been widely accepted. He claimed that parables arrest the hearer by their vividness or strangeness; they 'tease the mind into active thought'.

In 1947 Joachim Jeremias published the first edition of a major study of the parables. He modified Dodd's 'realized eschatology', insisting that for Jesus the kingdom of God was in the process of realization. Like Dodd, he attempted to link the parables to specific settings in the life of Jesus; in particular, he claimed that Jesus used parables as 'weapons of warfare' in response to the criticisms of opponents. Perhaps his most important contribution, however, was in two other areas. Jeremias had a wide knowledge of the cultural life of first-century Palestine, to which he linked the parables closely. He set out fully the ways the parables were modified in the course of their transmission. Parables which originally belonged to quite specific settings in the life of Jesus were adapted by the early church and by the evangelists in order to make them relevant for new circumstances in very different cultural settings outside Palestine. (Some examples were noted above on pp. 219–22.) For Jeremias, as for Dodd, the parables were an integral part of Jesus' proclamation of the kingdom of God.

In recent years discussion of the parables has been dominated by the work of several American scholars. Dan Otto Via (1967) was the first to reject Jeremias's severely historical approach, insisting that if parables are tied closely to specific settings in the life of Jesus there is a danger that they will be left in the past and fail to speak to us today. The parables are not just illustrations of ideas, they are literary works of art. Via analysed the plot movements within the parables, distinguishing between tragic and comic parables. In the former, people in dramatic encounters and conflicts move downward towards catastrophe, as, for example, in the ten maidens (Matt. 25: 1–13) and the wicked tenants (Mark 12: 1–9). In comic parables people move upwards towards well-being, as in the workers in the vineyard (Matt. 20: 1–16) and the prodigal son (Luke 15: 11–32). Via's emphasis on the literary and 'timeless' character of the parables was echoed by a number of writers, though his own interpretations of them tended to be rather vague and bland.

J. D. Crossan (1973) also used literary criticism in his stimulating discussion of the parables. In particular he stressed their poetic character. Unlike Via, he took their context in the life of Jesus seriously. Jesus 'was not crucified for parables but for ways of acting which resulted from the experience of God presented in the parables'. So although the parables are not illustrations of the teaching of Jesus on the kingdom, like the kingdom sayings they express Jesus' convictions about the reality of God. Crossan selected three key parables which were then used to interpret all the others: the hidden treasure (Matt. 13: 44), the pearl of great price (Matt. 13: 45), and the great fish (found only in the Gospel of Thomas, logion 8). On the basis of these key parables three categories were distinguished: parables of advent (which open up new possibilities), parables which speak of the reversal of man's past, and parables of action (which are expressions of the new world). Although this analysis is illuminating, the selection of three key parables was arbitrary.

Similar literary approaches have become popular in the last two decades or so. The metaphorical character of the narrative parables has been stressed strongly by several writers. They insist that the parables are not to be read as illustrations of religious truths. The parables are not merely about the kingdom of God, they possess a vitality and power in and of themselves: they convey something of the reality of the kingdom of God. The parables are not to be interpreted by their hearers, rather the hearers are to be interpreted by them.

There has also been renewed discussion of the allegorical features of the parables, of the allegorical explanations attached to some of them, and of Jülicher's claim that each parable makes only one point. Several writers have noted that parables in the Old Testament, Jewish apocalyptic writings, and rabbinic texts often include allegorical explanations. So why should Jesus not have interpreted his own parables in this way? No longer are all traces of allegory set aside as early church accretions which destroy the simplicity and power of the original allegory-free, 'single point' parables of Jesus. But how can one accept the value of allegory as a method of communication and yet avoid the arbitrary interpretations of many of the church fathers? This is an unresolved question.

Several writers have stressed the very close relationship between many of the parables and their present contexts in the gospels and have argued that they stem solely or largely from the evangelists' own hands. For example, in her literary study of the role of the parable of the sower in Mark's gospel, Mary Ann Tolbert (1989, p. 306–7) shows how closely this parable is related to Mark's overall storyline. However, she doubts whether more sophisticated forms of analysis will enable us to recover *any* pre-Marcan form of the parable of the sower; she doubts whether recovery of the original version of the parable told by Jesus will be possible. Not surprisingly, she also doubts whether a renewed quest for the historical Jesus will be successful. Here there are many questions to be asked.

How open-ended are the parables? May they be understood quite differently by every individual who hears them? By stressing their 'timeless' character, some recent interpreters have replaced arbitrary allegorical interpretation with an overemphasis on the individual's self-understanding as the key to interpretation.

The parables continue to fascinate. Their riddle-like qualities continue to tease. However, there is no clear consensus concerning appropriate methods or starting points for their interpretation. Indeed there seems to be a widening gap between those who want to recover their original setting in the Galilean ministry of Jesus, and those who underline their timeless, universal qualities and their close relationship to the aphorisms we shall discuss in a moment.

This gap must be bridged, in spite its width. Interpretation of the parables must take their first-century setting and their context in the gospels seriously, but it must not stop there. The parables were told by a prophet–teacher whose primary concern was the kingdom of God. The parables may be seen as one of the varied ways Jesus spoke about the 'sphere' of God's kingly rule and power. Jesus used an indirect and subtle method of communication which may well have been more effective than direct, dogmatic statements. For those who have ears to hear, the parables still convey something of the reality of God's kingly rule.

Aphorisms

There are far more aphorisms than parables in the gospels—over one hundred on most definitions of an aphorism. Aphorisms are pithy, arresting sayings which are complete in themselves. Unlike metaphors, they do not require a specific narrative context in order to make an impact. Aphorisms express vividly truths which are general to the experience of humankind; they have a 'timeless', universal quality—rather like the parables on some interpretations.

There are collections of aphoristic sayings in Proverbs, Ecclesiastes, and Ben Sirach, as well as in other Jewish writings. The aphorisms of the gospels belong to this 'wisdom' tradition. While some are (or may be) related to Jesus' proclamation of the kingdom, most are not. So this important strand of the teaching of Jesus reminds us that he was a wisdom teacher who had much in common with Jewish teachers of his time.

'The tree is known by its fruit' (Matt. 12: 33b). 'The labourer is worthy of his hire' (Matt. 10: 10b). 'When a woman is in labour, she has pain, because her hour has come. But when her child is born, she no longer remembers the anguish because of the joy of having brought a human being into the world' (John 16: 21). In all these examples an aphorism as a general truth makes a powerful point in its present context, but it could also make good sense in a very different context.

Several aphorisms are in the form of admonitions. For example, 'Do not store up for yourselves treasures on earth, where moth and rust consume and where thieves break in and steal; but store up for yourselves treasures in heaven, where neither moth nor rust consumes and where thieves do not break in and steal. For where your treasure is, there your heart will be also' (Matt. 6: 19–21 = Luke 12: 33b–34). 'Enter through the narrow gate; for the gate is wide and the road is easy that leads to destruction, and there are many who take it. For the gate is narrow and the road is hard that leads to life; and there are few who find it' (Matt. 7: 13–14 = Luke 13: 23–4; cf. also Matt. 5: 25–6 = Luke 12: 58–9).

Parables and aphorisms are closely related, not twins, but certainly siblings. As we noted above, the same Hebrew word (*māshal*) and the same Greek word (*parabolē*) are used for both. Aphorisms and parables both invite reflection and may even stimulate fresh lines of thought. As a method of communication they are less direct than straightforward statements, but they may often be more effective.

If Jesus' proclamation of the kingdom (and several other features of his ministry) indicate that he was an eschatological prophet, his aphorisms and many of his parables suggest that he was a wisdom teacher. Is one portrait more authentic than the other?

In his response to the request of some of the scribes and Pharisees for a sign, Jesus made an important implicit claim about himself, 'something greater than [the prophet] Jonah is here' and also 'something greater than [the wisdom teacher] Solomon is here' (Matt. 12: 38–42 = 11: 16, 29–32). So Jesus himself seems to have had no difficulty in juxtaposing 'prophet' and 'wisdom teacher'.

Several North American scholars, most of whom are members of the Jesus Seminar led by R. W. Funk, have recently argued that Jesus should be seen primarily as a wisdom teacher; J. D. Crossan (1991) has taken a further step and has claimed that Jesus was a Jewish Cynic. Cynicism arose among loosely organized groups of wandering philosophers in the fourth century BC; there was a revival about the time of Jesus.

The scholars who advocate this general approach note that some of the parables and aphorisms of Jesus are non-eschatological, i.e. they are not related at all to proclamation of the coming kingly rule of God. One can hardly object to this first step in the argument, though the claim that *only* these sayings are authentic to Jesus is unconvincing.

The next steps are quite implausible. The attempt to isolate a first and therefore primary non-eschatological layer of the traditions shared by Matthew and Luke (Q) is largely a case of finding what one is looking for. The appeal to the Gospel of Thomas as support for a wisdom portrait of the historical Jesus is even less plausible. In its present form Thomas is a fourth-century Gnostic collection in Coptic of 114 sayings of Jesus. Some of its traditions may be independent of the synoptic gospels, but it is also clear that many sayings are dependent on the synoptic gospels. In short, reconstruction of an early non-Gnostic Greek version of Thomas is hazardous, to say the least. (For further discussion of Thomas, see above pp. 123–30.)

There are some similarities between Jesus and the Cynics of his day: both moved from place to place conveying wisdom teaching, some of which was socially subversive. However, it is important to note that the first-century Cynics were very diverse in their teachings and behaviour, so parallels with Jesus become less impressive. There are in fact at least as many differences as similarities. While there were some Cynics in Galilee, there is no evidence that Jesus had direct contact with them. The Cynics were not noted for healings and exorcisms; as we shall see in the next chapter, miracles were a central part of the ministry of Jesus.

Those who portray Jesus primarily or solely as a wisdom teacher or Jewish Cynic have built dubious hypothesis upon dubious hypothesis.

Why? One cannot help observing that once again history is repeating itself: as has often happened in historical Jesus research, the reconstructed portrait of Jesus bears an uncanny resemblance to the researcher. A portrait of Jesus as a teacher of timeless aphorisms may be congenial to some today, but it does not do justice to the many-sided evidence we have for the actions, teaching, and intention of Jesus.

14

MIRACLES AND EXORCISMS

In the preceding chapters we saw that Jesus was both a prophet who called for a response to the coming kingly rule of God, and a wisdom teacher. Was Jesus also a healer and an exorcist? There are eighteen traditions in Mark which portray Jesus as a miracle-worker or exorcist. Most of these are retained by Matthew and Luke, who add two Q and several 'M' and 'L' traditions. In all, there are seventeen accounts of healings in the gospels, including three of revivification; there are six accounts of exorcisms. Eight further traditions are usually referred to as 'nature miracles'. These numbers do not include parallel passages or the many references to miracles in the evangelists' summary passages. The bald statistics confirm the prominence of miracles in the gospels.

As usual, we shall start with the gospels as we now have them. We shall consider the evangelists' use of miracle traditions before we ask whether Jesus performed miracles, and if so, why.

The evangelists and the miracle traditions

In later centuries Christian writers often pointed to the miracles of Jesus as 'proof' that he was the Son of God. So we might have expected the evangelists to have made rather more of the miracle traditions than in fact they do. On the whole the evangelists have not heightened the miraculous element found in the traditions they used. With the exception of the fourth evangelist, they have not developed full-scale theological explanations of the miracle stories. In comparison with many miracle stories found in ancient writings (and in writings from the early church), the evangelists have exercised notable restraint. For example, in the Infancy Gospel of Thomas which dates from the middle of the second century, the precocious child

Jesus is able to make birds out of mud and to reassemble instantly Mary's shattered water pitcher. There are many more similar tales in this apocryphal gospel.

Mark's opening accounts of the healings of Jesus are narrated and commented on in quite varied ways. In 1: 21–8 (and in many other passages) Mark links closely the teaching and the healing activity of Jesus: both are said to have been 'with authority'. The healing of Simon's mother-in-law is left devoid of any comment at all (1: 30–1). Confronted by a 'leper' with some kind of skin disease, Jesus is 'moved with anger' by the evidence of the disfigurement caused by Satan (1: 40–5). (The phrase 'moved with compassion' is found in many ancient manuscripts and in some modern translations, but this reading stems from embarrassment at a reference to the anger of Jesus found in a few manuscripts. In this case, as in many others, the 'more difficult', 'more embarrassing' reading is preferable, even though it is attested in only a few manuscripts.)

In Mark's account of the healing of the paralytic (2: 1–12) the authority of Jesus to forgive sins is given priority over his ability to heal. This passage is also notable for its emphasis on the faith of those who lowered the paralytic through the roof. A number of other miracle stories (but by no means all) refer to the faith of those whom Jesus healed. Faith is also mentioned in many pagan accounts of healings. However, in contrast to the synoptic gospels, where the individual's faith in God elicits the response of Jesus, in Graeco-Roman writings the miraculous events lead to faith.

Matthew retains Mark's varied ways of presenting miracle stories. In 8: 17 he expands Mark's first summary of the healings of Jesus with one of his 'formula' quotations of Scripture in order to underline their significance: 'This was to fulfil what was spoken through the prophet Isaiah, "He took our infirmities and bore our diseases."' In his account of the mission of the disciples, Matthew takes pains to stress that the disciples are given authority to perform exactly the same kind of miracles as Jesus (cf. 10: 8 with the miracle stories in chapters 8 and 9). Matthew also links explicitly the disciples' authority to heal with their proclamation of the kingdom of heaven (10: 7–8).

As we saw in Chapter 11, Luke emphasizes the prophetic role of Jesus. In the Old Testament miracles are associated with prophets such as Moses, Elijah, and Elisha. In a first-century collection of legends about the prophets, Jeremiah, Ezekiel, and Zechariah are described as miracle-workers. At the time of Jesus expectation of various types of prophets of the end-times was widespread; they were expected to be miracle-workers, like the prophets of old. So it comes as no surprise to find that Luke links (in part) the miracles of Jesus to his portrait of Jesus as a prophet. (This is done already, but less clearly, in Mark 6: 14–15.) This link is implied in the opening of Luke's account of the ministry of Jesus where Jesus aligns himself with Elijah and Elisha and their miracles (4: 23–7). Luke models his account of the raising of the widow's son at Nain on the account of the raising of the son of the widow of Zarephath by Elijah in 1 Kings 17: 8–24; in response to the miracle the crowd says, 'A great *prophet* has arisen among us! God has visited his people' (Luke 7: 16). On the road to Emmaus, Cleopas and his companion refer to Jesus as a 'prophet mighty in deed and word before God and the people' (Luke 24: 19).

A much more developed theological interpretation of the miracles is found in John's gospel. Only a small number of miracles are selected (cf. 20: 30); for no obvious reason there are no accounts of exorcisms or of healings of lepers. At the end of the first miracle story, the turning of water into wine, the evangelist comments, 'This, the first of his signs, Jesus did at Cana in Galilee, and manifested his glory; and his disciples believed in him' (2: 11). The miracle not only leads to faith, it 'manifests the glory of Jesus', i.e. it establishes Jesus' relationship to God.

At the end of the account of the healing of the royal official's son in Capernaum, the evangelist John comments: 'Now this was the second sign that Jesus did after coming from Judaea to Galilee' (4: 46–54). The healings which follow are not numbered in this way, but most of them introduce profound expositions of the significance of Jesus. The evangelist concludes the main body of the gospel with a comment addressed directly to the reader. This book (i.e. John's gospel) has recorded the signs which Jesus did 'so that you may come to believe that Jesus is the Messiah, the Son of God, and that through believing you may have life in his name' (20: 30). But even in the fourth gospel the signs of Jesus do not suffice if God does not give men and women eyes to see (12: 37–43).

Did Jesus perform miracles?

In antiquity miracles were not accepted without question. Graeco-Roman writers were often reluctant to ascribe miraculous events to the gods, and offered alternative explanations. Some writers were openly sceptical about miracles (e.g. Epicurus; Lucretius; Lucian). So it is a mistake to write off the miracles of Jesus as the result of the naivety and gullibility of people in the ancient world.

In Jesus' own lifetime follower and foe alike accepted that Jesus had unusual healing powers. The question was not, 'Did Jesus perform miracles?' for that was taken for granted. What was in dispute was on whose authority and with whose power Jesus performed unusual deeds. Were the miracles the result of the presence of God's kingly rule (Matt. 12: 28 = Luke 11: 20), or the result of Jesus' collusion with Beelzebul, the prince of demons (Mark 3: 22), or the result of his use of magical powers (cf. Justin Martyr, *Dialogue* 69: 6–7; *b. Sanh.* 43a and *b. Sanh.* 107b)?

The comments of Celsus, the philosopher and the first pagan critic of Christianity, are revealing. About AD 180 he wrote as follows (as recorded by Origen, *Contra Celsum* 1. 6): 'Christians get the power which they seem to possess by pronouncing the names of certain daemons and incantations . . . It was by magic that he [Jesus] was able to do the miracles which he appears to have done.' Celsus did not doubt that both Jesus and his followers performed miracles, but he attributed them to magical powers.

Writing a couple of decades earlier, Justin Martyr is also aware of the accusation that Jesus was a magician and claims that it was made in the lifetime of Jesus: 'Our Christ healed . . . and he raised dead men . . . and by his works he pressed the people of that day to recognize him. Yet when they saw these things come to pass, people said it was a display of magic art, for they even dared to say that *Jesus was a magician and a deceiver of the people*' (*Dialogue* 69. 6–7).

So was Jesus a magician? This question has been debated inconclusively by several scholars: not surprisingly, definitions are all-important. If magic is defined as the use of standard techniques, whether of word (primarily incantations) or act (e.g. touch, or the use of spittle), then there are some magical traits in the miracle traditions in the gospels.

Mark's story of the woman with a haemorrhage is the clearest example

(Mark 5: 24b–34). The woman came up behind Jesus and touched his cloak, confident that she would be made well if she could but touch his clothes. Jesus is aware that 'power has gone out from him' but does not know who touched him. When the woman tells him what has happened, Jesus says to her, 'Daughter, your faith has made you well.' In his redaction of this incident Matthew carefully avoids any suggestion that the woman is cured merely by touching Jesus' cloak (Matt. 9: 20–6).

However, there are more differences than similarities between the miracle traditions in the gospels and accounts of magical practices. In the gospels there are no lengthy incantations, no lists of esoteric names, and no references to the use of amulets. Nor is there any suggestion that a petitioner can force Jesus to perform a miracle against his will. In antiquity magic was often used for purely selfish ends (e.g. to win a horse race or a lover), and normally no lasting bonds were formed between the magician and his 'clients'.

While it is true that on some definitions miracle and magic are closely related, it is worth noting that in antiquity (as today) magic generally had strongly negative connotations. So magic is not a neutral term that can be used without further ado with reference to Jesus.

The powers of Jesus to heal and to exorcize were not unique. He gave his own disciples authority to heal and to exorcize (Mark 6: 7, 13; Matt. 10: 1; cf. Matt. 7: 22). Jesus himself refers to other exorcists who were able to cast out demons (Matt. 12: 27 = Luke 11: 19; cf. Acts 19: 11–17). There are reports of Jewish miracle-workers who lived at about the time of Jesus, though they are not common; rather surprisingly, they do not include cures of the deaf, the dumb, and the lame.

Today few scholars doubt that Jesus possessed unusual gifts as a healer, though of course varied explanations are offered. Some suggest that many of the illnesses and disabilities had psychosomatic roots. While this may well have been the case, we have no ways of investigating the matter further.

What was exorcism? G. H. Twelftree offers the following helpful definition (1993, p. 13): 'Exorcism was a form of healing used when demons or evil spirits were thought to have entered a person and to be responsible for sickness and was the attempt to control and cast out or expel evil spiritual beings or demons from people'. The phrase 'form of healing' is important, for the exorcisms in the gospels are very closely linked to the accounts of healing. The six exorcism traditions may puzzle modern readers, though they would not have baffled the first readers of the gospels. As we have just noted, others, including the disciples of Jesus, shared his ability to exorcize evil spirits.

The seven so-called nature miracles raise more acute problems than the healings and exorcisms: the cursing of the fig tree (Mark 11: 12–14, 20–1 = Matt. 21: 18–20); the miraculous catch of fish (Luke 5: 1–11; cf. John 21: 1–14); the walking on the water (Mark 6: 45–52 = Matt. 14: 22–33 = John 6: 16–21); the stilling of the storm (Mark 4: 35–41 = Matt. 8: 23–7 = Luke 8: 22–5); the changing of water into wine (John 2: 1–11); the two accounts of feedings of crowds (Mark 6: 32–44 and Mark 8: 1–10, and parallels). In terms of their structure these traditions are quite disparate, and most of them differ in several other respects from the miracle traditions. Four of them can be linked together loosely as 'gift' miracles (so, G. Theissen 1983), for they all record the provision of food (or wine), but this observation does not take us much further forward.

In one case there is a plausible explanation. The cursing of the fig tree is the only 'destructive' miracle in the gospels (Mark 11: 13–14; 20–1). Since a parable of a barren fig tree is recorded in Luke 13: 6–9, the miracle story may have 'grown' out of a parable Jesus told. But it is impossible to know just what may lie behind the other so-called nature miracles. A decision on their historicity will be determined largely by one's philosophical presuppositions and by one's overall assessment of the origin and development of the gospel traditions.

Why did Jesus perform miracles and exorcisms?

Given that Jesus possessed unusual gifts as a healer, why did he perform the particular miracles and exorcisms recorded in the gospels? As we have noted, it was very easy to 'write off' miracle workers in first-century Palestine as 'magicians', or to claim that their unusual abilities were the result of collusion with Beelzebul, the prince of demons (cf. Mark 3: 22). So why did Jesus run the risk of ridicule and rejection? The faith of the individual is mentioned in many but by no means all cases. Although the evangelists refer to the compassion of Jesus on occasion, they do not suggest that this was the main motive for all his miracles. The evangelists record that some of the miracles attracted crowds (e.g. Mark 1: 28), and this may have been one of the reasons the authorities eventually moved against Jesus. But the attraction of crowds is unlikely to have been the main reason why Jesus performed miracles.

By paying close attention to the individuals and the circumstances involved, we can gain important insights into the intention of Jesus. Jesus healed people with many kinds of disability. The lepers healed by Jesus may have had some kind of skin disease, i.e. not true leprosy, now known as Hansen's disease. In the eyes of many, touching a leper was a violation of purity regulations (Mark 1: 40–5 and parallels; Luke 17: 11–19; Lev. 13: 45–6; Josephus, *Against Apion* I. 279–86). As H. C. Kee has emphasized (1986, pp. 78–9), Jesus healed persons who were considered by some of his contemporaries to be 'off-limits' by the standards of Jewish piety, by reason of their race (Mark 7: 24–30), their place of residence (Mark 5: 1–20, in a tomb in pagan territory), or their ritual impurity (5: 25–34, a woman with menstrual flow). Many of the healings and exorcisms of Jesus were an indication of his full acceptance of those who were socially and religiously marginalized. (For further discussion of 'purity' and 'impurity' see pp. 260–5.)

The healing activity of Jesus aroused suspicion and hostility (cf. Mark 3: 22–7). Even John the Baptist was puzzled, for apparently he did not have healing powers (cf. John 10: 41). In his reply to John's query (Matt. 11: 4–6 = Luke 7: 22–3) Jesus claimed that his healing activity carried out among the marginalized was in fulfilment of the promises for the coming age referred to in Isa. 29: 18–19; 35: 5–6; 61: 1. In short, the healings were seen by Jesus as signs of the breaking-in of God's kingly rule, even though the phrase 'kingdom of God' is not used in Jesus' reply to John.

Jesus steadfastly refused to give a sign to his critics which would offer proof that his miracles were carried out as a result of his relationship to God, and not because he was in league with Beelzebul, the prince of demons, or because he was a false prophet (cf. Mark 8: 11–13; Matt. 12: 38–42 = Luke 29–31). It was possible to 'see' the miracles of Jesus and 'perceive' nothing (cf. John 12: 37). But Jesus insisted that those with eyes to see were 'blessed', for in his actions the hopes of the prophets of old were being fulfilled (Matt. 13: 16–17 = Luke 10: 23b–24).

Jesus stated explicitly that his exorcisms were signs that God's kingly rule was breaking in: 'If it is by the finger of God that I cast out demons, then has the kingdom of God come upon you' (Matt. 12: 28 = Luke 11: 20).

As Twelftree has emphasized in his detail study, the exorcisms are the kingdom of God in operation (Twelftree, 1993, p. 170). Since exorcisms were seen as a form of healing, we can be confident that Jesus saw the significance of his healings in terms of the arrival of God's kingly rule.

Like the parables, the miracles and exorcisms were 'signs' but not proof of the kingdom of God; 'outsiders' could 'see' and 'hear' but not 'perceive' and 'understand' (Mark 4: 10; 8: 18). The miracles, like many of the parables, were intended by Jesus to convey to those who had eyes to see and ears to hear the reality of God's kingly rule.

15

MESSIAH, SON OF GOD, SON OF MAN

What claims did Jesus make about himself? Until the rise of modern historical study of the gospels in the late eighteenth century, it was generally assumed that Jesus spoke openly about himself as a divine being. Jesus of Nazareth was the Son of God of the Christian creeds. Reference was often made to verses from the fourth gospel such as John 8: 58 and 17: 5. In the former, when Jesus says, 'Before Abraham was, I am' (John 8: 58), there is a clear echo of God's self-disclosure to Moses in Exodus 3: 14: 'I am who I am.' In John 17: 5 Jesus speaks of the glory which he had with the Father *before* the world was made.

The 'first' or 'old' quest for the historical Jesus (see pp. 164–5), however, underlined the gap between the ways Jesus spoke about himself in the fourth gospel and in the synoptic gospels. In the fourth gospel Jesus speaks regularly and in exalted language about himself and his relationship to God. In the synoptic gospels he does so rarely and then often rather reluctantly. So it was customary to claim that the synoptic gospels were much closer to the 'Jesus of history' than the fourth gospel.

As we saw in Chapter 3, however, in the early decades of the twentieth century it became clear that Mark's gospel is not a straightforward history or biography of the life of Jesus. A distinction may be drawn between the Christ of faith and the Jesus of history: i.e. between the synoptic evangelists' presentation of the *significance* of Jesus in the light of their post-Easter convictions and Jesus' own self-understanding. Matthew, Mark, and Luke have their own Christological emphases.

Scholars of all persuasions now agree that only with careful use of rigorous methods is it possible to isolate the earliest form of the traditions and so uncover Jesus' own self-understanding. This is a difficult task. In the synoptic gospels Jesus speaks frequently about God and his kingly rule; in only a small number of passages does Jesus make direct claims about himself. And to complicate matters, in those passages it is not always easy to separate the earliest form of the traditions from later reinterpretation.

The preceding chapters in Part II of this book have opened with discussion of the evangelists' emphases before turning to the historical Jesus. However, this pattern will not be followed in the present chapter. The evangelists' presentations of Jesus as Messiah–Christ and Son of God have already been set out in Chapters 3–6 on the individual gospels. In this chapter it will be more convenient to discuss possible differences between the evangelists' convictions and Jesus own self-understanding as we proceed. Several key questions lie behind the discussion. Can the roots of the evangelists' convictions concerning the significance of Jesus (i.e. their Christologies) be traced back to Jesus himself? Did Jesus refer to himself as the Messiah–Christ, Son of God, and Son of Man? If he did refer to himself in some or all of these ways, what did he mean?

Messiah–Christ

For most Christians today, to deny that Jesus is the Messiah, or the Christ, is akin to renouncing their Christian faith. They generally have in mind affirmations about Jesus such as: 'Christ died for our sins' (1 Cor. 15: 3); 'we have believed in Christ Jesus' (Gal. 2: 16); 'we have peace with God through our Lord Jesus Christ' (Rom. 5: 1). For Christians today, 'Christ' has become a shorthand way of referring to the significance of Jesus for them; it often has little or no relationship to the meaning of 'Christ' or 'Messiah' in the lifetime of Jesus.

This transition had already taken place by the time Paul wrote his letters, some twenty years after the crucifixion of Jesus. In nearly every passage in Paul's writings 'Christ' is a personal name. With no significant loss of meaning, 'Christ' can be replaced either with 'Son of God', or with 'Lord', or with 'Jesus'. In other words, at a very early period the term 'Messiah' or 'Christ' was filled with specifically Christian content.

But what did 'Messiah' mean to those who heard Jesus in Galilee or in Jerusalem? This is by no means an easy question to answer, since 'Messiah' was understood in quite diverse ways in first-century Judaism. The Hebrew word 'messiah' means an anointed person or thing. It is translated by *christos* (hence 'Christ') in the Greek translation of the Old Testament, the Septuagint (LXX).

Although the noun 'the messiah' does not occur in the Old Testament, it is found thirty-nine times in an adjectival sense. In a number of passages 'anointed one' is applied to the divinely appointed King. (See, for example, 1 Sam. 12: 3 (Saul) and 2 Sam 19: 22 (David).) In a few passages 'anointed one' is used of prophets (e.g. Isa. 61: 1) and of priests (Lev. 4: 3, 5, 16), but without further designation the term normally refers to the king of Israel.

In the later Old Testament period hopes for a 'messianic age' arose. Sometimes these hopes focused on a divinely appointed King of David's line—i.e. a Messiah. But in many passages, especially in Isa. 40–66, hopes for the future are expressed in general terms. There is often no explicit reference to an agent or Messiah through whom God would bring the longed-for new age of salvation.

In Jewish writings which can be dated to the two centuries before the time of Jesus there is even more diversity. In an important but fragmentary Qumran writing there is an expectation of an anointed prophet (11Q Melch. line 18); in this passage the herald of good tidings of Isa. 52: 7 is linked with the prophet anointed by the Spirit of Isa. 61: 1. The Qumran community, at least at some points in its history, seems to have expected 'the anointed ones of Aaron and Israel' (1QS 9: 11 and many other passages): i.e. *two* messiah figures, one a priestly figure (Aaron) and the other a Davidic king. The two Messiahs are God's agents in the end-time. As in other writings of the period, the community's expectation of the future is focused on God and the era of salvation he will inaugurate. Hence the two messiahs (who are human figures) are not sketched sharply as individuals.

In the Psalms of Solomon (which seem to have been collected in the first century BC, and which some scholars think are from Pharisaic circles) a future reign of an ideal Davidic king is described; in chapter 17 emphasis is placed on his military and political successes. The hopes expressed in the Psalms of Solomon may have been quite widespread. If so, then for many who heard Jesus, the hoped-for Messiah would have been a Davidic king who would sweep the Roman armies into the sea. As we shall see in Chapter 17 (pp. 286–8), it was as a messianic pretender of this kind that Jesus was crucified by the Romans. This view lies behind the mocking in Mark 15: 32: 'Let the Messiah, the King of Israel, come down from the cross now so that we may see and believe.' It has often been suggested that Jesus himself either avoided the term 'Messiah' or accepted it reluctantly and 'secretly' in order to avoid the charge that he was a Messiah who would use armed revolt in order to drive out the occupying Roman forces.

There are in fact very few passages in which Jesus himself claims quite explicitly to be 'the Christ'. There are no such sayings in Q. There are two key passages in Mark, but in both cases they show signs of later Christological reflection.

At two turning points in his presentation of the story and significance of Jesus, Mark portrays Jesus as the Messiah–Christ, the Son of God and the Son of Man, thus associating three Christological titles closely with one another. At the central point in Mark's drama, Jesus asks his disciples, 'Who do people say that I am?' (Mark 8: 27). Peter replies, 'You are the Christ.' Jesus neither accepts nor rejects the title. Mark immediately adds the enigmatic comment, 'And Jesus sternly ordered them not to tell anyone about him', and then notes, 'And Jesus began to teach them that the Son of Man must undergo great suffering . . . ' (8: 29–31). Peter is roundly rebuked when he protests that this understanding of Messiahship is inappropriate. A few verses later Jesus speaks of the coming of the Son of Man 'in the glory of *his Father*' (8: 38), an indirect way of referring to his role as Son of God. While this whole scene may reflect in part post-Easter Christian convictions about Jesus as the Christ, the rather ambiguous response of Jesus to Peter does not look like the retrojection of a later Christian confessional statement.

At the climax of Mark's story, in front of the 'whole council' (Sanhedrin) the high priest asks Jesus, 'Are you the Christ, the Son of the Blessed One [i.e. God]?' In response to the high priest, Jesus concedes that he is the Messiah (Mark 14: 62). But in some manuscripts Jesus replies, not, 'I am' (the Messiah), but, 'You have said that I am': those words are yours, not mine. Although this alternative reading is not found in the earliest manuscripts, it may in fact record the response of Jesus. An evasive or ambiguous response to the question, 'Are you the Christ?' is much more likely to have been replaced by some Christian scribes with a ringing affirmation, 'I am' than vice versa. As in 8: 31, Jesus prefers to speak of his role as Son of Man: 'you will see the Son of Man seated at the right hand of Power, and coming with the clouds of heaven' (14: 61–2).

From these two passages it is clear that for Mark the three terms

Messiah–Christ, Son of God, and Son of Man are important ways of spelling out the significance of Jesus for his readers. In short, for Mark (as for the other three evangelists) they are Christological titles which are closely related and which interpret one another.

Some scholars insist that Jesus did not claim to be Messiah and that his ministry was not messianic in any sense. There is certainly little explicit evidence that he did claim the title. But if Jesus repudiated the title completely and if none of his actions was understood by his followers to be messianic, then it becomes very difficult to explain why immediately after Easter his followers suddenly and strongly affirmed that he *was* the Christ. Messiah was not in fact a common title at the time of Jesus. The Easter experiences of the disciples would not have led the disciples to this conclusion, for there were no expectations that God would raise his Messiah from the dead. So it is highly likely that some of the actions and teaching of Jesus led his circles of followers to believe that he was in fact the promised Messiah.

Perhaps Jesus generally avoided the term because of its political implications for many of his hearers. While not denying that he was the promised Davidic king of Israel, he encouraged his hearers to understand Messiahship in quite new ways.

Or perhaps some of the actions and teachings of Jesus aroused strong messianic hopes, but Jesus himself deliberately avoided making an overt claim to be the Messiah. There is some Jewish evidence which suggests that the expected Messiah would remain silent about his Messiahship until he had completed his task and been vindicated by God (*b. San.* 98a; Justin Martyr, *Dialogue* 8: 4). An explanation along these lines would account for the diffidence of Jesus which the synoptic evangelists record and yet allow for the fact that some of his actions and sayings encouraged his disciples to believe that he was the Messiah. His followers would have seen the resurrection as God's *vindication* of his messiahship. Attractive though this possible solution is, the evidence for such Jewish views about the Messiah cannot be traced back with certainty any earlier than the first decades of the second century.

Son of God

In the Graeco-Roman world some heroes, rulers, and philosophers were called sons of God. In the Old Testament 'son of God' is used of angels or heavenly beings (e.g. Gen. 6: 2, 4; Deut. 32: 8; Job 1: 6–12), Israel or Israelites (e.g. Ex. 4: 22; Hosea 11: 1), and also of the king (notably in 2 Sam. 7: 14 and Psalm 2: 7). Two Qumran fragments (IQSa 2. 11 f. and 4QFlor. 1. 10 f.) describe the hoped-for Davidic Messiah in the language of divine sonship. This latter usage, which comes from just before the time of Jesus, is of particular interest since several New Testament writers link the Messiahship and Sonship of Jesus.

In view of this wide usage in Judaism and in the Graeco-Roman world, it is not surprising that 'Son of God' became one of the most important ways Christians spoke about the significance of Jesus. In the opening verses of Romans, where Paul may be citing a very early creed-like statement, he speaks about the 'gospel concerning his *Son*, who was descended from David according to the flesh and was declared to be *Son of God* with power . . . by his resurrection from the dead' (1: 3–4). Here, as in the Qumran fragments just referred to, a Davidic 'messianic' role and 'Son of God' are linked. As we have seen, Mark 14: 61–2 also links Jesus' Messiahship with his role as Son of God. But, in contrast to Mark, in Rom. 1: 4 Jesus becomes Son of God at the resurrection, not at his baptism.

As we saw in Chapter 3 (pp. 41–4), the evangelist Mark places particular emphasis on Jesus as the Son of God. Did Jesus refer to himself in this way? Or is this a confessional statement which first arose in the post-Easter church?

At the baptism of Jesus (1: 11) and again at the Transfiguration (9: 7), Jesus is referred to as 'my beloved Son' by the voice from heaven. The word 'beloved' may well be synonymous with a Jewish messianic term, 'the Chosen One'. Most scholars agree that the Aramaic or Hebrew word behind 'son' is 'servant'. So as the Spirit descends on Jesus at his baptism, Jesus is addressed by the voice from heaven in terms of Isaiah 42: 1: 'Behold my servant . . . my chosen . . . I have put my Spirit upon him.' So although Mark 1: 11 and 9: 7 affirm that Jesus is called by God to a special messianic task, the emphasis is on Jesus' role as the anointed servant, rather than as

Son of God. In any case the words are those of the voice from heaven, and are not a direct reflection of the self-understanding of Jesus.

There are in fact very few sayings in which Jesus refers to himself as God's Son. In Mark 13: 32 Jesus states that 'no one, not even the angels in heaven, nor the Son, but only the Father' knows the day or hour of the end-time. Since this verse concedes that Jesus is ignorant of the future and that he is subordinate to the Father, it is unlikely that the whole verse was created in the early church. On the other hand, since it is the only verse in Mark in which Jesus refers to himself as *the* Son in an absolute sense, its original form may have been '*a* Son', a phrase which, as we shall see, Jesus does seem to have used.

In the parable of the wicked husbandmen (Mark 12: 1–12) the servants sent to collect the fruit from the vineyard (Israel) are rejected and some are killed. Finally a beloved son, who is obviously Jesus himself, is sent. In its present form this parable has some allegorical features. In the past some scholars have assumed too readily that all traces of allegory must stem from the early church, not Jesus. But as we saw in Chapter 13 (p. 227), there is now a greater willingness to accept that some of the original parables of Jesus may have included some allegorical features. The original hearers of the parables would naturally have expected from their know-ledge of the scriptures that (for example) a king referred to God, a vineyard to Israel, and servants to the prophets. So in this case there is no reason to assign all the allegorical features of this parable to the early church.

Jesus alludes to his role as the 'final' prophet sent to Israel and as 'a beloved son'. The word 'beloved' may well have been added by the evangel-ist to make a link with the words of the voice from heaven at the baptism of Jesus (1: 11) and again at the Transfiguration (9: 7). But the parable's refer-ence to Jesus as '*a* son' (rather than '*the* son', as in later usage) is probably authentic. If so, then in this parable Jesus speaks indirectly of his role not merely as God's final messenger to Israel, but as God's Son. The parable hints that Sonship involves suffering and death. This latter theme becomes even more explicit at Mark 14: 36 where in Gethsemane Jesus addresses God directly as Abba, Father; to be God's Son is to be dedicated unconditionally to God's will, even to the point of death.

In two Q passages Jesus addresses God as Father and alludes to his own Sonship. As we saw on pp. 9–10, in the opening line of the Lord's prayer Jesus addresses God directly as Father and encourages his disciples to share his sense of Sonship. In Matt. 11: 27 = Luke 10: 22 Jesus thanks 'the Father, Lord of heaven and earth' in these words: 'All things have been handed over to me by my Father; and no one knows the Son except the Father, and no one knows the Father except the Son and any one to whom the Son chooses to reveal him.' As in the case of Mark 13: 32, the reference to Jesus as '*the* Son' suggests at least some reshaping in the early church, but that is no reason to assign the whole verse to the early church. Joachim Jeremias (1971, pp. 59–61) plausibly suggested that the original form of this saying on the lips of Jesus may have drawn a picture from everyday life:

> Just as only a father really knows his son,
> so only a son really knows his father.

Some such wording may well go back to Jesus. The saying would then be one of only a handful of indirect references Jesus made to himself as standing in a special relationship of sonship to God. It is, of course, impossible to say whether or not Jesus saw his relationship to God as unique.

Jesus did not speak of himself as 'the Son of God' in the ways which were developed in the post-Easter period. There are, however, a few sayings which suggest that he not only addressed God as Father in striking ways, but also spoke about his own relationship to God as his Son.

Son of Man

We have seen that there are only a handful of references in the synoptic gospels to Jesus as the Messiah–Christ and as the Son or Son of God. In sharp contrast, there are a large number of Son of man sayings. There are thirteen in Mark, twelve in Q, eight in Matthew's special material ('M'), six in Luke's special material ('L'), and eleven in John's gospel. 'Christ' and 'Son of God' are often found in confessional statements in the New Testament writings, but John 9: 35 is the only Son of Man saying which is used in that way. With only two exceptions (Acts 7: 56 and Rev. 14: 14), Son of Man is confined to the gospels. In the gospels the phrase is always found on the lips of Jesus. In the only exception (John 12: 34) the crowd asks Jesus: 'How can you say that the Son of Man must be lifted up? Who is this Son of Man?'

Readers of the gospels have often echoed the question, 'Who is this Son of Man?' Why is this phrase found so frequently on the lips of Jesus? How many of the Son of Man sayings can be traced back to Jesus himself? If Jesus did use these words, what did he mean by them? Do they provide clearer clues than 'Christ' or 'Son' to his self-understanding? Not surprisingly, there have been numerous attempts to answer these questions. Most scholars accept that the Son of Man sayings are the single most intractable problem facing serious students of the New Testament writings. In the paragraphs which follow we can do no more than sketch out the main issues at stake and assess the three most plausible solutions.

Broadly speaking, the Son of Man sayings fall into three categories (though the boundaries between the three groups are less clear than many have supposed). Seven sayings refer to the earthly activity of Jesus as Son of Man. 'The Son of Man has authority on earth to forgive sins' (Mark 2: 10); 'Foxes have holes, and birds of the air have nests; but the Son of Man has nowhere to lay his head' (Matt. 8: 20 = Luke 9: 58). A much larger number (though there are no examples in Q) refer to the suffering of the Son of Man. 'The Son of Man must suffer many things, and be rejected . . . ., and be killed . . .' (Mark 8: 31); 'Judas, would you betray the Son of Man with a kiss?' (Luke 22: 48). A number of sayings (which are especially prominent in Q) refer to the heavenly glory and future coming of the Son of Man. 'For whoever is ashamed of me and my words . . ., of him will the Son of Man also be ashamed, when he comes in the glory of his Father with the holy angels' (Mark 8: 38). 'For as the lightning comes from the east and flashes as far as the west, so will be the coming of the Son of Man' (Matt. 24: 27 = Luke 17: 24).

The Son of Man sayings in the John's gospel are distinctive; only a few of them are related even indirectly to the sayings in the synoptic gospels. The first Son of Man saying which comes as the climax of the fourth evangelist's extended prologue is notable: 'Very truly, I tell you, you will see heaven opened, and the angels of God ascending and descending upon the Son of Man' (1: 51). Here the Son of Man, like Jacob's ladder in Gen. 28: 12, is the link between heaven and earth. Several other Johannine Son of Man sayings portray Jesus in a similar way.

Son of Man in Old Testament and later Jewish writings

How would Jesus' hearers have understood 'Son of Man'? These words are used in several distinct senses in the Old Testament and later Jewish writings. Since the main solutions which have been proposed all appeal to *one* of these strands as the primary background for Jesus' own usage, we must sketch out the evidence.

(a) Ezekiel and Psalm 80. In some ninety-three passages in Ezekiel the prophet is addressed by God as 'Son of Man'. The phrase underlines the humanity of the prophet. Although some passages refer to the suffering of the prophet with his people (and might therefore provide a link with the second category sketched above), this is not always the case. In Psalm 80: 17 the one who 'sits at God's right hand' is identified with 'the son of Man' whom God has strengthened. This verse has occasionally been seen as the background for Mark 14: 62, the reply of Jesus to the high priest, and therefore influential on the development of Son of Man sayings. But most scholars accept that whatever the origin of this saying, it is to be interpreted in the light of Dan. 7: 13 rather than Psalm 80.

(b) In Daniel 7: 13 one 'like a Son of Man' comes with the clouds of heaven and is presented to the Ancient of Days (God). In the verses which follow in this passage the one 'like a Son of Man' is linked with the saints of the Most High who suffer (verses 18, 22, and 27). The obedience of the Son of Man (and those associated with him) leads through suffering to vindication and to a role as judge. Several scholars have argued that Son of Man sayings in the three categories noted above can be readily understood against the background of this passage.

(c) In chapters 37–71 of 1 Enoch (often known as the Parables or Similitudes of Enoch) there are a number of references to the Son of Man. In chapters 62 and 63 he is seated by the Lord of Spirits (God) on the throne of judgement (62: 2). The Son of Man is 'the elect one' (a term used elsewhere of the Messiah) who has 'been hidden from the beginning' and is revealed 'on that day' (of judgement) to the elect (62: 1, 6–7, 13). In the Similitudes the portrait of the Son of Man is related to Dan. 7: 13 ff., but there is considerable development. 'Son of Man' is now clearly a messianic title for a divine being.

(d) Although 'Son of Man' is used so frequently in the gospels, in Greek it is an awkward phrase. Hence there is general agreement that it is a clumsy translation of an Aramaic phrase *bar enash(a)*. But what did the Aramaic phrase which Jesus would have used mean? Unfortunately very few writings in Aramaic have survived from the time of Jesus. Several scholars claim that some rabbinic traditions put us in touch with first-century Aramaic usage. Here are two examples. The first passage refers to the death ('going') of human beings in general (including the speaker) and their passage into the next world. Rabbi Judah is challenging the traditional view that every man (or a son of man) passes into the next world in the same condition or status as he leaves the present world. 'It is said that Rabbi [Judah] was buried in a single sheet, because, he said, It is not as *bar enasha* (*the* son of man) goes that he will come again. But the Rabbis say, As *bar enash* (*a* son of man) goes, so he will come again' (j.Ket. 35a).

In the second example the phrase *bar nasha* seems to mean 'a man like me'. 'Rabbi Simeon ben Yohai said: If I had stood on Mount Sinai when the Torah was given to Israel, I would have asked the Merciful One to create two mouths for *bar nasha* [i.e. 'for me', or 'for a man like me'], one for the study of the Torah and one for the provision of all his needs' (j. Ber. 3b).

Three explanations

Three quite diverse explanations of the use of 'Son of Man' in the gospels have been based on differing assessments of the relevance and of the interpretation of these Old Testament and later Jewish passages. Rudolf Bultmann and several other scholars appeal primarily to the evidence of 1 Enoch and insist that at the time of Jesus 'Son of Man' was an apocalyptic messianic title. Since Jesus did not make any messianic claims (so the argument runs), the Son of Man sayings cannot go back to him. They originated as part of the apocalyptic fervour of the very earliest post-Easter communities and were further developed in the early church and by the evangelists. Some of the scholars who take this general approach allow that a few of the 'future' sayings are authentic. They insist that if Jesus spoke about the Son of Man, he used the phrase to refer to someone other than himself. Luke 12: 8 (= Matt. 10: 32) is often cited: 'And I tell you, every one who acknowledges *me* before men, *the Son of Man* also will acknowledge before the angels of God' (cf. also Mark 8: 38).

In recent years what may be termed the apocalyptic interpretation has been vigorously opposed, but it still has defenders. Scholars who reject this approach insist that there is no evidence that 'Son of Man' was a messianic or apocalyptic *title* at the time of Jesus. They insist that the Similitudes of Enoch are no earlier than the end of the first century AD and are therefore irrelevant. Although fragments of parts of 1 Enoch have been found in the Qumran caves (and must therefore date from before AD 70), no fragments of the Similitudes have been discovered. Hence this part of 1 Enoch with the Son of Man passages must have been added well after the time of Jesus to what is generally accepted as a composite work written over a long period of time. (This, however, is not a conclusive argument. Since the Qumran fragments are small in number, the absence of any fragments of the Similitudes may simply be a coincidence.)

Opponents of the apocalyptic interpretation also claim that it is almost impossible to believe that all (or nearly all) the Son of Man sayings were created by the early church. If so, why are they never used in confessional statements, and why are they always placed only on the lips of Jesus? It is difficult to accept that Jesus spoke of someone other than himself as Son of Man. If Jesus did so, what was his understanding of his own role and of his relationship to the other figure? Luke 12: 8 does not necessarily have to be interpreted as a reference to someone other than Jesus: it may be merely a circumlocution for 'I', or some other kind of self-reference on the part of Jesus. Since only a very few passages in the synoptic gospels suggest that Jesus was an apocalyptic prophet, this approach has to ignore many other sayings with good claims to authenticity.

Two rival alternative explanations of the 'Son of Man' sayings have been offered. Several scholars (most notably C. F. D. Moule and Morna Hooker) have appealed to Daniel 7 as the primary background for the Son of Man sayings in the gospels. Morner Hooker notes that the Son of man of Daniel 7 'is not simply one who appears at the end of time to act as judge: rather it is because he is Son of Man now—i.e. elect, obedient, faithful and there-fore suffering—that he will be vindicated as Son of Man in the future: the eschatological role of the Son of Man is based upon his obedient response to God now' (*The Son of Man in Mark*, 1967, p. 190). This general approach claims that some of the Son of Man sayings in all three categories go back to Jesus. 'Son of Man' on the lips of Jesus referred to the *role* of the Son of Man in Daniel 7; only later in Jewish writings and in further development of the sayings of Jesus did 'Son of man' become a *title*. The odd definite article 'the' at the beginning of the Greek phrase may be a pointer to its original sense: Jesus may have been referring to '*that*' well-known Danielic Son of Man.

Some scholars who also reject the apocalyptic interpretation offer yet another explanation. Some of them claim that since the sayings which most clearly allude to Daniel 7 are secondary, this passage is not the key to the problem. They appeal to Aramaic usage at the time of Jesus, especially to usage of the phrase in the rabbinic writings, two examples of which were noted above. The Aramaic phrase is said by some (e.g. Geza Vermes) to be simply a circumlocution for 'I'. If that is its origin, then it is difficult to account for the awkwardness of the Greek phrase: why was a simple 'I' not used in Greek? The odd very literal Greek translation does suggest that the Aramaic words were thought to be a little unusual and perhaps special.

Other scholars who appeal to Aramaic usage interpret it rather differently. The Aramaic phrase *bar enash(a)* is said to mean 'man or mankind in general' (Maurice Casey) or 'a person in my position' (Barnabas Lindars). Unfortunately the Aramaic evidence is not a magic wand which solves the Son of Man problem swiftly and easily. In spite of intensive discussion in recent years, there is still uncertainty about the dating of the traditions in the rabbinic writings which refer to 'Son of Man'. And in addition, many of these sayings are at least as difficult to interpret with precision as the Son of man sayings in the gospels!

Enough has been said to give the flavour of the main lines of recent discussion. The various arguments are complex. There is still no consensus. The most plausible explanations appeal either to the role of a human, suffering but eventually vindicated Son of Man in Daniel 7 or to an Aramaic phrase which may have meant 'a person in my position'. In either case the Son of Man sayings which Jesus is most likely to have used are *indirect* allusions to his role rather than bold claims to a particular title or status.

In this chapter we have seen just how difficult it is to separate the claims Jesus made about himself from their later development in the early church. Jesus spoke about his own role reluctantly. He rarely, if ever, referred explicitly to himself as Messiah. On the other hand, so many aspects of his actions and teaching were 'messianic' in a broad sense that we can understand how his followers claimed soon after Easter that Jesus was the promised Messiah. Jesus did refer to God as Father and occasionally to himself as a Son (of God); this 'self-understanding' was also developed considerably in the early church. The phrase 'Son of Man' had a similar history: Jesus used the phrase in various contexts to refer indirectly to himself; his followers developed his usage until the phrase eventually became a messianic title.

In other chapters in Part II of this book we have seen some of the other indirect claims Jesus made. In some ways they reveal more about Jesus' self-understanding than the terms 'Christ', 'Son of God', or 'Son of Man'. Two sayings in particular may be taken as characteristic of Jesus' self-understanding. In neither case is there an explicit claim to be Messiah, a Son or the Son of God, or Son of Man.

In Matt. 10: 40 = Luke 10: 16 (and cf. also John 13: 20) Jesus says to his disciples: 'Whoever welcomes you welcomes me, and whoever welcomes me welcomes the one who sent me.' Just as the disciples are sent on their mission with the authority of Jesus, he himself has been sent to Israel with the authority of God. Acceptance or rejection of Jesus is equated with acceptance or rejection of God. Jesus implies that he bears prophetic authority, but he does not appeal to particular titles. Jesus speaks about God only indirectly as the 'one who sent me', but the implicit claim which lies behind this saying is bold, to say the least.

When John the Baptist sent disciples to make inquiries about Jesus, he answered as follows: 'Go and tell John what you see and hear: the blind receive their sight, the lame walk, the lepers are cleansed, the deaf hear, the dead are raised, and the poor have the good news (gospel) proclaimed to them' (Matt. 11: 4–6 = Luke 7: 22–3 [Q]). With these words Jesus is alluding to Isaiah 29: 18–19; 35: 5; and 61: 1–2. The first two passages provide the general theme of an eschatological time when the deaf will hear, the blind see, and the lame walk. The climax comes with the allusion to Isaiah 61: 1, 'the poor have the good news (gospel) proclaimed to them'. Was Jesus hinting that he was an expected end-time prophet, or even that he was the Messiah? Although it has frequently been assumed that these words would have been understood as an indirect claim to be Messiah, until recently it has been difficult to cite clear-cut evidence that Isaiah 61: 1 was referred to the Messiah in Jewish circles at the time of Jesus.

The missing evidence has now turned up in a Qumran document, 4Q521, published in 1992. One of the 17 fragments opens in line 1 as follows: ' . . . heaven and earth will obey his Messiah' (fragment 2 ii). The lines which follow speak of care for the pious, righteous, the poor, the captives, the blind. And then in the very important line 12 we read, 'for he will heal the wounded, *give life to the dead, and preach good news to the poor.*'

The correspondence with Matthew 11: 4–6 (quoted above), with Isaiah 52: 7 and 61: 1 f. and with 11Q Melchizedek line 18 is striking. Although the fragment of 4Q521 quoted opens with a reference to the Messiah, it is not clear whether the one caring for the various needy groups is God or his agent, the Messiah. But in line 12 there is no doubt. As J. J. Collins has emphasized (1995, pp. 116–23) God does not usually 'preach good news'; this is the task of his herald or messenger. So in line 12 it is the Messiah who has the task of 'healing the wounded, giving life to the dead, and preaching good news to the poor,' as in Matthew 11: 4–6 quoted above.

In 4Q521 the Messiah 'preaches good news to the poor'. So we now have evidence that at the time of Jesus Isaiah 61: 1f., with its reference to the anointed prophet being sent to preach good news to the poor, was understood to refer to a *messianic prophet*. It is highly likely that when Jesus referred to his own actions and words in terms of this passage (and the related ones), he was making an *indirect* messianic claim.

16

CONFLICT

The evangelists

In all four gospels conflict between Jesus and various Jewish groups forms a central part of the evangelists' presentation of the story of Jesus. The evangelists all depict Jesus as at odds with religious leaders from the very outset of his ministry right up to his arrest and 'trial'.

Mark has placed a series of 'conflict' traditions near the beginning of his story (Mark 2: 1 to 3: 6). A further set of conflict stories is brought together from 11: 27 to 12: 44; they follow Jesus' so-called triumphal entry into Jerusalem and are all set in the temple or its precincts. The opponent are 'the chief priests, the scribes, and the elders' (11: 27), 'some Pharisees and some Herodians' (12: 13–14), 'some Sadducees' (12: 18–27), and finally 'scribes' (12: 28–40). In this section of Mark's gospel, all the various opponents of Jesus are brought onto the stage, group by group. In Mark's storyline these conflict traditions prepare the way for the plot to arrest Jesus by stealth (14: 1).

Matthew locates the origin of conflict between Jesus and his opponents even earlier: the birth of Jesus causes consternation to Herod and the Jerusalem authorities (Matt. 2). Herod's murderous intent is thwarted by God's provision for Jesus his Son (Matt. 2: 15). Although Matthew includes conflict traditions in 9: 1–17, reference to a plot against Jesus is held back (perhaps for dramatic purposes) until 12: 14. Only then are we set on the way to the arrest of Jesus.

Conflict and rejection are already announced in Luke's infancy narrative: Simeon warns Mary that her child will be 'a sign that will be opposed' (2: 34). In Luke's account of the opening scene in the Galilean ministry Jesus clashes with the members of the synagogue in Nazareth (Luke 4:

16–30). Luke retains intact (but with editorial modifications) Mark's first cycle of conflict stories (Luke 5: 17 to 6: 11). This section of Luke's gospel opens in even more dramatic fashion than the Marcan cycle of traditions which is being used. 'One day, while he was teaching, Pharisees and teachers of the law were sitting near by (they had come from every village of Galilee and Judaea and from Jerusalem); and the power of the Lord was with Jesus to heal' (5: 17; cf. Mark 2: 1, 6).

The Prologue to the fourth gospel notes that the Jesus 'came to what was his own, and his own people did not accept him' (John 1: 11; cf. 1: 5). The fourth evangelist places the 'cleansing' of the temple (2: 13–22) close to the opening of his dramatic story in order to underline the deep-seated conflict between Jesus and 'the Jews'. As we saw in Chapter 6 (pp. 114–15), there are references to 'the Jews' right through John's gospel.

In all four gospels conflict between Jesus and his critics is prominent not only at the opening of each evangelist's story, but also in its central sections and at its climax. Who were the opponents of Jesus? What were the issues at stake? Before we turn to these questions we must discuss briefly the origin of the conflict traditions.

The gospels were probably all written between AD 70 and 90, a period when many Christian groups were at odds with their Jewish neighbours. So it has often been suggested that the accounts in all four gospels of the disputes between Jesus and his opponents reflect the issues which divided Christians and Jews some five decades later. This is almost certainly the case, at least in part. In Matthew and John anti-Jewish polemic is strong; as we saw in Part I, both gospels reflect a rather painful parting of the ways between Christians and Jews.

However, there are reasons for hesitating to conclude that the gospels merely record disputes which took place decades after the lifetime of Jesus. Some of the gospel traditions record disputes over issues which (as far as we know) were not prominent in the post-Easter church (e.g. sabbath—Rom. 14: 6 is an exception; handwashing before meals, Mark 7: 1–8; Matt. 15: 1–9; Luke 11: 37–41). Some of the issues over which Jews who became Christians agonized are not found in the gospels; for example, the necessity of circumcision for Gentile Christians, and sharing meals with Gentiles (cf. Gal. 2: 1–14). The disputes between Jesus and his critics are so many, so various, and so deep-seated in the traditions used by the evangelists that it is unlikely that conflict traditions were all created in the early church.

In this chapter we shall concentrate on the disputes between Jesus (and his followers) and the Pharisees who are the most prominent opponents of Jesus in the gospels. First we must comment briefly on several other movements and groups in first-century Palestine. Before we proceed, however, it is important to stress strongly that it is no part of our intention to portray the various Jewish groups and parties in a poor light—and as a negative foil to Jesus and his followers. We also need to bear in mind that most Jews in Galilee and Judaea did not belong to any of the sects and groups we shall discuss. Members of these groups were the 'movers and shakers' of their day. Most Jews were peasants struggling to survive economically; their attitudes to observance of the law are likely to have varied considerably.

Jesus shared with his fellow-Jews (whether or not they belonged to the sects and groups we shall discuss) a commitment to Scripture and a determination to obey God's commandments as a response to God's revelation of himself and his call to Israel to be his people. What was at stake was the interpretation of Scripture and the status of later oral elaborations of the law ('the tradition of the elders' of Mark 7: 3, 5).

Essenes, Sadducees, 'zealots', and scribes

The Essenes have long puzzled scholars. There seem to have been Essene communities throughout the country, but they had largely cut themselves off from mainstream Jewish society. Philo and Josephus both state that there were 'more than four thousand Essenes.' They were devoted to the law of Moses and were particularly concerned with issues of purity as their response to God's holiness. Their strict procedures for admission as well as their communal lifestyle suggest that 'sect' is an appropriate way of describing them.

Most scholars now accept that the Qumran writings which were first discovered in caves along the Dead Sea in 1947 come from Essene groups who had withdrawn to the wilderness nearly two centuries before the time of Jesus. The Qumran covenanters (as they are often called) had isolated themselves from other Jews (whom they considered to be 'doomed'), in order to carry out the requirements of the law more faithfully than they believed was possible in 'corrupt' and 'impure' Jerusalem.

Before the discovery of the first Dead Sea Scrolls, we knew a little about Essene groups from Philo and Josephus, but we did not possess any of their own writings. If at least some of the Dead Sea Scrolls come from Essenes, we now know a great deal more about them. The writings of the Qumran Essenes were hidden in caves around the Dead Sea just prior to the outbreak in AD 66 of hostilities against the Romans. So we now have writings from a Jewish group which was prominent at the time of Jesus. (For a fuller discussion of the Dead Sea Scrolls, see pp. 152–4.)

Neither the Qumran Essenes nor any other Essene groups appear in the gospels. Perhaps this is not surprising, given that they deliberately isolated themselves from other groups. The differences between the Qumran Essenes and Jesus are striking. Both spoke harshly about the temple. But in contrast to Jesus, the Qumran Essenes rejected the sacrificial worship of the temple and replaced it with their own rituals; they believed that in the forthcoming eschatological war they would regain control over the temple and its worship. They believed that the renewal of Israel would come through their scrupulous observance of the law in a monastic-like community. Jesus sought the renewal of Israel along very different lines.

The Sadducees were aristocrats, many of whom belonged to, or were associated with, the priesthood (cf. Acts 5: 17). Josephus writes: 'They win over the wealthy. They do not have the people on their side' (*Antiquities* 13. 298). Once again there is a striking contrast with Jesus, who focused his teaching and his action on those on the margins of society. The Sadducees gave priority to the Pentateuch over the other two sections of Scripture, the prophets and the writings. Unlike the Pharisees, they rejected entirely the oral expositions of Torah which had been developed over the centuries. The Sadducean rejection of belief in bodily resurrection and in reward in a life to come is not surprising, for these beliefs arose only in the two centuries or so before the time of Jesus. On this issue they clashed with Jesus (Mark 12: 18–27) who, in this respect at least, was closer to the Pharisees. Some of the Sadducees were political leaders at the time of Jesus; they may have been the dominant group on the Sanhedrin which tried Jesus (Mark 14: 53), although the gospels do not mention this.

Our knowledge of the Sadducees is limited; all the information we have about them comes from people who were not Sadducees, many of whom were their opponents. With the triumph of the Romans in AD 70 they lost their power and importance. Several scholars have suggested that their demise was the outcome of their 'pro-Roman' stance, but this is no more than a possibility.

The 'zealots' are often mentioned in standard books on the New Testament writings as a fourth group in first-century Judaism alongside the Pharisees, the Essenes, and the Sadducees. Unlike the other three groups, the 'zealots' are said to have advocated the use of violence in order to rid the land of the Romans, the hated occupying power. However, the so-called 'zealots' were by no means the only Jews opposed to Roman rule. Many others (including some Pharisees) shared their objectives, if not their methods. In addition, the term 'zealots' is misleading, since there is no firm evidence before AD 66 (the outbreak of the Jewish uprising against the Romans) that there was a group or sect known as the 'zealots'. Nonetheless there is clear evidence that in the previous sixty years there were several (often competing) groups dedicated to the overthrow of the Romans. Their aims were both political and religious—indeed in first-century Palestine religion and politics are usually synonymous. The various resistance movements called for overt opposition to the Romans in order to restore the purity of the land of Israel, which had been defiled by some of the actions of the Romans. The so-called zealots were *zealous* for the law and for the purity of Israel.

It has been argued that Jesus was a zealot sympathizer. On this view, which is especially associated with S. G. F. Brandon, the evangelists have painted a portrait of a 'pacifist' Jesus to suit the period after AD 70 when Christians had to prove to the Romans that their movement was politically harmless. The 'real' Jesus is hidden by the evangelists' whitewash: he was in fact associated with the freedom fighters of his day. But, it is alleged, the whitewash is so thin that it reveals some tell-tale clues for the keen observer.

Brandon notes that one of disciples of Jesus is referred to as 'Simon, the Cananaean/zealot' (Mark 3: 18). The Greek word 'Cananaean' transliterates an Aramaic word which may mean no more than 'enthusiast'. In any case there is no evidence that once he became a disciple of Jesus, Simon retained any former sympathies with a group of 'enthusiasts' who may or may not have been freedom fighters. Brandon places a good deal of emphasis on what he takes to have been the original intention of Jesus on his entry into Jerusalem and 'cleansing' of the temple; we shall discuss his main points in Chapter 17, pp. 285–6. If Jesus taught his followers to 'love their enemies' (Matt. 5: 44 = Luke 6: 27, 35), how can he have been sympathetic to freedom fighters? Brandon dismisses this saying too readily as a creation of Matthew's. But this is a Q logion which antedates our written gospels; it has good claims to be accepted as a radical saying of Jesus with no more than limited precedent in first-century Jewish teaching.

Before we turn to the Pharisees we must refer briefly to the scribes, who are associated in the gospels both with the Pharisees and with the chief priests as opponents of Jesus. In some passages (e.g. Mark 2: 6; 3: 22; 9: 11; 12: 28–40) they are not linked with any other group. The primary role of the scribes (who are referred to in later Jewish writings as the sages or rabbis) was to teach the law (cf. Luke 5: 17; Acts 5: 34) and to administer justice. Many of the scribes were associated with the Pharisees (cf. Mark 2: 16; Acts 23: 9); some with the Sadducees. In so far as Jesus challenged some current assumptions about the meaning of Scripture, he was bound to have been in conflict with scribes. In the gospels nearly all the passages which refer to scribes as the sole opponents of Jesus are concerned with issues which might well have been raised by Pharisees.

The Pharisees

In Mark eight disputes between Jesus and the Pharisees are mentioned (2: 16–17, eating with tax-collectors and sinners; 2: 18–20, fasting; 2: 23–6, plucking corn on the sabbath; 3: 1–6, sabbath healing; 7: 1–8, eating with unwashed hands; 8: 11–13, request for a sign; 10: 2–9, divorce; 12: 13–17, paying taxes to Caesar). Matthew and Luke retain these traditions and add more.

Whereas Mark refers to the Pharisees as hypocrites only once (7: 6) and Luke not at all, Matthew has twelve such references (mainly in ch. 23). As we saw on pp. 75–6, Matthew's strong anti-Pharisaic polemic is related to the pain and hostility felt by a minority group which had recently parted company with Judaism. It is most unfortunate that this polemic has encouraged Christians of all generations to regard 'Pharisees' and 'hypocrites' as synonymous terms. In fact Matthew also refers to Christians as 'hypocrites' (7: 5 and 24: 51) and engages in vigorous polemic with 'unfaithful' Christians (e.g. 13: 36–43, 47–50; 22: 11–12; 23: 8–12). No doubt some individual Pharisees were hypocritical, but our earliest gospel, Mark, confirms that hypocrisy was not the basic issue at stake between Jesus and the Pharisees.

As in so many other respects, John's gospel differs. The Pharisees are much less prominent; they are just one part of 'the Jews', who, as representatives of the unbelieving world, are starkly contrasted with Jesus and his followers.

With the exception of Matt. 27: 62 and John 18: 3 (the two most 'anti-Jewish' gospels) the Pharisees are not mentioned in the accounts of the arrest, trial, and crucifixion of Jesus. In view of their prominence earlier in the gospels this is surprising. In the passion narratives the chief priests, scribes, and elders (in various combinations) are portrayed as the enemies of Jesus. There is in fact no direct link between Mark's account of the controversies of the ministry of Jesus and the issues raised at the trial of Jesus before the Sanhedrin. We shall return to this point in Chapter 17, pp. 285–6.

Who were the Pharisees? There is general agreement that at the time of Jesus the Pharisees were the most influential 'sect' or movement within Judaism (cf. Josephus, *Jewish War* 2. 8. 14, §162). In addition to the traditions about the Pharisees in the gospels, three further strands of evidence inform us about them: Josephus (writing as a Jewish historian in the final decades of the first century); the rabbinic writings (the earliest of which date, in written form, from *c.* AD 200); and Paul, who states that he was formerly a Pharisee (Phil. 3: 5). So we have plenty of evidence. Unfortunately it often seems to be contradictory. For example, the rabbinic writings (and the gospels) indicate that the Pharisees were particularly concerned with food laws, but Josephus says next to nothing about this, even though he claims to be a Pharisee himself.

The difficulties can be resolved to some extent by noting the purposes of the various writings. Josephus wrote in order to give his sophisticated Roman readers a favourable impression of Judaism. He is often very negative about the Pharisees. He presents them as a philosophical school and (apparently) decides to avoid adverse reactions by playing down their concern with food and purity laws. In agreement with the gospels, Paul, and the rabbinic writings, Josephus does, however, refer to the strictness and exactness with which they interpreted the law.

In recent decades rigorous historical methods have been used for the first time in study of the rabbinic writings. This work has been pioneered by the Jewish scholar Jacob Neusner. In numerous writings he has shown that two-thirds of the rabbinic traditions about the Pharisees before AD 70 deal with dietary laws: ritual purity for meals, and agricultural rules governing the fitness of food for consumption. According to Neusner, at the time of Jesus the Pharisees were attempting to replicate the temple cult in everyday life in the home; they were the 'missionaries' or 'religious enthusiasts' of their day.

These concerns for purity should not be understood (as they often have been by Christians) as pettifogging legalism. In Leviticus impurity or ritual defilement is related to a wide range of matters which include sexual morality and rules of diet. There were, of course, various ways in which 'purity' could be restored, including lustration rites (cf. Mark 1: 44). This concern for purity is profoundly religious in intention. It is directly related to God's command to be holy, for God himself is holy (see, for example, Lev. 11: 44).

At the time of Jesus some observed the laws of purity strictly, some did not. The Essenes and the Pharisees went further than most in their observance of the law. They extended some of the requirements of the law, usually in the light of other passages of Scripture. For example, Scripture does not prescribe ritual purity for the eating of ordinary meals (cf. Lev. 14: 46–7), though this is required of priests who eat the food specially dedicated in offerings to the Lord (Lev. 22: 3–9). Since all Israel was declared to be a 'kingdom of priests' (Ex. 19: 6), Qumran Essenes and probably Pharisees ate meals in a state of purity. The purity laws kept by priests in the temple were to be observed at the table of the ordinary Jew; thus, quite literally, Israel would be turned into a 'kingdom of priests and a holy nation'.

The Pharisees were concerned with the application of the will of God to the whole of life. Unlike the Essenes and (to a lesser extent) the Sadducees, they did not cut themselves off from society. Like Jesus, they were seeking the renewal of the whole of Israel, though of course they differed in how this was to be achieved.

Not all the traditions in the gospels are hostile to the Pharisees. Luke mentions that on two occasions Jesus was invited to dine with a Pharisee (7: 36; 14: 1) and that some Pharisees warned Jesus that Herod wanted to kill him (13: 31; cf. also Acts 5: 34). How can these favourable references to the Pharisees in Luke and our suggestion that Jesus shared some of their concerns be reconciled with the 'conflict' traditions in the gospels?

Sociologists have often observed that the closer the relationship between groups, the more intense the conflict. Some modern political parties provide ample illustration of this phenomenon. So it is by no means implausible to conclude that in many ways Jesus was closer to the Pharisees than to Qumran Essenes, groups of resistance fighters, or the Sadducees.

Sabbath, purity, and divorce

We turn now to three of the issues on which, according to the evangelists, Jesus and the Pharisees differed. Controversy over the sabbath is prominent in all the gospels. Mark includes two disputes (2: 23–8 and 3: 1–6) which both Matthew and Luke retain. Matthew expands these traditions (12: 1–14) and Luke adds two quite separate incidents (13: 10–17 and 14: 1–5). Two of John's discourses have as their starting point a sabbath dispute (5: 1–9 and 9: 1–7).

Along with all the various Jewish groups Jesus and his disciples normally kept the sabbath and attended the synagogue (see, for example, Mark 1: 21 and Luke 4: 16). But did Jesus occasionally flout the generally observed laws, as the evangelists insist? Or are these disputes a reflection of later controversies in the early church? Mark the evangelist underlines the importance of the conflict: he even makes a direct link between Jesus' healing of a man with a withered hand and a plot to destroy Jesus which was instigated by the Pharisees (3: 1–6). Mark does not, however, mention this dispute in his account of the trial of Jesus.

At the time of Jesus where there was danger to life, healings were permitted on the sabbath. The sabbath healings in the gospels, however, do not fall into that category. Since Jesus could have waited until the following day to heal, he does seem to have provoked conflict with those (especially Pharisees) who were keen to observe sabbath regulations meticulously. But there is a further complication. Some scholars have noted that in stories of healing on the sabbath in the synoptic gospels, Jesus always heals simply with a word: since no physical action was involved, sabbath law (it is alleged) was not transgressed. This line of argument is dubious. Not only is it based on silence (Jesus may well have used some form of 'physical action' which is not recorded) but it is also based on sabbath regulations which cannot be dated with confidence to the first century.

The pericope concerning the plucking of grain from a field on the sabbath is both interesting and complex (Mark 2: 23–8). It concludes with two bold pronouncements: 'the sabbath was made for humankind, and not humankind for the sabbath' (v. 27); 'the Son of Man is lord even of the sabbath' (v. 28). As we saw in the previous chapter, in their original form the 'Son of Man' sayings may have been an indirect way Jesus used to speak about his authority. If so, then in verse 28 Jesus may be defending himself (and his disciples) on the basis of the more general statement in verse 27: in exceptional circumstances Jesus could override sabbath regulations since the needs of individuals (or of Israel) took priority. Since it was permissible to pluck corn from the edge of a farmer's field, but not on the sabbath, Jesus is claiming that the circumstances were exceptional. But is mere hunger an 'exceptional circumstance'? In his defence Jesus claims support for his conduct from David's action when he and those with him were hungry. The argument is so sophisticated that it is unlikely to have been invented in the early church as a defence of Christian rejection of sabbath observance.

Taken as a whole, the sabbath controversies suggest that Jesus caused offence by acting against widely accepted interpretation of the the current laws, though he rarely if ever broke the law. Even if Jesus' healings on the sabbath did not technically break sabbath regulations, they caused deep offence. They fall into the same category as Jesus' failure to fast (Mark 2: 18–20): convention was flouted and this led to conflict. Flouting of convention can provoke conflict which is just as sharp as that caused by non-observance of laws.

The clearest rejection by Jesus of the plain teaching of the law is the saying attributed to him in Mark 7: 15: 'There is nothing outside a person which by going in can defile; but the things which come out of a person are what defile.' Mark states that this saying was a *parabolē* ('parable' or enigmatic saying—see above p. 219). Mark himself adds a note for his readers in order to underline the significance of this saying attributed to Jesus: 'Thus he declared all foods clean' (7: 19b). But did Jesus launch an all-out attack on a fundamental principle of the law and a continuing concern of many (perhaps even most) Jews at that time? Did he teach that from now on it was acceptable for any Jew to eat any kind of food?

Some scholars who are not noted for conservative views on the historicity of the gospel traditions use this saying as part of their argument that

Jesus repudiated the plain teaching of the Mosaic law. But Jesus is unlikely to have challenged directly basic biblical teaching concerning pure and impure food (Lev. 11; Deut. 14). This is the only passage in the gospels which suggests that he did so. And if he did so, then it is difficult to explain why in his crucial controversy with Paul, Peter retreated and sided with James and the 'false brethren' by refusing to eat with non-Jews (Gal. 2: 1–14).

Mark's comment, 'Thus he declared all foods clean' (v. 19b) may have been influenced by these later controversies in the early church. We know from 1 Cor. 10: 14–33 (and cf. also Rom. 14: 14) that there were also disputes concerning meat which had been slaughtered as part of a pagan sacrifice.

There is a plausible explanation of the enigmatic saying of Jesus on defilement (v. 15) which is more consistent with other traditions in the gospels than Mark's comment that Jesus rejected entirely not only Pharisaic but also biblical food laws. Jesus may have been using a pattern of speech which is attested elsewhere in the gospels: an apparent denial of one claim in favour of another means in fact 'not so much' the former 'as' (rather) the latter. Hence the intended meaning may have been: 'A person is *not so much* defiled by that which enters from outside *as* he is by that which comes from within.'

In other words, Jesus may not have rejected the view that defilement was caused by eating particular foods, or by touching a corpse. He may have insisted that defilement is caused *not so much* by physical contact with 'impure' objects or people, *as* by a person's own impure thoughts and desires (Mark 7: 20–3 and note also 7: 2). This is radical teaching, for it challenges accepted priorities and conventions. It is consistent with Jesus' attitude to sabbath laws and conventions. But what about divorce?

Of all the conflicts between Jesus and the Pharisees, perhaps that over permissible grounds for divorce is the most intriguing and problematic (Mark 10: 1–12 and cf. the Q saying behind Matt. 5: 32 and Luke 16: 18). In order to test Jesus, Pharisees asked, 'Is it lawful for a man to divorce his wife?' (Mark 10: 2). Jesus knew full well that his critics were divided on what precisely were the permissible grounds under which Moses 'allowed a man to write a certificate of dismissal and to divorce his wife' (10: 4 and cf. Deut. 24: 1–4). Jesus did not repudiate the law of Moses, but took a more stringent line—a line which may have been shared with a minority among his contemporaries. Jesus declared, 'Therefore what God has joined together [as man and wife], let no one separate [i.e. divorce]' (10: 9).

This saying has strong claims to authenticity, for it seems to have embarrassed Jesus' own followers. (For this criterion for authenticity, see above p. 175.) Immediately after the radical denial of divorce in verse 9, the disciples ask for clarification 'in the house'. Jesus replies, 'Whoever divorces his wife and marries another, commits adultery against her' (v. 11). Strictly speaking there is a contradiction between verse 9, 'no divorce', and verses 11–12, 'no remarriage following divorce'. Presumably the further teaching given in verses 11–12 'in the house' reflects *later* clarification of what should happen where the ideal of 'no divorce' is not attained among disciples of Jesus. If so, this would be in line with what we find elsewhere in early Christian writings.

Paul quotes Jesus' radical denial of divorce in 1 Cor. 7: 10 and 11b, but immediately indicates that in his own view there is a permissible ground for divorce (vv. 11a and 15). A Christian need not necessarily divorce an unbelieving partner (vv. 12–14), 'but if the unbelieving partner desires to separate, let it be so' (v. 15).

In Matthew's version of the teaching of Jesus on divorce recorded in Mark 10: 10–11 *porneia* is referred to as a permissible ground for divorce (5: 32 and 19: 9). The meaning of this key word is disputed; NRSV and REB translate 'unchastity', but precisely what was thought to constitute 'unchastity' is unclear. So whereas Jesus did not allow divorce, the law of Moses, current Pharisaic teaching, Paul, Matthew, and perhaps even Mark the evangelist, all allowed that in certain circumstances it was permissible.

The variations between Matthew, Mark, and Paul have caused great consternation to Christians for two thousand years. Until modern times most Christians followed the lead first given by Hermas the early second-century Christian writer: while divorce as separation is permissible, remarriage is not (*Mand.* 4. 1. 6).

Under the influence of Erasmus and the Reformers, an alternative approach first became popular in the sixteenth century. Matthew's version of the teaching of Jesus is given priority: following *porneia* ('unchastity') divorce is permissible. On this view, Mark is thought to be an abbreviation of the full and normative teaching of Matthew, which records accurately the original teaching of Jesus. But once we accept that Mark is our first written gospel and that Matthew is dependent on Mark, this view becomes untenable.

If careful historical study of the gospels is taken seriously, we have no option but to conclude that Jesus rejected divorce. In this case (unlike many others) it is possible to recover the original words of Jesus with a fair measure of confidence. But what did Jesus mean? Did he intend to lay down a clear legal ruling? If so, was his stringent demand only for disciples, or was it intended for people in general? If the latter, how do we square his 'harsh' ruling on divorce with his attitude of compassion shown to so many whose lives fell short of God's requirements? If Jesus did intend to legislate, then both Matthew, Paul, and perhaps Mark, have misunderstood his intention by allowing that in a given situation his absolute demand could be qualified.

As part of his reply to the Pharisees Jesus appealed to what is often known as the 'creation principle'. Jesus quoted from two passages in Genesis, giving them priority over the teaching of Moses. 'God made them male and female'; 'For this reason a man shall leave his father and mother and be joined to his wife, and the two shall become one' (Mark 10: 6–8, quoting Gen. 1: 27 and 2: 24). These quotations provide the specific theological context in which Jesus spoke about divorce. Jesus believed that in the coming (or already partly present) end-time, the conditions of the beginning time of creation would be restored. In other words, the coming of God's kingly rule would lead to a restoration of his original 'creation' intention ('the two shall become one'), which had been thwarted by people's 'hardness of heart' (Mark 10: 5). On this approach, the 'harsh' teaching of Jesus on divorce was for those prepared to respond to his proclamation of the kingly rule of God. The coming new age meant a radical break with current conventions. If this explanation is correct (and in the context of first-century Jewish teaching there is a good deal to be said for it), then Paul has accurately implemented a distinction implied by Jesus. Divorce is not permitted for those committed to discipleship of Jesus (with its radical implications), but it is permitted reluctantly for marriages between believers and unbelievers.

Whether or not this explanation of the 'harsh' teaching of Jesus is accepted, it is clear that, as on many other issues, Jesus and the Pharisees parted company in their attitudes to divorce. In this case Jesus was not defying or rejecting the law of Moses (though Jesus' teaching has often been wrongly understood to carry this implication). Rather Jesus was giving priority to one part of Scripture (Gen. 1: 24, 27) over another (Deut. 24: 1–4). In this case, as in others, Jesus frequently called for greater stringency than did the plain teaching of the law of Moses.

Did Jesus ever intend to repudiate the Mosaic law? On issues of sabbath observance and divorce Jesus parted company with some of the ways in which many (in particular Pharisees) interpreted the implications of the law. In these cases, the conflict revolved around differing interpretations of the will of God as revealed in Scripture. In some cases, such as fasting and hand-washing before meals, Jesus caused offence by rejecting well-established conventions which were not a matter of law at all. Jesus seems neither to have confirmed nor to have denied that eating impure food leads to ritual defilement. Instead he took the wind out of his opponents' sails by asserting that moral actions such as fornication, theft, murder, adultery, and avarice caused greater defilement than impure food (Mark 7: 21–3). In so doing, he was giving priority to one section of the law over another—just as he did in the case of divorce. But neither in this case nor in any other did Jesus reject the law of Moses.

17

THE LAST DAYS

Passion narratives in the four gospels

The four evangelists all record in some detail the last days of Jesus before his crucifixion and burial. In the final part of their stories they agree much more closely in the order of the events and in the content of the individual episodes than they do earlier. This is not surprising. It does not matter very much whether the incidents Mark records in 2: 1 to 3: 6, for example, happened early in the ministry of Jesus or not. Mark might well have included some of these stories in his collection of conflict traditions in chapter 12. But within the passion narratives the order of the individual episodes usually does matter. Mark could not have recorded the crucifixion of Jesus before referring to his arrest!

The missionary preaching and the worship of the earliest Christian communities focused on the death and resurrection of Jesus. Paul's account of the institution by Jesus of what Christians later called the Last Supper or Eucharist includes a reference to 'the night when Jesus was betrayed', the words of Jesus over the bread and the cup, and the command, 'Do this in remembrance of me' (1 Cor. 11: 24–5; see also Luke 22: 19). So it is reasonable to suppose that at their celebrations of the Last Supper, the first followers of Jesus recounted with particular care the events of the last days of Jesus in Jerusalem.

These considerations led several form critics who wrote in the 1920s and 1930s to suggest that behind all four gospels stands an early, coherent, and on the whole accurate account of the last days of Jesus. More recent studies have shown just how difficult it is to establish the precise extent of an original passion narrative to which some further episodes might have been added at a later stage. Indeed it has been argued by some that it was the evangelist Mark who first brought together originally independent accounts of the various episodes which now feature in his passion narrative. That seems unlikely simply because many of the individual episodes make sense only when set alongside others. The account of the arrest of Jesus (Mark 14: 43–50), for example, was probably linked from the very earliest period with the Sanhedrin hearing before the 'high priest, and all the chief priests, the elders, and the scribes' (Mark 14: 53–65).

Even if an early short passion narrative does lie behind all four gospels, the evangelists have all developed their own distinctive emphases both by their choice of supplementary traditions and by their reshaping and adaptation of the narratives. The passion narratives contain the same blend of 'story' and 'significance' as other parts of the gospels. Before we turn to some of the central episodes in the last days of Jesus, we shall consider briefly (as we have done in earlier chapters of Part II) the individual evangelists' contributions.

Mark opens his passion narrative with a solemn and formal introduction: 'It was two days before the Passover and the festival of Unleavened Bread. The chief priests and the scribes were seeking how to arrest Jesus by stealth and kill him' (14: 1). In the narratives which follow Mark develops themes to which he has drawn attention earlier in his gospel.

It has been said that the whole of Mark's gospel is a passion narrative with an extended introduction. Although this comment is an exaggeration, Mark prepares for the passion long before 14: 1. He refers to a plot to destroy Jesus as early as 3: 6. A similar threat is reported in 11: 18, immediately after the so-called cleansing of the temple. In 12: 12 once again we hear of the authorities' plot: they recognize that Jesus has told the parable of the wicked husbandmen against them. Jesus' own threefold predictions of his impending passion (8: 31; 9: 31; 10: 33) prepare the reader for the final act in the drama long before it takes place. In chapters 11–13 Mark emphasizes anti-temple and anti-Jerusalem themes which reach a climax in the accusation before the Sanhedrin that Jesus was heard to say these words: 'I will destroy this temple that is made with hands, and in three days I will build another, not made with hands' (14: 58). A second climax occurs with the note that at the death of Jesus 'the curtain of the temple was torn in two, from top to bottom' (15: 38). The temple is no longer the focal point of access to God; the 'new community' will itself be 'a temple not made with hands'.

In Chapter 3 (pp. 42–4) we saw that Mark's emphasis on Jesus as Son of God reaches its climax with the cry of the Roman centurion at the moment Jesus dies: 'Truly this man was God's Son' (15: 39). We also noted that Mark draws attention to the disciples' failure to understand Jesus (pp. 45–6). Finally they all forsake Jesus and flee (14: 50). Even the young man who 'followed Jesus' (at his arrest, but perhaps earlier) 'ran away naked' (14: 51–2). Peter 'follows at a distance' (14: 54) and then denies Jesus (14: 66–72). Mark does not call the inner circle of followers 'disciples' from the Gethsemane incident (14: 32) right through to the message of the mysterious young man sitting at the entrance to the empty tomb. The young man hints at the eventual restoration of the disciples. 'But go, tell his disciples and Peter that he is going ahead of you to Galilee; there you will see him, just as he told you' (16: 7). Mark ends not with a grand resurrection appearance, but with the fear of the women at the discovery of the empty tomb: the ending is as terse and enigmatic as many other parts of the gospel.

Matthew retains almost all of Mark's passion narrative. He adds some rather puzzling additional material such as the accounts of the death of Judas (27: 3–10), Pilate's wife's dream (27: 19), and the earthquake which occurred as Jesus died and which 'opened the tombs of the saints' (27: 52–4). Most of Matthew's characteristic emphases, which we noted in Chapter 4, can be readily observed in his reshaping of Marcan and other traditions in his passion narratives. Mark's Son of God Christology, for example, is strengthened still further. In his expanded version of Mark's account of the scene of the crucifixion, passers-by deride Jesus in words which recall Matthew's temptation narratives: '*If you are the Son of God*, come down from the cross' (27: 40; cf. 4: 3, 6). In words which have no parallel in Mark, the Jewish leaders continue the derision: 'Jesus trusts in God; let God deliver him now, if he wants to; for he said, "I am God's Son"' (27: 43). Readers of Matthew appreciate the irony: they know full well that the evangelist believes that Jesus *was* the Son of God. The additional taunts make the believing response of the Roman centurion all the more poignant: 'Truly this man was God's Son' (27: 54).

Matthew's anti-Jewish polemic and apologetic provide a second example of his reshaping of his traditions in line with his earlier emphases. The chief priests accept that they are responsible for the death of Jesus by taking the blood money returned by Judas (27: 3–10). In additions to Mark at 27: 19 and 24, Pilate's wife and Pilate himself acknowledge that Jesus is innocent. In stark contrast (in another addition to Marcan traditions) the people accept full responsibility for the death of Jesus: 'His blood be on us and on our children' (27: 25).

Perhaps in order to counter Jewish claims that the disciples of Jesus stole his body and pronounced him risen from the dead, Matthew records that the chief priests and the Pharisees pleaded (successfully) with Pilate to be allowed to place a secure guard of soldiers at the tomb (27: 62–6). On the discovery of the empty tomb, the guards were bribed by the chief priests to say that some of the disciples of Jesus 'came by night and stole him away while we were asleep'. 'This story', Matthew observes, 'is still told among the Jews to this day' (28: 11–15).

Luke follows Mark much less closely than Matthew. His passion narrative differs both in order and content at so many points that some scholars have argued that Luke possessed an independent non-Marcan passion narrative, which he filled out with a handful of Mark's traditions. Since Luke is usually reluctant to alter Mark, this suggestion is plausible. However, many scholars now accept that Mark, not an independent narrative, is the base on which Luke has built. On this view Luke has reshaped Mark quite considerably and has made use of a number of traditions to which he alone seems to have had access. On either view Luke's passion narrative is distinctive.

Luke takes pains to stress the innocence of Jesus. The three accusations which the Jewish leaders level against Jesus in Pilate's presence are carefully balanced by Pilate's threefold declaration that Jesus is innocent (compare 23: 2 with 23: 4, 14 and 22). Herod also concedes that Jesus is innocent (23: 15), as does one of the men crucified with Jesus (23: 41). In contrast to Mark and Matthew, the Roman centurion does not declare that Jesus is the Son of God, rather that he is innocent (23: 47). This theme is also prominent in Acts; see, for example, Acts 3: 13–16 and 13: 27–8. Luke's portrait of Paul is similar. Jewish authorities bring political charges against Paul, but Luke stresses that in Roman eyes he too is innocent (Acts 17: 5–9; 24: 1–9; 25: 7–8, 13–27; 26: 30–2). In his two volumes Luke takes pains to stress that as far as the Romans are concerned, Jesus and his followers are politically innocent.

Even more frequently than the other evangelists, Luke stresses the compassion of Jesus for those on the fringes of society. The same motif is prominent in his passion narrative. Jesus consistently shows sympathy for the various individuals and groups who enter the story: for the high priest's servant whose right ear was cut off by one of the disciples (22: 50–1); for Peter, in spite of his denials (22: 61–2); for the lamenting women who follow him to the place of crucifixion (23: 27–31); for one of the criminals crucified with him (23: 43).

From the betrayal by Judas (18: 2–11) right through to the burial of Jesus by Joseph of Arimathea (19: 38–42) John's passion narrative seems to be similar, at least in broad outline, to the synoptic gospels. But as is often the case, first appearances are deceptive. In John there is no account of the institution of the eucharist. Instead, at the final meal which Jesus shares with his disciples, he washes their feet (13: 1–20). Then, in a lengthy series of monologues in chapters 14–17 (usually known as the farewell discourses), Jesus prepares the disciples for the future. There is nothing comparable in the synoptic gospels, though arguably Luke 22: 24–38 is a partial exception.

In John there is no Gethsemane scene, simply a bald reference to a 'garden across the Kidron valley' which Jesus and his disciples entered only to be met by Judas with a band of soldiers and officers (18: 1–3). There is no trial by the Sanhedrin. Jesus is questioned informally by Annas (the father-in-law of Caiaphas, the high priest) 'about his disciples and his teaching' (18: 19) and then sent bound to Caiaphas. But there is no record at all of a hearing before Caiaphas.

Jesus remains serenely confident and totally dominates the proceedings from his arrest right through to his final cry of triumph from the cross, 'It is finished' (19: 30). As the arresting party confronts Jesus, he takes the initiative and asks, 'Whom are you looking for?' They answer, 'Jesus of Nazareth'. Jesus replies, 'I am he'. His words recall the way God speaks in numerous passages in the Old Testament, and, perhaps, God's revelation of himself to Moses: 'I am who I am' (Exod. 3: 14). At these words the arresting party 'stepped back and fell to the ground' (18: 4–6). The reader of John's passion narrative soon realizes that it is not Jesus who is on trial, but the various individuals and groups with whom he comes in contact. The death of Jesus is neither a tragedy (Mark) nor a sad and moving spectacle (Luke), but a royal triumph. Earlier in the gospel the evangelist has explained to the reader that the 'lifting up of Jesus on the cross' is not a disaster, but his exaltation to the Father (3: 13–14; 8: 28; 12: 31–6). (For further discussion of the Johannine passion narrative, see pp. 113–16.)

We now turn from the evangelists' reshaping and development of the earlier traditions on which they drew to the main episodes in the last days of the life of Jesus. We soon discover that two stories are interwoven. The dominant story concerns Jesus' entanglement with the Jewish and Roman authorities. This starts with the entry of Jesus into Jerusalem, and continues with the 'cleansing' of the temple, the betrayal by Judas, and the hearings before the Sanhedrin and Pilate; it reaches its climax with the eventual crucifixion of Jesus. There is another largely separate story: it concerns the relationship of Jesus with his disciples (the Last Supper, Peter's denials) and with God (Gethsemane, the final words from the cross); its climax comes with the discovery of the empty tomb and the appearances of the Risen Jesus to his disciples. In the remainder of this chapter we shall consider central questions from each of these stories. What did Jesus teach his disciples at the Last Supper? Why was Jesus put to death? What happened 'on the third day'?

The Last Supper

In addition to the accounts of the Last Supper in the synoptic gospels, Paul quotes a tradition which he received 'from the Lord' (1 Cor. 11: 23–6). This is the earliest written account of the last meal Jesus shared with his disciples. It is fifteen to twenty years earlier than Mark 14: 22–5, though of course the oral traditions which Paul and Mark used may be equally early. Many of the details in the tradition Paul quotes correspond to Luke's account in 22: 17–20. Some scholars believe that the verses in Luke represent an earlier form of the Pauline tradition; others claim that the reverse is true.

The matter is complicated by the existence in some manuscripts of Luke's gospel of a shorter account which omits verses 19b and 20. The longer account, which is found in very nearly all the earliest and most reliable manuscripts, is more clearly related to Paul's. It is not difficult to understand why a short 'untheological' original account in Luke might at some later point have been expanded in most manuscripts under the influence of 1 Cor. 11: 22–6. The short account has an unusual order which may well have been brought into line with the traditional order at a later stage. In the shorter account a reference to Jesus taking a *cup* and giving thanks

(v. 17) is followed by 'Then he took a loaf of *bread*, and when he had given thanks he broke it and gave it to them, saying, "This is my body"' (v. 19a).

The longer account includes these additional words in verses 19b and 20: '[This is my body] which is given for you. Do this in remembrance of me. And he did the same with the cup after the supper, saying, "This cup that is poured out for you is the new covenant in my blood."' These words are missing in only one major Greek manuscript (Codex Bezae) and in some early Latin translations. Of the various explanations for their omission, the following seem the most plausible. An early scribe may have been confused by the odd order of the longer account (cup, v. 17; bread, v. 19; cup, v. 20) so he decided to omit reference to the second cup. Or perhaps the omission of verses 19b and 20 from Codex Bezae has to be put down to some scribal idiosyncrasy; there are several puzzling omissions in this same manuscript in Luke 24.

Mark's account has been followed closely by Matthew, but also developed. Some of Matthew's additions clearly represent the influence of liturgical practice. Mark's simple 'Take, this is my body' (14: 22) becomes 'Take, *eat*, this is my body' (Matt. 26: 26). Mark's statement, 'all of them drank from it' (v. 23) becomes a command, 'Drink from it, all of you' (v. 27), which neatly balances the command 'Take, eat . . .'. There is also an important theological addition. Mark's reference to 'the blood of the covenant, which is poured out for many' (v. 24) is expanded (and, one might say, expounded) by 'for the forgiveness of sins' (v. 28).

The accounts of the last meal in the synoptic gospels and in 1 Corinthians 11 differ considerably in detail. By taking account of the liturgical and theological development of the traditions, it is possible to isolate an early tradition behind Mark–Matthew in which the focus is on the atoning death of Jesus, and another early form behind Luke–I Corinthians in which 'the new covenant' theme is dominant. Before we consider further the meaning of the original words of Jesus (in so far as they can be reconstructed), we must consider whether or not the Last Supper of Jesus with his disciples was a Passover celebration. If it was, then we may have an important clue to the interpretation of the actions and words of Jesus at that last meal.

In their accounts of the preparations for the last meal, the synoptic evangelists all state explicitly that it was a Passover meal. Passover was the high point in the Jewish religious year. Unless prevented by distance, every adult Jew kept Passover in Jerusalem. The population of Jerusalem was swollen fourfold by visitors. At Passover God's deliverance of his people from Egypt was recalled; hope for a coming new redemption was held keenly by many. Passover lambs were slaughtered ritually at the temple in the afternoon of the 'Day of Preparation' (14 Nisan) and then eaten in homes at the Passover meal that evening, 'the First Day of Unleavened Bread' (which was reckoned as the start of 15 Nisan).

The chronology implied in John's gospel differs. Jesus is crucified on the 'Day of Preparation' (John 19: 31), so his last meal with his disciples would have been held on 14 Nisan, twenty-four hours *before* the Passover. How is this discrepancy to be accounted for?

The fourth evangelist may have altered the chronology. He may have wanted his readers to appreciate the significance of the fact that Jesus died at the moment the Passover lambs were being slaughtered in the temple: Jesus is the lamb of God who takes away the sins of the world (cf. John 1: 29). If this is John's intention, it is odd that he does not make this profound theological point more explicitly.

Or it is possible that John's chronology is correct. If so, then in the course of the development of the tradition behind the synoptic gospels, the Last Supper, which was in fact held twenty-four hours before Passover, became an account of a Passover meal. (The various attempts to eliminate the difficulty by claiming that there were two calendars or two ways of reckoning days all seem forced and implausible.)

The accounts of the last meal in the synoptic gospels have been examined meticulously for tell-tale signs which might either confirm or rule out the possibility that it was a Passover meal. Joachim Jeremias has listed twelve reasons for identifying the Last Supper as a Passover. Not all his points are convincing, and some are more plausible than others. Nevertheless, the case remains strong. The main objection is that although there is a reference to the Passover lamb in the accounts of the preparations for the meal (Mark 14: 20 and Luke 22: 15), the lamb is conspicuous by its absence from the accounts of the meal itself. In other words, the original form of the tradition of the meal may not have been that of a Passover meal; the detailed account of the preparations may have been added at a later stage. In reply, it can be claimed that the earliest Christians who transmitted the accounts of the last meal were primarily interested in the words of Jesus over the bread and the cup. Hence reference to the Passover lamb may have dropped out of the tradition concerning the meal itself and been retained only in the account of the preparations for the meal.

The Mishnah (*m. Pesahim* x. 1–9) gives full details of the Passover *seder* or order of service. Although it dates in its written form from *c.* AD 200, at the time of Jesus it probably followed the summary given here. There were four main parts to the Passover meal.

1. The Preliminary Course:
   Blessing (*Kiddush*) spoken over the first cup of wine
   Dish of green herbs, bitter herbs and fruit sauce
   Serving of the meal and mixing of the second cup of wine

2. The Passover Liturgy
   The Passover narrative (*haggadah*, based on Exodus 12) was recited by the head of the household, in response to the youngest son's question, 'Why is this night different from all other nights?'
   Drinking of the second cup of wine
   Singing of Psalm 113

3. The Main Meal:
   Grace spoken over the unleavened bread, bitter herbs (Exodus 12: 8)
   Meal of lamb, unleavened bread, bitter herbs
   Grace over the third cup of wine

4. Conclusion:
   Singing of Psalms 114–18 (the great *hallel*)
   Praise over the fourth cup of wine

There are four probable indications in Mark's account of the meal itself (and not merely in the account of the preparations) that the Last Supper was a Passover meal. (i) Mark notes that the meal was eaten in the evening (14: 17); normal meals began in the late afternoon and rarely lasted beyond sunset. (ii) Mark implies that a dish had been taken before the bread was distributed (14: 20); this may be a reference to the preliminary course noted above. (iii) Mark mentions that the meal was concluded with the singing of a hymn (14: 26); this was probably the great *hallel*. (iv) But perhaps most important of all are the words of interpretation spoken by Jesus over the bread and the cup. While the Passover *haggadah* included comment on the significance of the various features of the meal, this did not accompany the distribution of the unleavened bread and a cup of wine, as do the words of Jesus. Here Jesus seems to be giving new significance to the central element in the Passover liturgy, the recalling of the past redemptive act of God at the Exodus and the hope of his future grace to Israel.

Can we more precise about the intention of Jesus? In its Marcan form the saying over the bread is terse: 'Take; this is my body' (14: 22). There is little doubt that Jesus indicates that the bread given to the disciples signifies the gift of the whole of himself (not simply his flesh). In Mark the saying over the cup fills out, as it were, this first saying by making explicit the implicit reference to the forthcoming death of Jesus. In the Luke–Paul tradition (which may well be the earliest form of the tradition) the gift of the bread (i.e. of Jesus himself) is 'for you' (the disciples). Jesus compares his death to that of a martyr.

In some first-century Jewish circles it was held that the death of a martyr atoned for the sins of Israel. The writer of 4 Maccabees (writing perhaps shortly before the time of Jesus) notes that through the death of martyrs 'our country was purified, they having as it were become a ransom for our nation's sin; and through the blood of these righteous men and the propitiation of their death, the divine Providence delivered Israel' (17: 21 f.). In his words over the bread Jesus almost certainly draws on this tradition. It is also probable (though this is disputed) that the phrase 'for you', like the 'for many' in the cup saying, alludes to the suffering servant of God in Isa. 53: 10–12 who gives himself as a sacrifice for sin and who bears the sins of many.

Although the words of Jesus over the cup differ in the various traditions, in all of them the blood (i.e. the forthcoming death of Jesus) is said to mark the making of a covenant. In 1 Cor. 11: 25 and Luke 22: 20 the covenant is said to be 'new'; this is probably a later expansion which echoes the reference in Jer. 31: 31–4 to the new covenant which God promised to make with his people. The primary background, however, is Exod. 24: 8–11, where, following a sacrifice, Moses takes the blood of the animal and sprinkles it upon the people with the words, 'See the blood of the covenant that the Lord has made with you.' In a Jewish exposition (targum) of this passage, the blood is said to cleanse the people from their sins. If this interpretation was known at the time of Jesus (and this is possible but not certain) the 'cup' saying of Jesus, like the 'bread' saying, may have referred to his forthcoming death as an atonement for sin.

We can be confident that the covenant theme was central in the words of Jesus over the cup. In Old Testament thought a covenant is a relationship which God enters into with his people: his promise to be their God carried the obligation that they would be his people and carry out his will. Even if Jesus did not use the word 'new' to describe the covenant, he implies that through his forthcoming death God is entering into a new relationship with his people.

Why was Jesus put to death?

It is by no means easy to determine why Jesus was put to death. The issues are complex and at crucial points there are gaps in our historical knowledge. The evangelists are not concerned with constitutional and legal niceties. They tell the story of the last days of Jesus very selectively, and only in so far as it meets the needs of Christian communities in their own day. There is Jewish and Roman evidence which may help to fill out the picture the evangelists sketch, but it is often difficult to decide which parts of that evidence are directly relevant.

The main issues are these. If the Romans were primarily responsible for the death of Jesus, did they act reasonably and with good cause? If so, then the Romans must have considered Jesus to be a dangerous political agitator and a threat to the stability they sought to impose as the occupying power. Or was there a gross miscarriage of Roman justice?

To what extent was there Jewish involvement in the downfall of Jesus? Was there a formal hearing before the Sanhedrin, or merely informal discussion? What were the accusations made against Jesus? How are those accusations related to the issues at stake between Jesus and his opponents *before* he went up to Jerusalem for the last time?

We must first consider whether or not the Jewish authorities were permitted to carry out capital punishment. If they were, they would almost certainly have stoned Jesus, for crucifixion was primarily a Roman form of execution. In other words, if the Sanhedrin did have the power of capital punishment, then apparently it was not used. Jewish involvement must have been minimal or non-existent. If, on the other hand, the Romans reserved for themselves the right to execute, then it remains possible that the Jewish authorities held either an informal hearing or a formal trial before handing the case over to the Romans.

So what was the precise relationship between the Romans and the Jerusalem leaders during the last days of Jesus? There is some Jewish evidence which suggests that the Sanhedrin was not competent to carry out capital punishment. An important passage in the Talmud (*j. Sanh.* 1: 1; 7: 2) notes that 'the right to try capital cases was taken from Israel forty years before the destruction of the temple'. The reference to forty years is probably a round number which refers to the beginning of direct rule by the Romans in AD 6. In John 18: 31 the Jewish leaders claim it is not lawful for them to put anyone to death, though it is not clear that this is intended as a historical comment; the verse which follows suggests otherwise. There is no explicit statement in Mark concerning the powers of the Sanhedrin in capital cases, but this gospel does assume that the Roman procurator held the right to carry out an execution.

There are, however, some accounts of executions which were carried out on the orders of the Sanhedrin between AD 6 and AD 70. Some scholars have appealed to them in order to argue that since the Jewish authorities could have put Jesus to death, their involvement with the death of Jesus was minimal. On closer inspection, however, not one of the cases offers firm support for this explanation. The Mishnah (*San.* 7.2) records that the daughter of a priest who had committed adultery was burned to death. But this was almost certainly during the reign of Agrippa I, when the Jews again had their own independent state for a short period between AD 41 and 44. A few years later, in AD 62, James the brother of Jesus was condemned by the Sanhedrin and stoned (Josephus, *Antiquities* xx. 200–3). But Josephus explains that the high priest acted illegally in presiding over this Sanhedrin decision; he was later deprived of his office as a result. Luke records the death of Stephen by stoning (Acts 7: 54–60). But although Acts 6: 11 to 7: 1 states that the accusations against Stephen were heard at a formal trial, Luke's account of his death implies that it was caused by the impulsive actions of a lynch mob rather than as a result of a formal legal decision. In the account of the woman caught in the act of adultery (John 7: 53 to 8: 11) there is no suggestion that the scribes and Pharisees intended to arrange a judicial hearing; they hoped to trick Jesus into giving a ruling which would allow them to condemn him. In short, both the Jewish and the Christian evidence seems to suggest that the Jews could try but not execute, though we cannot be certain about this.

It has often been alleged that Mark's account of the Sanhedrin trial cannot be historical because in five respects it infringed current procedures: the Sanhedrin met at night (and not during the daytime); it met on the eve of Passover, which was illegal; there was no second hearing to confirm the sentence of death; the trial was held in the house of the high priest, not in the Sanhedrin's regular hall of assembly; Mark implies that blasphemy was the central issue, but does *not* state that Jesus uttered the divine name, the form of blasphemy punishable by death. Luke's account contains at most only two 'infringements', but it is at least possible that Luke has himself made modifications in order to make his account of the Sanhedrin hearing more 'legal'. Debate over these alleged infringements has reached a stalemate simply because we do not know for certain what procedures were followed by the Sanhedrin at the time of Jesus. Mark's account does 'infringe' the laws which were codified in written form *c.* 200. But these laws probably represent Pharisaic practice, whereas at the time of Jesus the Sadducees dominated the Sanhedrin.

Scholars who deny that there was a Sanhedrin trial or informal hearing claim that the accounts in the synoptic gospels are part of a sustained early Christian tendency to switch responsibility for the death of Jesus from the Romans to the Jews. John's gospel shows that this is an over-simplification. Its passion narrative plays down the responsibility of Pilate and stresses that he was a puppet controlled by the Jewish leaders, yet there is no formal Sanhedrin hearing. The accounts in the synoptic gospels of a hearing or trial before the Sanhedrin are so imprecise that they are unlikely to have been invented at a later stage. Invention in the light of later anti-Jewish sentiments would probably have encouraged greater verisimilitude. The earliest Jewish sources, difficult though they are to date and to interpret in detail, do not deny Jewish involvement in the fate of Jesus, so this seems likely.

The accusations against Jesus

What then were the accusations against Jesus? Only once in the accounts of the hearing before the Sanhedrin is there a clear statement about the issue which led directly to Jesus' condemnation: blasphemy (Mark 14: 64). Mark clearly believes that a two-fold claim of Jesus before the high priest constituted blasphemy: the claim to be 'the Christ, the Son of the Blessed One', and the claim that the high priest would see 'the Son of Man sitting at the right hand of the Power, and coming with the clouds of heaven' (14: 61–2). But would such claims have been considered blasphemous? This too has to be left as an open question, since it is not possible to determine precisely how blasphemy was defined at the time of Jesus. It is probable that a claim to be a messiah would not have been considered blasphemous.

At first sight the twofold claim just noted does seem to be the product of early Christian reflection on the significance of Jesus. As we noted in Chapter 15, Jesus referred to his own role only rarely, and then most reluctantly. The explicit claim before the high priest (as he presided over the Sanhedrin) to be both Messiah and Son of God seems to be out of character with the rest of the synoptic traditions.

On the other hand there are some signs that Mark 14: 61–2 should not be dismissed too readily as an intrusion of later post-Easter Christian convictions about Jesus. The careful avoidance of the name of God by the use of the phrases 'the Blessed One' and 'the right hand of the Power', suggests traditional Jewish usage rather than later Christian confessional statements. As we noted on p. 243, some manuscripts suggest that Jesus' reply to the high priest's question, 'Are you the Christ, the Son of the Blessed', may have been 'You have said so' rather than 'I am'.

Luke's account is significantly different at this crucial point; it may put us in touch with an earlier form of the tradition. In Luke's account of the Sanhedrin hearing (22: 66–70), 'Messiah' and 'Son of God' are not juxtaposed and equated as in Mark. It is the claim, accepted only indirectly by Jesus, to be the Son of God which leads directly to the Sanhedrin's decision to condemn him and take him to Pilate.

Mark refers to a second accusation against Jesus: he claimed that he would destroy the temple and build another (14: 58). If blasphemy was defined in very wide terms, then this claim may have been considered to be not only outrageous, but blasphemous. It is hard to overestimate the importance of the temple for the religious and political life of Jerusalem. At the time of Jesus Jerusalem had a population of about 25,000, nearly half of whom were directly dependent on the temple for their livelihood. Three times a year large numbers of Jewish pilgrims travelled there from all over the Mediterranean world. Any serious threat to the temple would have been opposed vigorously both by the temple authorities and by the local inhabitants of Jerusalem.

According to Mark's account of the hearing before the Sanhedrin, false witnesses stood up and said, 'We heard him say, "I will destroy this temple that is made with hands, and in three days I will build another, not made with hands"' (Mark 14: 58). At the scene of the crucifixion passers-by deride Jesus, 'shaking their heads, and saying, "Aha! You who would destroy the temple and build it in three days, save yourself, and come down from the cross!"' (Mark 15: 29–30).

Did Jesus speak along these lines? Mark places the sayings on the lips of Jesus' opponents and thus implies that there was no truth in them at all. But at 13: 2 he himself records that Jesus did predict the destruction of the temple. As Jesus comes out of the temple he says to one of his disciples, 'Not one stone will be left here upon another; all will be thrown down.' These three Marcan sayings against the temple (and their parallels in Matthew) are unlikely to have been invented in the early decades of the early church; during those years completion of the building of the temple, not its destruction, went on apace.

Two other anti-temple sayings are relevant. (i) Luke does not include Mark 14: 58 and 15: 29–30, but in Acts 6: 14 he notes that false witnesses claimed that Stephen spoke against the temple: 'We have heard him say that this Jesus of Nazareth will destroy this place'. Luke himself, like Mark, regards the accusations as mischievous: both writers are reluctant to admit that Jesus made any such claim, but this partial 'cover-up' makes us suspect that he may well have done so, at least indirectly. (ii) Immediately after John's account of the 'cleansing of the temple' Jesus says to his Jewish critics, 'Destroy this temple, and in three days I will raise it up' (2: 19). As is often the case in the fourth gospel, the opponents of Jesus misunderstand his words—and this allows the evangelist to clarify their true meaning. John explains that Jesus was speaking about the temple of his body. Since John could hardly have allowed Jesus to say 'I will destroy this temple, my body', a saying very similar to the three we have noted seems to have been changed from 'I will destroy this temple . . .' to 'Destroy this temple' (my body).

The prediction of the destruction of the temple in Mark 13: 2 does not imply that Jesus himself will be involved and it does not mention a rebuilding of the temple. But the other four 'temple' sayings we have noted (Mark 14: 58; 15: 29; Acts 6: 14; John 2: 19) all mention rebuilding, and three of them (John 2: 19 is only a partial exception) do indicate that Jesus himself would be involved in the destruction of the temple.

Is Jesus likely to have claimed quite openly that he would destroy the temple and somehow be involved in its rebuilding? In the early decades of the first century some Jewish circles did expect that in the 'last days' God would provide a 'new temple', and thus the purity of Israel would be restored. A new temple clearly implies the destruction of the existing temple.

Perhaps Jesus spoke against the temple in the form of a riddle. The variations in the anti-temple sayings suggest that an original riddle-like saying may have been developed in different ways. No doubt many ignored the rather strange indirect attack on the temple Jesus seemed to be making. But some of the leaders of the religious 'establishment' would have recalled readily that Jesus had recently entered the temple and 'driven out those who were selling and those who were buying in the temple' (Mark 11: 15). Any hint, even in the form of a riddle, that the present temple might be destroyed and replaced by a new temple of some kind would be seen as a threat to the status quo.

Mark (followed by Matthew and Luke) implies that there was a direct link between the actions of Jesus in the temple and the hardening of opposition on the part of some of the Jerusalem authorities. This may well have been the case. The 'overturning of the tables of the money changers and the seats of those who sold doves' (Mark 11: 15) may have been an 'acted parable': a prophetic declaration of God's judgement on the temple (and, by implication, on Israel as a whole) and an expression of hope that God would soon replace it with some form of 'purified' new temple.

There are two alternative explanations of the actions of Jesus in the temple (Mark 11: 15–18 and parallels) which we must discuss briefly. On the traditional view, Jesus cleansed the temple. He protested against the actions of the money changers: their trade should not have been taking place within the precincts of the temple. Jesus was attempting to restore 'pure' worship of God by showing that much current worship was based on mere externals. Mark seems to have understood the actions of Jesus along these lines—as a protest against blatant abuses. He himself is probably responsible for the citations of Scripture (11: 17) which portray the temple as a 'den of robbers' (Jer. 7: 11), in sharp contrast to God's intention that the temple should be a 'house of prayer for all the nations' (Isa. 56: 7).

While there was certainly an element of protest in the actions of Jesus, the traditional view ignores the fact that buying and selling in the temple precincts was necessary in order to sustain temple worship. Overturning a few money tables would not have brought buying and selling to a halt: to do that one would have needed an army! Hence the actions of Jesus are better understood as more than a protest against the money changers; they were a prophetic gesture against the temple itself. Open denunciation would have led to instant dismissal as a mere madman. But by his riddle-like sayings about the destruction and rebuilding of the temple and his 'parabolic' actions in the temple precincts, Jesus expressed his opposition to the temple in whose precincts he taught and his hope for its 'rebuilding', though the form of that 'rebuilding' is left undefined. (On prophetic actions, see p. 199.) At the time there were several Jewish groups which, for diverse reasons, opposed the Jerusalem temple, so we need not be surprised that Jesus adopted such a radical stance.

S. G. F. Brandon has offered a very different explanation of the actions of Jesus in the temple. He claimed that Jesus was sympathetic to the zealots who were ready to use violence in order to be rid of the Roman occupying forces. Brandon argued that the evangelists have 'toned down' the actions of Jesus in the temple; Jesus intended to spark off a full-scale revolutionary uprising against the Romans. We noted above (pp. 259–60) some of the reasons why it is unlikely that Jesus was sympathetic to any group of activists eager to use violence against the Romans. In addition, Brandon fails to take sufficient account of the fact that at Passover time each year the Romans reinforced their garrison in Jerusalem. Large numbers of troops were stationed right beside the temple. Any suggestion of a major disturbance in the temple precincts would have drawn an immediate vigorous response.

It is possible that at a hearing before the Sanhedrin Jesus referred to himself (perhaps only indirectly) as Messiah and/or Son of God. Such claims may well have been considered to be intolerable—even blasphemous. But we have suggested that the words and actions of Jesus against the temple may have been the more immediate cause of his downfall. This latter suggestion allows us to link a little more readily the issues at stake between Jesus and the Pharisees and scribes on the one hand, and the central accusation against Jesus at the Sanhedrin hearing on the other. As we saw on pp. 263–8, Jesus parted company with *some* of the ways in which many (in particular Pharisees) interpreted the implications of the law. If so, it becomes more probable that his stance towards the temple was equally unconventional. Jesus expected that in the 'last days', which he believed to be imminent, the temple would be destroyed and replaced by some form of alternative access to God. In the eyes of the Jerusalem temple 'establishment', these views were provocative and outrageous.

Several issues concerning the Sanhedrin hearing have to be left as open questions; for several more only provisional answers can be given. We have suggested that the course of events *implied* by Mark is probably correct. At a hearing before the Sanhedrin (which may have been an informal discussion rather than a formal trial), the sayings of Jesus against the temple and his prophetic action in the temple itself were as crucial as a claim to be Messiah or Son of God. Following a decision against Jesus, his case was passed to the Romans.

A crucified Messiah–King

In antiquity crucifixion was the most savage and shameful form of capital punishment. It was so barbarous and inhumane that polite Romans did not talk about it. Crucifixion was carried out by the Romans especially on slaves, violent criminals, and rebellious subject peoples.

The crucifixion of Jesus was an acute embarrassment to his followers. At the time of Jesus there was no expectation that a Messiah would suffer or be crucified, so proclamation of a crucified Messiah made no sense at all to Jews who heard it. Markus Bockmuehl (1994, p. 55) notes that 'in the public mind this kind of ignominious death would have meant the end of any Messianic claim. A righteous man he might be—after all, even the highly regarded Maccabean martyrs had suffered a violent death. But he could not be the Messiah.'

To Greeks, proclamation of a recently crucified person was 'folly' (1 Cor. 1: 23). The reaction of Celsus, the second-century pagan critic of Christianity, was surely typical. He poked fun at Christians who claimed that Jesus was God's Son, 'although he was most dishonourably arrested and punished to his utter disgrace' (Origen, *Contra Celsum* 6. 10).

The first followers of Jesus could not possibly have invented the crucifixion of Jesus, for it left them open to ridicule. So there can be no doubt at all that Jesus was crucified by the Roman prefect Pilate as a political rebel. The disciples did not and could not gloss over this embarrassing fact. Very soon after what must have been a traumatic event for the disciples, they attached positive theological significance to the crucifixion of Jesus. About AD 50 Paul cites a much earlier tradition he had received: 'Christ died for our sins in accordance with the Scriptures' (1 Cor. 15: 3). Luke reports that on the day of Pentecost Peter claimed that the crucifixion of 'this Jesus' was part of God's definite plan: by raising Jesus from the dead, God reversed the actions of wicked men (Acts 2: 23–4). But even the positive ways the earliest Christians spoke about the death Jesus could not hide the shame of crucifixion.

There is equally little doubt about the historicity of the inscription on the cross. Similar wording is found in all four Gospels:

Mark 15: 26: 'The King of the Jews'

Matthew 27: 37: 'This is Jesus, the King of the Jews'

Luke 23: 38: 'The King of the Jews, this one'

John 19: 29: 'Jesus the Nazorean, the King of the Jews'.

The differences are not significant, but they do remind us that the gospels do not give us absolute accuracy.

The inscription placed above a crucified person was intended to provide information about the offence to passers-by, and to act as a deterrent. Mark's earliest and simplest wording is probably what was written. 'The King of the Jews' announced the charge made against Jesus: he was put to death for claiming to be king of the Jews and thus usurping Rome's authority. From the evangelists' point of view, the inscription was profoundly true: Jesus was indeed the Messiah–King. Nonetheless, the inscription, like the crucifixion itself, was deeply embarrassing, for it announced to all and sundry that Jesus had been condemned as a political upstart.

Why was Jesus put to death on a Roman cross? As soon as the possible explanations of this 'brute fact' are explored, we are brought face to face with the political and religious turmoil of the times. In first-century Palestine politics and religion were inseparable. A challenge to the religious status quo carried strong political overtones, and vice versa.

Were the Romans in fact justified in putting Jesus to death for political subversion? Surely not. We saw above (pp. 259–60) that Jesus did not advocate the use of violence against the despised Roman occupying power. Jesus was put to death by the Romans as a political criminal because he was considered wrongly to be a threat to the political stability of Judaea. His followers soon claimed that he was indeed a messianic king. But since a *crucified* Messiah-King was an embarrassment to them, they are unlikely to have invented the words over the cross, 'The King of the Jews' (Mark 15: 26).

'On the third day'

At the beginning of this chapter we noted that the distinctive emphases of the four evangelists are prominent in their passion narratives. This is also the case in the resurrection narratives. We have seen some examples in our discussion of aspects of the resurrection traditions in Mark (p. 53) and Matthew (pp. 73–4). As a further example, we may note that the varying geographical settings of the resurrection appearances are related to the wider concerns of the individual evangelists.

Mark implies that the disciples will see the risen Jesus in Galilee (16: 7); the prophecy of Jesus on the way to the Mount of Olives will be fulfilled: 'After I am raised up, I will go before you to Galilee' (14: 28). Matthew sets the final appearance of the risen Jesus on a mountain in Galilee (28: 16–20). Mountains are especially important in Matthew. The third of the three temptations faced by Jesus at the outset of his ministry of Jesus takes place 'on a very high mountain' (4: 8); the first discourse is set on a mountain (the Sermon on the Mount, chs. 5–7). Of his six references to mountains, three are from his own hand. So it is not surprising that his final scene is set on a mountain.

The appearances recorded by Luke in chapter 24 are all set in Jerusalem. The first part of Luke's story (i.e. Luke's gospel) ends where it began: in the temple in Jerusalem (cf. 2: 5–23 and 24: 53). The opening of Acts is set in Jerusalem: from there the Christian message is to be taken to the ends of the earth. In John 20 the resurrection traditions are set in Jerusalem and are interwoven with several Johannine themes. The later appendix in chapter 21 is set in Galilee, perhaps partly in order to bring the resurrection

traditions in this gospel closer to the geographical setting of the appearances in Mark and Matthew.

Once the redactional concerns of the individual evangelists are
accounted for, what can be said about the underlying traditions? What lies
behind the conviction of the four evangelists that God raised Jesus from
the dead 'on the third day'? Can the historian say anything about what
happened between the burial of Jesus in Joseph of Arimathea's tomb
(Mark 15: 46) and the appearances of Jesus to some of his followers (1 Cor.
15: 5–8; Matt. 28: 9–10, 17–18; Luke 24: 31, 34, 36–43; John 20: 14–18, 19–23,
26–9; 21: 7)?

The earliest written account of resurrection appearances is in 1 Cor. 15:
5–8; this letter dates from the early 50s AD. Here Paul mentions that at an
earlier stage he had *passed on* to the Corinthians a tradition which he
himself had *received*. Behind these verbs lie technical Jewish terms for the
careful transmission of tradition. Paul refers to appearances to Cephas
(Peter), to the twelve, and to 'more than five hundred at one time'. He also
lists appearances to James, to all the apostles, and to himself. In these verses
Paul is probably referring to two very early lists of recipients of resurrection appearances, one headed by Peter, and one by James, both of whom
were leaders of the early church.

Although the tradition Paul quotes goes back to the very earliest years of
the post-Easter church, in two respects it is out of line with the resurrection traditions in the gospels. Paul says nothing about the discovery of an
empty tomb; unlike the evangelists, he does not refer to appearances of the
risen Jesus to women followers.

Paul's silence about the empty tomb has been much discussed. On one
view, the sequence of verbs used by Paul, 'died', 'buried', 'raised' (1 Cor. 15:
3–4) must imply an empty tomb; a first-century Jew could not have understood this sequence of verbs in any other way. Paul's line of argument in
this chapter concerning the relationship between the resurrection of Jesus
and the Christian hope for general resurrection rests squarely on the
conviction that the known place of burial must have been empty.

This general approach is not embarrassed by Paul's failure to refer to
appearances to women. Paul knew full well that the testimony of women
counted for little, so not surprisingly, he referred only to appearances to
men. The evangelists were well aware of customary attitudes to the testimony of women, but they simply recorded the traditions they received,

even though they would have carried little weight in arguments with opponents.

An alternative view underlines Paul's silence about the empty tomb. It notes that all the earliest statements about the resurrection faith of the early church focus on the 'raising of Jesus' by God (see, for example, Rom. 1: 3; 6: 4), his appearances to followers (see the references above), or his exaltation (Phil. 2: 9; 1 Tim. 3: 16); in these 'credal' statements, reference to the empty tomb is conspicuous by its absence. Hence the empty tomb traditions are said to be a 'late apologetic development'. They were created in the early church in order to underpin or even 'prove' the validity of faith in the risen Lord.

However this latter approach fails to explain why the empty tomb traditions do not in fact attempt to offer 'proof' that Jesus was raised by God. The discovery of the tomb leads not to faith but to 'trembling and astonishment' (Mark 16: 8) and to 'perplexity' (Luke 24: 4; cf. John 20: 2). John 20: 8 is a clear exception. Peter and the 'beloved disciple' run to the tomb. The 'beloved disciple' wins the race but does not enter the tomb. Peter enters the tomb, but no reaction is recorded. In contrast, when the 'beloved disciple' enters the tomb, 'he saw and believed'. This tradition seems to be related to later rivalry concerning Peter and the beloved disciple. In the community for which the fourth evangelist wrote, Peter may be important, but the 'beloved disciple' takes precedence; he was the first disciple to reach the tomb and the first to believe.

The numerous differences in detail in the resurrection narratives lend support to the basic conviction the evangelists are intending to convey. 'Calculated deception should have produced greater unanimity', writes Sanders (1993, p. 280). 'Instead there seem to have been *competitors*: "I saw him first!" "No! I did."' Neither in the empty tomb nor in the appearance traditions are the evangelists attempting to *prove* their case. John, for example, explains that his primary concern is with faith that does not see, not proof (20: 29).

Given that the empty tomb traditions do not show signs of extensive early Christian theological development, their historicity should not be dismissed. But that does not mean that the historian can *prove* the validity of the Christian claim that God raised Jesus 'on the third day'. Other explanations of the empty tomb may be unlikely, but they can never be ruled out entirely. Some of the modern historians who accept that the traditions about the empty tomb are well grounded either leave open the *cause* of the empty tomb, or they claim that the disciples stole the body of Jesus.

This latter suggestion has a long history: Matthew knows that it is popular among non-Christian Jews in his own day, so he does his best to refute it. He explains that since the tomb was guarded by soldiers, it was not possible for the disciples to steal the body of Jesus; the guards were bribed by the authorities to say that the body was stolen while they were asleep (27: 64–6; 28: 11–15; cf. John 20: 13). In effect the soldiers are made to admit to dereliction of duty.

The New Testament writers stress that it was the appearances of the Risen Jesus which led to the resurrection faith of the first followers of Jesus and to their conviction that God had raised Jesus from the dead. Their claims about the Risen Jesus do not fit into any of the Jewish and Graeco-Roman ways of understanding post-mortem existence. They were *not* claiming that Jesus had been restored to normal human life only to die again in due course, as happened to the widow's son at Nain, for example (Luke 7: 11–16). Nor were they claiming that the Risen Jesus was some kind of ghost or apparition (cf. Mark 6: 49; Matt. 14: 26). In the Graeco-Roman world the apotheosis or deification of a ruler or hero was not unknown, but this pattern does not provide a parallel, for apotheosis was *of the soul*, not the body. It was confined to the elite on the grounds of their alleged virtue—and it often drew scorn and derision.

The early Christian claim was that God raised the crucified, dead, and buried Jesus 'on the third day' to a new form of existence, the precise nature of which Paul and the four evangelists describe in rather different ways. That claim can be neither confirmed nor denied with the use of historical lines of inquiry. Whether it may be accepted as plausible depends both on careful assessment of the resurrection traditions and on convictions about God.

18

WHO WAS JESUS OF NAZARETH?

In this book we have emphasized that the evangelists are concerned with both the story and the significance of Jesus of Nazareth. As we saw in Part I, the evangelists' claims about Jesus differ considerably in emphasis and in detail, yet they share a number of convictions. They all proclaim that Jesus is the Christ, the Son of God, and the fulfilment of Israel's hopes. The story of his life, death, and resurrection is the foundation of the Christian story.

The evangelists all believe that the teaching and actions of Jesus have continuing value for Christian life and faith in their own day. In the light of that firmly held view, they felt free to modify the traditions they received in order to allow them to be relevant to their different cultural and religious settings.

The four evangelists believe that the death of Jesus was not in vain. Jesus died a martyr's death 'for others'. Although they expound in different ways what 'for others' means, they agree that ultimately the death of Jesus is related to sin and to one's standing before God (see, for example, Mark 10: 45; 14: 24; Matt. 20: 28; 26: 28; Luke 22: 19–20; 24: 46–7; Acts 20: 28; John 1: 29).

The evangelists all believe that God raised Jesus from the dead 'on the third day'. They have written their gospels in the light of that conviction: in that sense their gospels 'breathe resurrection faith', to quote J. A. Bengel's dictum from the middle of the eighteenth century.

Are the evangelists' theological convictions about the significance of Jesus still meaningful today? Important though that question is for anyone interested in the truth claims of Christianity, we have not attempted to pursue it in this book. Our focus has been on the historical, theological, and literary dimensions of the text of the gospels in order to explore the question 'Who was Jesus of Nazareth?' In several parts of the book our agenda has been primarily historical. That latter phrase is chosen deliberately, for it is not possible to adopt a *purely* historical approach, from which the writer's own convictions and presuppositions have been carefully excluded. There is no such thing as 'pure' or 'neutral' history. I have written this book as a Christian, and that stance will inevitably shine through, even though it has been my aim to set out the evidence for readers with varied personal religious convictions.

Believer and non-believer may have to agree to part company on answers to the question 'Who *is* Jesus of Nazareth for us today?' If we ask 'Who *was* Jesus of Nazareth?', however, believer and non-believer can join hands. The believer will want to ask about the basis on which Christian faith stands. If she or he is wise, the sharp questions of the uncommitted scholar interested in the story of Jesus will be welcomed. The non-believer or the uncommitted inquirer will want to ask how it came about that Jesus of Nazareth made (and still makes) such a profound impact.

Historical reconstruction of the teaching and actions of Jesus is never easy, but it is not as difficult as some would have us believe. In this book attention has been drawn to the following basic principles on which careful assessment of the evidence must be based.

(i) In discussion of the teaching and actions of Jesus, one should always start with the evangelists' viewpoints. Reconstruction of the original form of traditions about Jesus is possible only after account has been taken of the stance of the evangelists and of the modifications they have introduced. Hence the title of this book: *The Gospels and* (only then) *Jesus*.

(ii) Traditions in the four gospels which were an embarrassment to the later followers of Jesus are particularly valuable, for they are most unlikely to have been invented by his followers. A number of examples were given in the later chapters.

(iii) In order to answer the question 'Who was Jesus of Nazareth?', it is necessary to set the teaching and actions of Jesus as firmly as possible in the context of first-century Judaism. In our discussion of the ways one might assess the evidence of the gospels, we referred to this principle as 'historical plausibility'. In Part II we frequently compared and contrasted Jesus with various contemporary Jewish movements and 'sects'. In some ways we are caught in a circle as we attempt to do this. We can only make progress in our understanding of the story of Jesus by increasing our knowledge of first-century Judaism. But on any view, some of our best evidence for Judaism at the time of Jesus is found in the gospels.

(iv) In several chapters in Part II more weight than is customary has been given to traditions which are strongly critical of Jesus. Some of the polemical comments discussed come from the second half of the second century (Trypho as quoted by Justin Martyr; Celsus as quoted by Origen), but they have deep roots. In his own lifetime Jesus was considered by some to be deeply offensive. Both his teaching and his actions drew criticism. Were his exorcisms and healing miracles signs that God's kingly rule was breaking into history, or were they the result of his collusion with the prince of demons? Was Jesus a prophet sent by God, or was he a false prophet who was deceiving Israel? The polemical traditions confirm that as Jesus moved from village to village in Galilee the relationship of Jesus to God was a central issue.

(v) Attention has been given to a further principle. In order to appreciate fully the significance of the actions and teaching of Jesus, the aftermath should not be neglected. We shall return to this point in a moment.

When these principles are taken seriously, some of the results are surprising. In first-century Galilee and Judaea there were other prophets; one of the most influential was John the Baptist. There were other healers and exorcists. There were other teachers who had circles of disciples, and some who told parables. But it is not easy to find in first-century Judaism any other prophet–teacher who had healing gifts and who frequently used parables and aphorisms in teaching both crowds and a circle of followers. In the light of our limited knowledge it would be rash to claim that these varied gifts and qualities mark Jesus out as unique among his contemporaries. But we need have no hesitation in describing Jesus as 'unconventional' in the context of his religious and social world.

It is most important not to emphasize one or more of these strands at the expense of the others. Some scholars have tended to single out a handful of actions or sayings of Jesus as authentic, and have then given them undue prominence in their historical reconstructions. It is all too easy for the modern scholar to make Jesus in his or her own image—and that has been happening ever since the opening of the 'first' or 'old' quest for the historical Jesus. This danger can be avoided only by assessing all the evidence equally rigorously—even the less congenial parts.

In the early church there were similar problems. Some Christians fastened on to one strand of the evidence and developed lopsided portraits of Jesus. In some circles he was seen as a miracle-worker, or even as a 'divine being' whose feet hardly touched the ground. In other circles he was seen as a wisdom and ethical teacher, but sometimes (as in the Gospel of Thomas) with no inkling that his teaching was part of his prophetic call for the renewal of Israel. And in still other circles he was seen as a revealer of Gnostic secrets whose most significant teaching was given following his resurrection.

We have seen that while certainty often eludes us, we do know a good deal about Jesus of Nazareth. With careful use of sound historical methods it is possible to rule out some of the more fanciful views which have been proposed. Historians, whether Christian or not, are able to confirm that Jesus did exist and that the evangelists' portraits, for all their differences, are not wholly misleading. The similarities in those portraits are more striking than the differences.

What holds the various strands of evidence together? What gives the story coherence? These questions may be addressed from two angles. We may ask how the various parts of the story are related to one another. In Chapters 13 and 14, for example, we discussed whether the parables and the miracles are related to Jesus' proclamation of the kingly rule of God. In Chapter 17 we asked whether the issues which arose at the trial of Jesus in Jerusalem were related to the disputes between Jesus and Pharisees and scribes in Galilee.

The coherence of the story of Jesus may be considered from another angle. What was the intention of Jesus? Is there one single aim or one overriding principle which lies behind all his teaching and actions? Christians have traditionally used the phrase 'the ministry of Jesus' to refer to his overall intention. Some contemporary theologians have used the phrase 'Jesus, the man for others' as a way of summing up his primary aim. While Jesus certainly did minister to the needs of others, to see Jesus primarily as a pastor *par excellence* hardly does justice to the many-sided evidence. How would we then explain his downfall?

The key to the story is its ending and its aftermath. Jesus went up to Jerusalem for the last time not simply in order to 'minister' to its inhabitants. He went to Jerusalem in order to confront the religio-political establishment with his claim that the kingdom of God was at hand. On the basis of his convictions about the presence, power, and will of God, Jesus called for a reordering of Israel's priorities. In that sense he sought the renewal of Judaism. Renewal movements generally involve a rediscovery of basic principles and a call for loyalty to an inherited tradition. The 'Jesus movement' was no exception. In due course what Jesus and his followers intended as a 'recall to basics' led to the parting of the ways between Christianity and Judaism—but that is another story.

Jesus certainly did not intend to found a new religion. He did not repudiate Scripture—far from it. And he did not call in question the law of Moses, though on occasion he emphasized some Scriptural principles at the expense of others. But he did challenge established conventions and priorities. Jesus believed that he had been sent by God as a prophet to declare authoritatively the will of God for his people: acceptance or rejection of him and of his message was equivalent to acceptance or rejection of God (Matt. 10: 40 = Luke 10: 16). The stakes really were that high!

What about the aftermath? The impact of a religious or political leader can be judged in part by the eventual outcome of that person's distinctive aims. Only with hindsight some years after the death of a prominent person can his or her achievement be assessed adequately. So too with Jesus of Nazareth, though this point has been regularly overlooked in most recent 'historical Jesus' studies.

We have insisted (with E. P. Sanders, see above p. 176) that it is quite in accord with sound historical method to look closely at the 'aftermath of Jesus' in the post-Easter period. It is often said that where there is smoke there is fire. In the three or so decades immediately after the resurrection the swirling smoke is easy to find, but what about the fire?

In the very conservative religious and social climate of the first century followers of Jesus made profound claims about him and took radical steps in his name. Two points are particularly relevant in the present context.

(i) In spite of the monotheistic heritage his followers refused to abandon, at a very early point in the post-Easter period they began to *worship* Jesus and to speak about him in ways that had been reserved for God. For this there was no direct precedent—and hardly a precedent of any kind.

A hymn which Paul probably inherited from his predecessors speaks of God's exaltation of Jesus Christ (following death on a cross) 'so that at the name of Jesus every knee should bend . . . and every tongue confess that Jesus Christ is Lord . . .' (Phil. 2: 6–11). Here is a clear example of very early Christian worship of Jesus—and some Christians still use a version of these words in modern hymns of worship.

In his letter to Christians in Corinth Paul acknowledges that there are many gods and many lords and then states firmly in a creed-like passage, 'Yet for us' (followers of Jesus):

There is one God, the Father, from whom are all things and for whom we exist, And one Lord, Jesus Christ, through whom are all things and through whom we exist.   (1 Cor. 8: 6)

Here statements about God and Christ are not merely juxtaposed, they are carefully set out in parallel. How could all this have happened if Jesus of Nazareth was merely a sage or a conventional teacher?

As we saw in Chapter 15, at some points there is no pre-Easter precedent for many of the later claims about the significance of Jesus; at other points there are clear and important lines of continuity. Perhaps the most significant example of the latter is the claim that Jesus is the Son of God. Although Jesus did not speak of himself as 'the Son of God' in the ways which were developed in the post-Easter period, there are a few sayings which suggest that he not only addressed God as Father in striking ways, but also spoke about his own relationship to God as his Son.

(ii) Paul's letter to the Galatians (c. AD 53) reveals that there were deep and painful divisions among the followers of Jesus over acceptance of non-Jews into their circles. Paul's own view was clear: circumcision was not required of Gentiles as an entry rite into the people of God; Jews and Gentiles should share table fellowship with one another openly and freely; the 'works of the law' were the very antithesis of 'faith in Christ'. In his face-to-face confrontation with Peter at Antioch (Gal. 2: 11–14), Paul may have lost the battle; in the long run his views won the day.

Why did Paul take such a firm stand? One possible answer might be that as a Jew proud of his heritage he was doing no more than some other Jews of his day had been doing for some time, i.e. welcoming Gentiles freely without insisting on circumcision as commanded by the law of Moses. Plenty of evidence indicates that in Paul's day Judaism with its monotheism and high ethical standards was an attractive religion to many non-Jews.

Although first-century Judaism was not a missionary religion, Gentiles who wished to associate themselves with local Jewish communities were welcome; they were often known as 'God-fearers'. But this phenomenon, important though it is, does not explain why Paul acted as he did.

Paul and his co-workers were not merely accepting Gentiles as 'associates', as 'sympathizers', but as equals in every possible way: in Christ, the customary distinctions between Jew and Gentile had been abolished (Gal. 3: 28). For this, there was no precedent in Judaism. Although full conversion of Gentile proselytes did take place from time to time, circumcision of males, keeping the sabbath, and observing purity regulations were always the marks of full conversion, and, even then, proselytes were not considered to be on all fours with 'born Jews'.

Paul's own explanation of the origin of his Gentile 'law-free' mission is clear: he was called by God to proclaim Jesus as the Son of God among the Gentiles (Gal. 1: 15–16). This insight may well have come to Paul as a bolt from the blue, but nonetheless the historian will want to ask about its earlier roots.

At this point there is a surprise. Jesus himself said nothing at all about circumcision. From time to time he accepted the faith of individual Gentiles, for example, the Roman centurion at Capernaum (Matt. 8: 5–13 = Luke 7: 1–10 [Q]). But Jesus did not call non-Jews into discipleship. He confined his teaching and his healings very largely to Israel (e.g. Matt. 10: 5; 15: 24; Mark 7: 24–30). So Jesus did not directly pave the way for later developments.

Is there no connection at all between the actions and words of Jesus and the later full acceptance of Gentiles? A mission to Gentiles is deeply embedded in resurrection traditions (Matt. 28: 19; Luke 24: 47; Acts 1: 8; John 20: 21), but this link seems to have been made later, for the disciples did not embark on a mission to Gentiles immediately after Easter Day.

So we still have a puzzle. It is not hard to find the smoke, but where is the fire? In deliberately turning repeatedly to socially and religiously marginalized people Jesus made a profound impact on his followers. As we saw in Chapter 12 (pp. 214–17), the list is long. These traditions were transmitted orally by followers of Jesus over a long period, and eventually their deeper significance was discerned.

In commenting on his confrontation with Peter at Antioch, Paul notes that he and Peter are both Jews by birth, and not Gentile 'sinners'. He then insists that a person's standing before God is established not by 'works of the law' (including circumcision), but by faith in Jesus Christ (Gal. 2: 15–16). The immediate issue was table fellowship: Gentile 'sinners' were to be accepted at table freely. Surely Jesus' own action in sharing table fellowship with tax collectors and sinners (Mark 2: 16–17; Matt. 11: 19 = Luke 7: 34 [Q]) lies in the background, even though we cannot trace a direct link.

The issue of table fellowship was closely related to the question of pure and impure food. In Chapter 16 (pp. 264–5) we saw that Jesus is unlikely to have launched a wholesale attack on Jewish purity regulations, one of the pillars of the law. However, Jesus provoked reflection on priorities by saying, 'A person is *not so much* defiled by that which enters from outside *as* by that which comes from within . . . ' (i.e. by impure, evil thoughts and desires: Mark 7: 20–3).

Both by his deeds and his words Jesus paved the way, albeit indirectly, for some of the radical steps taken in the immediate post-Easter period which are sketched in the preceding paragraphs. By searching for the fire behind the smoke, we are able to uncover some of the most striking and distinctive features of the actions and teaching of Jesus of Nazareth.

Finally, we must revisit *the* key question. How are we to account for the post-Easter developments for which these is little or no pre-Easter precedent? Shortly after his crucifixion Jesus was *worshipped* by his followers. Language and attributes began to be used of Jesus which had been reserved for God alone in Scripture (i.e. the Old Testament) and in later Jewish writings. The whole story of Jesus was read against the backdrop of Scripture and seen as its fulfilment.

The historian will find it difficult if not impossible to offer explanations for these startling developments. The first followers of Jesus, however, had their own answers. They are set out most clearly in John's Gospel at 2: 22; 12: 16; 14: 26; 15: 26; 16: 13; 20: 9, and related passages: only in the light both of Resurrection faith and of the gift of the Spirit was it possible to understand the full significance of the story of Jesus.

BIBLIOGRAPHY

This Bibliography lists suggestions for further reading which complement the present book. Publications which are marked with an asterisk are suitable for more advanced study.

Reference works

Anchor Bible Dictionary (New York: Doubleday, 6 vol., 1992). Unsurpassed for historical and archaeological information; not always strong on theological topics.

A Dictionary of Biblical Interpretation, ed. R. J. Coggins and J. L. Houlden (London: SCM, 1990). Useful entries on different methods of interpretation.

Dictionary of Biblical Interpretation, ed. J. H. Hayes (Nashville: Abingdon, 2 vols., 1999). Focuses on the history of interpretation.

Dictionary of Jesus and the Gospels, ed. J. B. Green, S. McKnight, and I. H. Marshall (Downers Grove: InterVarsity, 1992). Lengthy articles on major topics.

[Several one-volume Bible dictionaries and one-volume Bible commentaries include helpful articles on individual gospels and on topics referred to in this book. They are not listed in this Bibliography.]

PART I: THE FOUR GOSPELS

General

Blomberg, Craig, *Jesus and the Gospels* (Nashville: Broadman & Holman, 1997).

Burridge, R. A., *Four Gospels, One Jesus?* (London: SPCK, 1994).

Hooker, Morna D., *Beginnings: Keys that Open the Gospels* (London: SCM, 1997).

Marsh, Clive, and Moyise, Steve, *Jesus and the Gospels* (London: Cassell, 1999).

Tuckett, C. M., *Reading the New Testament: Methods of Interpretation* (London: SPCK, 1987).

Introductions

'Introductions' discuss the origin, authorship, structure, and date of biblical writings; they are not necessarily introductory!

Brown, Raymond E., *An Introduction to the New Testament* (New York: Doubleday, 1996). A very fine, well-balanced textbook.

Collins, R. F., *Introduction to the New Testament* (London: SCM, 1983).

Ehrman, Bart D., *The New Testament. A Historical Introduction to the Early Christian Writings* (New York and Oxford: Oxford University Press, 1997).

Guthrie, Donald, *New Testament Introduction* (Leicester: Apollos, 4th edn., 1990). Very detailed; conservative approach.

Johnston, L. T., *The Writings of the New Testament* (London: SCM, London 1986).

Martin, R. P., *New Testament Foundations* (Exeter: Paternoster, 2 vols., 1975, 1978).

Schnelle, Udo, *The History and Theology of the New Testament Writings* (London: SCM, 1998). Now the standard German introduction; includes references to English-language scholarship.

Synopses (which set out the text of the gospels in columns)

*Aland, K. (ed.), *Synopsis of the Four Gospels* (Stuttgart: German Bible Society, 1972). This includes the RSV as well as the Greek text.

Barr, A., *A Diagram of Synoptic Relationships* (Edinburgh: T & T Clark, new edn., 1995). This large coloured chart sets out clearly the relationships between the synoptic gospels.

Funk, R. (ed.), *New Gospel Parallels* 2 vols., (Philadelphia: Fortress, 1985).

Sparks, H. F. D., (ed.), *A Synopsis of the Four Gospels*, Parts I and II (London: Black, 1974).

Throckmorton, B. H., Jr. (ed.), *Gospel Parallels: A Synopsis of the First Three Gospels* (York and London: Nelson, 3rd edn., 1967).

Chapter 1: From the Gospels to Jesus

Evans, C. F., *The Lord's Prayer* (London: SCM, rev. edn., 1999).

Jeremias, Joachim, *The Prayers of Jesus* (London: SCM, 1967).

Chapter 2: What is a Gospel?

*Stanton, G. N., *A Gospel for a New People. Studies in Matthew* (Edinburgh: T&T Clark, 1992). Chapters 2, 3, and 4 discuss redaction critical, literary critical, and social scientific approaches to the gospels—with special reference to Matthew.

The gospels as biographies

Aune, D. E., *The New Testament in its Literary Environment* (Philadelphia: Westminster Press, 1987).

*Burridge, R. A., *What are the Gospels? A Comparison with Graeco-Roman Biography* (Cambridge: Cambridge University Press, 1992).

*Stanton, G. N., *Jesus of Nazareth in New Testament Preaching* (Cambridge: Cambridge University Press, 1974). Ch. 5 discusses ancient biographical writing.

Marcan priority

*Bellinzoni, A. J., (ed.), *The Two-Source Hypothesis* (Macon: Mercer University Press, 1985). A collection of essays from various viewpoints.

*Farmer, W. R., *The Synoptic Problem* (London and New York: Macmillan, 2nd edn., 1976). Classic exposition of the Griesbach hypothesis.

*Styler, G. M., 'The Priority of Mark', in C. F. D. Moule, *The Birth of the New Testament* (London: Black, 3rd edn., 1981).

*Tuckett, C. M., *The Revival of the Griesbach Hypothesis* (Cambridge: Cambridge University Press, 1983). Critical but fair appraisal.

The Q hypothesis

*Catchpole, D. R., *The Quest for Q* (Edinburgh: T&T Clark, 1993). Includes detailed refutation of the view that Luke used Matthew.

*Kloppenborg, J. S., *The Formation of Q* (Philadelphia: Fortress, 1987). Influential attempt to trace stages in the composition of Q.

*Piper, R. A. (ed.), *The Gospel behind the Gospels: Current Studies on Q* (Leiden: Brill, 1995).

*Tuckett, C. M., *Q and the History of Early Christianity* (Edinburgh: T&T Clark, 1996).

*Tuckett, C. M., (ed.), *Synoptic Studies* (JSOT Press, Sheffield 1984).

Form criticism

Taylor, V., *The Formation of the Gospel Tradition* (London: Macmillan, 1953). Classic exposition of form critical approach to the gospels.

Redaction criticism

Bornkamm, G., 'The Stilling of the Storm in Matthew', in G. Bornkamm, G. Barth, and H. J. Held, *Tradition and Interpretation in Matthew* (London: SCM, 1963).

*Rohde, J., *Rediscovering the Teaching of the Evangelists* (London: SCM, 1968).

Literary criticism

Powell, Mark A., *What is Narrative Criticism?* (Minneapolis: Fortress, 1990).
Rhoads, D., and Michie, D., *Mark as Story: An Introduction to the Narrative of a Gospel* (Philadelphia: Fortress, 1982).
[See also entries below under individual gospels.]

Chapter 3: Mark's Gospel

Commentaries

*Guelich, R. A., *Mark 1:–8: 26* (Word Biblical Commentary; Dallas: Word, 1989).
*Gundry, R. H., *Mark. A Commentary on his Apology for the Cross* (Grand Rapids: Eerdmans, 1992). Substantial; stimulating.
Hooker, Morna D., *The Gospel According to St Mark* (Black's NT Commentaries; London: Black, 1991). The finest one-volume commentary available.
*Marcus, Joel, *Mark 1–8* (Anchor Bible; New York: Doubleday, 2000). Thorough and judicious; highly commended.
Nineham, D. E., *The Gospel of St Mark* (Harmondsworth: Penguin, 1963). Succinct and clear form critical approach.

Studies

Bauckham, R. J. (ed.), *The Gospels for All Christians: Rethinking the Gospel Audiences* (Edinburgh: T&T Clark, 1998).
Best, E., *Following Jesus: Discipleship in the Gospel of Mark* (Sheffield: JSOT Press, 1981).
—— *Mark: The Gospel as Story* (Edinburgh: T&T Clark, 1983).
*Hengel, M., *Studies in the Gospel of Mark* (London: SCM Press, 1985).
Hooker, M. D., *The Message of Mark* (London: Epworth, 1983).
*Kee, H. C., *Community of the New Age: Studies in Mark's Gospel* (London: SCM, 1977).
Kingsbury, J. D., *The Christology of Mark's Gospel* (Philadelphia: Fortress, 1983).
*Marshall, C. D., *Faith as a Theme in Mark's Narrative* (Cambridge: Cambridge University Press, 1989; pb. 1994). A fine study from a narrative critical viewpoint.
Martin, R. P., *Mark—Evangelist and Theologian* (Exeter: Paternoster, Exeter, 1979). Careful discussion of Marcan scholarship up until the end of the 1970s.
*Telford, W. R. (ed.), *The Interpretation of Mark* (Edinburgh: T&T Clark, 2nd edn., 1995). Major essays, with the editor's own 60-page helpful assessment of Marcan scholarship.

Telford, W. R., *The Theology of the Gospel of Mark* (Cambridge: Cambridge University Press, 1999). A helpful guide, with good bibliography.

*Tuckett, C. M. (ed.), *The Messianic Secret* (SPCK, London, 1983). Major essays.

Chapter 4: Matthew's Gospel

Commentaries

*Davies, W. D., and Allison, D. C., *Matthew* (ICC; Edinburgh: T&T Clark, 3 vols., 1988–97). Detailed study of the Greek text.

France, R. T., *The Gospel according to St. Matthew* (Leicester: Inter-Varsity, 1985).

*Gundry, R. H., *Matthew, a Commentary on his Literary and Theological Art* (Grand Rapids: Eerdmans, 2nd edn., 1994). Redaction critical approach.

*Hagner, D. A., *Matthew* (Word Biblical Commentary; Dallas: Word, 2 vols., 1993 and 1995). Lucid and thorough.

*Luz, U., *Matthew 1–7* (Edinburgh: T&T Clark, 1989). Only the first of the four German volumes has been translated as yet; already a classic.

Schweizer, E., *The Good News According to Matthew* (London: SPCK, 1976).

Senior, D. A., *Matthew* (Nashville: Abingdon, 1998). A very useful 'middle level' commentary.

Studies

*Bauer, D. R., and Powell, M. A. (eds.), *Treasures New and Old. Contributions to Matthean Studies* (Atlanta: Scholars, 1996). Essays by leading specialists.

*Bornkamm, G., Barth G., and Held, H. J., *Tradition and Interpretation in Matthew* (London: SCM, London, rev. edn. 1983). Important pioneering redaction critical studies.

Brown, R. E., *The Birth of the Messiah: A Commentary on the Infancy Narratives in Matthew and Luke* (London: Chapman, 2nd edn., 1993). Detailed, but accessible.

Carter, Warren, *Matthew: Story Teller, Interpreter, Evangelist* (Peabody: Hendrickson, 1996). Excellent introduction.

—— *What are they Saying about Matthew's Sermon on the Mount?* (New York: Paulist, 1994).

France, R. T., *Matthew: Evangelist and Teacher* (Exeter: Paternoster, 1989).

*Guelich, R. A., *The Sermon on the Mount* (Waco: Word, 1982). Detailed commentary.

Howell, D. B., *Matthew's Inclusive Story* (Sheffield: Sheffield Academic Press, 1990). Detailed narrative critical study.

*Kilpatrick, G. D., *The Origins of the Gospel according to Matthew* (Oxford: Clarendon, 1946). A classic study.

Kingsbury, J. D., *Matthew as Story* (Philadelphia: Fortress, 2nd edn., 1988). Pioneering narrative critical exposition.

*—— *Matthew: Structure, Christology and Kingdom* (Philadelphia: Fortress, 1975).

Lambrecht, Jan, *The Sermon on the Mount* (Wilmington: Michael Glazier, 1985).

Luz, Ulrich, *The Theology of the Gospel of Matthew* (Cambridge: Cambridge University Press, 1995).

Overman, J. A., *Church and Community in Crisis: The Gospel according to Matthew* (Valley Forge: Trinity Press International, 1996)

*—— *Matthew's Gospel and Formative Judaism* (Minneapolis: Fortress, 1990).

*Saldarini, A. J., *Matthew's Christian-Jewish Community* (Chicago: University of Chicago Press, 1994).

*Sim, David C., *The Gospel of Matthew and Christian Judaism: The History and Social Setting of the Matthean Community* (Edinburgh: T&T Clark, 1998).

*Stanton, G. N., *A Gospel for a New People. Studies in Matthew* (Edinburgh: T&T Clark, 1992).

*—— (ed.), *The Interpretation of Matthew* (Edinburgh: T&T Clark, 2nd edn., 1995). Major essays on Matthew, with the editor's appraisal of recent Matthean scholarship.

Strecker, G., *The Sermon on the Mount* (London: T&T Clark, 1988).

Chapter 5: Luke's Gospel

Commentaries

Danker, F. W., *Luke* (Philadelphia: Fortress, 2nd edn., 1987).

Ellis, E. E., *The Gospel of Luke* (London: Oliphants, 1966).

Evans, C. F., *Saint Luke* (London: SCM, 1990). Full of insights.

Fitzmyer, J. A., *The Gospel According to Luke* (Anchor Bible; Garden City: Doubleday, 2 vols., 1981 and 1985).

*Green, Joel, *The Gospel of Luke* (Grand Rapids: Eerdmans, 1995).

Lieu, Judith, *The Gospel of Luke* (London: Epworth, 1997).

*Nolland, J., *Luke* (Word Biblical Commentary; Waco: Word, 3 vols., 1989–1993).

Schweizer, E., *The Good News According to St Luke* (London: SPCK, 1984).

Talbert, C. H., *Reading Luke: A Literary and Theological Commentary on the Third Gospel* (Crossroad, New York, 1984).

Tannehill, R. C., *Luke* (Nashville: Abingdon, 1996).

Studies

Barrett, C. K., *Luke the Historian in Recent Study* (London: Epworth, 1961). A classic short study.

*Conzelmann, H., *The Theology of St Luke* (London: Faber, 1960). Influential redaction critical study.

Fitzmyer, J. A., *Luke the Theologian* (New York: Paulist, 1989).

Green, Joel B., *The Theology of the Gospel of Luke* (Cambridge: Cambridge University Press, 1995).

*Jervell, J., *Luke and the People of God* (Minneapolis: Augsburg, 1972).

Knight, J., *Luke's Gospel* (Routledge Readings; London: Routledge, 1998).

*Maddox, R., *The Purpose of Luke–Acts* (Edinburgh: T&T Clark, 1982).

*Marshall, I. H., *Luke, Historian and Theologian* (Exeter: Paternoster, 1970).

*Moessner, David P. (ed.), *Jesus and the Heritage of Israel. Luke's Narrative Claim upon Israel's Legacy* (Harrisburg: Trinity Press International, 1999). Excellent set of essays by leading specialists.

Powell, Mark A., *What are they Saying about Luke?* (New York: Paulist, 1989).

Richardson, N., *The Panorama of Luke* (London: Epworth, 1982).

Schweizer, E., *Luke: A Challenge to Present Theology* (London: SPCK, 1982).

*Tannehill, R. C., *The Narrative Unity of Luke–Acts* I (Philadelphia: Fortress, 1986).

*Tuckett, C. M. (ed.), *Luke's Literary Achievement* (Sheffield: Sheffield Academic Press, 1995).

Chapter 6: John's Gospel

Commentaries

*Barrett, C. K., *The Gospel According to St John* (London: SPCK, 1978). A classic; always worth consulting.

*Beasley-Murray, G. R., *John* (Word Biblical Commentary; Waco: Word, 1987).

Brown, R. E., *The Gospel According to John* (Anchor Bible; Garden City: Doubleday, 2 vols., 1966 and 1970).

*Bultmann, R., *The Gospel of John* (Oxford: Blackwell, 1971). Stimulating and influential.

Lindars, B., *The Gospel of John* (New Century Bible; London: Oliphants, 1972).

Smith, D. Moody, *John* (Nashville: Abingdon, 1999). Fine one-volume commentary by a leading specialist.

Talbert, C. H., *Reading John: A Literary and Theological Commentary on the Fourth Gospel and the Johannine Epistles* (New York: Crossroad, 1992).

Studies

*Ashton, J. A., *Studying John: Approaches to the Fourth Gospel* (Oxford: Clarendon, 1994). Includes criticism of some narrative critical approaches.

*—— *Understanding the Fourth Gospel* (Oxford: Clarendon, 1991). Important wide-ranging scholarly study.

*—— (ed.), *The Interpretation of John* (Edinburgh: T&T Clark, 2nd edn., 1997). Major essays, with the editor's appraisal of recent scholarship.

*Brown, R. E., *The Community of the Beloved Disciple* (London: Chapman, 1979).

*Culpepper, R. A., *Anatomy of the Fourth Gospel. A Study in Literary Design* (Philadelphia: Fortress, 1983).

*Fortna, R. T., *The Fourth Gospel and its Predecessor. From Narrative Source to the Present Gospel* (Edinburgh: T&T Clark, 1988).

*Gardner-Smith, P., *Saint John and the Synoptic Gospels* (Cambridge: Cambridge University Press, 1938). Still worth consulting.

*Harvey, A. E., *Jesus on Trial: A Study in the Fourth Gospel* (London: SPCK, 1976).

*Hengel, M., *The Johannine Question* (Philadelphia: Trinity Press International, 1989).

Käsemann, Ernst, *The Testament of Jesus: A Study of the Gospel of John in the Light of Chapter 17* (London: SCM, 1968).

Kysar, R., *John's Story of Jesus* (Philadelphia: Fortress, 1984).

Lindars, B., *Behind the Fourth Gospel* (London: SPCK, 1971).

*Martyn, J. Louis, *History and Theology in the Fourth Gospel* (Nashville: Abingdon, rev. edn., 1979). Important influential study.

*Painter, John, *The Quest for the Messiah: The History, Literature and Theology of the Johannine Community* (Edinburgh: T&T Clark, rev. edn., 1993).

Pryor, John W., *John: Evangelist of the Covenant People* (London: Darton, Longman and Todd, 1992).

Smalley, S., *John—Evangelist and Interpreter* (Exeter: Paternoster, 1978).

*Smith, D. M., *Johannine Christianity: Essays on its Sources, Setting, and Theology* (Columbia: University of South Carolina Press, 1984).

—— *The Theology of the Gospel of John* (Cambridge: Cambride University Press, 1995). Excellent, lucid introduction to the evangelist's theological themes.

*Stibbe, Mark, *John's Gospel* (Routledge Readings; London: Routledge, 1994). Discusses a wide range of literary approaches.

Chapter 7: Why Four Gospels?

*Charlesworth, James H., and Evans, Craig A., 'Jesus in the Agrapha and Apocryphal Gospels' in Bruce Chilton and Craig A. Evans (eds.), *Studying the Historical Jesus* (Leiden: Brill, 1994), pp. 479–534.

*Crossan, John Dominic, *Four Other Gospels. Shadows on the Contours of Canon* (Minneapolis: Winston, 1985). A very different approach from the present book.

Elliott, Keith, *The Apocryphal New Testament* (Oxford: Clarendon, 1993). The standard collection of the texts in translation.

Evans, Craig, *Noncanonical Writings and New Testament Interpretation* (Peabody: Hendrickson, 1992).

Jeremias, J., *Unknown Sayings of Jesus* (London: SPCK, 1964).

*Layton, B. (ed.), *The Gnostic Scriptures: A New Translation with Annotations and Introductions* (Garden City: Doubleday, 1987).

*Robinson, J. M. (ed.), *The Nag Hammadi Library in English* (Leiden: Brill, 1977).

*Tuckett, C. M., *Nag Hammadi and the Gospel Tradition* (Edinburgh: T&T Clark, 1986).

The Gospel of Thomas

*Patterson, Stephen J., *The Gospel of Thomas and Jesus* (Sonoma: Polebridge, 1993). Thorough, though rather one-sided on Thomas's dependence on the canonical gospels.

*Tuckett, C. M., 'Thomas and the Synoptics', *Novum Testamentum* 30 (1988), pp. 132–57.

The fourfold gospel

*Bruce, F. F., *The Canon of Scripture* (Glasgow: Chapter House, 1988).

*Campenhausen, H. von, *The Formation of the Christian Bible* (Philadelphia: Fortress, 1972).

*Gamble, Harry Y., *The New Testament Canon: Its Making and Meaning* (Philadelphia: Fortress, 1985).

*Metzger, B. M., *The Canon of the New Testament* (Oxford: Clarendon, 1987).

*Stanton, G. N., 'The Fourfold Gospel', *New Testament Studies* 43 (1997), pp. 317–46.

PART II: JESUS IN GOSPEL TRADITION

General Books about Jesus

Allison, Dale C., *Jesus of Nazareth: Millenarian Prophet* (Minneapolis: Fortress, 1998).

Bockmuehl, Markus, *This Jesus* (Edinburgh: T&T Clark, 1994). An excellent clear introduction.

—— (ed.), *The Cambridge Companion to Jesus* (Cambridge: Cambridge University Press, 2001). A wide-ranging set of essays by leading specialists.

Borg, Marcus J., *Conflict, Holiness and Politics in the Teachings of Jesus* (New York: Edwin Mullen, 1984).

—— *Jesus: A New Vision* (San Francisco: Harper, 1987).

Bornkamm, G., *Jesus of Nazareth* (London: Hodder, 1960). Influential; still important.

*Chilton, B. D., and Evans, C. A., (eds.), *Studying the Historical Jesus* (Leiden: Brill, 1994). Wide-ranging, important essays.

*Chilton, Bruce, *Pure Kingdom: Jesus' Vision of God* (London: SPCK, 1996).

*Crossan, J. D., *The Historical Jesus* (San Francisco: Harper, 1991). A major rather idiosyncratic study.

*Dahl, Nils Alstrup, 'The Problem of the Historical Jesus', in *Jesus the Christ*, ed. D. H. Juel (Minneapolis: Fortress, 1991), pp. 81–112.

Dodd, C. H., *The Founder of Christianity* (London: Collins, 1971).

Fredriksen, Paula, *Jesus of Nazareth, King of the Jews: A Jewish Life and the Emergence of Christianity* (London: Macmillan, 2000).

Harvey, A. E., *Jesus and the Constraints of History* (London: Duckworth, 1982).

*Jeremias, J., *New Testament Theology I: The Proclamation of Jesus* (London: SCM Press, 1971). A magisterial study of the teaching of Jesus.

*Leivestad, R., *Jesus in his own Perspective* (Minneapolis: Augsburg, 1987).

*McKnight, Scot, *A New Vision for Israel. The Teachings of Jesus in National Context* (Grand Rapids/Cambridge: Eerdmans, 1999).

*Meier, John P., *A Marginal Jew* (New York: Doubleday, 2 vols., 1991, 1994). Thorough and judicious; when complete, Meier's trilogy will be unsurpassed.

*Meyer, B. F., *The Aims of Jesus* (London: SCM, 1979). Important, often overlooked study.

*Riches, J., *Jesus and the Transformation of Judaism* (London: Darton, Longman and Todd, 1980).

Sanders, E. P., *The Historical Figure of Jesus* (London: Allen Lane, 1993). An abbreviated and more wide-ranging version of his 1985 book.

*—— *Jesus and Judaism* (London: SCM, 1985). Fine, very influential study.

*Theissen, Gerd, and Merz, Annette, *The Historical Jesus: A Comprehensive Guide* (London: SCM, 1998). Plenty of good material, but not all easy to digest.

Vermes, Geza, *Jesus the Jew* (London: SCM, 2nd edn., 1983).

Witherington, Ben III, *The Jesus Quest* (Downers Grove: Intervarsity, 1995).

*Wright, N. T., *Jesus and the Victory of God* (London: SPCK, 1996). Major study.

Chapter 8: What do we know about Jesus of Nazareth?

Did Jesus exist?

*Wells, G. A., *The Jesus Legend* (Chicago: Open Quest, 1996). The author's most recent attempt to deny the existence of Jesus.

Literary evidence from outside the gospels

*Mason, Steve, *Josephus and the New Testament* (Peabody: Hendrickson, 1992). Excellent introduction.

Van Voorst, Robert, *Jesus Outside the New Testament* (Grand Rapids: Eerdmans, 2000). Discusses a wide range of evidence carefully.

The Dead Sea Scrolls

Betz, Otto, and Riesner, Rainer, *Jesus, Qumran and the Vatican: Clarifications* (New York: Crossroad, 1994). Assesses critically attempts to forge links between the Dead Sea Scrolls and earliest Christianity.

*Charlesworth, James H. (ed.), *Jesus and the Dead Sea Scrolls* (New York: Doubleday, 1992). Essays by leading specialists; includes a good Bibliography.

Fitzmyer, J. A., *Responses to 101 Questions on the Dead Sea Scrolls* (London: Chapman, 1992). Very useful introduction by a leading specialist.

*García Martínez, Florentino, *The Dead Sea Scrolls Translated* (Leiden: Brill, 1994). The most complete translation available; includes excellent introduction and bibliographical references.

*Golb, Norman, *Who Wrote the Dead Sea Scrolls?: The Search for the Secret of Qumran* (New York: Scribner, 1995).

Shanks, Herschel (ed.), *Understanding the Dead Sea Scrolls* (London: SPCK, 1993). Introductory essays by a number of specialists.

VanderKam, James C., *The Dead Sea Scrolls Today* (Grand Rapids: Eerdmans, 1994). Up to date, with balanced judgements.

Vermes, G., *The Complete Dead Sea Scrolls in English* (London: Allen Lane, 1999). A new edition of a widely used translation; reliable and helpful.

Archaeological evidence

Avigad, N., *The Herodian Quarter in Jerusalem* (Jerusalem: Keter, 1991). Deserves to be more widely known.

McRay, John, *Archaeology and the New Testament* (Grand Rapids: Baker, 1991).

Meyers E. M. and Strange, J. F., *Archaeology, the Rabbis and Early Christianity* (London: SCM Press, 1981). An authoritative study.

Rousseau, J. J., and Arav, Rami, *Jesus and His World. An Archaeological and Cultural Dictionary* (Minneapolis: Fortress, 1995). Reliable guide.

Chapter 9: Assessing the Evidence

Gerhardsson, B., *The Origins of the Gospel Traditions* (London: SCM, 1979).

*—— *Memory and Manuscript. Oral Tradition and Written Transmission in Rabbinic Judaism and Early Christianity* (Grand Rapids: Eerdmans; 1st edn., 1961; rev. edn., 1998).

Neill, Stephen and Wright, N. T., *The Interpretation of the New Testament, 1861–1986* (Oxford: Oxford University Press, rev. edn., 1988). Includes an accessible account of quests of the historical Jesus.

Powell, M. A., *Jesus as a Figure in History: How Modern Historians View the Man from Galilee* (Louisville: Westminster, 1998).

*Stanton, G. N., 'Form Criticism Revisited', in M. D. Hooker and C. J. A. Hickling (eds.), *What About the New Testament?* (London: SCM, 1975), pp. 13–27.

Chapter 10: John the Baptist

*Hollenbach, Paul, 'The Conversion of Jesus: From Jesus the Baptizer to Jesus the Healer', *Aufstieg und Niedergang der römischen Welt*, II. 25. 1 (Berlin: de Gruyter, 1982), pp. 196–219. A useful survey of recent discussion.

*Taylor, Joan E., *The Immerser: John the Baptist within Second Temple Judaism* (Grand Rapids: Eerdmans, 1997). Fresh insights.

*Webb, Robert, 'John the Baptist and his Relationship to Jesus', in B. Chilton and C. A. Evans (eds.), *Studying the Historical Jesus* (Leiden: Brill, 1994), pp. 179–230.

*—— *John the Baptizer and Prophet: A Social-Historical Study* (Sheffield: JSOT, 1991). A fine study.

*Wink, W., *John the Baptist in the Gospel Tradition* (Cambridge, Cambridge University Press, 1968). Clear exposition of the evangelists' portraits of John.

Chapter 11: Prophet and Teacher

*Hengel, M., *The Charismatic Leader and his Followers* (Edinburgh: T&T Clark, 1981).

Hooker, Morna D., *The Signs of a Prophet. The Prophetic Actions of Jesus* (London: SCM, 1997).

Tannehill, Robert C., *The Sword of his Mouth. Forceful and Imaginative Language in Synoptic Sayings* (Philadelphia: Fortress, 1975).

Chapter 12: The Kingdom of God

Beasley-Murray, G. R., *Jesus and the Kingdom of God* (Exeter: Paternoster, 1986).
*Chilton, B. D., *God in Strength* (Sheffield: JSOT Press, 1987).
*—— (ed.), *The Kingdom of God in the Teaching of Jesus* (London: SPCK, 1984).
  Major essays.
*Kümmel, W. G., *Promise and Fulfilment* (London: SCM, 1957). Influential study.
Ladd, G. E., *The Presence of the Future* (London: SPCK, 1974).
Perrin, N., *The Kingdom of God in the Teaching of Jesus* (London: SCM, 1976).

Chapter 13: Parables and Aphorisms

Blomberg, Craig L., *Interpreting the Parables* (Leicester: Apollos, 1990).
*Crossan, J. D., *In Parables* (San Francisco: Harper, 1973).
Dodd, C. H., *The Parables of the Kingdom* (London: Nisbet, 1935 and many later
  editions).
*Jeremias, J., *The Parables of Jesus* (London: SCM, 3rd edn., 1972).
Lambrecht, J., *Once More Astonished: The Parables of Jesus* (New York: Crossroad,
  rev. edn., 1983).
Stein, R. H., *An Introduction to the Parables of Jesus* (Philadelphia: Westminster, 1981).
Tolbert, Mary Ann, *Sowing the Gospel. Mark's World in Literary-Historical
  Perspective* (Minneapolis: Fortress, 1989).
*Via, D. O., *The Parables: Their Literary and Existential Dimension* (Philadelphia:
  Fortress, 1967).
*Young, Brad H., *The Parables: Jewish Tradition and Christian Interpretation*
  (Peabody: Hendrickson, 1998).

Chapter 14: Miracles and Exorcisms

*Kee, H. C., *Miracle in the Early Christian World* (New Haven: Yale, 1983).
*—— *Medicine, Miracle and Magic in New Testament Times* (Cambridge:
  Cambridge University Press, 1986).
Theissen, Gerd, *The Miracle Stories of the Early Christian Tradition* (Edinburgh:
  T & T Clark, 1983).
*Twelftree, G. H., *Jesus the Exorcist: A Contribution to the Study of the Historical
  Jesus* (Peabody: Hendrickson, 1993).

Chapter 15: Messiah, Son of God, Son of Man

*Casey, M., *Son of Man* (London: SPCK, 1979).
*Collins, John J., *The Sceptre and the Star: The Messiahs of the Dead Sea Scrolls and
  other Ancient Literature* (New York: Doubleday, 1995).

Dunn, J. D. G., *Christology in the Making* (London: SCM, 1980).

*Hengel, M., *The Son of God* (London: SCM, 1976).

Hooker, Morna D., *The Son of Man in Mark* (London: SPCK, 1967).

*Lindars, B., *Jesus Son of Man* (London: SPCK, 1983).

*Moule, C. F. D., *The Origin of Christology* (Cambridge: Cambridge University Press, 1977).

Witherington III, Ben, *The Christology of Jesus* (Minneapolis: Fortress, 1990).

Chapter 16: Conflict

*Bammel E. and Moule, C. F. D. (eds.), *Jesus and the Politics of his Day* (Cambridge: Cambridge University Press, 1984). Wide-ranging essays, partly in response to S. G. F. Brandon's theories.

*Brandon, S. G. F., *Jesus and the Zealots* (Manchester: Manchester University Press, 1967).

Hengel, Martin, *Was Jesus a Revolutionist?* (Philadelphia: Fortress Press, 1971).

*—— *The Zealots* (Edinburgh: T&T Clark, 1988).

Saldarini, Anthony J., *Pharisees, Scribes and Sadducees in Palestinian Society* (Edinburgh: T&T Clark, 1988).

Chapter 17: The Last Days

Passion narratives in the four gospels

Brown, R. E., *The Death of the Messiah* (New York: Doubleday, 2 vols., 1994). Major study, but eminently readable.

*Carroll, John T. and Green, Joel B., *The Death of Jesus in Early Christianity* (Peabody: Hendrickson, 1996).

*Green, Joel, *The Death of Jesus: Tradition and Interpretation in the Passion Narratives in the Four Gospels* (Tübingen: Mohr, 1988).

*Hengel, Martin, *The Cross of the Son of God* (London: SCM, 1986).

Matera, F. J., *Passion Narratives and Gospel Theologies* (New York: Paulist, 1986).

The Last Supper

*Jeremias, J., *The Eucharistic Words of Jesus* (London: SCM, 1966).

Marshall, I. H., *Last Supper and Lord's Supper* (Exeter: Paternoster, 1980).

Schweizer, E., *The Lord's Supper According to the New Testament* (Philadelphia: Fortress, 1967).

Why was Jesus put to death?

*Bammel, E. (ed.), *The Trial of Jesus* (London: SCM, 1970).

*Blinzler, J., *The Trial of Jesus* (Newman: Westminster, 1959).

*Catchpole, D. R., *The Trial of Jesus* (Leiden: Brill, 1971).

Légasse, Simon, *The Trial of Jesus* (London: SCM, 1997).

Rivkin, Elias, *What Crucified Jesus?* (London: SCM, 1984). An evocative study by a Jewish scholar.

*Winter, P., *On the Trial of Jesus* (Berlin: de Gruyter, 1953).

'On the third day'

Barton, S., and Stanton, G. N., *Resurrection* (London: SPCK, 1994). Wide-ranging essays; good bibliography.

Brown, R. E., *The Virginal Conception and Bodily Resurrection of Jesus* (London: Chapman, 1993).

Catchpole, D. R., *Resurrection People. Studies in the Resurrection Narratives of the Gospels* (London: Darton, Longman & Todd, 2000). Perceptive.

*Evans, C. F., *Resurrection and the New Testament* (London: SCM, 1970).

Moule, C. F. D., (ed.), *The Significance of the Message of the Resurrection for Faith in Jesus Christ* (London: SCM, 1968).

Perkins, P., *Resurrection: New Testament Witness and Contemporary Reflection* (London: Chapman, 1984).

Chapter 18: Who was Jesus of Nazareth?

*Dunn, J. D. G., *The Partings of the Ways between Christianity and Judaism and their Significance for the Character of Christianity* (London: SCM, 1991).

*Hurtado, Larry, *One God, One Lord: Early Christian Devotion and Ancient Jewish Monotheism* (Edinburgh: T&T Clark, 2nd edn., 1998). How did followers of Jesus come to worship him?

INDEX OF PASSAGES CITED

GENERAL INDEX